Guide to Careers in

Federal Law Enforcement

Guide to Careers in
Federal Law
Enforcement

PROFILES OF 225 HIGH-POWERED POSITIONS AND SUREFIRE TACTICS FOR GETTING HIRED

Thomas H. Ackerman

Sage
Creek
Press

TRAVERSE CITY, MICHIGAN

The views expressed in this book do not necessarily represent the views of any organization, department or agency of the United States government. Editorial inquiries should be addressed to:

Hamilton Burrows Press
2843 East Grand River, Suite 250A
East Lansing, MI 48823
e-mail: inquiries@federalcareers.com
Web: www.federalcareers.com

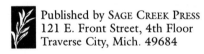Published by SAGE CREEK PRESS
121 E. Front Street, 4th Floor
Traverse City, Mich. 49684

Publisher's Cataloging-in-Publication Data
Ackerman, Thomas H.
    Guide to careers in federal law enforcement: profiles of 225 high-powered positions and surefire tactics for getting hired / Thomas H. Ackerman -- Traverse City, Mich.: Sage Creek Press, 1999.
        p.   cm.
    Includes index.
    ISBN 1-890394-33-5
    1. Law enforcement—vocational guidance—United States. 2. Civil service positions—United States. I. Title.
HV8143 .A35   1999   98-88127
363.2'023'73   dc—21   CIP

PROJECT COORDINATION BY JENKINS GROUP, INC.

03 02 01 00 ◆ 5 4 3 2 1

Printed in the United States of America

In memory of
Supervisory Special Agent
Charles R. "Bob" Thomas, Jr.,
my friend and mentor.

CONTENTS

CAREER PROFILES

CAREER PROFILES
Alphabetical by Department or Agency

INTRODUCTION

CAREERS IN FEDERAL LAW ENFORCEMENT OFFER PROSPECTS for challenge and diversity found in few other areas of work. Federal agencies employ a multitude of investigators, police and other law enforcement officers, compliance inspectors, security and technical support specialists, correctional and court officers, and other personnel in a wide range of careers which are suited to a variety of interests. Federal law enforcement careers also offer prestige, excellent salaries and benefits, and opportunities for travel, mobility, specialization and advancement.

While the goals of federal agencies differ, and their authorities cover broad geographic areas, the scope of most agencies is specific and limited. Some have enforcement duties that deal with criminal or regulatory matters, while others focus on security, civil enforcement, military affairs, or intelligence. In a nutshell, the federal system offers something for practically everyone.

THE FEDERAL LAW ENFORCEMENT EMPLOYMENT OUTLOOK

Growing concern over crime and increased vigilance in protecting our nation's borders, coupled with the need to replace personnel who retire or transfer to other occupations, will result in thousands of appointments to federal law enforcement positions in years to come.

A more security-conscious society and concern about terrorism will heighten the need for highly-trained security specialists to design and maintain effective security systems for the protection of federal office buildings, courts, military installations, nuclear power plants, airports, banks, hospitals, museums, and other government facilities.

Federal criminal investigators – who comprise the seventh-largest white-collar occupational group in the federal government – will be hired to combat the flow of illegal drugs, fraud in government programs, and threats to national security. Opportunities for uniformed law enforcement officers should also be plentiful.

According to a recent study by the U.S. Department of Labor, employment of correctional officers is expected to increase up to 35 percent through the year 2006, as additional officers are hired to supervise and control a growing prison inmate population. Increasing public concern over the spread of crime and illegal drugs, the adoption of mandatory sentencing guidelines calling for longer prison terms, and reduced parole for inmates, will spur demand for correctional officers.

A continuation of the trend toward increased use of civilians in technical support positions by law enforcement agencies will create employment opportunities in years to come for non-sworn personnel as well, such as civil and compliance investigators, safety inspectors, forensic examiners, seized property custodians, and communications personnel. Non-sworn technical and investigative personnel in the federal service are also highly trained and well paid. For example, the average salaries of Customs Import Specialists, Railroad Safety Inspectors, Mine Safety and Health Inspectors, and Air Safety Investigators ranged from $50,802 to $68,027 in 1998.

WHY THIS BOOK WAS WRITTEN

I have spoken to countless college students, law enforcement and security officers, and others seeking criminal justice careers who are knowledgeable about municipal police work and hiring processes, although are unaware of the variety of opportunities which exist in federal law enforcement.

Through my experience as a federal agent, police officer, training academy instructor, lecturer at the college level, and in attending career fairs and criminal justice conferences nationwide, I have found that most job seekers are familiar with Special Agent careers at the nation's largest agencies, such as the FBI, Marshals Service, DEA, Customs Service, and Secret Service. Few, however, are aware of the broad range of careers which exist within these organizations – including security specialists, forensic chemists, document analysts, photographers, intelligence specialists, radio dispatchers, uniformed officers, pilots, and others – and even fewer know about opportunities with smaller agencies.

More than 130 federal agencies employ thousands of law enforcement, investigative, security, compliance, and technical support personnel in rewarding careers that relatively few job seekers will ever learn about. In fact, positions with lesser-known, well-respected agencies, such as the USDA Animal and Plant Health Inspection Service, EPA Criminal Investigation Division, Bureau of Land Management, National Marine Fisheries Service, Administrative Office of the U.S. Courts, and National Zoological Park Police are among the best-kept secrets in law enforcement. Consider the following examples:

♦ The National Park Service employs uniformed River Rangers to conduct back-country patrols on white-water rivers, enforce federal and state laws, and carry out search and rescue missions.

♦ Field Investigators with the National Indian Gaming Commission investigate gaming activities on Indian land in an effort to shield these operations from corruption and organized crime.

♦ Wildlife Inspectors of the U.S. Fish and Wildlife Service intercept shipments of protected wildlife and wildlife products which violate federal laws and international treaties.

♦ Physical Security Specialists with the U.S. Capitol Police design, install, and maintain electronic security systems for the protection of the Capitol Building and other congressional buildings in the Washington, D.C. area.

♦ Amtrak Police Officers respond to emergency incidents and perform law enforcement functions at more than 500 train stations in 45 states, and over a rail system of 24,500 route miles.

♦ Special Agents of the National Highway Traffic Safety Administration organize and manage multi-agency task force operations which target automobile dealerships that are involved in vehicle odometer fraud.

I have also discovered that many job aspirants are either misinformed, confused, intimidated, or overwhelmed with the Federal hiring process, or simply do not know where to obtain information about position qualification requirements, application and testing procedures, vacancy announcements, or other details. In addition, many job seekers are unaware that Federal law enforcement agencies regularly recruit personnel through special hiring programs for college students, veterans of the Armed Forces, and Native Americans, and that co-op positions or good grades in college can lead to a fast-track ticket to employment.

In the Federal personnel system, which rewards attention to detail and jumping through the right hoops at the right time, it is common for candidates to overshadow more highly qualified applicants by conducting superior job search campaigns and knowing the ropes. A thorough understanding and careful navigation of the hiring process are crucial to outshining the competition and landing a career in Federal law enforcement. This book was written for those seeking to gain a competitive edge.

HOW TO USE THIS BOOK

Guide to Careers in Federal Law Enforcement is organized in three parts. Part I provides an overview of the federal civil service system, salary and benefits, specific strategies for standing out from the crowd, special hiring programs, and sources of information. Part II includes profiles of 225 careers with 131 agencies, divided among ten occupational categories. Summaries of the primary basic training programs for federal law personnel are presented in Part III. The appendices provide a listing of occupational classifications related to law enforcement, a sample job vacancy announcement, a copy of the OF-612 Application for Employment, various salary schedules, a form which can be used to keep track of agency contacts, and an exhaustive list of action verbs that are targeted to law enforcement applications and resumes.

Except for those who are well-versed in the federal civil service process, all readers should review chapters one through five in order, as each progresses in a step-by-step fashion through the hiring process and builds upon previous chapters. On the other hand, chapters six through fifteen need not be read in order. Instead, move freely between the various categories of occupations according to your career interests.

Each career profile includes a summary of the agency's primary purpose, a brief description of the primary responsibilities, basic qualification requirements, and a summary of initial and in-service training. Nearly every profile includes a World Wide Web address, with the exception of a handful of agencies which did not have a Web site at the time of publication. E-mail addresses of agencies that correspond with the public in this manner are also provided.

Rather than providing exhaustive histories of the agencies or summaries of famous cases – which are of little value during a serious job search – career profiles in this book are intended to provide a basis for making informed career choices, without superfluous details. They do not, however, provide absolutely everything there is to know about each position. Candidates seeking details about recruiting plans or other information should contact the agencies directly. Most agencies prefer written inquiries as opposed to telephone calls, and will usually respond within two to three weeks.

Finally, after reading this book and mapping out a career search campaign, carefully follow the strategies and devote as much time as possible toward reaching your goal. Also, refer to this book periodically as a navigational aid to stay on course. Above all, remember that the agencies will not come to you – you must seek them out and demonstrate what you have to offer. In the final analysis, successful candidates are those who are armed with reliable information and undaunted perseverance. This book provides the information. The perseverance is up to you.

Chapter One

THE FEDERAL CIVIL SERVICE SYSTEM

> And so, my fellow Americans, ask not what your
> country can do for you – ask what you can do for your country.
> – JOHN FITZGERALD KENNEDY

T HE FEDERAL GOVERNMENT IS THE NATION'S LARGEST EMPLOYER, with nearly three million personnel serving throughout the United States and abroad in more than 2,000 different occupations. Federal employees are classified into a wide range of occupational groups and appointment classifications, and are compensated under a variety of pay systems. Hiring procedures also vary from one agency to another, as the federal civil service system does not revolve around a standard or unified hiring process or personnel system. Although hiring procedures vary, all are based upon common principles, and all agencies are required to observe certain laws and regulations to ensure that job applicants are evaluated objectively.

This chapter provides an overview of the federal civil service system, including personnel administration, types of federal service, occupational classifications, experience requirements, job vacancy announcements, application formats, written examinations, applicant ratings, and special hiring programs.

PERSONNEL ADMINISTRATION

The U.S. Office of Personnel Management

The United States Office of Personnel Management (OPM) is the President's advisor for operating and continuously improving the government's system of human resource management. To ensure compliance with personnel laws and regulations, OPM supports agencies in hiring and examining processes in accordance with *Merit System Principles* to ensure that hiring and retention decisions are based on objective job-related criteria and procedures, and that all applicants receive equal opportunity for employment. The OPM provides employment information and job vacancy announcements for many government positions, administers written examinations for certain jobs at the request of agencies, and establishes basic qualification standards for all federal occupations. OPM also operates the nation's largest retirement programs, which together cover more than five million active and retired federal employees; administers the Federal Employees Health Benefits Program; sets investigation policy for the federal personnel security program, and provides for personnel investigations relating to suitability and security; sets standards for information that goes into employees' Official Personnel Files at agencies; and provides policy direction and guidance on appointments, promotions, reassignments, reinstatements, temporary and term employment, Veterans' Preference, career transition, and other provisions.

TYPES OF FEDERAL SERVICE

The federal civil service system includes all appointive positions in the executive, judicial, and legislative branches of the federal government, except military positions of the uniformed services. Civil service components consist of the *Competitive Service*, the *Excepted Service,* and the *Senior Executive Service.* The rights, benefits, entitlements, appointment procedures, and job protections of federal personnel are determined based upon the variety of service and appointment held. This section provides an overview of the types of federal civilian employment and many of the rules under which federal personnel serve.

Competitive Service Appointments

Federal positions normally filled through open competitive examination under civil service rules and regulations established by OPM are categorized in the *Competitive Service.* The competitive examination process involves the evaluation of applicants based on their education, experience, and other qualifications, and sometimes includes written tests. Positions in the executive branch of the federal government, which includes most civilian government positions, are in the competitive service unless they are specifically excluded from it. In the competitive service, appointment procedures, merit promotion requirements, and qualification standards are prescribed by law or by OPM, and apply to all agencies.

Excepted Service Appointments

Executive branch positions which are filled outside of competitive civil service processes are in the *Excepted Service.* Agencies that hire personnel through excepted service processes are authorized either under federal law, by Presidential Order, or by OPM to establish independent hiring processes to fill certain positions. In the excepted service, only basic requirements are prescribed by law or regulation, and each agency develops specific requirements and procedures for its own jobs. Many agencies hire employees in the competitive service for some jobs and in the excepted service for others. Positions in the legislative and judicial branches are included in the excepted service unless they are specifically included in the competitive service.

Excepted Agencies

While many federal agencies fill position vacancies in both the competitive and excepted service, some are completely excluded from competitive civil service procedures and have their own hiring systems and evaluation criteria. Agencies that operate independent employment systems are known as *Excepted Agencies.* Application forms or information on employment with excepted agencies are not provided by OPM. Applicants who are interested in employment with an excepted agency should contact that agency directly.

Major excepted agencies include the Administrative Office of the U.S. Courts, Agency for International Development, Central Intelligence Agency, Defense Intelligence Agency, Federal Bureau of Investigation, Federal Reserve Board, General Accounting Office, National Security Agency, Nuclear Regulatory Commission, Postal Service, Department of State, Tennessee Valley Authority, Supreme Court of the United States, and Library of Congress.

Senior Executive Service Appointments

The Civil Service Reform Act (CSRA) established the Senior Executive Service (SES) in 1979 to ensure that executive management of the government is responsive to the needs, policies, and goals of the nation. It was set up as a "third" service, completely separate from the existing competitive and excepted services. The SES covers most managerial, supervisory, and policy positions in the executive branch which are classified above GS-15 and which do not require Senate confirmation.

Permanent Appointments

Permanent appointments in the competitive service are classified as either *Career-Conditional* or *Career.* Career-conditional appointments are generally used for initial appointments into the competitive service. Once an employee completes three years of continuous service under a career-conditional appointment, their appointment is converted to career status. Permanent employees may work full-time or part-time work schedules; are eligible for retirement benefits, health insurance, and life insurance; and earn annual and sick leave.

Temporary and Term Appointments

Temporary appointments are made not to exceed one year, although may be extended for an additional year. The work of temporary appointees must not be permanent in nature. Temporary employees may work full-time or part-time work schedules and earn annual and sick leave, although employees on temporary appointments of one year or less are not entitled to retirement benefits, health insurance, or life insurance.

Term appointments are made for periods of more than one year but may not exceed four years. These appointments may be appropriate, for example, when there is project work to be completed, an extraordinary workload, or an agency reorganization. Term employees may work full-time or part-time work schedules. They also earn annual and sick leave, and are eligible for retirement benefits, health insurance, and life insurance.

Competitive Status

Federal employees serving in either career or career-conditional appointments in the competitive service have what is known as *Competitive Status*. While many job vacancies are open to competition from the general public, others are open only to applicants with competitive status, or in some cases only to employees of the agency which is filling the position. Applicants with competitive status are commonly known as *Status Applicants*. Job applicants who are not federal employees, and federal employees who do not qualify for competitive status, are known as *Non-Status* applicants.

Reinstatement Eligibility

Reinstatement Eligibility allows certain former federal employees to apply for federal jobs open only to status candidates, which allows them to reenter the competitive service workforce without competing with the general public in civil service examination processes. Former federal employees with career status and former career-conditional employees who qualify for Veterans' Preference maintain reinstatement eligibility for life. In addition, most nonveterans who were career-conditional employees are eligible for reinstatement for three years after their date of separation. Excepted Service appointees do not have reinstatement eligibility.

FEDERAL OCCUPATIONAL CLASSIFICATIONS

Occupational Groups and Series

OPM has established occupational groups and series that are used to classify federal positions. These classifications are made in terms of the variety or subject matter of the work, the level of difficulty or responsibility, and qualification requirements. Position classifications ensure similar treatment for positions within a class in personnel and pay administration. Occupational groups have been established for white-collar positions, which are classified under the General Schedule, as well as blue-collar jobs, which fall under the Wage Grade designation.

The largest category of occupations relating to law enforcement is found in the *Investigation Group*, which includes positions classified in the GS-1800 through GS-1899 series, such as criminal investigators, general and compliance investigators, compliance inspectors and specialists, Border Patrol Agents, and others. The next-largest category falls under the *Miscellaneous Occupations Group*, which includes police and correctional officers, fingerprint specialists, park rangers, and security specialists classified in the GS-0000 through GS-0099 series. A complete schedule of occupational groups for positions represented in this book is shown in Appendix 1.

EXPERIENCE REQUIREMENTS

Qualification standards for federal law enforcement positions typically specify requirements for experience that is either *General* or *Specialized* in nature. Qualifying general and specialized experience varies widely in its degree of specialty from one occupational series to another, and also between salary grades within an occupational series. In addition, position qualification standards often require that a certain amount of the experience be at a level of difficulty and responsibility equivalent to the next lower grade level in the federal service. Job vacancy announcements usually provide detailed descriptions of qualifying general and specialized experience.

General Experience

General Experience is usually required at grade levels where the specific knowledge and skills needed to perform the duties of a position are not prerequisites, but where applicants must have demonstrated the ability to acquire the particular knowledge and skills. For some occupations, any progressively responsible work experience may be qualifying. Others require experience that provided a familiarity with the subject matter or processes of the occupation, or of the equipment used on the job, although not to the extent required of specialized experience.

Specialized Experience

Specialized Experience is that which has equipped an applicant with the particular knowledge, skills, and abilities to successfully perform the duties of the position, and which is in or directly related to the line of work of the position. For example, qualifying specialized experience for GS-0083 Police Officer positions at the GS-4 level and above is defined as:

> *Experience that provided knowledge of a body of basic laws and regulations, law enforcement operations, practices, and techniques and involved responsibility for maintaining order and protecting life and property. Creditable specialized experience may have been gained in work on a police force; through service as a military police officer; in work providing visitor protection and law enforcement in parks, forests, or other natural resource or recreational environments; in performing criminal investigative duties; or in other work that provided the required knowledge and skills.*

Candidates who possess a bachelor's degree but no specialized experience in the career field of the position sought generally are eligible for appointment at the GS-5 level. Positions at or above the GS-7 level typically require one year of specialized experience equivalent to the next lower grade level. This means, for example, that in order to qualify for a position at GS-12, an applicant must have had at least one year of specialized experience equivalent to GS-11.

In many cases, applicants may substitute graduate-level education for specialized experience in order to qualify for federal law enforcement careers at the GS-7 level and above. In lieu of specialized experience, one year of graduate study is normally qualifying for appointment to GS-7. Similarly, a master's degree or two years of graduate study may be substituted for specialized experience when applying for positions at the GS-9 level, and a Ph.D. or three years of graduate education may be substituted for specialized experience when seeking positions at the GS-11 level. In addition, applicants without specialized experience who achieved high academic standing during undergraduate studies qualify for many federal law enforcement jobs at the GS-7 level (see *Special Hiring Programs and Provisions: Superior Academic Achievement*).

JOB VACANCY ANNOUNCEMENTS

Federal agencies seeking to fill job vacancies disseminate detailed *Vacancy Announcements*, sometimes referred to as *job postings,* which provide position details and information concerning qualification requirements, selection criteria, and the application process. While the format varies from one agency to another, most vacancy announcements consist of essentially the same components, which are discussed below. An example of a vacancy announcement is shown in Appendix 2.

Position Title

The official title of an advertised position is always indicated near the top of the vacancy announcement, and is usually followed by the occupational series of the position. *Official titles,* which are determined by federal position classification standards, sometimes differ from *working titles* of law enforcement and other personnel. For example, Criminal Investigators in the GS-1811 series are commonly known by their working title of *Special Agent.* Working titles are sometimes referenced in narrative portions of vacancy announcements.

Occupational Series and Salary Grade

The occupational series and salary grade are usually listed adjacent to the position title, in a format such as: *GS-1811-07*. In this example, the position is classified in the GS-1811 *Criminal Investigator* series, with a salary grade of GS-7. When only one salary grade is indicated (as above), applicants must meet the minimum qualifications for the specified grade level and cannot be hired at any other grade. Many vacancy announcements specify a range of salary grades, such as GS-1811-07/09/11. A vacancy advertised in this manner may be filled at the highest grade level for which appointees are qualified.

Full Performance Level

Vacancy announcements may also indicate a salary grade at the *Full Performance Level* of a position. This is the highest grade to which one could expect to advance without competition, provided that their job performance was satisfactory. For example, in the case of a Criminal Investigator hired at GS-7, and where the Full Performance Level is GS-12, advancement to GS-9, GS-11, and GS-12 would normally occur at one-year intervals without undergoing testing or competition from other candidates.

Announcement Number

Virtually all vacancy announcements include an identifying number which facilitates the processing of application materials and recordkeeping functions. Announcement numbers provide a ready reference for personnel specialists to the exact position title, salary grade, opening and closing dates, location of duty station, and other pertinent data. Job applicants should always record announcement numbers on application forms, supplemental qualification statements, and other application materials.

Opening and Closing Dates

The period in which applications are accepted for federal job vacancies is marked by the *Opening* and *Closing Dates* of vacancy announcements. Opening dates are sometimes referred to as "issue dates" or "announcement dates." This is the first day in which candidates are permitted to submit application materials. Application closing dates are not as straightforward, however, and may be interpreted differently from one agency to another. For example, some agencies require that all job application materials be *received* by the human resources office on or before the closing date, while others permit applicants to have their materials *postmarked* no later than the closing date. Announcements must remain open for a minimum of three days, although most law enforcement announcements are posted for two to four weeks.

Organization and Location of Position

The name of the organization filling the position and location of the duty station are included under this heading. When vacancies exist in more than one geographic location, or "nationwide," applicants must specify where they are willing to work.

Appointment Tenure

Vacancy announcements indicate whether positions are to be filled as full-time permanent, part-time, temporary, or term appointments. The vast majority of federal law enforcement positions are filled as full-time permanent appointments, although agencies such as the National Park Service hire officers for part-time or temporary work.

Number of Vacancies

Employing agencies often indicate the number of vacancies to be filled under a particular vacancy announcement. Some agencies fill multiple vacancies under the same announcement, while others issue multiple announcements when filling more than one position.

Area of Consideration

This section specifies who is eligible to apply for a particular vacancy, such as competitive status or non-status candidates, employees of the department or agency issuing the vacancy announcement, or those who qualify under special hiring programs such as Outstanding Scholars, Veterans, Native Americans, and others. Positions which are open to the general public are often indicated by the terms "All Sources" or "Non-Status" in the Area of Consideration block, although current federal employees may also apply for these positions.

Statement of Position Duties

The vast majority of vacancy announcements provide an overview of the primary duties and responsibilities of positions being filled. These statements range from a single sentence which provides little or no useful information, to full-page descriptions which include specific details of assignments and tasks performed on the job.

Qualification Requirements

An outline of the basic eligibility standards is incorporated under this heading. These may include a combination of general and specialized experience, education, training, medical requirements, minimum and maximum age, and other standards. Applicants must meet the minimum qualification requirements in order to be eligible for further consideration in the application process. Positions advertised under multiple salary grades usually include a breakdown of minimum requirements for each grade. Qualification requirements are often summarized in a format similar to the following example:

> *To qualify for appointment at the GS-5 level, applicants must have completed a four-year course of study above high school leading to a bachelor's degree, OR have three years of general experience which was equivalent to at least GS-4 in the Federal service.*

> *For GS-7, applicants must have completed one full year of graduate level education, or have attained superior academic achievement during undergraduate studies, OR have one year of specialized experience which was equivalent to at least GS-5 in the Federal service.*

Minimum qualification standards are used by personnel management specialists to evaluate candidates' qualifications for positions, and to eliminate those who are not eligible for further consideration because they fail to meet basic requirements.

Evaluation Criteria

A description of specific evaluation criteria or special qualifications are often indicated under headings such as *Knowledge, Skills, and Abilities, Quality Ranking Factors, Selection Criteria,* or *Selective Placement Factors.* Applicants who meet basic eligibility requirements are rated on the basis of whether they possess specific attributes listed under these headings for positions being filled.

Knowledge, Skills, and Abilities (KSA's) are the attributes required to perform a job and are generally demonstrated through qualifying experience, education, and training.

Quality Ranking Factors are KSA's that could be expected to significantly enhance performance in a position, but are not considered essential for satisfactory performance. Applicants who possess such KSA's may be ranked above those who do not, but no one may be rated ineligible solely for failure to possess such KSA's.

Selective Placement Factors, on the other hand, are KSA's or special qualifications that are in addition to the minimum requirements in a qualification standard, but are determined to be essential to perform the duties and responsibilities of a particular position. In other words, these KSA's are mandatory requirements, and applicants who do not meet all Selective Placement Factors are ineligible for further consideration.

Selection Criteria normally are outlined for specific salary grade levels of vacant positions. For example, a recently posted vacancy announcement for a GS-1811 Criminal Investigator (Special Agent) position at the GS-7 level specified selection criteria under the heading of "Knowledge, Skills, and Abilities," as follows:

1. *Knowledge of investigative techniques, principals, detection methods, and equipment.*

2. *Knowledge of criminal law and rules of criminal procedure.*

3. *Skill in both oral and written communication.*

4. *Ability to analyze and evaluate facts, evidence, and related information and arrive at sound conclusions.*

5. *Ability to deal effectively with individuals and groups at all levels of government and the private sector.*

While the KSA's referenced above are fairly typical of Criminal Investigator positions at the GS-7 level, vacancy announcements for the same job series and salary grade may vary widely from one agency to another depending upon the nature of positions being filled and agency requirements. In other words, while some vacancy announcements describe selection criteria in detail, others may present KSA's in less explicit terms, as shown in the following example which was used for a GS-1811 Criminal Investigator position at the GS-7 level:

1. *Skill in oral communication.*

2. *Skill in written communication.*

3. *Ability to investigate.*

Supplemental Qualifications Statements

When applying for most federal law enforcement jobs, applicants are required to submit a *Supplemental Qualifications Statement* along with their application forms or a résumé that describes their education, experience, training, accomplishments, and awards as they relate to the selection criteria. Vacancy announcements usually include instructions pertaining to the format of these statements.

Conditions of Employment

Agencies utilize this section to advise prospective applicants of special conditions under which hiring and continued employment may be based. For example, appointment and retention may be contingent upon passing medical examinations, urinalysis screening for illegal drugs, psychological assessments, written aptitude tests, physical fitness screening, training programs, personal interviews, a polygraph examination, or a pre-employment background investigation. Most agencies require suitability for a security clearance, and many require their personnel to travel extensively or relocate to other duty stations.

How to Apply

This section provides detailed instructions relating to application forms and supporting documentation to be submitted, the format of supplemental qualifications statements, addresses to which materials should be sent, and other information concerning the application process. Candidates are often directed to send application materials to a human resources office which is located at a site other than the duty station or unit where employment is sought.

Contact Information

Vacancy announcements usually indicate an address and sometimes a particular person to direct questions or other inquiries. In some cases, a telephone number is provided for access to information regarding the status of the application process, although oftentimes callers are connected only to recorded information lines.

APPLICATION FORMATS

Federal job applicants have several choices when applying for employment consideration, including the *Optional Application for Federal Employment* (OF-612), a résumé, the *Standard Form 171 Application for Federal Employment* (SF-171), or any other written format of choice. In addition, applications may be submitted on-line or over the telephone for certain positions, and some agencies utilize specialized application forms. This section provides an overview of application format options.

OF-612 Optional Application for Federal Employment

The OF-612 Application form replaced the SF-171 in 1995 as the standard written format for applying for federal employment. Unlike the cumbersome SF-171, which took hours to complete, the OF-612 is easier to fill out and is printed on two sides of a single sheet of paper. This form requires applicants to describe their employment experience, educational background, and other qualifications, such as job-related training cours-es, skills, certificates and licenses, honors, awards, and special accomplishments. An OF-612 Application form is shown in Appendix 3.

The Federal Résumé

Along with replacement of the SF-171 application came new rules allowing applicants to submit résumés for job consideration. The *Federal Résumé*, however, differs significantly from those utilized in the private sector. While a corporate résumé presents a brief synopsis of an applicant's background, a Federal résumé goes into greater detail and must include specific data which is not normally included in résumés submitted to private industry. Applicants who fail to provide the required information are often eliminated from further consider-ation. In addition to the information requested in job vacancy announcements, Federal résumés must provide essentially the same information as requested in the OF-612 application, including the following:

Job Information — Vacancy announcement number, position title, and salary grade applied for.

Personal Information — Full name, complete mailing address, daytime and evening telephone numbers, Social Security number, country of citizenship, veterans' preference eligibility, reinstatement eligibility, and highest Federal civilian grade held (including dates).

Education — Highest grade completed, name and complete address of high school attended, date of diplo-ma or GED; name and complete address of colleges or universities attended, total credits earned (specify whether semester or quarter credits), majors, type and year of any degrees received. Include a copy of college transcript(s) if requested to do so in vacancy announcements.

Paid and Nonpaid Work Experience — Titles of jobs held (including series and grade, if federal), starting and ending dates (month and year), salary, number of hours per week, employer's name and complete address, supervisor's name and telephone number (indicate whether or not supervisor may be contacted), description of duties and accomplishments. Prepare a separate entry for each job.

Other Qualifications — Title and dates of job-related training courses; examples of job-related skills; title and dates of job-related certificates and licenses held; details of honors, awards, and special accomplishments.

SF-171 Application for Federal Employment

The Standard Form 171 was created in an effort to standardize job application forms at a time when agencies were using a wide assortment of agency-specific forms. Until January 1995, when it was replaced by the OF-612, applicants had no choice but to submit an SF-171 when applying for most federal jobs. While the SF-171 is on its way to becoming obsolete, it is still utilized for job transfers and promotions by current federal employees. Although agencies cannot require an SF-171 for positions open to the public, applicants may still use this form to apply for most federal jobs.

Telephone Application Processing System

Many agencies accept employment applications over the telephone via the OPM Telephone Application Processing System (TAPS), which provides a simple method of applying for federal job vacancies twenty-four hours a day, seven days a week. Applicant information is entered through a combination of touchtone tele-phone keypad and recorded voice responses, including demographic, geographic, and job preference data, along with qualifying education and experience information. This data is downloaded nightly to a local area network and processed. Applicants are evaluated electronically through a rating instrument created for each position, and are referred to agencies for additional processing. TAPS telephone numbers, which vary from one position to another, are provided in job vacancy announcements.

On-line Application

The U.S. Office of Personnel Management provides a service which allows job applicants to complete an elec-tronic application for employment and submit it on-line for certain federal positions. Applicants must have a copy of the vacancy announcement and the Supplemental Qualification Statement for the job in which they are applying in order to complete the application. There is no charge for this service. Additional details are available from the OPM World Wide Web site at: http://www.usajobs.opm.gov.

WRITTEN EXAMINATIONS

A few federal law enforcement agencies require candidates to pass a written examination in order to receive further consideration in the application process. Some examinations are job-specific and are administered only within particular agencies, such as those for Border Patrol Agents, FBI Special Agents, and Postal Police Officers, while others are generic in nature. Vacancy announcements normally indicate whether written exams are required. An overview of many of the exams utilized for law enforcement positions is included below.

Treasury Enforcement Agent Examination

The Treasury Enforcement Agent (TEA) Examination is administered to candidates for Treasury Enforcement Agent positions, which includes Special Agents of the United States Customs Service; Secret Service Special Agents; Bureau of Alcohol, Tobacco and Firearms Special Agents; as well as Special Agents and Internal Security Inspectors of the Internal Revenue Service. The TEA exam is also given to Deputy United States Marshal candidates, and is utilized by a number of other agencies and departments. The exam is divided into three parts which measure verbal reasoning, arithmetic reasoning, and analytical abilities. Passing scores range from 70 to 100 points before the addition of Veterans' Preference points.

FBI Special Agent Examination

Qualified applicants for Special Agent positions with the Federal Bureau of Investigation (FBI) are administered a battery of written examinations in the first phase of the selection process. These exams consist of a Biographical Data Inventory, a three-part Cognitive Ability Test, and a Situational Judgment Test. The FBI Special Agent Examination is scored on a "pass or fail" basis, and applicants are not provided with their numeric scores.

The Biographical Data Inventory measures critical skills and abilities, which include ability to organize, plan, and prioritize; ability to maintain a positive image; ability to evaluate information and make judgment decisions; initiative and motivation; ability to adapt to changing situations; and physical requirements. Time limits established for this segment allow most candidates to finish without being rushed.

The Cognitive Ability Test consists of three parts which are timed separately under stringent time limits. This test measures mathematical reasoning, data analysis and interpretation skills, mathematical knowledge, attention to detail, and ability to evaluate information and make decisions. Many individuals are unable to finish this segment in the time allocated.

In the Situational Judgment Test, candidates are faced with descriptions of problem situations and are asked to choose their *most likely* and *least likely* courses of action among a number of alternatives. This test measures critical skills and abilities, such as the ability to organize, plan, and prioritize; ability to relate effectively with others; ability to maintain a positive image; ability to evaluate information and make judgment decisions; ability to adapt to changing situations; and integrity. Time limits for this portion of the test are not particularly demanding for most candidates.

U.S. Postal Police Officer Examination

The Postal Police Officer Examination is a multiple-choice test which focuses on reading comprehension, name and number comparison proficiency, and arithmetic reasoning. Reading comprehension questions require candidates to draw inferences and distinguish between essential and peripheral information presented in narrative passages. Name and number comparison questions require candidates to examine a series of similar names and numbers to determine which are different or alike. The arithmetic reasoning section requires analysis of information in order to solve problems which are presented in both verbal and numeric form. A minimum score of 70 percent (exclusive of veterans' preference) is required to be placed on a register of eligibles.

U.S. Border Patrol Agent Examination

All Border Patrol Agent candidates must pass a four-part general aptitude examination, and those who are not fluent in the Spanish language must also pass an artificial language test. The general aptitude exam consists of multiple-choice questions pertaining to vocabulary and reading comprehension, English grammar, general knowledge and judgment, and logical reasoning. The artificial language aptitude exam does not test knowledge of the Spanish language; rather, it is used to predict the ability to learn a foreign language.

U.S. Park Police Officer Examination

Candidates for the position of U.S. Park Police Officer who meet minimum experience, education, and age requirements must pass a three-part written examination which is administered by OPM. This exam takes approximately two and one-half hours to complete, and consists of 100 multiple-choice questions which measure aptitude in name and number comparison, reading comprehension, and mathematical reasoning. Passing examination scores are converted into a numerical rating which ranges from 70 to 100 prior to the addition of veterans' preference points.

APPLICANT RATINGS

Written Examination Ratings

Agencies that require applicants to take a written examination typically place those who achieve passing scores on a register of eligibles according to their scores. Those who qualify for Veterans' Preference receive either five or ten additional points, depending upon their level of preference. Many agencies maintain eligibility registers for a period of months or even years, from which candidates may be called upon to complete additional phases in the selection process.

Application Ratings

Applications which have been received (or submitted) prior to the closing date are screened by personnel specialists to determine whether candidates meet minimum qualification requirements. Some agencies also use a self-assessment questionnaire as an initial screening tool. Applicants who are lacking required education, experience, training, or other requirements are eliminated from further consideration. Remaining applications are evaluated and graded in a numerical scoring process based on qualifications. In some cases, agencies also screen out minimally qualified applicants at this point in the process.

Applications that survived the initial screening process are then reviewed by a *Rating Panel* which usually consists of agency staff members who hold positions at or above the grade level of the job being filled. At this point, applicants are further evaluated and are assigned numerical scores for each element of the position selection criteria. After all applications have been reviewed by each member of the panel, the total scores are calculated and divided by the number of panel members to reach an average score which is known as a *Rating*. Depending upon the number of positions being filled and agency procedures, a certain number of candidates with the highest scores are then placed on a list of eligibles which is commonly known as the *Best Qualified List*. These candidates are then referred to the office which will conduct the remainder of the selection process, which normally includes personal interviews, background investigations, and final selections.

SPECIAL HIRING PROGRAMS AND PROVISIONS

The federal government administers a number of special hiring programs that provide preference in hiring for certain groups. Of particular interest to those seeking careers in law enforcement are programs and provisions which apply to college graduates, veterans, and Native Americans, including the following:

The Outstanding Scholar Program

Federal agencies have always looked to educational institutions to recruit candidates who have the skills needed to meet its future staffing needs. The Outstanding Scholar Program is a special hiring authority that is used to attract talented students to certain entry-level positions in the competitive service at the GS-5 and GS-7 grade levels. Applicants who meet Program requirements may be offered a direct appointment by a federal agency without having to go through competitive examining procedures. The direct appointment process cuts through most of the red tape and can save weeks or months of time.

To qualify for consideration, an applicant must be a college graduate and have maintained a grade point average (GPA) of 3.45 or better on a 4.0 scale for all *undergraduate* coursework, or have graduated in the upper 10 percent of their graduating class in the college, university or major subdivision (such as the College of Liberal Arts or the School of Criminal Justice). A college degree in any major is qualifying for most of the career fields covered under the Outstanding Scholar Program. A few, however, require some coursework in subjects related to the job. Application may be made a few months before graduation, provided that GPA or class standing requirements are met at such time as a job offer is extended.

Primary law enforcement and investigative career fields covered under the Outstanding Scholar Program include: Park Ranger (GS-0025); Security Administration (GS-0080); Intelligence (GS-0132); Wage and Hour Compliance (GS-0249); Internal Revenue Officer (GS-1169); General Investigations (GS-1810); Criminal Investigations (GS-1811); Game Law Enforcement (GS-1812); Immigration Inspection (GS-1816); Alcohol, Tobacco, and Firearms Inspection (GS-1854); Import Specialist (GS-1889); and Customs Inspector (GS-1890).

Superior Academic Achievement

College students who have achieved high academic standing during *undergraduate* study may qualify for appointment at the GS-7 level for many federal jobs under *Superior Academic Achievement* provisions, even if they are lacking job-related experience. Under this provision, unlike the Outstanding Scholar Program, candidates must follow normal competitive hiring procedures and are not eligible for direct appointment.

The Superior Academic Achievement provision applies to those who have completed (or expect to complete within nine months) all the requirements for a bachelor's degree from an accredited college or university. (Students in their senior year of study can apply for positions prior to graduation for consideration based on their grades at the time of application.) Qualification is based upon either class standing, grade-point average, or honor society membership, as follows:

Class Standing — Applicants must be in the upper third of their graduating class in the college, university or major subdivision (such as the College of Liberal Arts or School of Criminal Justice) based upon completed courses.

Grade Point Average — Applicants must have a grade point average of 2.95 or higher out of a possible 4.0 for all courses completed at the time of application or during the last two years of the curriculum; OR a 3.45 or higher out of a possible 4.0 for all courses completed in the major field of study at the time of application or during the last two years of the curriculum.

Honor Society Membership — Applicants who have membership in one of the national honor societies (other than freshman or sophomore societies) recognized by the Association of College Honor Societies.

Many of the careers which are featured in this book provide for appointment under Superior Academic Achievement provisions. For these positions, eligibility is specified under the Qualifications heading of applicable career profiles.

Veterans' Preference Credit

Since the time of the Civil War, veterans of the armed forces have been given some degree of preference in appointments to federal jobs. By law, veterans who are disabled or who served on active duty during certain time periods are entitled to preference over nonveterans in hiring from competitive lists of eligibles. Preference applies in hiring from civil service examinations and for most excepted service jobs.

Veterans meeting the criteria for preference and who are found eligible (achieve a score of 70 or higher either by a written examination or an evaluation of their experience and education) have either five or ten points added to their numerical ratings depending upon the nature of their preference. Additional details relating to veterans' preference requirements are normally included in vacancy announcements.

Veterans' Readjustment Appointment

The Veterans' Readjustment Appointment (VRA) is a special authority through which agencies can appoint eligible veterans without competitive examination. Candidates need not have been on a list of eligibles, but must meet the basic qualification requirements of the position. Agencies can use the VRA authority to fill positions up through the GS-11 grade level, or at the equivalent grade level under other pay systems. VRA appointments are in the excepted service for a two-year period. Conversion to a permanent (career or career-conditional) status is granted after satisfactory completion of the two-year service period and any education or training requirements.

In order to qualify, candidates must have served on active duty for more than 180 days, all or any part of which occurred after August 4, 1964, and received other than a dishonorable discharge. Some veterans who served fewer than 180 days are also eligible, including those who were discharged or released from active duty as a result of a service-connected disability, as well as Reserve and Guard members who were ordered to active duty under certain circumstances. Vacancy announcements typically include details relating to VRA eligibility.

Thirty Percent or More Disabled Veteran Program

Federal agencies have the authority to provide noncompetitive appointments to veterans who have a service-connected disability of 30 percent or more. Unlike the VRA Program, which limits appointments up to the GS-11 grade, qualifying candidates may be appointed to any salary grade for which they are qualified, without limitation. Candidates must meet all qualifications of the position to which they are appointed, which may include achieving a passing score on a written examination. Appointments are considered temporary for a period of at least sixty days, after which conversion to permanent status may be granted provided that performance was satisfactory.

Native American Preference

In accordance with the Indian Reorganization Act of 1934, preference in filling employment vacancies is given to qualified Native American candidates for all positions in the Bureau of Indian Affairs (BIA), and to other positions in the Department of the Interior directly and primarily related to providing services to Indians. Initial appointments under the Act are in the excepted service. Conversion to a career appointment in the competitive service is granted after three years of continuous service and satisfactory performance. Law enforcement careers in the BIA include Correctional Officers, Police Officers, Radio Telecommunication Operators, and Special Agents.

Chapter Two

Salary And Benefits

If you enjoy what you do,
you'll never work another day in your life.
– CONFUCIUS

EDERAL LAW ENFORCEMENT PERSONNEL ENJOY COMPETITIVE SALARIES and a wide range of fringe benefits surpassing those provided by many state and municipal government agencies and firms in the private sector. A recent study conducted by the Congressional Budget Office found that federal benefits are superior to those of large companies in private industry. In addition to health and life insurance, paid holidays, vacation and sick leave, travel allowances, and injury compensation benefits provided to federal employees, many federal law enforcement officers are also covered under special salary and benefit programs. This chapter provides an overview of salary structures and the primary benefits available to sworn and non-sworn federal law enforcement personnel.

FEDERAL PAY SYSTEMS

Federal law enforcement personnel are covered by a number of different pay systems, including some established by individual laws and others by administrative determination. The three statutory pay systems for federal white-collar employees are those of the General Schedule, the Foreign Service, and a system that covers certain employees in the Veterans Health Administration of the Department of Veteran Affairs (VA). Salaries under these systems are governed by policies and principles set forth in the United States Code. The majority of federal law enforcement personnel are covered under the General Schedule pay system. Special Agents and Regional Security Officers of the State Department's Bureau of Diplomatic Security are covered under the Foreign Service pay system. The Veterans Health Administration provides pay plans for VA medical staff.

The General Schedule Pay System

Approximately three-quarters of federal employees are covered under the General Schedule (GS) pay system, including most white-collar personnel in the executive branch and in certain agencies of the legislative branch. The General Schedule consists of fifteen grades, each broadly defined in terms of difficulty and responsibility of the work and the qualifications required for its performance, ranging from GS-1 through GS-15. A salary range of ten steps is provided within each grade, with employees normally starting at step one within a particular grade at entry level. Within-grade advancement to the next step normally occurs after fifty-two weeks of service in the first three steps in a grade, after 104 weeks in steps four through six, and after 156 weeks in steps seven and above. To qualify for advancement to the next higher step an employee must demonstrate work at an acceptable level of competence. Those who demonstrate high quality performance may advance more rapidly within their grades by being granted additional "quality step increases."

An employee may receive only one such increase, however, during any fifty-two week period. A chart which illustrates General Schedule salary grades and steps is shown in Appendix 4.

Administratively Determined Pay Systems

Administratively determined pay systems are those for which Congress has authorized heads of agencies to establish compensation for the entire agency or for particular groups of positions without regard to the General Schedule. Some of the agencies administratively establish their own schedules of rates, while others use the General Schedule grade and step structure although they are not required to do so. Many federal law enforcement personnel are compensated under administratively determined pay systems, although not nearly as many as those covered under the General Schedule.

Other Major Pay Systems

Other major pay systems include the Federal Wage System, which includes the Wage Grade Schedule for certain blue-collar employees; the Senior Executive Service, which covers most management and supervisory positions above the GS-15 level; the Executive Schedule, which covers top officials in the executive branch; and several pay schedules which are administered by the United States Postal Service. These and a number of other pay systems do not apply to the vast majority of federal law enforcement personnel, although agencies such as the Postal Inspection Service are covered under such a system.

LOCALITY PAYMENTS

Federal employees covered under the General Schedule and many other pay systems receive locality-based comparability payments, known as *Locality Pay,* for the difference between prevailing federal and private sector salaries in the geographic location where they are employed. More than thirty metropolitan areas in the United States are designated as qualifying for Locality Pay. Personnel employed in all other areas of the country receive Locality Pay according to the rate established for those in the "Rest of United States" category. Locality Pay rates are adjusted annually. The Salary Schedule shown in Appendix 4 provides an itemization of Locality Pay rates.

LAW ENFORCEMENT SALARY RATES AND ADJUSTMENTS

Law Enforcement Salary Rates

The Federal Law Enforcement Pay Reform Act of 1990 established Special Salary Rates for law enforcement officers at grades GS-3 through GS-10, including pay enhancements which range from one to seven salary steps above General Schedule rates. For example, a police officer who is appointed at grade GS-5 *step one* under the Special Rate would receive a starting salary equal to GS-5 *step eight* in the General Schedule. Similarly, Special Rate GS-7 *step six* is equivalent to GS-7 *step ten* in the General Schedule, and so on. Salary for personnel below GS-3 and above GS-10, however, follow the General Schedule. Special Salary Rates apply to criminal investigators, police officers, correctional officers, field personnel assigned to Federal correctional institutions and military detention or rehabilitation facilities, and certain other law enforcement officers and security specialists. A chart which illustrates Special Salary Rates for law enforcement officers is shown in Appendix 5.

Special Pay Adjustments

The Federal Law Enforcement Pay Reform Act also established Special Pay Adjustments for law enforcement officers in selected metropolitan areas, such as Boston, Los Angeles, New York, San Diego, and San Francisco. These adjustments are administered in the same manner as Locality Pay, although officers receive only the higher of the two, not both. Pay Adjustments apply to all grades, and range from eight to 16 percent of basic pay rates.

PREMIUM PAY

Law Enforcement Availability Pay (LEAP)

Congress enacted the Law Enforcement Availability Pay (LEAP) Act of 1994 to compensate federal criminal investigators for substantial amounts of unscheduled overtime duty which they routinely perform, and to ensure the availability of criminal investigators for unscheduled duty based upon the needs of employing agencies. As a result, the vast majority of personnel in the GS-1811 (Criminal Investigating) and GS-1812 (Game Law Enforcement) series receive a salary premium fixed at 25 percent of basic pay. For example, a criminal investigator whose base salary is $52,000 per year receives an additional 25 percent ($13,000) in LEAP, resulting in a total annual salary of $65,000.

In order to qualify for LEAP, investigators are expected to work, or be available to work, an average of two hours of duty above every regular eight-hour work day. LEAP is a guaranteed employee entitlement that agencies must provide as long as required conditions are met. Some agencies, such Offices of Inspectors General that employ fewer than five criminal investigators, may elect not to cover criminal investigators or are otherwise exempt from LEAP provisions. A Salary Schedule which incorporates LEAP is shown in Appendix 6.

Administratively Uncontrollable Overtime (AUO)

To compensate employees for irregular or occasional overtime work inherent in certain occupations, many agencies provide Administratively Uncontrollable Overtime (AUO) pay to qualifying personnel. AUO is a form of premium pay which ranges from 10 to 25 percent of basic pay depending upon the average number of hours of overtime work performed per week. Qualifying employees must work at least three hours but not more than five hours of overtime per week to receive 10 percent AUO pay; over five but not more than seven hours to receive 15 percent; over seven but not more than nine hours to receive 20 percent; and more than nine hours to receive 25 percent. AUO is paid to Border Patrol Agents and certain other officers, investigators, technicians, and specialists who are involved in field investigative and enforcement activities. Personnel who receive LEAP are not eligible for payment of AUO.

Paid Holidays

Federal employees receive paid leave for ten holidays annually, including: New Years Day, Martin Luther King's Birthday, Washington's Birthday, Memorial Day, Independence Day, Labor Day, Columbus Day, Veterans Day, Thanksgiving Day, and Christmas Day. If a holiday falls on Saturday, the previous Friday is observed as the legal holiday for employees whose basic workweek is Monday through Friday. Similarly, holidays which fall on Sunday are observed on the following Monday. In the case of employees whose basic workweek is other than Monday through Friday, when a holiday falls on a non-workday, these personnel receive paid leave on the first workday before the holiday. Employees who must work on a holiday receive Holiday Pay, which is 100 percent of their rate of basic pay (double time).

Other Premium Pay

Certain personnel receive overtime pay for work performed beyond a standard workday or service week; compensatory time off in lieu of overtime pay; night shift differential pay; and Sunday premium pay when their regularly scheduled workweek includes Sunday.

DEATH AND DISABILITY BENEFITS

Congress enacted the Public Safety Officers' Benefits Act and the Federal Law Enforcement Dependents Assistance Act to provide benefits to the families of officers whose deaths or disabilities are the result of injuries sustained in the line of duty.

Public Safety Officers' Benefits Program

Federal law enforcement officers are eligible for death and disability benefits under the Public Safety Officers' Benefits (PSOB) Act, which was enacted to assist in the recruitment and retention of law enforcement officers and firefighters. The Act was designed to offer peace of mind to men and women seeking careers in public safety and to make a strong statement about the value American society places on the contributions of those who serve their communities in potentially dangerous circumstances.

The PSOB Program provides a one-time financial payment to the eligible survivors of public safety officers whose deaths are the direct and proximate result of a traumatic injury sustained in the line of duty. The Program provides the same benefit to those who have been permanently and totally disabled by a catastrophic personal injury sustained in the line of duty if that injury permanently prevents them from performing any gainful work. Since 1988, the benefit has been adjusted annually to reflect the percentage of change in the Consumer Price Index. For fiscal 1998, the benefit was $141,556.

Law enforcement officers eligible for PSOB Program benefits include, but are not limited to, police, corrections, probation, parole, judicial, and other law enforcement officers of federal, state, county, and local public agencies, as well as the District of Columbia, the Commonwealth of Puerto Rico, and any U.S. territory or possession.

Federal Law Enforcement Dependents Assistance Program

Congress enacted the Federal Law Enforcement Dependents Assistance (FLEDA) Act of 1996 to provide financial assistance for higher education to the spouses and children of federal law enforcement officers killed or disabled in the line of duty. FLEDA benefits are intended for the sole purpose of paying for educational expenses, including tuition, room and board, books, supplies and fees for dependents who attend a qualifying program of education at an eligible institution. Assistance under the Program is available for a period of forty-five months of full-time education or training or for a proportional period for a part-time program.

Funeral Leave for Law Enforcement Officers

Federal law enforcement officers may be excused from duty, without loss of pay or leave, to attend the funeral of a fellow federal law enforcement officer who was killed in the line of duty. Attendance at such a service is considered to be an official duty, and employing agencies are authorized under the United States Code to pay the costs of travel and subsistence for those who attend.

RETIREMENT BENEFITS

Traditional Retirement Benefits

Most federal civilian employees are eligible to receive an unreduced retirement annuity at age sixty with twenty years of service, and at age sixty-two with five years of service. With thirty years of service, personnel who are covered under the Federal Employees' Retirement System (FERS), which includes most who were hired after December 31, 1983, may retire at age fifty-five to fifty-seven depending upon their year of birth. Employees who are covered under the Civil Service Retirement System (CSRS), the predecessor to FERS, may retire at age fifty-five with thirty years of service. There is no mandatory retirement age for federal civilian employees unless they are covered under special retirement provisions for law enforcement officers, firefighters, or air traffic controllers.

Special Law Enforcement Retirement

The majority of fully-commissioned federal law enforcement officers are covered under special provisions which provide for voluntary and mandatory retirement at an earlier age than other government employees. These provisions apply only to personnel who serve in certain "covered" positions, including most criminal investigators, police officers, correctional officers, field personnel assigned to federal correctional institutions and military detention or rehabilitation facilities, and certain other law enforcement officers and security specialists.

Qualifying law enforcement personnel who are covered under FERS may receive an unreduced retirement annuity at the age of fifty with twenty years of federal law enforcement service, or at an earlier age with twenty-five years of such service. Those covered under CSRS may also retire at age fifty with twenty years of service, although are not permitted to retire at an earlier age. Retirement is mandatory for law enforcement officers covered under both systems at the age of fifty-seven.

In most cases, personnel serving in covered positions must be appointed prior to their thirty-seventh birthday. Applicants over the age of thirty-seven who have previous service creditable under special law enforcement retirement provisions sufficient to allow them to retire at age fifty-seven with twenty years of creditable service may also be eligible. The maximum entry age for covered positions is an exception to the provisions against age discrimination contained in the Age Discrimination in Employment Act of 1967.

Federal Thrift Savings Plan

The Federal Thrift Savings Plan (TSP) is a retirement savings and investment plan for federal personnel which provides the same type of savings and tax benefits that many private corporations offer their employees under 401(k) plans. The TSP offers tax-deferred investment earnings, a choice of investment funds, a loan program, portable benefits upon leaving government service, and a choice of withdrawal options.

Employees covered under FERS may contribute up to 10 percent of their basic pay each pay period to a TSP account. Contributions by FERS employees are either partially or fully matched by the government, depending upon the percentage of income contributed. CSRS personnel may contribute up to 5 percent of their basic pay, although they do not receive any agency matching contributions. Employee contributions, agency matching funds, and earnings on all TSP accounts are deferred from income taxes until funds are withdrawn.

OTHER BENEFITS

Life Insurance

Most federal civilian personnel are eligible to participate in the Federal Employees' Group Life Insurance (FEGLI) Program, a plan which offers both life insurance and accidental death and dismemberment coverage. Premiums are based upon the employee's age, and are paid through regular payroll deductions. FEGLI policies build no cash or loan value, and participants are not permitted to borrow against life insurance benefits. Participants may purchase additional life insurance to cover eligible family members, although accidental death and dismemberment coverage is not included.

Healthcare Benefits

The Federal Employees Health Benefits (FEHB) Program provides healthcare insurance coverage to eligible employees through the largest employer-sponsored health insurance program in the world. The FEHB Program offers the widest selection of health plans in the country, including managed fee-for-service plans, point of service plans, and health maintenance organization programs. Enrollees are granted coverage without medical examinations or restrictions relating to age or physical condition, and may elect self-only or self-and-family protection. The government contributes between sixty and 75 percent toward the total cost of premiums depending upon the plan selected. Employees pay their share of premiums through a payroll deduction.

Sick Leave

All full-time federal civilian personnel earn thirteen days of paid sick leave per year, in four-hour increments each biweekly pay period. Sick leave may be used for medical, dental, or optical examination or treatment; for incapacitation; to prevent the exposure of communicable diseases; to conduct adoption-related activities; to provide care for ill family members; or to make arrangements necessitated by the death of a family member or attend the funeral of a family member. In addition, employees may take up to twelve weeks of unpaid leave for similar purposes under provisions of the Family and Medical Leave Act of 1993.

Annual Leave

Federal employees accumulate paid Annual Leave for vacations or other purposes based upon their years of federal service. Annual leave accrues at the rate of thirteen days per year for employees with fewer than three years of service, at twenty days per year for those with three to fifteen years service, and twenty-six days per year for personnel with more than fifteen years of service. Employees are normally prohibited from carrying forward more than 240 hours of annual leave from year to year.

Travel Allowances

Federal civilian employees who travel on official business normally receive reimbursement for transportation and lodging expenses plus a daily allowance for meals and incidental expenses (M&IE). Most hotel chains and many independent establishments offer discounted lodging rates for government travelers. M&IE allowances are paid at a government-wide flat daily rate which varies from one locality to another.

Chapter Three

STANDING OUT FROM THE CROWD

The difference between a successful person and others is not
a lack of strength, not a lack of knowledge, but rather a lack of will.
– VINCE LOMBARDI

YOUR LIKELIHOOD OF SUCCEEDING IN ANY CAREER SEARCH depends considerably on your ability to stand out from the crowd. In order to gain an edge in the highly competitive federal law enforcement application process, you must fully understand the federal civil service process and be able to communicate, both orally and in writing, that you are the best choice.

This concept may not be as simple as it appears. Standing out from the crowd does not necessarily mean that you must always be better qualified than other candidates. More often it means you have invested wisely in getting organized, targeting your career search, maintaining detailed records, evaluating your career skills and carefully matching them to targeted positions, networking, crafting an application or résumé using the right terminology, and performing well during employment interviews. It is a well-known fact that agencies do not always select the best qualified candidates – they often choose those who have invested the time and effort to conduct more effective job search campaigns.

This chapter provides details of specific strategies you can use to launch a successful campaign and land a rewarding career in federal law enforcement.

GETTING ORGANIZED

Perhaps the most important aspect of the job search is to get organized – and running a close second is to *stay* organized. Getting organized consists not only of gathering and arranging job search materials, but also involves targeting your career search, learning about the federal civil service process, and maintaining meticulous records of personal contacts and important information along the way. Time invested in these tasks will allow you to conduct a more efficient and productive campaign.

Targeting Your Career Search

The first step in the search process is to define your goals and target the type of career want. This will allow you to focus your search on a particular field or position and to cover territory more efficiently. Each of the ten career categories in this book provides a wide range of positions from which to choose. Set your sights on positions within one or two of these categories and then target your search efforts according to your career interests.

Learning About the Federal Hiring Process

Since the federal civil service process differs substantially from hiring procedures in the private sector, it is important to understand how the system works prior to navigating your way through the process. Reading this book is a good first step, as it provides an overview of civil service procedures and offers many tips and techniques for conducting your search. Since hiring processes sometimes change, you can also obtain pamphlets from individual agencies, speak to recruiters about the state of their hiring processes, and also visit agency World Wide Web sites for further information. In addition, some trade periodicals, such as *Federal Jobs Digest* and *Federal Career Opportunities*, publish articles which include advice for federal job-seekers (see Chapter Five).

Assembling Job Search Materials

After defining your goals, gather career search materials, such as high school and college transcripts, diplomas, certificates and awards, employment performance evaluations, military discharge documents, professional and character reference lists, blank application forms, and other information which you may use to compose a résumé, complete an application, or take to an interview. It is much less stressful to locate these materials in advance than to search for them on the day that an application is due or an hour before attending an interview.

Maintaining a Record of Agency Contacts

Among the most important aspects of an efficient and successful career search is to maintain good records of all contacts with prospective employers and others who can assist you with your career search. Candidates should record the details of each contact, including the date, agency name, telephone number, names of those contacted and their titles, results of the contact, and any other comments or special notes. An aggressive career search campaign should include numerous contacts which must remain organized and readily available for future reference and follow up. A handy *Agency Contact Record* which can be photocopied and used for this purpose is provided in Appendix 7.

NETWORKING

Establishing and Maintaining Personal Contacts

While networking is an important strategy in any career search, it can be an especially effective tool when attempting to get into the vast federal workforce. Networking consists of periodic contact with college professors and advisors, career placement office staff, federal agency personnel specialists, family members, friends, and any others who may become aware of hiring opportunities and sources of information. Contact should also be made with law enforcement personnel with whom you have come to know during the course of internships, co-op positions or career fairs. Becoming active in professional organizations is also an excellent way of establishing communication with criminal justice professionals. Let your contacts know what your goals are and ask for referrals to others who may be able to help you. Expanding your contact base is fundamental to successful networking.

APPLICATION FORMS AND RÉSUMÉS

Standing out from the crowd depends largely on your ability to assemble a comprehensive written application package which emphasizes your skills and attributes. An effective application or résumé starts with a thorough evaluation of your strengths, accomplishments, and career skills. In order to be competitive you must carefully match your skills to the targeted position and create a powerful written account of what you have to offer the agency. Using dynamic and industry-specific terminology will also make an impact.

Choosing an Application Format

Except in circumstances in which candidates are required to apply electronically or over the telephone for certain positions, federal job applicants must decide whether to submit an application form or a résumé.

Many Federal employees who were hired before 1995 are most comfortable with the SF-171 application form since they have already used it when applying for employment or promotions. These employees often decide to continue using the SF-171 in lieu of composing résumés or switching to the OF-612 application.

On the other hand, many applicants who have no experience with the SF-171 decide to steer clear of this form and opt for the less cumbersome and more user-friendly OF-612, as it takes less time to complete. The OF-612 is a good choice, although users should use continuation sheets or attachments in order to provide sufficient details relating to employment experience and other qualifications.

Résumés are appropriate for those who are adept at documenting their background without the structure inherent in formal application forms. This format provides for flexibility and the opportunity to emphasize skills and accomplishments in a unique manner. It is important to realize, however, that a *Federal résumé* differs significantly from those used in the private sector. As discussed in Chapter One, Federal résumés must include specific personal data, job information, and other details which are not normally included in résumés submitted to private industry. In addition, while one-page résumés are the rule of thumb in the private sector, a one-page federal résumé would not sufficiently cover the elements and detail required of federal job applicants in most situations.

While there are subtle advantages to one application format or the other depending upon your background, the format you choose is far less important than the content of your application package.

Evaluating Your Career Skills

The first step in putting together an effective résumé or application is to evaluate your background and experience to determine what career skills you have to offer. Carefully analyze the tasks you performed and your accomplishments at each job you held and create an exhaustive list of the skills you developed. Do not limit the list to full-time employment experience; also include any part-time or volunteer work, internship experience, and co-op positions. Make a list of all professional memberships, achievements, awards, certificates, licenses, leadership activities, proficiency in foreign languages, special skills, public speaking experience, and other activities.

If you have little or no experience related to the field you are seeking to enter, also list any extracurricular activities and hobbies, as skills developed during these endeavors may also be applied to certain careers. Examine each item on the list and think about the skills or talents they require. All jobs, internships, extracurricular activities, hobbies, and other pursuits require particular knowledge, skills and abilities – many of which are transferable to careers in law enforcement. Write them all down. Also list the schools, training seminars, and workshops you attended (including dates and locations), and any degrees, honors, fellowships, and certificates received. The quality of the finished product depends largely upon the depth and thoroughness of your effort in this step.

Matching Your Skills to the Position

Once you have prepared a list of your career skills, you can match your skills to those needed for the positions you are applying for when preparing applications or résumés. Use the following strategies to put together a winning package:

Customize Every Résumé or Application. It is critical that you tailor every résumé or application to the specific requirements of each targeted position. Job vacancy announcements include a listing of the required or preferred knowledge, skills and abilities (KSA's). Study the qualifications and tailor your application or résumé to the KSA's of the position, highlighting all education, training, experience, talents and accomplishments that demonstrate your ability to perform the job skills. Do not make the mistake of providing generic job descriptions which present little or no information about your individual accomplishments. Instead, describe your specific responsibilities and achievements and place emphasis on skills which are applicable to the job you are applying for.

Don't Undersell Yourself. Among the biggest mistakes that federal job applicants make is to undersell themselves. As a result, they lose consideration for employment, not because they were not qualified; but, because they failed to spell out their qualifications in writing. This is often a result of their misunderstanding of the federal job application rating process, under which applicants are scored based on the information provided in their applications or résumés. Rating panel members are forbidden from making assumptions or using personal knowledge in the rating process, no matter what positions you held. They may use only the written information that is provided by applicants. In other words, unless it is clearly spelled out on your application or résumé, you will not receive credit for it.

Sweat the Details. Federal job applicants should always describe in detail any experience and accomplishments that are related in any way to the career they are pursuing. Sit down and think carefully about all of your work experience and the skills you performed, regardless of the career field. Many jobs that are unrelated to criminal justice require skills which are applicable to careers in law enforcement, investigations, corrections, security, and compliance work. For example, record all of your experience which involved interacting with the public, gathering and organizing information, resolving complaints, troubleshooting, solving problems, writing reports, making oral presentations, using computers, establishing and attaining goals, following organizational policies and procedures, and coordinating projects with other people or organizations. Also highlight any experience which demonstrates communication skills, initiative, leadership, dependability, persistence, innovation, skill in problem solving, and ability to perform in stressful situations. You will be more competitive if you can demonstrate that you have experience which is related to the responsibilities of the position you are applying for, even if your experience has nothing to do with law enforcement or careers in the criminal justice system.

Listing and Describing Internships

Unless you have extensive experience related to the position you're applying for, you should list any job-related internships as separate positions on your application or résumé. Indicating internships on a list of extracurricular activities without providing details is of little value.

Since internships often represent the only job-related experience for many recent college graduates and those making a career change, it is critical that you describe exactly *what you did* rather than what you *observed*. Under separate headings for each internship, provide complete details of your activities and place emphasis on the specific tasks you performed and any accomplishments. Include a description of activities, such as operating technical equipment and communications devices, assisting with investigations, conducting surveillance, performing patrol duties, reviewing financial records and other documents, participating in personal interviews, assisting with trial preparation, answering inquiries from the public, searching databases, and solving problems. These and other tasks performed during internships should not be overlooked, as they often provide valuable hands-on experience which is directly related to the careers you are seeking.

Using Targeted Action Verbs

Whenever possible, use simple and concise phrases instead of long-winded sentences to describe your background and experience. Phrases which begin with well-chosen *action verbs* provide power and direction to résumés, application forms, and cover letters. Choose words which emphasize experience, skills, and activities *that are related to the targeted position*. Targeted action verbs are highly effective in conveying leadership, responsibility, and accomplishment. An extensive list of action verbs which are useful for federal résumés and application forms is shown in Appendix 8.

Completing Application Forms

It is very important that you fill out application forms completely and follow all instructions carefully. Do not omit any requested information, and make sure that all information provided is correct. Applicants are often eliminated from consideration for jobs because they failed to follow application directions or omitted pertinent information.

Getting a Second Opinion

After you have completed your application or résumé it is wise to have it proofread and critiqued by an objective person, such as a college faculty member, career placement office advisor, professional in the field of the career you are seeking, family member, or friend. Have them check for appearance, format, grammar, punctuation, style, misspelled words, and typographical errors. Many colleges and universities offer this service free of charge to enrolled students and alumni.

Using Cover Letters

Job seekers should always send cover letters with résumés or applications as a way of introducing themselves and explaining how their talents will benefit the organization. A cover letter should convey serious interest and enthusiasm, and must be short (no more than one page) and to the point. It should capture the reader's attention, follow a business letter format, identify the position sought, and highlight the sender's credentials and any unique qualifications. Cover letters must be individually tailored for each position. Candidates who qualify under special hiring programs, such as those for veterans or the Outstanding Scholar Program, should always highlight this in their cover letters.

PERSONAL INTERVIEWS

The application process for the majority of federal law enforcement careers includes one or more personal interviews. Agencies often conduct interviews to further assess competitive applicants toward the end of the application process, and to allow candidates an opportunity to learn more about the targeted position and the agency. Since virtually all careers in federal law enforcement require confidence and interpersonal skills, both of these attributes are evaluated carefully by interviewers. Personal interviews provide knowledgeable and well-prepared applicants with a golden opportunity to showcase their qualifications. Utilize the following strategies to make a positive impression.

Interview Preparation

Learn as Much as Possible about the Organization. Job applicants who take the time to learn about the agency and the position are far more likely to adequately articulate what they have to offer, while also sending the message that they are serious about a career with the organization. Many applicants conduct no more than minimal research about the careers they are seeking, and it shows. Employers take notice of those who have – or have not – done their homework.

Review Your Résumé or Application. Since many interview questions are based on information provided in résumés and applications, it is important to review these documents in advance. Interviewers often start off by confirming information which was provided by applicants months prior to the interview. Brush up on the details so as not to provide contradictory information.

Prepare Answers to Broad Questions about Yourself. Most interviews include a number of broad questions pertaining to education, work experience, job-related skills, and career goals. To avoid surprises, review these areas prior to interviews and anticipate probable questions.

Be Prepared to Ask Questions. A one-way job interview which consists only of questions asked by the employer and none by the applicant is more of an interrogation than an interview. An exchange of information is appropriate for virtually all job interviews, and applicants should be prepared to ask meaningful questions about the agency and the position.

During the Interview

Focus on the Positive. Candidates should always answer questions in a direct and positive manner, and speak positively of present and former employers. Express a positive attitude and interest in the position using information you gathered to prepare for the interview. Explain how your experience, education, and training will make you productive in the shortest time with minimal supervision. Sell yourself with specific examples of your skills and accomplishments.

Listen Carefully. Candidates who perform well during job interviews owe much of their success to good listening skills. Those who make an effort to listen attentively for information about the position and the agency tend to ask better questions, which sets them apart from others. Always listen carefully and take a brief moment to think about each question before responding.

Ask Questions During the Interview. Employers expect applicants to ask questions about the agency, working conditions, training programs, advancement opportunities, job performance measures, and other issues.

Having the confidence to ask appropriate questions during an interview will not only make a positive impression, but will also allow you to become more informed about the agency and the position.

After the Interview

Provide Requested Information. Always provide copies of references, certificates, diplomas, transcripts, or any other credentials or requested information as soon as possible after an interview.

Send a Follow-up Letter. Write a brief letter of appreciation after every interview. Thank the participants for their time and reiterate your interest in the position. Mail follow-up letters within twenty-four hours of the interview.

Evaluate Your Performance. In an effort to make each interview a learning experience, evaluate your performance by asking yourself whether you prepared adequately, presented your qualifications effectively, listened well, asked appropriate questions, and learned all that you needed to know about the position. After answering these questions as objectively as possible, make a list of specific ways you can improve, and review the list before your next interview.

PERSEVERANCE

Stay the Course

Searching for a position in federal law enforcement is not only hard work, but often a lengthy and discouraging process. While competition for these prestigious careers is intense, the rewards are plentiful for those who take an organized approach and stick with it. Utilize your personal network, keep good records, contact as many agencies as possible, and try every method you can to get your foot in the door. You must exercise steady persistence in spite of difficulties, obstacles or setbacks along the way. In order to stand out from the crowd you must remain focused on your goal. If you are qualified and determined, your perseverance will pay off.

Chapter Four

THE FOUR QUICKEST WAYS TO GET HIRED

Even if you are on the right track,
you'll get run over if you just sit there.
– WILL ROGERS

THE ROAD TO A CAREER IN FEDERAL LAW ENFORCEMENT CAN BE a fast track for candidates who either qualify for certain hiring programs or strategically place themselves in the right place at the right time. The fast track is often traveled by college graduates with good grades, those who held a co-op position or wisely invested their time in an internship related to their field of interest, as well as current and former federal employees who have served in any occupation. Among the primary benefits of these pathways over traditional approaches is that they usually allow qualifying candidates to compete in applicant pools that are considerably smaller. Carefully examine each of the following strategies and utilize as many as you qualify for.

FAST TRACK NUMBER ONE

Apply as an Outstanding Scholar

The Outstanding Scholar Program is perhaps the best kept secret in the federal law enforcement job search arena. This program allows agencies to hire college graduates at the GS-5 or GS-7 levels directly, without having to conduct competitive examining processes. In other words, direct appointments can be made even when no formal job vacancy announcements have been issued, and without administering written examinations or implementing other competitive hiring procedures. Many agencies prefer to hire personnel though the Outstanding Scholar Program because it allows them to recruit bright candidates while also eliminating most of the time-consuming tasks associated with competitive appointment processes.

While most positions in federal law enforcement do not specify a minimum college grade point average in order to qualify, in many cases position vacancies are open only to Outstanding Scholar candidates. As a result, job seekers who qualify under the Program are more likely to land a career in federal law enforcement simply because they are eligible for a common pathway of entry which is not available to others.

Outstanding Scholar applicants must have graduated with a grade point average (GPA) of 3.45 or better on a 4.0 scale for all undergraduate coursework, or have graduated in the upper 10 percent of their graduating class in the college, university or major subdivision (such as the College of Liberal Arts or the School of Criminal Justice). Candidates may apply any time after graduation, or a few months before graduation as long as they meet GPA or class standing requirements at the time a job offer is made.

Qualifying Law Enforcement Positions
The Outstanding Scholar Program is applicable only for certain positions. In addition to careers in business,

finance, management, personnel, and other administrative fields, a number of law enforcement and investigative career vacancies are filled under the Program, such as:

Park Ranger, Mounted Park Ranger, and River Ranger (GS-0025); Industrial Security Specialist, Information Security Specialist, Personnel Security Specialist, Physical Security Specialist, and Security Specialist (GS-0080); Intelligence Operations Specialist, Intelligence Research Analyst, Intelligence Research Specialist, and Intelligence Specialist, (GS-0132); Wage and Hour Compliance Specialist (GS-0249); Internal Revenue Officer (GS-1169); Civil Investigator and Investigator (GS-1810); Criminal Investigator, Deputy U.S. Marshal, Detective, Internal Security Inspector, and Special Agent (GS-1811); Fish and Wildlife Special Agent and Special Agent Pilot (GS-1812); Immigration Inspector (GS-1816); Alcohol, Tobacco and Firearms Inspector (GS-1854); Customs Import Specialist (GS-1889), and Customs Inspector (GS-1890).

How to Apply as an Outstanding Scholar

For openings which are restricted to Outstanding Scholar applicants that are advertised though formal vacancy announcements, Program details are usually specified under the *Area of Consideration* heading of these announcements. Agencies may also hire personnel under the Program without advertising vacancies.

Whether responding to a formal job vacancy announcement or sending unsolicited résumés or other materials to agencies, those who qualify under the Outstanding Scholar Program should *always* attach a cover letter which explains that they qualify under the Program, and should also attach a photocopy of their college transcript. In many cases, agencies that do not have current job vacancies will take notice of candidates who qualify under the Program and will retain these materials for further consideration once an opening occurs.

FAST TRACK NUMBER TWO

Acquire Federal Competitive Status

As discussed in Chapter One, federal employees who are serving in either career or career-conditional appointments in the competitive service have *competitive status*, and all other job seekers are classified as *non-status candidates*. A substantial proportion of job vacancies in federal law enforcement are open only to applicants with competitive status (known as *status applicants*), or in some cases only to employees of the agency that is filling the position. In other words, federal personnel are eligible to compete for many jobs in what amounts to an internal job market, and non-status candidates are effectively shut out of the process. In addition, many *former* federal employees also have reinstatement eligibility, which allows them to reenter the competitive service workforce without competing with the general public in civil service examination processes.

In consideration of the clear advantage held by federal employees in obtaining certain jobs, it only makes sense that in order to compete on a level playing field one must first acquire a position *somewhere* in the federal system. This strategy is utilized by many candidates who are serious about landing a federal law enforcement career and are willing to invest a year or two in a job that may not have been their first choice, although serves its purpose in providing competitive status. Once on the inside, these employees have access to internal job postings and also learn about job vacancies with other agencies that often go unnoticed by those outside of the government, and can apply for jobs that are not open to competition from the general public.

Obtain a Position Related to Law Enforcement

Although accepting a job in a field unrelated to law enforcement will extend competitive status, it is best for applicants to seek employment which is in some way related their career of choice. For example, if your goal is to become a Special Agent with the U.S. Customs Service and you have an opportunity to accept a position as a Customs Inspector, then take the job! Once inside the organization you will have the opportunity to watch for postings for Special Agent vacancies which may be open only to federal employees or, better yet, only to Customs Service personnel. Similarly, accepting a position as a Federal Police Officer, Probation Officer, Security Specialist, Dispatcher, or any other position related to law enforcement will not only result in competitive status, but should also allow you to gain experience related to the position you hope to apply for down the road. Accepting such a position also affords an opportunity to interact with law enforcement personnel from other agencies, and to find out about openings with their agencies as well.

Obtain Federal Employment in any Field

Even accepting federal employment in a position which is not related to law enforcement will provide competitive status, experience, and also the opportunity to apply for other positions which are open only to federal personnel or those of the employing agency. This strategy is especially appropriate for those who are either unemployed or underemployed. Unless you already have a good job and law enforcement experience, waiting empty-handed for your ultimate career appointment to come along makes little sense. Instead of passing up the opportunity to accept a federal job which is not your first choice, you should strongly consider getting your foot in the door first – and gaining experience and competitive status in doing so.

FAST TRACK NUMBER THREE

Obtain a Co-op Position

Many federal law enforcement agencies offer cooperative education (co-op) opportunities for college students which provide meaningful work experience and often lead directly to employment after graduation. Most of these programs are available to undergraduate students in their junior or senior year of study, and to graduate students pursuing a master's or Ph.D. degree. Depending on the program format and recruiting needs of employing agencies, students normally alternate between periods of paid work experience and classroom study for at least two academic terms, and sometimes for up to two years. Co-op participants usually earn a salary which is either slightly below or equal to that of the entry level for the occupation in which they serve. College credit is awarded in most cases.

Gain Valuable Experience

Co-op programs enable college students to integrate classroom instruction with practical professional experience in their major field of study which is not available in the classroom. Participants normally perform many of the primary duties of an occupation under the supervision of experienced personnel. For example, many Federal investigative agencies allow co-op students to participate in virtually every aspect of criminal investigations, including tasks such as performing record checks, participating in interviews, reviewing financial records and creating spreadsheets, conducting surveillance, operating technical investigative equipment, participating in intelligence gathering activities, assisting with the execution of search warrants, recovering and processing evidence, and meeting with Assistant United States Attorneys. In many instances, co-op students also participate in training exercises along with full-time personnel.

Whether in the public or private sectors, most employers prefer to hire college graduates who also have professional experience related to the jobs which they are filling. Co-op employment allows participants to graduate with firsthand experience under their belts, which provides an advantage over applicants without experience when seeking employment after graduation.

Co-op Positions Often Lead Directly to Employment

Many federal law enforcement agencies utilize co-op programs as a primary recruiting strategy, and convert student participants to full-time employees upon graduation. In most cases, these agencies allocate funds prior to bringing co-op participants on board with the expectation of filling anticipated job vacancies down the line. Undergraduate students who perform satisfactorily in their co-op experience typically are offered employment at the completion of their senior year, while graduate students sometimes have an opportunity to hire on prior to graduation. On the other hand, participants are under no obligation to accept employment. Those who do not hire on at the conclusion of their co-op participation still gain valuable experience which will be helpful when seeking employment elsewhere.

Application Process

Placement into co-op positions is usually very competitive. In addition to screening processes that are conducted by participating colleges and universities, federal law enforcement agencies usually require co-op candidates to undergo a formal application process which includes personal interviews, a background investigation, drug testing, and sometimes a medical examination. In most cases, candidates must also submit application forms and academic transcripts.

Information concerning co-op opportunities with federal law enforcement agencies is available from college cooperative education offices, job placement offices, or criminal justice faculty. Many college criminal justice departments also have co-op program advisors or coordinators on staff who can answer questions and assist students in obtaining co-op positions.

FAST TRACK NUMBER FOUR

Serve in a Criminal Justice Internship

In a similar manner to co-op positions, criminal justice internships also provide an opportunity for students to enhance their education and make practical application of classroom theory. Internships usually involve one academic term of unpaid field study in which students observe and participate in various tasks associated with a career in their academic major. This experience allows students to explore their career interests under actual working conditions, and to make informed choices before moving into the workforce. Internship opportunities tend to be more plentiful than co-op positions.

Although internships are not usually designed to lead directly to employment, many lead to employment *indirectly.* In other words, internship experience allows students to showcase their skills and potential, and also to get their foot in the door when seeking employment after college. As a result, interns gain the inside track with the agency they served, and often have an advantage over applicants who are unknown. In addition, interns who perform well sometimes acquire referrals to other agencies seeking qualified candidates.

Variety of Internship Opportunities

Criminal justice internships cover disciplines such as uniformed law enforcement, criminal investigation, intelligence, behavioral sciences, juvenile justice, probation and parole, forensic sciences, court administration, corrections, security, radio communications, research, and many others. While responsibilities vary depending upon the agency and type of work involved, interns perform tasks such as searching databases; examining financial records; observing undercover activities; organizing intelligence information; observing interviews with victims or witnesses; participating in search warrant execution; assisting with investigations and surveillance operations; analyzing evidence; observing legal proceedings; performing patrol duty (sometimes in uniform); assisting with prisoner handling, transportation, and processing; performing laboratory tests; operating security equipment; assisting with security surveys; creating audiovisual materials; operating communications equipment; conducting research projects; participating in training programs; and completing various clerical assignments.

A wide variety of federal agencies have provided internships to college students in the past including: USDA Forest Service; USDA Office of Inspector General; Central Intelligence Agency; EPA Criminal Investigation Division; Federal Protective Service; HUD Office of Inspector General; U.S. Park Police; Drug Enforcement Administration; Federal Bureau of Investigation; U.S. Immigration and Naturalization Service; U.S. Marshals Service; U.S. Postal Inspection Service; Bureau of Alcohol, Tobacco and Firearms; U.S. Customs; Internal Revenue Service; U.S. Secret Service; Federal Law Enforcement Training Center; State Department Bureau of Diplomatic Security; and State Department Office of Inspector General, among others.

Professional Networking

Criminal justice internships enable students to establish valuable contacts with professionals in the field which can lead to a successful job search. By interacting with those on the inside, interns can find out about advertised and unadvertised job vacancies, obtain advice, and seek referrals to other individuals or agencies. In many cases, these contacts can significantly reduce the amount of time it takes to obtain employment, and may mean the difference between landing a great career or none at all.

Internship Selection and Placement

Selection processes for internships can be very competitive, and placement opportunities vary from year to year and from one school to another. Agencies often require intern candidates to submit application forms, transcripts, an essay, and other materials anywhere from four months to one year in advance. Background checks are usually required. Students should inquire about internship opportunities early in their academic careers in order to properly plan for this experience, and should apply for these positions as early as possible in the application process. Most college criminal justice programs have internship coordinators or advisors on staff who can provide guidance and specific details about placement opportunities.

Chapter Five

SOURCES OF FEDERAL EMPLOYMENT INFORMATION

Knowledge is of two kinds. We know a subject
ourselves, or we know where we can find information upon it.
– SAMUEL JOHNSON

FEDERAL LAW ENFORCEMENT AGENCIES ARE ALWAYS SEARCHING for talented individuals to fill vacancies in critical occupations. Information on career opportunities in the federal workforce is available from a variety of resources which range from the information superhighway to more traditional sources. The key to finding out about job vacancies is knowing where to look.

Recruiting information can be obtained from career periodicals and newspapers which are geared exclusively to federal job seekers, telephone-based systems which provide up-to-date details on job vacancies, high-tech World Wide Web sites which utilize sophisticated search capabilities, and resources such as newspaper classified advertisements and agency personnel offices. This chapter provides an overview of many sources of information which will make your federal law enforcement career search more productive.

THE U.S. OFFICE OF PERSONNEL MANAGEMENT

The United States Office of Personnel Management (OPM) maintains an extensive collection of information pertaining to federal employment and civil service procedures. The public may access this information free of charge either at OPM service centers, on-line via the World Wide Web, via computer modem access to an electronic bulletin board, or through automated telephone response and FAX systems. The OPM Web site is located at: http://www.opm.gov/.

Federal Job Information Touch-Screen Computers

OPM manages a computer-based system utilizing touch-screen technology that provides job posting information. These kiosks, located nationwide, provide information on current worldwide federal job opportunities, and also allow users to request application packages. Touch-Screen Computer kiosks are located at OPM Federal Employment Information Centers in major cities around the country, at many state employment service centers and social service agencies, and within job placement offices at some colleges and universities.

Federal Job Opportunities Bulletin Board

This electronic bulletin board contains electronic want ads for the federal government, job search tips, salary information, information on job fairs, and much more. Users can scan open vacancy announcements while on-line or download them to a computer. This site can be accessed with a personal computer and modem by calling (912) 757-3100; or through the Internet (Telnet only) at: fjob.opm.gov. This service is available twenty-four hours a day, seven days a week.

FedFax Document Information System

OPM also provides an automated service which allows users to obtain employment-related documents and forms via fax machine twenty-four hours a day, seven days a week. To use this system, contact FedFax by using a touch-tone telephone, fax machine or computer fax-modem, then follow the prompts to receive an *Index of Available Documents*. A copy of this list will be sent instantly, along with instructions for obtaining dozens of documents relating to federal employment opportunities, qualification requirements, applications, special hiring programs, benefits, and other subjects. To access the system, contact FedFax at any of the following locations: Atlanta (404-331-5267); Denver (303-969-7764); Detroit (313-226-2593); San Francisco (415-744-7002); or Washington, D.C. (202-606-2600).

Career America Connection

The OPM Career America Connection is a telephone-based system that provides instant access to current information on federal job opportunities worldwide, student employment programs, salary and benefits information, special recruitment messages, employment policies and procedures, examinations, and more. Users are guided through a series of prompts allowing searches for position vacancies by occupational category, job series, or position title. Copies of vacancy announcements, application packages, forms, and other information can also be obtained through this service. Requested information is normally mailed or faxed within twenty-four hours. Career America Connection can be reached by telephone at 912-757-3000, twenty-four hours a day, seven days a week.

RESOURCES ON THE WORLD WIDE WEB

The World Wide Web offers a vast supply of information which can be very helpful in your job search. Extensive background information on federal law enforcement agencies and careers can be obtained by conducting keyword searches using popular Internet search engines such as Infoseek, Yahoo, Excite, and Lycos, among others. Search engines also provide links to job vacancy announcements which are posted on OPM's *USA Jobs* Web site. If you do not have a computer or Internet access, you can log onto the Web at many public and college libraries. Web resources are available twenty-four hours a day, seven days a week.

USA Jobs Web Site

One of the best resources for federal career information is the *USA Jobs* Web site, which is maintained by OPM. This site provides users with access to information on current job openings listed in the Federal Jobs Database, full text vacancy announcements, salary schedules, answers to frequently asked questions about federal employment and special hiring programs, and other information. Users can search for job vacancies by title, occupational category or series, department or agency, or geographic area. This site also allows users to print hard copies of vacancy announcements and other documents. Serious job hunters should make the *USA Jobs* Web site a regular stop on the road to landing a federal law enforcement career. *USA Jobs* operates twenty-four hours a day, seven days a week, and may be accessed at: http://www.usajobs.opm.gov/.

FedWorld Information Network

FedWorld was established by the National Technical Information Service, an agency of the U.S. Department of Commerce, to serve as the on-line locator service for a comprehensive inventory of information disseminated by the federal government. The FedWorld Information Network supports a federal job announcement database which uses files created by the Office of Personnel Management in Macon, Georgia. This search engine allows users to search for job vacancy information by keyword, occupational series, salary grade, or geographic area. FedWorld may be accessed on the Web at: http://www.fedworld.gov/.

Federal Agency Web Sites

Many federal law enforcement agencies maintain Web sites which provide a general overview and history of the organization, information relating to specific careers, an overview of recruiting processes, and a listing of current job opportunities. Some also provide recruiting bulletins, profiles of famous cases, summaries of enforcement activities, training information, internal search engines, links to other sources of information, and access to policy manuals, reports, strategic plans and other documents. Agency Web site addresses are indicated at the end of each career profile included in this book.

IG Net

IG Net is a Web site which is dedicated to the work of more than sixty Inspector General agencies that conduct investigations, inspections, and audits. This site provides an extensive listing of job vacancies in the Inspector General community, full text vacancy announcements, salary schedules, information on training seminars and workshops, a profile of the Inspector General Criminal Investigator Academy, a search engine, and links to home pages of various agencies and other on-line resources. Considering that many of the best careers in federal law enforcement are with Inspector General agencies, this Web site should be viewed regularly during your career search. Access the *IG Net* site at: http://www.ignet.gov/ignet/.

CAREER PERIODICALS AND NEWSPAPERS

Federal Career Opportunities

Each sixty-four page issue of *Federal Career Opportunities* contains details of thousands of federal job vacancies from entry level through the Senior Executive Service which are located nationwide and overseas. Listings are organized first by department or agency, and then by General Schedule (GS) series classification. Every issue also includes several articles pertaining to federal hiring practices, employment trends, recruiting drives, and other related subjects. An on-line version is also accessible by subscription. *Federal Career Opportunities* is published every two weeks and is available from: Federal Research Service, 243 Church Street NW, P.O. Box 1059; Vienna, VA 22183. Phone: 800-822-5027. World Wide Web: http://www.fedjobs.com/.

Federal Jobs Digest

The *Federal Jobs Digest* newspaper is published every two weeks with details of thousands of federal job vacancies located nationwide and overseas. Each thirty-two page publication also includes around a dozen articles and features relating to agency hiring plans, advice on preparing federal résumés and application forms, and news items related to federal employment. The *Federal Jobs Digest* Web site also provides job vacancy information on-line, recruiting information, and access to various job search services. *Federal Jobs Digest* is available in bookstores, or from: Breakthrough Publications, 310 North Highland Avenue; Ossining, NY 10562. Phone: 800-824-5000. World Wide Web: http://www.jobsfed.com/.

The Federal Times

The Federal Times is a weekly newspaper which is devoted to the issues and events that impact the federal workplace. Each twenty-four page issue includes dozens of articles relating to federal salary and benefits, actions in Congress and OPM, legal updates, and other news and information of interest to federal employees and job applicants. Informative articles pertaining to federal law enforcement matters appear regularly in this publication. *The Federal Times* normally includes a listing of approximately 100 current job vacancies in all career areas which are open to current or former federal employees. Subscription information is available from: *Federal Times*, 6883 Commercial Drive; Springfield, VA 22159. Phone: 800-368-5718. World Wide Web: http://www.federaltimes.com/.

Newspaper Classified Advertisements

Many federal agencies advertise job vacancies in the classified section of various local and national newspapers such as the *New York Times, Washington Post, Wall Street Journal, Los Angeles Times, USA Today, Chicago Tribune,* and *Detroit News.* These advertisements often provide few details beyond the job title, basic qualifications, application deadline, and contact information. Some agencies also provide a brief outline of position duties, salary and benefits, number of vacancies, Web site information, and other details. Newspaper classified ads should not be overlooked as a resource for federal job vacancy information.

OTHER SOURCES OF INFORMATION

Federal Agency Personnel Offices

Information pertaining to current job vacancies, minimum requirements, recruiting plans, training, and other employment-related matters is available from virtually all federal agency personnel offices. While the majority of these offices are located within their headquarters operations in and around Washington, D.C., recruiting information may be obtained from many regional and local offices nationwide. Many federal agency personnel offices also operate twenty-four hour employment hotlines which provide current job vacancy details and other recruiting information over the telephone.

State Employment Service Centers

State Employment Service Centers or Employment Security Offices also provide information relating to current federal job vacancies. Some offices have OPM Touch-Screen Computers on site, while others provide personal computers with Internet service which allow access to the OPM Web site.

College Career Placement Offices

Most colleges and universities provide career placement services to their students and alumni. Career placement offices usually provide information relating to job vacancies in business, nonprofit organizations, and government agencies. Many also provide career counseling services, conduct mock interviews, maintain career resource libraries, sponsor job search workshops and career fairs, and arrange on-campus interviews. Visit career placement offices early in your academic pursuits to take full advantage of these services.

Professional Organizations

Professional and trade organizations are excellent resources for finding out about job vacancies and establishing contacts with professionals in the field. Most of these groups hold regular meetings, conduct training seminars and conferences, and publish informative journals or newsletters. Some also offer career placement services and maintain job hotlines. Many well-known criminal justice organizations offer special membership categories and reduced rates for students, such as the Academy of Criminal Justice Sciences, American Correctional Association, American Society of Criminology, American Society for Industrial Security, and International Association of Law Enforcement Intelligence Analysts, among others. Active membership in professional organizations also demonstrates interest and involvement in the field.

Career Fairs

Career fairs remain an integral part of the recruiting effort for many agencies who are seeking the best and brightest candidates. Attending career fairs provides a unique opportunity for job-seekers to learn about federal law enforcement agencies and employment opportunities, to meet professionals in the field, and to develop a networking contact base. While all career fairs have professionals on hand to answer questions and pass out literature, some also conduct on-the-spot employment interviews or mock interviews. Obtain business cards from those who represent agencies you are interested in, and inquire about other individuals you may contact for further information.

Chapter Six

CRIMINAL INVESTIGATORS

You can get a lot more done with a kind word
and a gun, than with a kind word alone.
– AL CAPONE

FEDERAL CRIMINAL INVESTIGATORS IN THE UNITED STATES are among the most highly respected and thoroughly trained law enforcement officers in the world. While duties vary widely by the size and type of agency, these personnel conduct complex investigations which involve a broad range of criminal offenses; examine business and financial records associated with white-collar crime investigations; monitor court-authorized wiretaps; conduct surveillance; track the importation and interstate movement of drugs, contraband, stolen property, and other goods; infiltrate criminal organizations; execute search and arrest warrants; serve subpoenas; provide security for high-ranking officials and diplomats; and participate in sensitive undercover assignments. Investigations are often carried out through large-scale task force operations which involve federal, state and local law enforcement and regulatory agencies.

Criminal investigators must have a knowledge of investigative techniques, laws of evidence, rules of criminal procedure, precedent court decisions, search and seizure, and constitutional rights. They must also maintain close working relationships with Assistant United States Attorneys. Interaction with confidential informants and liaison with other law enforcement officers and sources of information are critical to the success of investigative operations.

This chapter includes profiles of criminal investigators with seventy-one agencies, of which nearly all are authorized to carry firearms and make arrests. Many are granted this authority through statutory laws, including those who serve in agencies such as the FBI, U.S. Marshals Service, USDA Office of Inspector General, DEA, and U.S. Postal Inspection Service. Certain criminal investigators without statutory authority are deputized by the Justice Department. Most criminal investigators are also covered under special retirement provisions for law enforcement officers, and receive 25 percent Law Enforcement Availability Pay in addition to their base salary.

The vast majority of criminal investigators are classified in the GS-1811 series under the working title of Special Agent, although criminal investigators also serve under the titles of Deputy U.S. Marshal, Detective, Internal Security Inspector, Investigator, and Postal Inspector.

CRIMINAL INVESTIGATOR (GS-1811)
OFFICE OF INSPECTOR GENERAL
DEFENSE INFORMATION SYSTEMS AGENCY
U.S. DEPARTMENT OF DEFENSE

Overview: The Defense Information Systems Agency (DISA), a combat support agency of the Defense Department, is responsible for planning, developing, and supporting command, control, communications, and information systems that serve the needs of the National Command Authorities under all conditions of peace and war. Agency field operations include the White House Communications Agency; Defense Information Technology Contracting Organization; DISA Space Command, and others. DISA Office of Inspector General (OIG) Criminal Investigators conduct sensitive and complex criminal and general investigations of federal laws concerning fraud, waste, abuse, or mismanagement in DISA programs and operations. Investigations often focus on allegations of fraud pertaining to Agency contracts and procurement, and violations of the Uniform Code of Military Justice (UCMJ). Operations may be conducted jointly with other Defense Department investigative divisions and various federal, state, or local law enforcement agencies. This is a civilian position and does not require active duty military service.

Qualifications: Applicants must be U.S. citizens. Eyesight requirements include "sufficiently good vision in each eye, with or without correction." Corrected or uncorrected near vision must be sufficient to read printed material the size of typewritten characters. Hearing loss must not exceed 35 decibels at 1000, 2000, and 3000 Hz. Requirements for appointment to GS-5 level include completion of a four-year course of study leading to a bachelor's degree, OR three years general experience, one year of which was equivalent to GS-4; for GS-7, one full year of graduate education, or superior academic achievement during undergraduate studies, OR one year of specialized experience equivalent to GS-5; for GS-9, a master's degree or two years of graduate education, OR one year of specialized experience equivalent to GS-7; for GS-11, a Ph.D. or equivalent doctoral degree, or three years of graduate education, OR one year of specialized experience equivalent to GS-9; and for GS-12 and above, one year of specialized experience equivalent to the next lower grade level. In some cases, qualifying education may be substituted for experience, and vice versa. Tentative appointees must qualify for a security clearance and pass a background investigation.

Training: DISA-OIG Criminal Investigators attend the eight-week Criminal Investigator Training Program at the Federal Law Enforcement Training Center in Glynco, Georgia (see Chapter 16). In-service training may include courses relating to the Uniform Code of Military Justice, criminal law, Defense Information Systems operations and investigations, computer software, contract fraud, financial investigations, procurement fraud, personnel investigations, interviewing and interrogation, and other subjects.

Contact: Office of Inspector General, Defense Information Systems Agency, 701 South Courthouse Road; Arlington, VA 22204. Phone: 703-607-6900. World Wide Web: http://www.disa.mil/cmd/disacmda.html.

DEPUTY UNITED STATES MARSHAL (GS-1811)
UNITED STATES MARSHALS SERVICE
U.S. DEPARTMENT OF JUSTICE

Overview: Deputy United States Marshals serve many vital federal law enforcement functions including: *Federal Court Security*, which involves personal protection of judges, responding to threats against court personnel and property, and security of court facilities; *Fugitive Investigations*, including those who have escaped from custody, violated parole conditions, failed to appear in court, or who are wanted by law enforcement agencies; *Protection of Federal Witnesses*, including federal and state witnesses who risk their lives to testify for the government in organized crime cases; *Prisoner Transportation and Custody*, including surface and air transportation of detainees between courts, prisons and deportation sites; and *Managing Seized Assets*, including the custody, sale and auction of property seized during drug investigations and other criminal cases. Selected Deputy U.S. Marshals also participate in the Marshals Service Special Operations Group, a tactically trained mobile reaction force which responds to emergency situations of national significance requiring federal intervention. Deputy U.S. Marshals are authorized to conduct surveillance and undercover operations, carry firearms, make arrests, execute search warrants and serve subpoenas. Investigations may be conducted jointly with agencies such as the DEA; Bureau of Alcohol, Tobacco and Firearms; USDA Office of Inspector General; IRS Criminal Investigation Division; Customs Service; FBI; and other federal, state, or local law enforcement agencies. This position is covered under special retirement provisions for law enforcement officers and qualifies for 25 percent Law Enforcement Availability Pay.

Qualifications: Applicants must be U.S. citizens, at least twenty-one years of age, and under the age of thirty-seven. (Candidates over age thirty-seven who have previous service creditable under special law enforcement retirement provisions may also be eligible.) Requirements include completion of a four-year course of study leading to a bachelor's degree, OR three years of responsible work experience, OR an equivalent combination of education and experience. Eyesight requirements include uncorrected vision no worse than 20/200 (Snellen), and corrected vision of 20/20 in one eye and 20/40 in the other eye. Corrected or uncorrected near vision must be sufficient to read printed material the size of typewritten characters. A history of Radial Keratotomy surgery may be disqualifying. Hearing loss must not exceed 30 decibels at levels of 500, 1000, 2000, and 3000 cycles per second. Deputy U.S. Marshals normally enter service at the GS-5, GS-7 or GS-9 level. Candidates must pass the Treasury Enforcement Agent Examination (see Chapter One), personal interview, drug screening test and medical exam; and qualify for a security clearance.

Training: Deputy U.S. Marshals attend the eight-week Criminal Investigator Training Program at the Federal Law Enforcement Training Center (FLETC) in Glynco, Georgia (see Chapter 16). Recruits then complete a six-week intensive U.S. Marshals Service Basic Training School at FLETC, which focuses on fugitive investigations, court security, prisoner transportation, witness protection, asset seizure, and other functions carried out by the Marshals Service. A variety of related in-service courses are also attended.

Contact: Office of Human Resources, United States Marshals Service, 600 Army Navy Drive; Arlington, VA 22202. Phone: 202-307-9000. World Wide Web: http://www.usdoj.gov/marshals/.

DETECTIVE (GS-1811)
NAVAL AIR SYSTEMS COMMAND POLICE DEPARTMENT
U.S. DEPARTMENT OF DEFENSE

Overview: The U.S. Naval Air Systems Command (USNASC) provides material support to the Navy and Marine Corps for aircraft, airborne weapon systems, avionics, photographic and support equipment, ranges, and targets. USNASC civilian police Detectives conduct criminal and administrative investigations pertaining to Naval personnel and firms conducting business with the Naval Air Warfare Center. Investigations often pertain to violations of Navy and Department of Defense (DoD) Standards of Conduct and the Uniform Code of Military Justice; fraudulent claims for line-of-duty injury compensation; sonic boom investigations involving damage allegedly caused by aircraft noise; and crimes such as drug possession and domestic assault involving Naval personnel. Detectives also review audit reports produced by the Defense Contract Audit Agency, DoD Office of Inspector General, and Government Accounting Office. Detectives are authorized to conduct surveillance and undercover operations, carry firearms, make arrests, execute search warrants and serve subpoenas. Many investigations are conducted with Special Agents of the Naval Criminal Investigative Service and Defense Criminal Investigative Service, and other federal, state, or local law enforcement agencies. This is a civilian position and does not require active duty military service.

Qualifications: Applicants must be U.S. citizens, at least twenty-one years of age, and under the age of thirty-seven. (Candidates over age thirty-seven who have previous service creditable under special law enforcement retirement provisions may also be eligible.) Eyesight requirements include "sufficiently good vision in each eye, with or without correction." Corrected or uncorrected near vision must be sufficient to read printed material the size of typewritten characters. Hearing loss must not exceed 35 decibels at 1000, 2000, and 3000 Hz. Requirements for appointment to GS-5 level include completion of a four-year course of study leading to a bachelor's degree, OR three years general experience, one year of which was equivalent to GS-4; for GS-7, one full year of graduate education, or superior academic achievement during undergraduate studies, OR one year of specialized experience equivalent to GS-5; for GS-9, a master's degree or two years of graduate education, OR one year of specialized experience equivalent to GS-7; for GS-11, a Ph.D. or equivalent doctoral degree, or three years of graduate education, OR one year of specialized experience equivalent to GS-9; and for GS-12 and above, one year of specialized experience equivalent to the next lower grade level. In some cases, qualifying education may be substituted for experience, and vice versa. Tentative appointees must qualify for a security clearance, and pass a drug screening test and medical exam.

Training: USNASC Detectives attend either a state-certified police academy training program in the state where they will be employed, or the eight-week Criminal Investigator Training Program at the Federal Law Enforcement Training Center in Glynco, Georgia (see Chapter 16). In-service training may include courses in Navy and Defense Department operations, report writing, child sexual abuse, interviewing and interrogation, legal issues and updates, supervision and leadership, computer software, first aid and CPR, firearms proficiency, arrest techniques, and defensive tactics.

Contact: Naval Air Systems Command Police Department, Washington Naval Yard, Building 111, 901 M Street SE; Washington, DC 20388. Phone: 202-433-8800. World Wide Web: http://www.navy.mil/.

DETECTIVE
AMTRAK POLICE DEPARTMENT
NATIONAL RAILROAD PASSENGER CORPORATION

Overview: The Amtrak Police Department is a vital component of the National Railroad Passenger Corporation (NRPC), a government corporation established to develop the potential for modern rail service and meet the nation's intercity passenger transportation needs. Amtrak serves more than 500 station locations in 45 states, and operates trains over a system of approximately 24,500 route miles. With police personnel assigned to 29 field locations in 16 states and the District of Columbia, the Amtrak Police Department serves as the law enforcement and security arm of the NRPC, performing crime prevention functions and providing protection of railroad passengers, property, and personnel. Police Detectives investigate a wide range of crimes occurring on trains, train station property, and other facilities owned or controlled by Amtrak, including offenses such as assault, larceny, burglary, robbery, weapons offenses, murder, drug trafficking, arson, vandalism, and bomb threats. Detectives also perform uniformed patrol duty, as needed, and are authorized to conduct surveillance and undercover operations, carry firearms, make arrests, execute search warrants and serve subpoenas. Salary for this position does not fall under the General Schedule pay system, although it is similar to GS-1811 Special Agent positions of other agencies.

Qualifications: Applicants must have U.S. citizenship or the right to work in the United States; be at least twenty-one years of age at the time of appointment; have a valid driver's license; and possess an associates degree or at least sixty semester credits from an accredited college or university. (A bachelor's degree is preferred.) No wavier will be granted for the substitution of previous work experience or training. Applicants must submit a résumé and employment application form and pass a written examination, personal interview, background investigation, psychological evaluation, medical examination, and drug screening test.

Training: Depending upon availability of training, Amtrak Police Detectives attend either the eight-week Criminal Investigator Training Program at the Federal Law Enforcement Training Center in Glynco, Georgia (see Chapter 16), or a state-certified criminal investigator training program at a police academy in the state where they will be employed. In-service training may include courses in surveillance techniques, undercover operations, firearms and drug interdiction, computer crime, criminal and civil law, intelligence gathering, interviewing techniques, first aid and CPR, firearms proficiency, arrest techniques, and defensive tactics.

Contact: Human Resources, Amtrak Police Department, 30th Street Station, North Tower; Philadelphia, PA 19104. Phone: 215-349-1108. World Wide Web: http://www.Amtrak.com/.

ENLISTED SPECIAL AGENT
ARMY CRIMINAL INVESTIGATION COMMAND
U.S. DEPARTMENT OF THE ARMY

Overview: The U.S. Army Criminal Investigation Command (Army-CID) was organized to provide investigative services to all levels of the Army. Using modern investigative techniques, equipment, and systems, Army-CID concerns itself with every level of the Army throughout the world in which criminality can or has occurred. The Army-CID provides a full range of investigative support to all Army elements; conducts sensitive and special interest investigations; and provides personal security for the Secretary of Defense and other Defense Department officials. Enlisted Special Agents of the Army-CID conduct investigations of serious crimes committed by Army personnel ranging from assault to homicide, drug trafficking, fraud, and terrorism. To support these missions, the Army-CID operates forensic laboratories, a crime records center, and a polygraph program. Enlisted Special Agents are battle-ready, and provide front-line support to Army divisions during operational deployments. They are also authorized to conduct surveillance and undercover operations, carry firearms, make arrests, execute search warrants and serve subpoenas. While the Army-CID maintains a staff of civilian criminal investigators (see *Special Agent, Army Criminal Investigation Command*), Enlisted Special Agent positions are staffed by active duty enlisted soldiers.

Qualifications: Candidates for Enlisted Special Agent positions must be twenty-one years of age and currently serving in the Army, with at least two years of service. Additional requirements include U.S. citizenship; six months experience with a military police unit, or completion of a six-month internship with a CID unit, or one year of experience with a civilian police force; no record of psychological or pathological personality disorders; no record of unsatisfactory credit; suitable character as established by a background investigation; no civil court or court-martial convictions; physical fitness; normal color vision; sixty semester hours of college credit; and willingness to complete a thirty-six month tour of duty upon completion of Apprentice Special Agent training. Promotion to Warrant Officer Special Agent requires twenty-four months as an Enlisted Special Agent demonstrating exceptional performance, a bachelor's degree (although this requirement may be waived to sixty semester hours if otherwise fully qualified), and demonstrated potential to serve in a supervisory capacity. All Special Agents must maintain a top-secret security clearance.

Training: Enlisted Special Agents attend a fifteen-week Apprentice Special Agent Course at the U.S. Military Police School in Fort McClellan, Alabama, which covers subjects such as criminal law, crime scene processing, physical and testimonial evidence, property and person crimes, drug trafficking, report writing, and protective services. In-service training may include courses in hostage negotiation, terrorism on military installations, child abuse investigation, criminal and civil law, first aid and CPR, firearms proficiency, arrest techniques, and defensive tactics. Additional courses may also be completed at facilities such as the FBI National Academy, Metropolitan Police Academy at Scotland Yard, Federal Law Enforcement Training Center, and Army Logistics Management College.

Contact: U.S. Army Criminal Investigation Command, 5611 Columbia Pike; Falls Church, VA 22041. Phone: 703-756-1232. World Wide Web: http://www.belvoir.army.mil/cidc/.

INTERNAL SECURITY INSPECTOR (GS-1811)
IRS INSPECTION DIVISION
U.S. DEPARTMENT OF THE TREASURY

Overview: The Inspection Division of the Internal Revenue Service (IRS) employs Internal Security Inspectors to conduct criminal and non-criminal investigations involving serious violations by IRS personnel, while also protecting the Service from outside attempts to corrupt, threaten or assault members of its workforce. Investigations of IRS personnel focus on offenses such as bribery, acceptance of gratuities, extortion attempts initiated by Service employees against taxpayers, unlawful disclosure of tax information, embezzlement, conspiracy, conflict of interest, illegal drug activities, theft of government property, and abuses of authority. Inspectors also investigate impersonation of and assaults upon IRS personnel; conduct background investigations of applicants seeking IRS employment; provide personal protection for the IRS Commissioner and other IRS officials; and occasionally assist the Secret Service with Presidential protective operations. Inspectors are authorized to conduct surveillance and undercover operations, carry firearms, make arrests, execute search warrants and serve subpoenas. Many investigations are conducted jointly with other federal, state, or local law enforcement agencies. This position is covered under special retirement provisions for law enforcement officers and qualifies for 25 percent Law Enforcement Availability Pay.

Qualifications: Applicants must be U.S. citizens, at least twenty-one years of age, and under the age of thirty-seven. (Candidates over age thirty-seven who have previous service creditable under special law enforcement retirement provisions may also be eligible.) Eyesight requirements include uncorrected distant vision of at least 20/200 (Snellen) in each eye, correctable to 20/30 in one eye and 20/20 in the other; normal depth perception and peripheral vision; the ability to distinguish shades of color; and near vision sufficient to read Jaeger type 2 at 14 inches. Hearing loss must not exceed 30 decibels at 500, 1000, 2000 Hz. Applicant must be able to hear the whispered voice at fifteen feet without a hearing aid. Requirements for appointment to GS-5 include completion of a four-year course of study leading to a bachelor's degree, OR three years general experience, one year of which was equivalent to GS-4; for GS-7, one full year of graduate education, or superior academic achievement during undergraduate studies, OR one year of specialized experience equivalent to GS-5; for GS-9, a master's degree or two years of graduate education, OR one year of specialized experience equivalent to GS-7; for GS-11, a Ph.D. or equivalent doctoral degree, or three years of graduate education, OR one year of specialized experience equivalent to GS-9; and for GS-12 and above, one year of specialized experience equivalent to the next lower grade level. In some cases, qualifying education may be substituted for experience, and vice versa. Tentative appointees must qualify for a security clearance and pass a drug screening test, medical exam, and the Treasury Enforcement Agent Examination (see Chapter One).

Training: IRS Internal Security Inspectors attend the eight-week Criminal Investigator Training Program at the Federal Law Enforcement Training Center in Glynco, Georgia (see Chapter 16), followed by a four-week Internal Security Inspector Basic School which includes subjects such as internal investigations, report writing, photography, and interviewing techniques. In-service training may include courses in surveillance and undercover operations, technical investigative equipment, computer crime, law, interviewing, administrative investigations, first aid and CPR, arrest techniques, defensive tactics, and firearms proficiency.

Contact: IRS Inspection Division, Department of the Treasury, 1111 Constitution Avenue NW; Washington, DC 20224. Phone: 202-622-5000. World Wide Web: http://www.irs.treas.gov/.

INVESTIGATOR
OFFICE OF INSPECTOR GENERAL
CENTRAL INTELLIGENCE AGENCY

Overview: The Central Intelligence Agency (CIA) collects, evaluates, and disseminates vital information on political, military, economic, scientific, and other developments abroad needed to safeguard national security. Investigators of the CIA Office of Inspector General (OIG) investigate allegations of waste, fraud, abuse, mismanagement, and violations of federal law pertaining to CIA programs and operations. Investigations are often related to official misconduct by Agency personnel, conflict of interest, time and attendance fraud, misuse of government property, contract fraud, bribery, kickbacks, embezzlement, and international investigations. CIA-OIG Investigators also investigate CIA employee grievances that have reached the appeal level, and appeals of decisions of various Agency boards. Investigators are authorized to conduct surveillance and serve subpoenas. Joint investigations may be conducted with agencies such as the FBI, State Department Bureau of Diplomatic Security, DEA, Defense Criminal Investigative Service, and other federal, state, or local law enforcement agencies. While the CIA-OIG fills Investigator positions in the excepted service and utilizes internal occupational series codes, the Agency follows the General Schedule salary scale for this position. Appointment is normally at the GS-12 level.

Qualifications: Applicants must be U.S. citizens and possess a bachelor's degree from an accredited college or university. Competitive applicants should have significant criminal investigative experience, preferably with a federal law enforcement agency; strong research and analytical capabilities; exceptional written and verbal communication skills; and the ability to produce coherent, articulate, and well-organized reports that are sometimes complex and lengthy. Applicants must also qualify for a security clearance and pass a multistage interview, background investigation, polygraph interview, and medical examination.

Training: Initial training for CIA-OIG Investigators includes a four-week program conducted by Agency staff which focuses on CIA policies and procedures, an overview of the criminal justice system, federal court processes, criminal law, rules of evidence, Inspector General subpoena authority, evidence processing and control, fraud, bribery and gratuities, conflict of interest, financial investigations, interviewing techniques, civil proceedings, internal briefings, trial preparation, and Financial Crimes Enforcement Network operations. In-service training may include courses which focus on computer fraud, white-collar crime, personnel misconduct, contractor fraud, legal issues and updates, and various courses offered by the Federal Law Enforcement Training Center or FBI Academy.

Contact: Office of Inspector General, Central Intelligence Agency; Washington, DC 20505. Phone: 703-874-2555. World Wide Web: http://www.odci.gov/cia/.

INVESTIGATOR
OFFICE OF INSPECTOR GENERAL
CORPORATION FOR NATIONAL SERVICE

Overview: The Corporation for National Service (CNS) awards grants for national service programs to address the nation's education, human, public safety, and environmental needs. The Corporation carries out its mission through three major program areas, including AmeriCorps, Learn and Serve America, and National Senior Service Corps. Investigators of the CNS Office of Inspector General (OIG) conduct investigations involving alleged or suspected violations of federal laws and regulations affecting the CNS, its contractors and grantees, and their employees. Investigations often relate to improprieties on the part of CNS employees, contractor and grantee representatives, and volunteers; fraud and abuse in the administration of CNS programs involving offenses such as embezzlement, false claims, misappropriation of funds, and violations of standards of ethical conduct; and other criminal and non-criminal activity affecting CNS operations. Primary responsibilities include interviewing witnesses, investigative targets, and informants; obtaining sworn statements; gathering documentary evidence; analyzing testimony and evidence; preparing and submitting reports and recommendations; maintaining liaison with other federal, state and local law enforcement agencies; referring cases to the U.S. Department of Justice; and serving as a witness before grand juries and in other court proceedings. Investigations may be conducted jointly with agencies such as the FBI, Defense Criminal Investigative Service, Health and Human Services OIG, the U.S. Office of Special Counsel, and other federal, state, or local law enforcement agencies. Salary for this position does not fall under the General Schedule pay system, although it is similar to GS-1811 Special Agent positions of other federal agencies.

Qualifications: CNS-OIG Investigator positions are filled in the excepted service, with entry-level salary bands at the NY-2 and NY-3 level, although eligibility requirements are similar to those of criminal investigators employed by agencies in the competitive service. Requirements for appointment to grade NY-2 are similar to positions filled at grades GS-7 through GS-10, while requirements for grade NY-3 are similar to positions at grades GS-11 through GS-13. In some cases, qualifying education may be substituted for experience, and vice versa.

Training: Newly appointed CNS-OIG Investigators who have not completed formal investigative training attend the three-week Inspector General Basic Training Program at the Federal Law Enforcement Training Center in Glynco, Georgia (see Chapter 16). In-service training may include courses relating to grant administration, white-collar crime, cooperative agreements, financial investigations, computer fraud, personnel misconduct investigations, and other subjects.

Contact: Office of Inspector General, Corporation for National Service, 1201 New York Avenue NW - Suite 8100; Washington, DC 20525. Phone: 202-606-5000. World Wide Web: http://www.cns.gov/.

INVESTIGATOR (GS-1811)
OFFICE OF ENFORCEMENT
U.S. NUCLEAR REGULATORY COMMISSION

Overview: The U.S. Nuclear Regulatory Commission (NRC) licenses and regulates civilian use of nuclear energy to protect public health and safety and the environment. Special Agents of the NRC Office of Enforcement conduct sensitive and complex investigations of violations, accidents, or incidents occurring at or related to facilities which are licensed by the NRC. Investigations often focus on wilful violations of federal laws and regulations by NRC licensees, contractors, and vendors, including public utilities that operate nuclear power plants or processors; hospitals that use nuclear materials; manufacturers of radioactive materials used in nuclear power, medicine, and other industries; laboratories which handle and dispose of radioactive materials and waste; and organizations that utilize industrial radiography in construction, oil and gas, utility, and aerospace applications. Results of investigations are used in criminal prosecutions and civil enforcement actions. Many investigations are conducted jointly with other law enforcement and regulatory agencies. This position is covered under special retirement provisions for law enforcement officers and qualifies for 25 percent Law Enforcement Availability Pay.

Qualifications: Applicants must be U.S. citizens, at least twenty-one years of age, and under the age of thirty-seven. (Candidates over age thirty-seven who have previous service creditable under special law enforcement retirement provisions may also be eligible.) Eyesight requirements include "sufficiently good vision in each eye, with or without correction." Corrected or uncorrected near vision must be sufficient to read printed material the size of typewritten characters. Hearing loss must not exceed 35 decibels at 1000, 2000, and 3000 Hz. Requirements for appointment to GS-5 level include completion of a four-year course of study leading to a bachelor's degree, OR three years general experience, one year of which was equivalent to GS-4; for GS-7, one full year of graduate education, or superior academic achievement during undergraduate studies, OR one year of specialized experience equivalent to GS-5; for GS-9, a master's degree or two years of graduate education, OR one year of specialized experience equivalent to GS-7; for GS-11, a Ph.D. or equivalent doctoral degree, or three years of graduate education, OR one year of specialized experience equivalent to GS-9; and for GS-12 and above, one year of specialized experience equivalent to the next lower grade level. In some cases, qualifying education may be substituted for experience, and vice versa. Tentative appointees must pass a background investigation and qualify for a security clearance.

Training: Initial training for NRC Special Agents includes the eight-week Criminal Investigator Training Program at the Federal Law Enforcement Training Center in Glynco, Georgia (see Chapter 16). In-service training may include courses concerning nuclear reactor construction and operations, radiography systems, quality assurance, radiation safety, nuclear reactor security systems, white-collar crime, interviewing techniques, and other topics.

Contact: Office of Personnel, U.S. Nuclear Regulatory Commission, Washington, DC 20555. Phone: 800-952-9678 or 301-415-7516. World Wide Web: http://www.nrc.gov/.

POSTAL INSPECTOR
UNITED STATES POSTAL INSPECTION SERVICE
U.S. POSTAL SERVICE

Overview: As the law enforcement arm of the United States Postal Service, the Postal Inspection Service exercises investigative jurisdiction over more than 200 postal-related statutes pertaining to assaults against the Postal Service or its employees and misuse of the nation's postal system. Investigations conducted by Postal Inspectors focus on crimes such as mail fraud, mail theft, possession of stolen mail, assaults upon Postal personnel in the performance of their duties, burglary of Postal facilities, robbery of letter carriers, bombs and explosives sent through the mails, trafficking in narcotics and other controlled substances through the mails, counterfeiting of postmarks and postage stamps, theft of postal money orders and postage stamps, use of the mails to distribute child pornography, embezzlement, and money laundering. Inspectors are authorized to conduct surveillance and undercover operations, carry firearms, make arrests, execute search warrants and serve subpoenas. Investigations may be conducted jointly with agencies such as the Postal Service OIG, Agriculture Department OIG, FBI, Justice Department OIG, Immigration and Naturalization Service, IRS Criminal Investigation Division, Health and Human Services OIG, Labor Department OIG, Transportation Department OIG, and other agencies. This position is covered under special retirement provisions for law enforcement officers and qualifies for 25 percent Law Enforcement Availability Pay. Salary for this position does not fall under the General Schedule pay system, although it is similar to GS-1811 Special Agent positions of other agencies.

Qualifications: Applicants must be U.S. citizens, at least twenty-one years of age, and under the age of thirty-seven; in good physical and mental condition; and possess a bachelor's degree. (Candidates over age thirty-seven who have previous service creditable under special law enforcement retirement provisions may also be eligible.) Eyesight requirements include uncorrected distant vision of at least 20/100 (Snellen) in both eyes, correctable to 20/30 in one eye and 20/40 in the other, and good color perception. A history of Radial Keratotomy surgery is disqualifying. Hearing requirements include ability to hear at ordinary conversation levels from fifteen feet without a hearing aid. Weight must be proportionate to height. Applicants must have experience or expertise in at least one of the following areas: *Postal Service Systems*, including two years of Postal Service experience in a supervisory or specialized capacity; *Internal Audit*, including that of a Certified Public Accountant, Certified Management Accountant, Certified Internal Auditor, or Certified Information Systems Auditor, and two years experience conducting internal audits; *Law Enforcement*, including two years experience as a criminal investigator with statutory authority to make arrests; *Military Officers*, including active-duty and former commissioned military officers who apply within two years from their date of separation, served at least two years on active duty as an officer, and received an honorable discharge; or *Foreign Language Expertise*, including fluency in certain foreign languages. Applicants must pass a written exam, polygraph, drug screening test, medical exam, background investigation, and personal interview.

Training: Postal Inspectors attend a 16-week Basic Training Program at the Postal Inspector Training Academy in Potomac, Maryland (see Chapter 16). In-service training may include courses which focus on subjects such as criminal law, search and seizure, court procedures, postal regulations and operations, investigative techniques, arrest techniques, firearms proficiency, and defensive tactics.

Contact: U.S. Postal Inspection Service, 475 L'Enfant Plaza SW; Washington, DC 20260. Phone: 202-268-4267. World Wide Web: http://www.usps.gov/websites/depart/inspect/.

SPECIAL AGENT (GS-1811)
OFFICE OF INSPECTOR GENERAL
U.S. AGENCY FOR INTERNATIONAL DEVELOPMENT

Overview: The U.S. Agency for International Development (USAID) administers U.S. foreign economic and humanitarian assistance programs worldwide in the developing world, Central and Eastern Europe, and the New Independent States of the former Soviet Union. USAID Office of Inspector General (OIG) Special Agents investigate procurement and contract fraud, including violations of the Procurement Integrity Act, a federal law aimed at enforcing ethical conduct in the government contracting process, as well as embezzlement of project funds, theft of commodities and government property, and serious misconduct by USAID personnel. USAID-OIG Special Agents are authorized to conduct surveillance and undercover operations, carry firearms, make arrests, execute search warrants and serve subpoenas. Investigations may be conducted jointly with agencies such as the USDA Office of Inspector General, IRS Criminal Investigation Division, U.S. Immigration and Naturalization Service, State Department Bureau of Diplomatic Security, FBI, and other federal, state, or local law enforcement agencies. Special Agents are authorized to conduct surveillance and undercover operations, carry firearms, make arrests, execute search warrants and serve subpoenas. This position is covered under special retirement provisions for law enforcement officers and qualifies for 25 percent Law Enforcement Availability Pay.

Qualifications: Applicants must be U.S. citizens, at least twenty-one years of age, and under the age of thirty-seven. (Candidates over age thirty-seven who have previous service creditable under special law enforcement retirement provisions may also be eligible.) Eyesight requirements include "sufficiently good vision in each eye, with or without correction." Corrected or uncorrected near vision must be sufficient to read printed material the size of typewritten characters. Hearing loss must not exceed 35 decibels at 1000, 2000, and 3000 Hz. Requirements for appointment to GS-5 level include completion of a four-year course of study leading to a bachelor's degree, OR three years general experience, one year of which was equivalent to GS-4; for GS-7, one full year of graduate education, or superior academic achievement during undergraduate studies, OR one year of specialized experience equivalent to GS-5; for GS-9, a master's degree or two years of graduate education, OR one year of specialized experience equivalent to GS-7; for GS-11, a Ph.D. or equivalent doctoral degree, or three years of graduate education, OR one year of specialized experience equivalent to GS-9; and for GS-12 and above, one year of specialized experience equivalent to the next lower grade level. In some cases, qualifying education may be substituted for experience, and vice versa. Tentative appointees must qualify for a top-secret security clearance, and pass a drug screening test and medical exam.

Training: USAID-OIG Special Agents attend the eight-week Criminal Investigator Training Program at the Federal Law Enforcement Training Center in Glynco, Georgia (see Chapter 16). In-service training may include courses pertaining to USAID program investigations, international issues and events, white-collar crime, search and seizure, criminal and civil law, computer hardware and software, financial investigations, personnel misconduct, firearms proficiency, arrest techniques, and defensive tactics.

Contact: Personnel Services, Office of Inspector General, U.S. Agency for International Development, Room 510; Washington, DC 20523. Phone: 703-875-4352. World Wide Web: http://www.info.usaid.gov. E-mail: pinquiries@usaid.gov.

SPECIAL AGENT (GS-1811)
FOREST SERVICE
U.S. DEPARTMENT OF AGRICULTURE

Overview: Special Agents of the USDA Forest Service investigate criminal activity on 191 million acres of national forests, grasslands and land utilization projects located in 44 states, the Virgin Islands, and Puerto Rico. Investigations may focus on timber theft, arson, accidents, unauthorized mining claims, violations of the Archeological Resources Protection Act, embezzlement, theft of government funds, and infractions of regulations by Forest Service personnel. In cooperation with other agencies in carrying out the National Drug Control Strategy, USDA Forest Service Special Agents also investigate the use and production of narcotics and controlled substances on National Forest System lands, including offenses such as marijuana cultivation, weapons and booby trap violations, and the production of illegal drugs in clandestine laboratories. USDA Forest Service Special Agents are authorized to conduct surveillance and undercover operations, carry firearms, make arrests, execute search warrants and serve subpoenas. Investigations may be conducted jointly with agencies such as the USDA Office of Inspector General, DEA, National Guard, and other federal, state, or local law enforcement and regulatory agencies. This position is covered under special retirement provisions for law enforcement officers and qualifies for 25 percent Law Enforcement Availability Pay.

Qualifications: Applicants must be U.S. citizens, at least twenty-one years of age, and under the age of thirty-seven. (Candidates over age thirty-seven who have previous service creditable under special law enforcement retirement provisions may also be eligible.) Eyesight requirements include "sufficiently good vision in each eye, with or without correction." Corrected or uncorrected near vision must be sufficient to read printed material the size of typewritten characters. Hearing loss must not exceed 35 decibels at 1000, 2000, and 3000 Hz. Requirements for appointment to GS-5 level include completion of a four-year course of study leading to a bachelor's degree, OR three years general experience, one year of which was equivalent to GS-4; for GS-7, one full year of graduate education, or superior academic achievement during undergraduate studies, OR one year of specialized experience equivalent to GS-5; for GS-9, a master's degree or two years of graduate education, OR one year of specialized experience equivalent to GS-7; for GS-11, a Ph.D. or equivalent doctoral degree, or three years of graduate education, OR one year of specialized experience equivalent to GS-9; and for GS-12 and above, one year of specialized experience equivalent to the next lower grade level. In some cases, qualifying education may be substituted for experience, and vice versa. Tentative appointees must qualify for a security clearance, and pass a drug screening test and medical exam.

Training: Forest Service Special Agents attend the eight-week Criminal Investigator Training Program at the Federal Law Enforcement Training Center (FLETC) in Glynco, Georgia (see Chapter 16), followed by a two-week course at FLETC which covers various aspects of Forest Service law enforcement operations. In-service training may include courses relating to controlled substance investigations, drug enforcement operations, non-lethal control techniques, impact weapons, aerosol subject restraints, emergency vehicle operation, criminal and civil law, survival and rescue tactics, photography, firearms, or completion of the FBI National Academy training program.

Contact: For further information, contact the regional or local Forest Service office where employment is sought, or: USDA Forest Service, P.O. Box 96090; Washington, DC 20090. Phone: 202-720-3760. World Wide Web: http://www.fs.fed.us. E-mail: mailroom/wo@fs.fed.us.

SPECIAL AGENT (GS-1811)
OFFICE OF INSPECTOR GENERAL
U.S. DEPARTMENT OF AGRICULTURE

Overview: Special Agents of the U.S. Department of Agriculture (USDA) Office of Inspector General (OIG) investigate fraud and other violations of federal law relating to USDA programs and operations, including those concerned with food assistance, food safety and inspection, farm subsidies and loans, federal crop insurance, rural housing programs, smuggling of animal and plant products, and Forest Service contracting operations, among others. Particular emphasis is given to the investigation of food stamp trafficking, which often focuses on the unlawful exchange of food stamps for cash, contraband, or other goods. USDA-OIG Special Agents also investigate allegations of serious official misconduct by Department personnel, including offenses such as embezzlement, conflict of interest, misuse of official position, bribery, extortion, collusion with program participants, and misuse or theft of government property. Investigations frequently involve undercover operations, electronic surveillance, and collecting intelligence information from informants and law enforcement sources. USDA-OIG Special Agents are also responsible for providing personal security for the Secretary of Agriculture and other USDA officials, and are authorized to carry firearms, make arrests, execute search warrants and serve subpoenas. Joint investigations may be conducted with agencies such as the USDA Forest Service, U.S. Fish and Wildlife Service, DEA, Postal Inspection Service, FBI, Customs Service, IRS, Secret Service, and other law enforcement and regulatory agencies. This position is covered under special retirement provisions for law enforcement officers and qualifies for 25 percent Law Enforcement Availability Pay.

Qualifications: Applicants must be U.S. citizens, at least twenty-one years of age, and under the age of thirty-seven. (Candidates over age thirty-seven who have previous service creditable under special law enforcement retirement provisions may also be eligible.) Eyesight requirements include "sufficiently good vision in each eye, with or without correction." Corrected or uncorrected near vision must be sufficient to read printed material the size of typewritten characters. Hearing loss must not exceed 35 decibels at 1000, 2000, and 3000 Hz. Requirements for appointment to GS-5 level include completion of a four-year course of study leading to a bachelor's degree, OR three years general experience, one year of which was equivalent to GS-4; for GS-7, one full year of graduate education, or superior academic achievement during undergraduate studies, OR one year of specialized experience equivalent to GS-5; for GS-9, a master's degree or two years of graduate education, OR one year of specialized experience equivalent to GS-7; for GS-11, a Ph.D. or equivalent doctoral degree, or three years of graduate education, OR one year of specialized experience equivalent to GS-9; and for GS-12 and above, one year of specialized experience equivalent to the next lower grade level. In some cases, qualifying education may be substituted for experience, and vice versa. Tentative appointees must qualify for a security clearance, and pass a background investigation, drug screening test and medical exam.

Training: USDA-OIG Special Agents attend the eight-week Criminal Investigator Training Program at the Federal Law Enforcement Training Center in Glynco, Georgia (see Chapter 16). In-service training may focus on USDA program investigations, undercover operations, criminal and civil law, white-collar crime, employee integrity investigations, interviewing techniques, firearms proficiency, arrest techniques, defensive tactics, and other subjects.

Contact: USDA Office of Personnel, Room 31-W, Jamie L. Whitten Building, 1400 Independence Ave. SW; Washington, DC 20250. Phone: 202-720-5781. World Wide Web: http://www.usda.gov/oig/.

SPECIAL AGENT (GS-1811)
BUREAU OF EXPORT ADMINISTRATION
U.S. DEPARTMENT OF COMMERCE

Overview: The Commerce Department's Bureau of Export Administration (DOC-BXA) directs the nation's export control policy, and carries out functions such as processing license applications, conducting foreign availability studies to determine when products should be decontrolled, and enforcing U.S. export laws. DOC-BXA Special Agents conduct investigations relating primarily to alleged or suspected violations of the Export Administration Act of 1979. In the interests of national security and foreign policy, DOC-BXA investigations focus on the illegal export of strategically sensitive non-agricultural commodities and technology. Particular attention is given to technological goods which may be utilized in the development of chemical, biological or nuclear weapons, or related missile delivery systems, as well as shipment of products to embargoed destinations such as Iraq, North Korea and Cuba, or to terrorist-designated nations such as Libya, Iran, Sudan, and Syria. Special Agents are authorized to serve subpoenas. Investigations may be conducted jointly with the FBI, Defense Department, Customs Service, and other federal, state, or local law enforcement and regulatory agencies. This position is covered under special retirement provisions for law enforcement officers and qualifies for 25 percent Law Enforcement Availability Pay.

Qualifications: Applicants must be U.S. citizens, at least twenty-one years of age, and under the age of thirty-seven. (Candidates over age thirty-seven who have previous service creditable under special law enforcement retirement provisions may also be eligible.) Eyesight requirements include "sufficiently good vision in each eye, with or without correction." Corrected or uncorrected near vision must be sufficient to read printed material the size of typewritten characters. Hearing loss must not exceed 35 decibels at 1000, 2000, and 3000 Hz. Requirements for appointment to GS-5 level include completion of a four-year course of study leading to a bachelor's degree, OR three years general experience, one year of which was equivalent to GS-4; for GS-7, one full year of graduate education, or superior academic achievement during undergraduate studies, OR one year of specialized experience equivalent to GS-5; for GS-9, a master's degree or two years of graduate education, OR one year of specialized experience equivalent to GS-7; for GS-11, a Ph.D. or equivalent doctoral degree, or three years of graduate education, OR one year of specialized experience equivalent to GS-9; and for GS-12 and above, one year of specialized experience equivalent to the next lower grade level. In some cases, qualifying education may be substituted for experience, and vice versa. Tentative appointees must qualify for a security clearance, and pass a drug screening test and medical exam.

Training: DOC-BXA Special Agents attend the eight-week Criminal Investigator Training Program at the Federal Law Enforcement Training Center in Glynco, Georgia (see Chapter 16). In-service training may include courses in missile technology; nuclear, biological and chemical weapons; identification and handling of chemical materials; international treaty obligations; investigative techniques; criminal and civil law; first aid and CPR; firearms proficiency; arrest techniques; and defensive tactics.

Contact: Bureau of Export Administration, Department of Commerce, 14th Street and Constitution Avenue NW; Washington, DC 20230. Phone: 202-482-2252. World Wide Web: http://www.bxa.doc.gov.

SPECIAL AGENT (GS-1812)
NATIONAL MARINE FISHERIES SERVICE
NATIONAL OCEANIC AND ATMOSPHERIC ADMINISTRATION
U.S. DEPARTMENT OF COMMERCE

Overview: As a component of the National Oceanic and Atmospheric Administration (NOAA), the National Marine Fisheries Service (NMFS) administers programs which support the domestic and international conservation and management of living marine resources. Special Agents of the NMFS Office of Enforcement investigate violations of federal laws pertaining to the conservation and protection of ocean fisheries, marine mammals, and endangered species of fish and wildlife. In order to monitor compliance with international treaties and agreements, NMFS Special Agents conduct surveillance of foreign fishing operations within a protected 200-mile conservation and fishery management territory along the U.S. coastline to enforce applicable laws and regulations. Investigations often include undercover operations involving extensive covert investigative procedures. Responsibilities also include representing the Agency at public meetings and seminars. Special Agents are authorized to board surface vessels and aircraft within the protected zone, carry firearms, make arrests, execute search warrants and serve subpoenas. Many operations are conducted jointly with the U.S. Fish and Wildlife Service, Coast Guard Investigative Service, Customs Service, FBI, and other federal, state, or local law enforcement and regulatory agencies. This position is covered under special retirement provisions for law enforcement officers and qualifies for 25 percent Law Enforcement Availability Pay.

Qualifications: Applicants must be U.S. citizens, at least twenty-one years of age, and under the age of thirty-seven. (Candidates over age thirty-seven who have previous service creditable under special law enforcement retirement provisions may also be eligible.) Eyesight requirements include distant vision of at least 20/200 (Snellen) in each eye without correction, and at least 20/20 in each eye with correction. Normal depth perception, peripheral vision, and ability to distinguish shades of color are required. Hearing loss must not exceed 30 decibels at 500, 1000, and 2000 Hz; and 40 decibels at 3000 Hz. Requirements for appointment to GS-5 level include completion of a four-year course of study leading to a bachelor's degree, OR three years general experience, one year of which was equivalent to GS-4; for GS-7, one full year of graduate education, or superior academic achievement during undergraduate studies, OR one year of specialized experience equivalent to GS-5; for GS-9, a master's degree or two years of graduate education, OR one year of specialized experience equivalent to GS-7; for GS-11, a Ph.D. or equivalent doctoral degree, or three years of graduate education, OR one year of specialized experience equivalent to GS-9; and for GS-12 and above, one year of specialized experience equivalent to the next lower grade level. In some cases, qualifying education may be substituted for experience, and vice versa. Tentative appointees must qualify for a security clearance, and pass a drug screening test and medical exam.

Training: NMFS Special Agents attend the eight-week Criminal Investigator Training Program at the Federal Law Enforcement Training Center in Glynco, Georgia (see Chapter 16). In-service training may include courses in fish and wildlife identification, international treaty obligations, first aid and CPR, drug enforcement, search and seizure, investigative techniques, criminal and civil law, arrest techniques, defensive tactics, and firearms proficiency.

Contact: Office of Enforcement, NOAA/National Marine Fisheries Service, Department of Commerce, 8484 Georgia - Suite 415; Silver Spring, MD 20910. Phone: 301-427-2300. World Wide Web: http://www.nmfs.gov.

SPECIAL AGENT (GS-1811)
OFFICE OF INSPECTOR GENERAL
U.S. DEPARTMENT OF COMMERCE

Overview: The U.S. Department of Commerce (DOC) encourages, serves, and promotes the nation's international trade, economic growth, and technological advancement. The Department provides a wide variety of programs through the competitive free enterprise system. DOC Office of Inspector General (OIG) Special Agents conduct investigations to identify fraud and other forms of criminal or improper activity in DOC programs and operations. Investigations often focus on allegations of embezzlement, conflicts of interest, kick-backs, or other fraudulent activities affecting labor laws and DOC programs, grants, contracts, contractors and their employees. DOC-OIG Special Agents also investigate misconduct by DOC personnel involving offenses such as bribery, conflict of interest, collusion, use of public office for personal gain, and violations of DOC standards of conduct. Special Agents are authorized to conduct surveillance and undercover operations, carry firearms, make arrests, execute search warrants and serve subpoenas. Investigations may be conducted jointly with agencies such as the FBI and other federal, state, or local law enforcement agencies. This position is covered under special retirement provisions for law enforcement officers and qualifies for 25 percent Law Enforcement Availability Pay.

Qualifications: Applicants must be U.S. citizens, at least twenty-one years of age, and under the age of thirty-seven. (Candidates over age thirty-seven who have previous service creditable under special law enforcement retirement provisions may also be eligible.) Eyesight requirements include "sufficiently good vision in each eye, with or without correction." Corrected or uncorrected near vision must be sufficient to read printed material the size of typewritten characters. Hearing loss must not exceed 35 decibels at 1000, 2000, and 3000 Hz. Requirements for appointment to GS-5 level include completion of a four-year course of study leading to a bachelor's degree, OR three years general experience, one year of which was equivalent to GS-4; for GS-7, one full year of graduate education, or superior academic achievement during undergraduate studies, OR one year of specialized experience equivalent to GS-5; for GS-9, a master's degree or two years of graduate education, OR one year of specialized experience equivalent to GS-7; for GS-11, a Ph.D. or equivalent doctoral degree, or three years of graduate education, OR one year of specialized experience equivalent to GS-9; and for GS-12 and above, one year of specialized experience equivalent to the next lower grade level. In some cases, qualifying education may be substituted for experience, and vice versa. Tentative appointees must qualify for a security clearance, and pass a drug screening test and medical exam.

Training: DOC-OIG Special Agents attend the eight-week Criminal Investigator Training Program at the Federal Law Enforcement Training Center in Glynco, Georgia (see Chapter 16). In-service training may include courses in DOC program investigations, personnel misconduct investigations, financial investigations, computer hardware and software, investigative techniques, legal issues and updates, first aid and CPR, firearms proficiency, arrest techniques, and defensive tactics.

Contact: Office of Inspector General, Department of Commerce, Room 7616, 14th Street and Constitution Avenue NW; Washington, DC 20230. Phone: 202-482-0934. World Wide Web: http://www.osec.doc.gov/oig/.

SPECIAL AGENT (GS-1811)
AIR FORCE OFFICE OF SPECIAL INVESTIGATIONS
U.S. DEPARTMENT OF DEFENSE

Overview: The United States Air Force Office of Special Investigations (AFOSI) provides major criminal, fraud, counterintelligence and special investigative services for the protection of Air Force and Defense Department resources, technology, and personnel worldwide. AFOSI Special Agents investigate crimes such as espionage, sabotage, terrorism, assault, rape, arson, burglary, drug trafficking, homicide, malicious destruction of government property, contract fraud, and violations of the Uniform Code of Military Justice. Special Agents also provide personal security for Air Force officials and their guests, and are authorized to conduct surveillance and undercover operations, carry firearms, make arrests, execute search warrants and serve subpoenas. Investigations may be conducted jointly with agencies such as the Bureau of Alcohol, Tobacco and Firearms; Secret Service; FBI; State Department; NASA Office of Inspector General, and other federal, state, or local, and foreign law enforcement agencies. Special Agents serve in 154 locations worldwide, including all major Air Force installations and a variety of special operating locations. This position is covered under special retirement provisions for law enforcement officers and qualifies for 25 percent Law Enforcement Availability Pay. While this position is staffed by civilian personnel, AFOSI also maintains a staff of military active duty Special Agents.

Qualifications: Applicants must be U.S. citizens, at least twenty-one years of age, and under the age of thirty-seven. (Candidates over age thirty-seven who have previous service creditable under special law enforcement retirement provisions may also be eligible.) Eyesight requirements include "sufficiently good vision in each eye, with or without correction." Corrected or uncorrected near vision must be sufficient to read printed material the size of typewritten characters. Hearing loss must not exceed 35 decibels at 1000, 2000, and 3000 Hz. Requirements for appointment to GS-5 level include completion of a four-year course of study leading to a bachelor's degree, OR three years general experience, one year of which was equivalent to GS-4; for GS-7, one full year of graduate education, or superior academic achievement during undergraduate studies, OR one year of specialized experience equivalent to GS-5; for GS-9, a master's degree or two years of graduate education, OR one year of specialized experience equivalent to GS-7; for GS-11, a Ph.D. or equivalent doctoral degree, or three years of graduate education, OR one year of specialized experience equivalent to GS-9; and for GS-12 and above, one year of specialized experience equivalent to the next lower grade level. In some cases, qualifying education may be substituted for experience, and vice versa. Tentative appointees must qualify for a security clearance, and pass a drug screening test and medical exam.

Training: Air Force OSI Special Agents attend an eleven-week Basic Special Investigators Course at the U.S. Air Force Special Investigations Academy at Andrews Air Force Base in Maryland (see Chapter 16). In-service training may include courses relating to protective service operations, drug trafficking, economic crime, terrorism, investigative techniques, technical investigative equipment, and counterintelligence.

Contact: Headquarters, Air Force OSI, 500 Duncan Avenue, Bolling AFB, Washington, DC 20332. Phone: 202-297-5352. World Wide Web: http://www.af.mil/.

SPECIAL AGENT (GS-1811)
ARMY CRIMINAL INVESTIGATION COMMAND
U.S. DEPARTMENT OF DEFENSE

Overview: Civilian Special Agents of the U.S. Army Criminal Investigation Command (Army-CID) investigate offenses concerning Army contracting, procurement and acquisition programs. Investigations often pertain to civilian contractors that research, develop, test, manufacture and install weapons systems or equipment for the Army, and focus on offenses such as product substitution, overcharging for goods and services, misappropriation of funds, falsification of contractor certified payrolls, charging personal expenses to Department contracts, bribery, embezzlement, antitrust violations, racketeering, and organized crime. Army-CID Special Agents are authorized to conduct surveillance and undercover operations, carry firearms, make arrests, execute search warrants and serve subpoenas. Investigations may be conducted jointly with other Defense Department organizations, the FBI, and other agencies. This position is covered under special retirement provisions for law enforcement officers and qualifies for 25 percent Law Enforcement Availability Pay. While this position is staffed by civilian personnel, the Army-CID also maintains a staff of Special Agents who are enlisted soldiers or warrant officer soldiers (see *Enlisted Special Agent*).

Qualifications: Applicants must be U.S. citizens, at least twenty-one years of age, and under the age of thirty-seven. (Candidates over age thirty-seven who have previous service creditable under special law enforcement retirement provisions may also be eligible.) Eyesight requirements include "sufficiently good vision in each eye, with or without correction." Corrected or uncorrected near vision must be sufficient to read printed material the size of typewritten characters. Hearing loss must not exceed 35 decibels at 1000, 2000, and 3000 Hz. Requirements for appointment to GS-5 level include completion of a four-year course of study leading to a bachelor's degree, OR three years general experience, one year of which was equivalent to GS-4; for GS-7, one full year of graduate education, or superior academic achievement during undergraduate studies, OR one year of specialized experience equivalent to GS-5; for GS-9, a master's degree or two years of graduate education, OR one year of specialized experience equivalent to GS-7; for GS-11, a Ph.D. or equivalent doctoral degree, or three years of graduate education, OR one year of specialized experience equivalent to GS-9; and for GS-12 and above, one year of specialized experience equivalent to the next lower grade level. In some cases, qualifying education may be substituted for experience, and vice versa. Tentative appointees must qualify for a top-secret security clearance, and pass a drug screening test and medical exam.

Training: Army-CID Special Agents attend a fifteen-week Apprentice Special Agent Course at the U.S. Military Police School in Fort McClellan, Alabama, which covers subjects such as criminal law, crime scene processing, physical and testimonial evidence, property and person crimes, drug trafficking, report writing, and protective operations. In-service training may include courses in hostage negotiation, terrorism on military installations, child abuse investigation, criminal and civil law, financial investigations, procurement fraud, first aid and CPR, firearms proficiency, arrest techniques, and defensive tactics. Additional courses may also be completed at the FBI National Academy, Metropolitan Police Academy at Scotland Yard, Federal Law Enforcement Training Center, and Army Logistics Management College.

Contact: U.S. Army Criminal Investigation Command, 5611 Columbia Pike; Falls Church, VA 22041. Phone: 703-756-1232. World Wide Web: http://www.belvoir.army.mil/cidc/.

SPECIAL AGENT (GS-1811)
NAVAL CRIMINAL INVESTIGATIVE SERVICE
U.S. DEPARTMENT OF DEFENSE

Overview: The Naval Criminal Investigative Service (NCIS) provides criminal investigative, counterintelligence, law enforcement and physical security, information and personnel security support to the Navy and Marine Corps worldwide, both ashore and afloat. NCIS Special Agents are stationed at more than 150 locations around the world, as well as on aircraft carriers and other major combatants. NCIS Special Agents are responsible for the investigation of offenses committed by or against the personnel or property of the Navy or Marine Corps, including federal crimes and violations of the Uniform Code of Military Justice. Investigations are divided among several disciplines including: *General Crimes*, such as homicide, rape, robbery, child abuse, larceny, vandalism, and arson; *White-Collar Crimes*, such as procurement fraud; *Computer Crimes*, involving malicious virus incidents, hackers, and criminal manipulation of software; *Counterintelligence*, relating to terrorist threats, espionage, sabotage, and security violations; and *Drug Interdiction*, involving the trafficking of illegal narcotics. NCIS Special Agents also perform technical investigative services such as polygraph examinations, electronic surveillance, and forensic laboratory procedures; and provide personal security for the Secretary of the Navy, senior military commanders, foreign dignitaries and other officials. NCIS Special Agents are authorized to carry firearms. Joint operations are conducted with other Defense Department agencies, the FBI, NASA Office of Inspector General, and other federal, state, or local law enforcement agencies. This position is covered under special retirement provisions for law enforcement officers and qualifies for 25 percent Law Enforcement Availability Pay. Appointment is normally at the GS-7 or GS-9 level, with progression to the journeyman level of GS-12. This is a civilian position and does not require active duty military service.

Qualifications: Applicants must be U.S. citizens, at least twenty-one years of age, and under the age of thirty-seven; have good communication skills; and possess a bachelor's degree from an accredited college or university. Applicants must submit a writing sample and achieve passing scores on the NCIS Special Agent Applicant Examination, personal interviews, a background investigation, medical exam, drug screening test, and a polygraph examination. Appointees must be willing to serve at any of the 150 worldwide offices, including locations throughout the United States, overseas, or on aircraft carriers or other major combatants. Candidates with special skills such as fluency in a foreign language, computer skills, military or law enforcement experience, an advanced degree, or academic excellence are encouraged.

Training: NCIS Special Agents attend the eight-week Criminal Investigator Training Program at the Federal Law Enforcement Training Center (FLETC) in Glynco, Georgia (see Chapter 16), followed by an eight-week NCIS course at FLETC which includes instruction in the NCIS report-writing system, databases, and courses related to specific job tasks. In-service training may include courses which focus on drug interdiction, investigative techniques, counterintelligence, law, procurement fraud, first aid and CPR, firearms proficiency, defensive tactics, arrest techniques, and other subjects.

Contact: Naval Criminal Investigative Service, 716 East Sicard Street SE, Building 111, Washington Navy Yard; Washington, DC 20388. Phone: 202-433-9162. World Wide Web: http://www.ncis.navy.mil/.

SPECIAL AGENT (GS-1811)
DEFENSE CRIMINAL INVESTIGATIVE SERVICE
OFFICE OF INSPECTOR GENERAL
U.S. DEPARTMENT OF DEFENSE

Overview: Special Agents of the Defense Criminal Investigative Service (DCIS) investigate violations of federal laws committed by Department of Defense (DoD) personnel and contractors. Often complex and sensitive, DCIS contract and procurement investigations focus on fraud relating to major construction projects, product substitution, cost mischarging and defective pricing, collusion, commercial bribery, and kickbacks. DCIS Special Agents also investigate DoD fraud in DoD programs, unlawful disclosure of classified information, larceny, embezzlement, sex offenses, antitrust violations, gambling, confidence games, use or distribution of narcotics, organized crime, labor law provisions, and misconduct by DoD personnel. Special Agents are authorized to conduct surveillance and undercover operations, carry firearms, make arrests, execute search warrants and serve subpoenas. Investigations may be conducted jointly with other DoD investigative divisions, the FBI, NASA Office of Inspector General, Transportation Department OIG, and other federal, state, or local law enforcement agencies. This position is covered under special retirement provisions for law enforcement officers and qualifies for 25 percent Law Enforcement Availability Pay. This is a civilian position and does not require active duty military service.

Qualifications: Applicants must be U.S. citizens, at least twenty-one years of age, and under the age of thirty-seven. (Candidates over age thirty-seven who have previous service creditable under special law enforcement retirement provisions may also be eligible.) Eyesight requirements include "sufficiently good vision in each eye, with or without correction." Corrected or uncorrected near vision must be sufficient to read printed material the size of typewritten characters. Hearing loss must not exceed 35 decibels at 1000, 2000, and 3000 Hz. Requirements for appointment to GS-5 level include completion of a four-year course of study leading to a bachelor's degree, OR three years general experience, one year of which was equivalent to GS-4; for GS-7, one full year of graduate education, or superior academic achievement during undergraduate studies, OR one year of specialized experience equivalent to GS-5; for GS-9, a master's degree or two years of graduate education, OR one year of specialized experience equivalent to GS-7; for GS-11, a Ph.D. or equivalent doctoral degree, or three years of graduate education, OR one year of specialized experience equivalent to GS-9; and for GS-12 and above, one year of specialized experience equivalent to the next lower grade level. In some cases, qualifying education may be substituted for experience, and vice versa. Tentative appointees must qualify for a security clearance, and pass a drug screening test and medical exam.

Training: DCIS Special Agents attend the eight-week Criminal Investigator Training Program at the Federal Law Enforcement Training Center in Glynco, Georgia (see Chapter 16). In-service training may include courses in Defense Department program investigations, construction fraud, white-collar crime, procurement fraud, personnel misconduct, search and seizure, interviewing techniques, legal issues and updates, firearms proficiency, arrest techniques, and defensive tactics.

Contact: Personnel and Security Directorate, Office of Inspector General - DCIS, Department of Defense, 400 Army Navy Drive; Arlington, VA 22202. Phone: 301-713-2239. World Wide Web: http://www.defenselink.mil/ig/.

SPECIAL AGENT (GS-1811)
OFFICE OF INSPECTOR GENERAL
U.S. DEPARTMENT OF EDUCATION

Overview: The United States Department of Education (ED) establishes policy for, administers, and coordinates most federal assistance to education. Special Agents of the ED Office of Inspector General (OIG) investigate fraud, waste and abuse in programs and operations administered or financed by the Department.

Investigations often focus on allegations of fraud involving Education Department contractors, grantees, educational or financial institutions, or individuals participating in Department programs. ED-OIG Special Agents perform internal investigations relating to allegations of misconduct by Education Department personnel, including offenses such as embezzlement, bribery, and conflict of interest. Special Agents are authorized to conduct surveillance and undercover operations, carry firearms, make arrests, execute search warrants and serve subpoenas. These personnel also participate in Justice Department intergovernmental fraud task forces, and conduct investigations jointly with agencies such as the IRS Criminal Investigation Division, FBI, and other federal, state, or local law enforcement agencies. This position is covered under special retirement provisions for law enforcement officers and qualifies for 25 percent Law Enforcement Availability Pay.

Qualifications: Applicants must be U.S. citizens, at least twenty-one years of age, and under the age of thirty-seven. (Candidates over age thirty-seven who have previous service creditable under special law enforcement retirement provisions may also be eligible.) Eyesight requirements include "sufficiently good vision in each eye, with or without correction." Corrected or uncorrected near vision must be sufficient to read printed material the size of typewritten characters. Hearing loss must not exceed 35 decibels at 1000, 2000, and 3000 Hz. Requirements for appointment to GS-5 level include completion of a four-year course of study leading to a bachelor's degree, OR three years general experience, one year of which was equivalent to GS-4; for GS-7, one full year of graduate education, or superior academic achievement during undergraduate studies, OR one year of specialized experience equivalent to GS-5; for GS-9, a master's degree or two years of graduate education, OR one year of specialized experience equivalent to GS-7; for GS-11, a Ph.D. or equivalent doctoral degree, or three years of graduate education, OR one year of specialized experience equivalent to GS-9; and for GS-12 and above, one year of specialized experience equivalent to the next lower grade level. In some cases, qualifying education may be substituted for experience, and vice versa. Tentative appointees must qualify for a security clearance, and pass a drug screening test and medical exam.

Training: ED-OIG Special Agents attend the eight-week Criminal Investigator Training Program at the Federal Law Enforcement Training Center in Glynco, Georgia (see Chapter 16). In-service training may include courses which focus on employee integrity investigations, Education Department program investigations, procurement fraud, financial investigations, law enforcement procedures, criminal and civil law, first aid and CPR, arrest techniques, defensive tactics, and firearms proficiency.

Contact: Office of Inspector General, Department of Education, 600 Independence Avenue SW; Washington, DC 20202-1510. Phone: 202-205-5770. World Wide Web: http://www.vais.net~edoig/.

SPECIAL AGENT (GS-1811)
OFFICE OF INSPECTOR GENERAL
U.S. DEPARTMENT OF ENERGY

Overview: The Department of Energy (DOE) manages programs pertaining to energy conservation and research, fossil energy, radioactive waste management, national security, and pipeline construction projects. DOE Office of Inspector General (OIG) Special Agents investigate fraud, waste, abuse, and mismanagement in these and other programs and operations of the Department which require large budget outlays and may fall victim to fraudulent activity. Program fraud investigations often focus on DOE contractors or grantees, and include offenses such as falsification of contractor certified payrolls, overcharging for goods and services, charging non-qualifying expenses to Department contracts, misappropriation of funds, violation of project construction permits, theft of government property, and participation in DOE contracts by debarred firms. Special Agents also investigate DOE personnel misconduct, including violations such as embezzlement, theft of office equipment and supplies, and fraudulent travel reimbursement claims. Special Agents are authorized to conduct surveillance and undercover operations, carry firearms, make arrests, execute search warrants and serve subpoenas. Investigations may be conducted jointly with agencies such as the FBI, IRS Criminal Investigation Division, EPA, and other federal, state, or local law enforcement and regulatory agencies. This position is covered under special retirement provisions for law enforcement officers and qualifies for 25 percent Law Enforcement Availability Pay.

Qualifications: Applicants must be U.S. citizens, at least twenty-one years of age, and under the age of thirty-seven. (Candidates over age thirty-seven who have previous service creditable under special law enforcement retirement provisions may also be eligible.) Eyesight requirements include "sufficiently good vision in each eye, with or without correction." Corrected or uncorrected near vision must be sufficient to read printed material the size of typewritten characters. Hearing loss must not exceed 35 decibels at 1000, 2000, and 3000 Hz. Requirements for appointment to GS-5 level include completion of a four-year course of study leading to a bachelor's degree, OR three years general experience, one year of which was equivalent to GS-4; for GS-7, one full year of graduate education, or superior academic achievement during undergraduate studies, OR one year of specialized experience equivalent to GS-5; for GS-9, a master's degree or two years of graduate education, OR one year of specialized experience equivalent to GS-7; for GS-11, a Ph.D. or equivalent doctoral degree, or three years of graduate education, OR one year of specialized experience equivalent to GS-9; and for GS-12 and above, one year of specialized experience equivalent to the next lower grade level. In some cases, qualifying education may be substituted for experience, and vice versa. Tentative appointees must qualify for a security clearance, and pass a drug screening test and physical exam.

Training: DOE-OIG Special Agents attend the eight-week Criminal Investigator Training Program at the Federal Law Enforcement Training Center in Glynco, Georgia (see Chapter 16). In-service training may include courses in DOE program investigations, procurement fraud, personnel misconduct, financial investigations, search and seizure, computer hardware and software, firearms proficiency, legal issues and updates, first aid and CPR, arrest techniques, and defensive tactics.

Contact: Office of Inspector General, Department of Energy, 1000 Independence Avenue SW; Washington, DC 20585. Phone: 202-586-5000. World Wide Web: http://www.hr.doe.gov/ig/.

SPECIAL AGENT (GS-1811)
CRIMINAL INVESTIGATION DIVISION
OFFICE OF CRIMINAL ENFORCEMENT, FORENSICS AND TRAINING
U.S. ENVIRONMENTAL PROTECTION AGENCY

Overview: Special Agents of the EPA Office of Criminal Enforcement, Forensics and Training, Criminal Investigation Division (EPA-CID), investigate violations of environmental laws that pose a threat to human health and the environment, particularly those relating to air, water and land resources. Investigations focus on hazardous waste disposal practices and industrial discharges associated with the Clean Air Act, Clean Water Act, Resource Conservation and Recovery Act, Safe Drinking Water Act, Toxic Substances Control Act, and other environmental statutes. Primary responsibilities include conducting interviews; developing sources of information and confidential informants; obtaining and reviewing documentary and other evidence; coordinating investigative activities with United States Attorneys; and testifying before grand juries and in subsequent criminal proceedings. EPA-CID Special Agents participate in a multitude of nationwide crime task forces; conduct investigations jointly with the FBI and other federal, state, or local law enforcement and regulatory agencies; and are authorized to conduct surveillance and undercover operations, carry firearms, make arrests, execute search warrants and serve subpoenas. This position is covered under special retirement provisions for law enforcement officers and qualifies for 25 percent Law Enforcement Availability Pay.

Qualifications: Applicants must be U.S. citizens, at least twenty-one years of age, and under the age of thirty-seven. (Candidates over age thirty-seven who have previous service creditable under special law enforcement retirement provisions may also be eligible.) Eyesight requirements include "sufficiently good vision in each eye, with or without correction." Corrected or uncorrected near vision must be sufficient to read printed material the size of typewritten characters. Hearing loss must not exceed 35 decibels at 1000, 2000, and 3000 Hz. A bachelor's degree is required, although acceptable experience in law enforcement or the environmental field may be considered in lieu of a degree. Requirements for appointment to GS-5 level include completion of a four-year course of study leading to a bachelor's degree, OR three years general experience, one year of which was equivalent to GS-4; for GS-7, one full year of graduate education, or superior academic achievement during undergraduate studies, OR one year of specialized experience equivalent to GS-5; for

GS-9, a master's degree or two years of graduate education, OR one year of specialized experience equivalent to GS-7; for GS-11, a Ph.D. or equivalent doctoral degree, or three years of graduate education, OR one year of specialized experience equivalent to GS-9; and for GS-12 and above, one year of specialized experience equivalent to the next lower grade level. In some cases, qualifying education may be substituted for experience, and vice versa. Tentative appointees must qualify for a security clearance, and pass a drug screening test and medical exam.

Training: EPA-CID Special Agents attend the eight-week Criminal Investigator Training Program at the Federal Law Enforcement Training Center in Glynco, Georgia (see Chapter 16), as well as a seven-week EPA Basic Environmental Investigation Course. In-service training may include courses pertaining to EPA laws and regulations, enforcement operations, criminal and civil law, interviewing techniques, firearms proficiency, arrest techniques, and defensive tactics.

Contact: EPA Office of Criminal Enforcement, 401 M Street SW; Washington, DC 20460. Phone: 202-564-2480. World Wide Web: http://www.es.epa.gov/oeca/oceft/cid/. E-mail: public-access@epamail.epa.gov.

SPECIAL AGENT (GS-1811)
OFFICE OF INSPECTOR GENERAL
U.S. ENVIRONMENTAL PROTECTION AGENCY

Overview: The mission of the Environmental Protection Agency (EPA) is to control and abate pollution in areas of air, water, solid waste, pesticides, radiation, and toxic substances. Special Agents of the EPA Office of Inspector General (OIG) conduct investigations which focus on fraud, waste and abuse in programs and operations administered or financed by the Agency. Often complex and sensitive in nature, EPA-OIG investigations revolve around violations of federal statutes pertaining to large interstate corporate entities and subsidiaries, grants, and contracts; violations of Federal Clean Air Act standards and asbestos removal projects; bid-rigging activities related to EPA contracts; bribery of EPA personnel; and intricate conspiracies. Investigations also focus on official misconduct by Agency personnel, including offenses such as collusion, conflict of interest, kickbacks, and embezzlement of federal funds. Special Agents are authorized to conduct surveillance and undercover operations, carry firearms, make arrests, execute search warrants and serve subpoenas. Investigations may be conducted jointly with agencies such as the FBI and other federal, state, or local law enforcement and regulatory agencies. This position is covered under special retirement provisions for law enforcement officers and qualifies for 25 percent Law Enforcement Availability Pay.

Qualifications: Applicants must be U.S. citizens, at least twenty-one years of age, and under the age of thirty-seven. (Candidates over age thirty-seven who have previous service creditable under special law enforcement retirement provisions may also be eligible.) Eyesight requirements include "sufficiently good vision in each eye, with or without correction." Corrected or uncorrected near vision must be sufficient to read printed material the size of typewritten characters. Hearing loss must not exceed 35 decibels at 1000, 2000, and 3000 Hz. Requirements for appointment to GS-5 level include completion of a four-year course of study leading to a bachelor's degree, OR three years general experience, one year of which was equivalent to GS-4; for GS-7, one full year of graduate education, or superior academic achievement during undergraduate studies, OR one year of specialized experience equivalent to GS-5; for GS-9, a master's degree or two years of graduate education, OR one year of specialized experience equivalent to GS-7; for GS-11, a Ph.D. or equivalent doctoral degree, or three years of graduate education, OR one year of specialized experience equivalent to GS-9; and for GS-12 and above, one year of specialized experience equivalent to the next lower grade level. In some cases, qualifying education may be substituted for experience, and vice versa. Tentative appointees must qualify for a security clearance, and pass a drug screening test and medical exam.

Training: EPA-OIG Special Agents attend the eight-week Criminal Investigator Training Program at the Federal Law Enforcement Training Center in Glynco, Georgia (see Chapter 16). In-service training may include courses which focus on environmental crimes and investigations, EPA program regulations, white-collar crime, personnel misconduct, criminal and civil law, firearms proficiency, arrest techniques, and defensive tactics.

Contact: Office of Inspector General, U.S. Environmental Protection Agency, 401 M Street SW; Washington, DC 20460. Phone: 202-260-1109. World Wide Web: http://www.epa.gov/oigearth/. E-mail: public-access@epamail.epa.gov.

SPECIAL AGENT (GS-1811)
OFFICE OF INSPECTOR GENERAL
EQUAL EMPLOYMENT OPPORTUNITY COMMISSION

Overview: In an effort to eliminate employment discrimination in the United States, the Equal Employment Opportunity Commission (EEOC) conducts investigations of alleged discrimination, makes determinations based on gathered evidence, attempts conciliation when discrimination has taken place, files lawsuits, and conducts voluntary assistance programs for employers, unions and community organizations. EEOC Office of Inspector General (OIG) Special Agents perform complex investigations involving fraud, waste and abuse pertaining to Commission programs and operations, as well as misconduct by its personnel. Investigations often focus on highly sensitive matters and prominent individuals, and involve offenses such as conflict of interest, collusion, mismanagement, theft of government property, falsification of records and documents, and non-compliance with requirements of legislation and administrative regulations relating to Commission programs. Investigations may be conducted jointly with agencies such as the FBI, Office of Personnel Management, General Accounting Office, and other federal, state, or local law enforcement and regulatory agencies.

Qualifications: Applicants must be U.S. citizens. Eyesight requirements include "sufficiently good vision in each eye, with or without correction." Corrected or uncorrected near vision must be sufficient to read printed material the size of typewritten characters. Hearing loss must not exceed 35 decibels at 1000, 2000, and 3000 Hz. Requirements for appointment to GS-5 level include completion of a four-year course of study leading to a bachelor's degree, OR three years general experience, one year of which was equivalent to GS-4; for GS-7, one full year of graduate education, or superior academic achievement during undergraduate studies, OR one year of specialized experience equivalent to GS-5; for GS-9, a master's degree or two years of graduate education, OR one year of specialized experience equivalent to GS-7; for GS-11, a Ph.D. or equivalent doctoral degree, or three years of graduate education, OR one year of specialized experience equivalent to GS-9; and for GS-12 and above, one year of specialized experience equivalent to the next lower grade level. In some cases, qualifying education may be substituted for experience, and vice versa. Tentative appointees must pass a background investigation and qualify for a security clearance.

Training: EEOC-OIG Special Agents attend the eight-week Criminal Investigator Training Program at the Federal Law Enforcement Training Center (FLETC) in Glynco, Georgia (see Chapter 16). In-service training may include the three-week Inspector General Basic Training Program at FLETC, and courses which focus on communication skills, accounting methods, contract fraud investigation, employee misconduct investigation, undercover operations, legal issues and updates, financial investigations, and law enforcement skills.

Contact: Personnel Office, Equal Employment Opportunity Commission, 1801 L Street NW; Washington, DC 20507. Phone: 202-663-4306. World Wide Web: http://www.eeoc.gov/.

SPECIAL AGENT (GS-1811)
OFFICE OF INSPECTOR GENERAL
FARM CREDIT ADMINISTRATION

Overview: The Farm Credit Administration (FCA) is responsible for ensuring the safe and sound operation of the banks, associations, affiliated service organizations, and other entities that collectively comprise what is known as the Farm Credit System, and for protecting the interests of the public and those who borrow from Farm Credit institutions or invest in Farm Credit securities. The FCA Office of Inspector General (OIG) is an independent agency which is responsible for the regulation, examination and supervision of lending institutions that are chartered under the Farm Credit Act of 1971. FCA-OIG Special Agents conduct sensitive and complex criminal and general investigations concerning fraud, waste, abuse, or mismanagement in FCA programs and operations. Program investigations focus on farm operating and real estate loans provided to farmers, ranchers, commercial fishermen, and rural homeowners by lending institutions incorporated in the Farm Credit System. FCA-OIG Special Agents also perform employee integrity investigations, which involve offenses such as bribery, theft of government property, embezzlement, conflict of interest, or abuse of authority. Special Agents are authorized to conduct surveillance and undercover operations, carry firearms, make arrests, execute search warrants and serve subpoenas. Investigations may be conducted jointly with other federal, state, or local law enforcement agencies. This position is covered under special retirement provisions for law enforcement officers and qualifies for 25 percent Law Enforcement Availability Pay.

Qualifications: Applicants must be U.S. citizens, at least twenty-one years of age, and under the age of thirty-seven. (Candidates over age thirty-seven who have previous service creditable under special law enforcement retirement provisions may also be eligible.) Eyesight requirements include "sufficiently good vision in each eye, with or without correction." Corrected or uncorrected near vision must be sufficient to read printed material the size of typewritten characters. Hearing loss must not exceed 35 decibels at 1000, 2000, and 3000 Hz. Requirements for appointment to GS-5 level include completion of a four-year course of study leading to a bachelor's degree, OR three years general experience, one year of which was equivalent to GS-4; for GS-7, one full year of graduate education, or superior academic achievement during undergraduate studies, OR one year of specialized experience equivalent to GS-5; for GS-9, a master's degree or two years of graduate education, OR one year of specialized experience equivalent to GS-7; for GS-11, a Ph.D. or equivalent doctoral degree, or three years of graduate education, OR one year of specialized experience equivalent to GS-9; and for GS-12 and above, one year of specialized experience equivalent to the next lower grade level. In some cases, qualifying education may be substituted for experience, and vice versa. Tentative appointees must qualify for a security clearance, and pass a drug screening test and medical exam.

Training: FCA-OIG Special Agents attend the eight-week Criminal Investigator Training Program at the Federal Law Enforcement Training Center in Glynco, Georgia (see Chapter 16). In-service training may include courses in FCA program updates and investigations, legal issues and updates, white-collar crime, computer hardware and software, employee integrity investigations, firearms proficiency, first aid and CPR, arrest techniques, and defensive tactics.

Contact: Office of Inspector General, Farm Credit Administration, 1501 Farm Credit Drive; McLean, VA 22102. Phone: 703-883-4030. World Wide Web: http://www.fca.gov/.

SPECIAL AGENT
OFFICE OF INSPECTOR GENERAL
FEDERAL DEPOSIT INSURANCE CORPORATION

Overview: The Federal Deposit Insurance Corporation (FDIC) promotes and preserves public confidence in U.S. financial institutions by insuring bank and thrift deposits; by examining state-chartered banks that are not members of the Federal Reserve System for safety, soundness, and compliance with consumer protection laws; and by liquidating assets of failed institutions to reimburse the insurance funds for the cost of failures. FDIC Office of Inspector General (OIG) Special Agents investigate violations of federal statutes or regulations relating to matters under FDIC jurisdiction, with particular emphasis on white-collar crime. Investigations often focus on fraud committed by FDIC contractors, and include offenses such as falsification of contractor certified payrolls, billing the FDIC for work that was not performed, altering invoices from subcontractors, overcharging for goods and services, charging personal expenses to FDIC contracts, misappropriation of funds, bribery, embezzlement, and kickbacks. Special Agents are authorized to conduct surveillance and undercover operations, carry firearms, make arrests, execute search warrants and serve subpoenas. Investigations may be conducted jointly with agencies such as the FBI, Secret Service, and other federal, state, or local law enforcement and regulatory agencies. This position is covered under special retirement provisions for law enforcement officers and qualifies for 25 percent Law Enforcement Availability Pay. Salary for this position does not fall under the General Schedule pay system, although it is similar to GS-1811 Special Agent positions of other agencies.

Qualifications: Applicants must be U.S. citizens, at least twenty-one years of age, and under the age of thirty-seven. (Candidates over age thirty-seven who have previous service creditable under special law enforcement retirement provisions may also be eligible.) Eyesight requirements include "sufficiently good vision in each eye, with or without correction." Corrected or uncorrected near vision must be sufficient to read printed material the size of typewritten characters. Hearing loss must not exceed 35 decibels at 1000, 2000, and 3000 Hz. Requirements for appointment to CG-5 level include completion of a four-year course of study leading to a bachelor's degree, OR three years general experience, one year of which was equivalent to CG-4; for CG-7, one full year of graduate education, or superior academic achievement during undergraduate studies, OR one year of specialized experience equivalent to CG-5; for CG-9, a master's degree or two years of graduate education, OR one year of specialized experience equivalent to CG-7; for CG-11, a Ph.D. or equivalent doctoral degree, or three years of graduate education, OR one year of specialized experience equivalent to CG-9; and for CG-12, one year of specialized experience equivalent to CG-11. In some cases, qualifying education may be substituted for experience, and vice versa. Tentative appointees must pass a background investigation and medical exam.

Training: FDIC-OIG Special Agents attend the eight-week Criminal Investigator Training Program at the Federal Law Enforcement Training Center in Glynco, Georgia (see Chapter 16). In-service training may include various courses conducted by the National Association of Certified Fraud Examiners, SIG Arms Academy, Air Force Office of Special Investigations, FBI, and various state and local police academies.

Contact: Office of Inspector General, Federal Deposit Insurance Corporation, 550 17th Street NW; Washington, DC 20429. Phone: 202-393-8400 or 800-695-8052. World Wide Web: http://www.fdic.gov/.

SPECIAL AGENT (GS-1811)
OFFICE OF INSPECTOR GENERAL
FEDERAL EMERGENCY MANAGEMENT AGENCY

Overview: Special Agents of the Federal Emergency Management Agency (FEMA) Office of Inspector General (OIG) conduct investigations to detect fraud, waste, abuse, and corruption in FEMA programs and operations. Investigations often focus on fraud committed by contractors and disaster relief recipients following major natural disasters and human-caused emergencies. Typical allegations involve false claims by disaster assistance applicants who use fictitious names and addresses; disaster assistance recipients victimized by contractors who inflate repair fees; unlawful filing of applications for disaster relief for losses which were not incurred; embezzlement of funds by Emergency Food and Shelter Program grantees; and various forms of insurance fraud and theft of government property. Investigations also focus on official misconduct by Agency personnel, including offenses such as bribery, collusion, conflict of interest, kickbacks, and embezzlement of federal funds. Specialists such as engineers, auditors, and personnel with expertise in other disciplines are sometimes called upon to assist FEMA-OIG Special Agents with investigations, as needed. Special Agents are authorized to conduct surveillance and undercover operations, carry firearms, make arrests, execute search warrants and serve subpoenas. Investigations may be conducted jointly with agencies such as the U.S. Postal Inspection Service, FBI, IRS Criminal Investigation Division, and other federal, state, or local law enforcement and regulatory agencies. This position is covered under special retirement provisions for law enforcement officers and qualifies for 25 percent Law Enforcement Availability Pay.

Qualifications: Applicants must be U.S. citizens, at least twenty-one years of age, and under the age of thirty-seven. (Candidates over age thirty-seven who have previous service creditable under special law enforcement retirement provisions may also be eligible.) Eyesight requirements include "sufficiently good vision in each eye, with or without correction." Corrected or uncorrected near vision must be sufficient to read printed material the size of typewritten characters. Hearing loss must not exceed 35 decibels at 1000, 2000, and 3000 Hz. Requirements for appointment to GS-5 level include completion of a four-year course of study leading to a bachelor's degree, OR three years general experience, one year of which was equivalent to GS-4; for GS-7, one full year of graduate education, or superior academic achievement during undergraduate studies,

OR one year of specialized experience equivalent to GS-5; for GS-9, a master's degree or two years of graduate education, OR one year of specialized experience equivalent to GS-7; for GS-11, a Ph.D. or equivalent doctoral degree, or three years of graduate education, OR one year of specialized experience equivalent to GS-9; and for GS-12 and above, one year of specialized experience equivalent to the next lower grade level. In some cases, qualifying education may be substituted for experience, and vice versa.

Training: FEMA-OIG Special Agents attend the eight-week Criminal Investigator Training Program at the Federal Law Enforcement Training Center in Glynco, Georgia (see Chapter 16). In-service training may include the Inspector General Basic Training Program at the Federal Law Enforcement Training Center (see Chapter 16), as well as courses which focus on FEMA program investigations, white-collar crime, management and leadership, procurement fraud, financial investigations, firearms proficiency, investigative techniques, search and seizure, criminal and civil law, first aid and CPR, arrest techniques, and defensive tactics.

Contact: Office of Inspector General, Federal Emergency Management Agency, 500 C Street SW; Washington, DC 20472. Phone: 202-646-4600. World Wide Web: http://www.fema.gov/ig/.

**SPECIAL AGENT
OFFICE OF INSPECTOR GENERAL
FEDERAL RESERVE BOARD**

Overview: The Board of Governors of the Federal Reserve System determines general monetary, credit, and operating policies for the System as a whole, and formulates the rules and regulations necessary to carry out the purposes of the Federal Reserve Act. The Board's principal duties consist of monitoring credit conditions; supervising the Federal Reserve Banks, member banks, and bank holding companies; and regulating the implementation of certain consumer credit protection laws. Special Agents of the Federal Reserve Board Office of Inspector General (OIG) investigate allegations of wrongdoing, including administrative, civil, and criminal misconduct related to the programs and operations administered or financed by the Board, as well as violations of Board personnel standards of conduct. Investigations focus on offenses involving theft or misuse of funds or Board property; false statements, documents, or claims; bribery; acceptance of gratuities; conflicts of interest; preferential treatment; disclosure of classified or confidential information; and other unlawful acts. Special Agents are authorized to conduct surveillance and undercover operations, and serve subpoenas. Investigations may be conducted jointly with agencies such as the FBI and other federal and state law enforcement and regulatory agencies. This position is covered under special retirement provisions for law enforcement officers. Salary does not fall under the General Schedule pay system, although it is similar to GS-1811 Special Agent positions of other agencies that do not receive Law Enforcement Availability Pay.

Qualifications: Applicants must be U.S. citizens, at least twenty-one years of age, and under the age of thirty-seven. (Candidates over age thirty-seven who have previous service creditable under special law enforcement retirement provisions may also be eligible.) While Federal Reserve Board OIG Special Agent positions are filled in the excepted service, qualification requirements are similar to GS-1811 Special Agents of federal law enforcement agencies in the competitive service.

Training: Federal Reserve Board OIG Special Agents attend the eight-week Criminal Investigator Training Program at the Federal Law Enforcement Training Center (FLETC) in Glynco, Georgia (see Chapter 16). In-service training may include courses such as the three-week Inspector General Basic Training Program at FLETC (see Chapter 16); instruction relating to Board program investigations, procurement fraud, legal issues and updates, or personnel misconduct; or courses presented by the Association of Certified Fraud Examiners, the Institute for Internal Auditors, or the Financial Fraud Institute at FLETC.

Contact: Office of Inspector General, Board of Governors of the Federal Reserve System, Twentieth Street and Constitution Avenue NW; Washington, DC 20551. Phone: 202-452-3000. World Wide Web: http://www.ignet.gov/ignet/internal/frb/oighome.html

SPECIAL AGENT (GS-1811)
OFFICE OF SPECIAL INVESTIGATIONS
U.S. GENERAL ACCOUNTING OFFICE

Overview: The United States General Accounting Office (GAO) was established to independently audit government agencies, and serves as the investigative arm of the United States Congress. The GAO Office of Special Investigations (OSI) conducts congressional oversight investigations of alleged violations of federal criminal law, misconduct, and serious abuse, including all matters concerning the receipt, disbursement and use of public funds. GAO-OSI Special Agents conduct complex and sensitive investigations of government programs and activities, prepare written reports and detailed analyses, and assist GAO auditors and evaluators when they encounter possible criminal and civil misconduct. Fraud investigations focus on programs that receive federal funds, such as those concerned with healthcare, defense, and national security. GAO-OSI also investigates conflicts of interest and mismanagement relating to government contracting and procurement activities; fraud pertaining to government grants, loans, and entitlements; violations of federal standards of ethical conduct and Departmental ethics regulations by federal employees and government officials; and the integrity of federal law enforcement and investigative programs. Investigations may be conducted jointly with the FBI, various Inspector General offices, and other federal, state, or local law enforcement agencies. This position is covered under special retirement provisions for law enforcement officers and qualifies for 25 percent Law Enforcement Availability Pay.

Qualifications: Applicants must be U.S. citizens, at least twenty-one years of age, and under the age of thirty-seven. (Candidates over age thirty-seven who have previous service creditable under special law enforcement retirement provisions may also be eligible.) Eyesight requirements include uncorrected distant vision of at least 20/200 (Snellen), correctable to 20/30 in one eye and 20/20 in the other; normal depth perception and peripheral vision; the ability to distinguish shades of color; and near vision sufficient to read Jaeger type 2 at 14 inches. Hearing loss must not exceed 30 decibels at 500, 1000, and 2000 Hz. Also required is the ability to hear the whispered voice at fifteen feet in each ear. Requirements for appointment to GS-5 level include completion of a four-year course of study leading to a bachelor's degree, OR three years general experience, one year of which was equivalent to GS-4; for GS-7, one full year of graduate education, or superior academic achievement during undergraduate studies, OR one year of specialized experience equivalent to GS-5; for GS-9, a master's degree or two years of graduate education, OR one year of specialized experience equivalent to GS-7; for GS-11, a Ph.D. or equivalent doctoral degree, or three years of graduate education, OR one year of specialized experience equivalent to GS-9; and for GS-12 and above, one year of specialized experience equivalent to the next lower grade level. In some cases, qualifying education may be substituted for experience, and vice versa.

Training: GAO-OSI Special Agents attend the eight-week Criminal Investigator Training Program at the Federal Law Enforcement Training Center in Glynco, Georgia (see Chapter 16). In-service training may include courses which focus on Defense Department programs, government program investigations, healthcare fraud, interviewing techniques, legal issues and updates, financial investigations, and procurement fraud.

Contact: Office of Special Investigations, U.S. General Accounting Office, 441 G Street NW; Washington, DC 20548. Phone: 202-512-3000 or 800-967-5426. World Wide Web: http://www.gao.gov/. E-mail: recruit@gao.gov.

SPECIAL AGENT (GS-1811)
FEDERAL PROTECTIVE SERVICE
U.S. GENERAL SERVICES ADMINISTRATION

Overview: The Federal Protective Service (FPS) is responsible for security and law enforcement operations in and around all federal buildings and facilities which are under the control of the U.S. General Services Administration. Special Agents are assigned to the Criminal Investigation Section, which is a division of the FPS Police Bureau. These personnel conduct a wide range of criminal investigations concerning theft, vandalism, robbery, burglary, arson, gambling, bomb threats, assault, rape, weapons offenses, illegal use and possession of narcotic substances and other drugs, homicide, and other crimes. FPS Special Agents also conduct pre-employment background investigations of FPS Police Officer candidates. Investigations and task force operations may be conducted jointly with agencies such as the FBI, Drug Enforcement Administration, U.S. Marshals Service, and other federal, state, or local law enforcement agencies. FPS Special Agents are authorized to conduct surveillance and undercover operations, carry firearms, make arrests, execute search warrants, and serve subpoenas. This position is covered under special retirement provisions for law enforcement officers and qualifies for 25 percent Law Enforcement Availability Pay.

Qualifications: Applicants must be U.S. citizens, at least twenty-one years of age, and under the age of thirty-seven. (Candidates over age thirty-seven who have previous service creditable under special law enforcement retirement provisions may also be eligible.) Eyesight requirements include "sufficiently good vision in each eye, with or without correction." Corrected or uncorrected near vision must be sufficient to read printed material the size of typewritten characters. Hearing loss must not exceed 35 decibels at 1000, 2000, and 3000 Hz. Requirements for appointment to GS-5 level include completion of a four-year course of study leading to a bachelor's degree, OR three years general experience, one year of which was equivalent to GS-4; for GS-7, one full year of graduate education, or superior academic achievement during undergraduate studies, OR one year of specialized experience equivalent to GS-5; for GS-9, a master's degree or two years of graduate education, OR one year of specialized experience equivalent to GS-7; for GS-11, a Ph.D. or equivalent doctoral degree, or three years of graduate education, OR one year of specialized experience equivalent to GS-9; and for GS-12 and above, one year of specialized experience equivalent to the next lower grade level. In some cases, qualifying education may be substituted for experience, and vice versa. Tentative appointees must qualify for a security clearance, and pass a drug screening test, physical exam, and background investigation.

Training: FPS Special Agents attend the eight-week Criminal Investigator Training Program at the Federal Law Enforcement Training Center in Glynco, Georgia (see Chapter 16). In-service training may include courses which focus on white-collar crime, financial fraud, forensic photography, arson investigation, computer investigative techniques, race and sex offenses, interpersonal violence, homicide investigation, legal issues and updates, firearms proficiency, arrest techniques, and defensive tactics, among others.

Contact: Federal Protective Service, General Services Administration, 18th and F Streets NW; Washington, DC 20405. Phone: 202-501-0907. World Wide Web: http://www.gsa.gov/pbs/fps/fps.htm.

SPECIAL AGENT (GS-1811)
OFFICE OF INSPECTOR GENERAL
U.S. GENERAL SERVICES ADMINISTRATION

Overview: The U.S. General Services Administration (GSA) is responsible for the management of government property and records; construction and management of buildings; procurement and distribution of supplies; operation of transportation and travel management programs; stockpiling of strategic materials; and management of data processing resources. GSA Office of Inspector General (OIG) Special Agents conduct criminal and non-criminal investigations pertaining to GSA contracts, contractors and their employees; falsification of contractors' certified payrolls; fraudulent deviation from contract specifications; manipulation of books and records of the business transactions of individuals, partnerships, corporations, and other entities; and statutes affecting labor law provisions. Special Agents also investigate violations of laws and Standards of Conduct by GSA personnel, such as bribery, collusion, conflict of interest, embezzlement, and larceny. Special Agents are authorized to conduct surveillance and undercover operations, carry firearms, make arrests, execute search warrants and serve subpoenas. Investigations may be conducted jointly with agencies such as the FBI, Defense Criminal Investigative Service, and other federal, state, or local law enforcement agencies. This position is covered under special retirement provisions for law enforcement officers and qualifies for 25 percent Law Enforcement Availability Pay.

Qualifications: Applicants must be U.S. citizens, at least twenty-one years of age, and under the age of thirty-seven. (Candidates over age thirty-seven who have previous service creditable under special law enforcement retirement provisions may also be eligible.) Eyesight requirements include "sufficiently good vision in each eye, with or without correction." Corrected or uncorrected near vision must be sufficient to read printed material the size of typewritten characters. Hearing loss must not exceed 35 decibels at 1000, 2000, and 3000 Hz. Requirements for appointment to GS-5 level include completion of a four-year course of study leading to a bachelor's degree, OR three years general experience, one year of which was equivalent to GS-4; for GS-7, one full year of graduate education, or superior academic achievement during undergraduate studies, OR one year of specialized experience equivalent to GS-5; for GS-9, a master's degree or two years of graduate education, OR one year of specialized experience equivalent to GS-7; for GS-11, a Ph.D. or equivalent doctoral degree, or three years of graduate education, OR one year of specialized experience equivalent to GS-9; and for GS-12 and above, one year of specialized experience equivalent to the next lower grade level. In some cases, qualifying education may be substituted for experience, and vice versa. Tentative appointees must qualify for a security clearance, and pass a background investigation, drug screening test and physical exam.

Training: GSA-OIG Special Agents attend the eight-week Criminal Investigator Training Program at the Federal Law Enforcement Training Center in Glynco, Georgia (see Chapter 16). In-service training may include courses concerning GSA program investigations, contract and procurement fraud, computer hardware and software, criminal and civil law, personnel misconduct, financial investigations, first aid and CPR, firearms proficiency, arrest techniques, and defensive tactics.

Contact: Office of Inspector General, General Services Administration, 18th and F Streets NW; Washington, DC 20405. Phone: 202-708-5082. World Wide Web: http://www.gsa.gov/.

SPECIAL AGENT
OFFICE OF INSPECTOR GENERAL
U.S. GOVERNMENT PRINTING OFFICE

Overview: With operations centered around the largest general printing plant in the world, the U.S. Government Printing Office (GPO) produces and procures printed and electronic publications for Congress and the departments and establishments of the federal government. Special Agents of the GPO Office of Inspector General (OIG) investigate violations of federal law concerning GPO programs and operations, including fraud committed by printing and supply contractors, as well as misconduct by GPO personnel. Investigations revolve around procurement fraud, false statements and claims, bribery, conflict of interest, illegal drug activity, assault, workers' compensation fraud, employment discrimination, theft of GPO funds and property, misappropriation of funds, and other offenses. GPO-OIG Special Agents are authorized to conduct surveillance and undercover operations, carry firearms, make arrests, execute search warrants and serve subpoenas. Investigations may be conducted jointly with other federal, state, or local law enforcement agencies. This position is covered under special retirement provisions for law enforcement officers. Although salary does not fall under the General Schedule pay system, salaries for grades PG-5 through PG-12 are similar to GS-5 through GS-12.

Qualifications: Applicants must be U.S. citizens, at least twenty-one years of age, and under the age of thirty-seven. (Candidates over age thirty-seven who have previous service creditable under special law enforcement retirement provisions may also be eligible.) Requirements for appointment to PG-5 level include completion of a four-year course of study leading to a bachelor's degree, OR three years general experience, one year of which was equivalent to PG-4; for PG-7, one full year of graduate education, or superior academic achievement during undergraduate studies, OR one year of specialized experience equivalent to PG-5; for PG-9, a master's degree or two years of graduate education, OR one year of specialized experience equivalent to PG-7; for PG-11, a Ph.D. or equivalent doctoral degree, or three years of graduate education, OR one year of specialized experience equivalent to PG-9; and for PG-12 and above, one year of specialized experience equivalent to the next lower grade level. In some cases, qualifying education may be substituted for experience, and vice versa. Applicants are rated on the basis of their knowledge, skills, and abilities related to the position, as well as relevant experience, education, training, supervisory appraisal, and job-related awards. Tentative appointees must qualify for a security clearance, and may be required to pass a physical examination and drug screening test.

Training: GPO-OIG Special Agents attend the eight-week Criminal Investigator Training Program at the Federal Law Enforcement Training Center in Glynco, Georgia (see Chapter 16). In-service training may include courses which cover GPO program and financial investigations, computer fraud, contract and procurement fraud, money laundering, asset forfeiture, legal issues and updates, first aid and CPR, firearms proficiency, arrest techniques, and defensive tactics.

Contact: Employment Branch, Government Printing Office, 732 North Capitol Street NW; Washington, DC 20401. Phone: 202-512-1118. World Wide Web: http://www.gpo.gov/. E-mail: wwwadmin@www.access.gpo.gov.

SPECIAL AGENT (GS-1811)
FOOD AND DRUG ADMINISTRATION
U.S. DEPARTMENT OF HEALTH AND HUMAN SERVICES

Overview: Special Agents of the Food and Drug Administration (FDA) Office of Criminal Investigations (OCI) investigate violations of federal law relating to FDA programs and operations, such as those pertaining to the Food, Drug and Cosmetic Act; Federal Anti-Tampering Act; Prescription Drug Marketing Act; and the Safe Medical Device Act. The FDA-OCI has the primary responsibility for criminal investigation of tampering and threat incidents involving products regulated by the FDA. The purpose of these investigations is to determine whether tampering has occurred; the seriousness of the problem; the quantity of affected products on the market; the source of the tampering; and to remove contaminated products from consumers or commerce. Special Agents also investigate misconduct and violations of laws by FDA personnel relating to Administration programs and operations, including offenses such as bribery, conflict of interest, embezzlement, or misappropriation of federal funds. Special Agents are authorized to conduct surveillance and undercover operations, carry firearms, make arrests, execute search warrants and serve subpoenas. Investigations may be conducted jointly with agencies such as the Health and Human Services OIG, Customs Service, U.S. Fish and Wildlife Service, USDA Animal and Plant Health Inspection Service, USDA Office of Inspector General, FBI, and other federal, state, or local law enforcement and regulatory agencies. This position is covered under special retirement provisions for law enforcement officers and qualifies for 25 percent Law Enforcement Availability Pay.

Qualifications: Applicants must be U.S. citizens, at least twenty-one years of age, and under the age of thirty-seven. (Candidates over age thirty-seven who have previous service creditable under special law enforcement retirement provisions may also be eligible.) Eyesight requirements include "sufficiently good vision in each eye, with or without correction." Corrected or uncorrected near vision must be sufficient to read printed material the size of typewritten characters. Hearing loss must not exceed 35 decibels at 1000, 2000, and 3000 Hz. Requirements for appointment to GS-5 level include completion of a four-year course of study leading to a bachelor's degree, OR three years general experience, one year of which was equivalent to GS-4; for GS-7, one full year of graduate education, or superior academic achievement during undergraduate studies, OR one year of specialized experience equivalent to GS-5; for GS-9, a master's degree or two years of graduate education, OR one year of specialized experience equivalent to GS-7; for GS-11, a Ph.D. or equivalent doctoral degree, or three years of graduate education, OR one year of specialized experience equivalent to GS-9; and for GS-12 and above, one year of specialized experience equivalent to the next lower grade level. In some cases, qualifying education may be substituted for experience, and vice versa. Tentative appointees must qualify for a security clearance, and pass a drug screening test and medical exam.

Training: FDA-OCI Special Agents attend the eight-week Criminal Investigator Training Program at the Federal Law Enforcement Training Center in Glynco, Georgia (see Chapter 16). In-service training may include courses in FDA program investigations, legal issues and updates, FDA regulations, investigative techniques, criminal and civil law, first aid and CPR, arrest techniques, defensive tactics, and firearms proficiency.

Contact: Office of Human Resources, Food and Drug Administration, 5600 Fishers Lane; Rockville, MD 20857. Phone: 301-827-4120. World Wide Web: http://www.fda.gov/.

SPECIAL AGENT (GS-1811)
OFFICE OF INSPECTOR GENERAL
U.S. DEPARTMENT OF HEALTH AND HUMAN SERVICES

Overview: The U.S. Department of Health and Human Services (HHS) is the federal government's principal agency for protecting the health of Americans and providing essential human services. The Department includes more than 300 programs, which cover a wide spectrum of activities, and is the largest grant-making agency in the federal government. Special Agents of the HHS Office of Inspector General (OIG) conduct investigations to identify fraud and other forms of criminal or improper activity in HHS programs and operations. Investigations often focus on Food and Drug Administration programs, and fraud committed by Medicare and Medicaid providers, such as hospitals, nursing homes, doctors, and medical equipment companies. Fraud investigations may involve allegations of embezzlement, contract and procurement fraud, kickbacks, and using false identities or otherwise filing false claims to obtain government benefits. Investigations also focus on official misconduct by Department personnel, including offenses such as bribery, collusion, and conflict of interest. Special Agents are authorized to conduct surveillance and undercover operations, carry firearms, make arrests, execute search warrants and serve subpoenas. Investigations may be conducted jointly with agencies such as the Secret Service, IRS Criminal Investigation Division, U.S. Postal Inspection Service, FBI, and other federal, state, or local law enforcement and regulatory agencies. This position is covered under special retirement provisions for law enforcement officers and qualifies for 25 percent Law Enforcement Availability Pay.

Qualifications: Applicants must be U.S. citizens, at least twenty-one years of age, and under the age of thirty-seven. (Candidates over age thirty-seven who have previous service creditable under special law enforcement retirement provisions may also be eligible.) Eyesight requirements include "sufficiently good vision in each eye, with or without correction." Corrected or uncorrected near vision must be sufficient to read printed material the size of typewritten characters. Hearing loss must not exceed 35 decibels at 1000, 2000, and 3000 Hz. Requirements for appointment to GS-5 level include completion of a four-year course of study leading to a bachelor's degree, OR three years general experience, one year of which was equivalent to GS-4; for GS-7, one full year of graduate education, or superior academic achievement during undergraduate studies, OR one year of specialized experience equivalent to GS-5; for GS-9, a master's degree or two years of graduate education, OR one year of specialized experience equivalent to GS-7; for GS-11, a Ph.D. or equivalent doctoral degree, or three years of graduate education, OR one year of specialized experience equivalent to GS-9; and for GS-12 and above, one year of specialized experience equivalent to the next lower grade level. In some cases, qualifying education may be substituted for experience, and vice versa. Tentative appointees must qualify for a security clearance, and pass a drug screening test and medical exam.

Training: HHS-OIG Special Agents attend the eight-week Criminal Investigator Training Program at the Federal Law Enforcement Training Center in Glynco, Georgia (see Chapter 16). In-service training may include courses in HHS program investigations, Medicare and Medicaid fraud, search and seizure, interviewing techniques, criminal and civil law, white-collar crime, procurement fraud, first aid and CPR, firearms proficiency, arrest techniques, and defensive tactics.

Contact: Office of Inspector General, Department of Health and Human Services, 1040 Cohen Building, 330 Independence Avenue SW; Washington, DC 20201. Phone: 202-619-0146. World Wide Web: http://www.dhhs.gov/progorg/oig/.

SPECIAL AGENT (GS-1811)
OFFICE OF INSPECTOR GENERAL
U.S. DEPARTMENT OF HOUSING AND URBAN DEVELOPMENT

Overview: The U.S. Department of Housing and Urban Development (HUD) is the principal federal agency responsible for programs concerned with the nation's housing needs, fair housing opportunities, and improvement and development of the nation's communities. Special Agents of the HUD Office of Inspector General

(OIG) conduct criminal, civil, and administrative investigations of irregularities in connection with housing programs funded by HUD. Offenses investigated include fraud relating to HUD Single Family and Multifamily Housing and other Department programs, false statements, theft of government property, bribery, kickbacks, racketeering, money laundering, forgery, embezzlement, extortion, organized crime, narcotics transactions, gang activity in public housing projects, violent crimes, and official misconduct by Department personnel. Investigations may be highly sensitive, involving national organizations with strong political action programs, where there is a high degree of visibility and Congressional or Executive interest. Special Agents are authorized to conduct surveillance and undercover operations, carry firearms, make arrests, execute search warrants and serve subpoenas. Investigations may be conducted jointly with agencies such as the DEA, IRS Criminal Investigation Division, U.S. Postal Inspection Service, FBI, and other federal, state, or local law enforcement agencies. This position is covered under special retirement provisions for law enforcement officers and qualifies for 25 percent Law Enforcement Availability Pay.

Qualifications: Applicants must be U.S. citizens, at least twenty-one years of age, and under the age of thirty-seven. (Candidates over age thirty-seven who have previous service creditable under special law enforcement retirement provisions may also be eligible.) Eyesight requirements include "sufficiently good vision in each eye, with or without correction." Corrected or uncorrected near vision must be sufficient to read printed material the size of typewritten characters. Hearing loss must not exceed 35 decibels at 1000, 2000, and 3000 Hz. Requirements for appointment to GS-5 level include completion of a four-year course of study leading to a bachelor's degree, OR three years general experience, one year of which was equivalent to GS-4; for GS-7, one full year of graduate education, or superior academic achievement during undergraduate studies, OR one year of specialized experience equivalent to GS-5; for GS-9, a master's degree or two years of graduate education, OR one year of specialized experience equivalent to GS-7; for GS-11, a Ph.D. or equivalent doctoral degree, or three years of graduate education, OR one year of specialized experience equivalent to GS-9; and for GS-12 and above, one year of specialized experience equivalent to the next lower grade level. In some cases, qualifying education may be substituted for experience, and vice versa. Tentative appointees must qualify for a security clearance, and pass a drug screening test and medical exam.

Training: HUD-OIG Special Agents attend the eight-week Criminal Investigator Training Program at the Federal Law Enforcement Training Center in Glynco, Georgia (see Chapter 16). In-service training may include courses concerning HUD program investigations, law enforcement procedures, computer hardware and software, search and seizure, legal issues and updates, financial investigations, procurement fraud, first aid and CPR, firearms proficiency, arrest techniques, and defensive tactics.

Contact: HUD Office of Inspector General, 451 Seventh Street SW; Washington, DC 20201. Phone: 202-708-0430. World Wide Web: http://www.hud.gov/oig/oigindex.html.

SPECIAL AGENT (GS-1811)
BUREAU OF INDIAN AFFAIRS
U.S. DEPARTMENT OF THE INTERIOR

Overview: The Bureau of Indian Affairs (BIA) is the principal bureau within the federal government responsible for the administration of federal programs for recognized Indian tribes, and for promoting Indian self-determination. In addition, the Bureau has a trust responsibility emanating from treaties and other agreements with Native groups. Operating from BIA offices nationwide, BIA Special Agents investigate violations of federal, state, tribal, and local laws on Indian reservations, such as assault, burglary, auto theft, child sexual abuse, murder, rape, robbery, drug trafficking, fraud, and criminal activity related to gaming operations and other legitimate businesses operating within Indian country. Investigations often involve surveillance and undercover operations under hazardous conditions. Special Agents are authorized to carry firearms, make arrests, execute search warrants and serve subpoenas. Many investigations are conducted jointly with other law enforcement agencies at the federal, state, local, and tribal levels. This position is covered under special retirement provisions for law enforcement officers and qualifies for 25 percent Law Enforcement Availability Pay.

Qualifications: Under the Indian Reorganization Act of 1934, qualified Indian applicants are given hiring preference for BIA positions, although applications from non-Indian candidates are encouraged. Applicants must be U.S. citizens, at least twenty-one years of age, and under the age of thirty-seven. (Candidates over age thirty-seven who have previous service creditable under special law enforcement retirement provisions may also be eligible.) Eyesight requirements include "sufficiently good vision in each eye, with or without correction." Corrected or uncorrected near vision must be sufficient to read printed material the size of typewritten characters. Hearing loss must not exceed 35 decibels at 1000, 2000, and 3000 Hz. Requirements for appointment to GS-5 level include completion of a four-year course of study leading to a bachelor's degree, OR three years general experience, one year of which was equivalent to GS-4; for GS-7, one full year of graduate education, or superior academic achievement during undergraduate studies, OR one year of specialized experience equivalent to GS-5; for GS-9, a master's degree or two years of graduate education, OR one year of specialized experience equivalent to GS-7; for GS-11, a Ph.D. or equivalent doctoral degree, or three years of graduate education, OR one year of specialized experience equivalent to GS-9; and for GS-12 and above, one year of specialized experience equivalent to the next lower grade level. In some cases, qualifying education may be substituted for experience, and vice versa. Tentative appointees must qualify for a security clearance, and pass a drug screening test and medical exam.

Training: BIA Special Agents attend the eight-week Criminal Investigator Training Program at the Federal Law Enforcement Training Center in Glynco, Georgia (see Chapter 16). In-service training may include courses in tribal matters, tribal and criminal law, civil law, fish and game laws, drug trafficking investigations, search and seizure, technical investigative equipment, undercover operations, financial investigations, first aid and CPR, firearms proficiency, arrest techniques, and defensive tactics.

Contact: Office of Personnel, Bureau of Indian Affairs, 1849 C Street NW; Washington, DC 20240. Phone: 202-208-3710. World Wide Web: http://www.doi.gov/bureau-indian-affairs.html.

SPECIAL AGENT (GS-1811)
BUREAU OF LAND MANAGEMENT
U.S. DEPARTMENT OF THE INTERIOR

Overview: The Bureau of Land Management (BLM) administers public lands within a framework of the Federal Land Policy and Management Act of 1976, and other laws. The surface acres under Bureau management comprise one-eighth of America's land surface and amount to 41 percent of the land under federal ownership. BLM Special Agents are responsible for the investigation of criminal activities relating to 270 million acres of public lands and resources managed by the Bureau, as well as 300 million acres where mineral rights are owned by the federal government. Investigations focus on offenses such as timber theft, destruction or theft of archaeological artifacts, unlawful sale or treatment of wild horses or burros, violation of conservation laws, marijuana cultivation, and other criminal acts occurring on Bureau-managed forests and ranges. Field work is often conducted in remote areas, at high altitudes, and over rugged terrain where climatic conditions are variable and extreme. Special Agents are authorized to conduct surveillance and undercover operations, carry firearms, make arrests, execute search warrants and serve subpoenas. Many investigations are conducted jointly with other law enforcement agencies at the federal, state, and local levels. This position is covered under special retirement provisions for law enforcement officers and qualifies for 25 percent Law Enforcement Availability Pay.

Qualifications: Applicants must be U.S. citizens, at least twenty-one years of age, and under the age of thirty-seven. (Candidates over age thirty-seven who have previous service creditable under special law enforcement retirement provisions may also be eligible.) Eyesight requirements include "sufficiently good vision in each eye, with or without correction." Corrected or uncorrected near vision must be sufficient to read printed material the size of typewritten characters. Hearing loss must not exceed 35 decibels at 1000, 2000, and 3000 Hz. Requirements for appointment to GS-5 level include completion of a four-year course of study leading to a bachelor's degree, OR three years general experience, one year of which was equivalent to GS-4; for GS-7, one full year of graduate education, or superior academic achievement during undergraduate studies,

OR one year of specialized experience equivalent to GS-5; for GS-9, a master's degree or two years of graduate education, OR one year of specialized experience equivalent to GS-7; for GS-11, a Ph.D. or equivalent doctoral degree, or three years of graduate education, OR one year of specialized experience equivalent to GS-9; and for GS-12 and above, one year of specialized experience equivalent to the next lower grade level. In some cases, qualifying education may be substituted for experience, and vice versa. Tentative appointees must qualify for a security clearance, and pass a drug screening test and medical exam.

Training: BLM Special Agents attend the eight-week Criminal Investigator Training Program at the Federal Law Enforcement Training Center in Glynco, Georgia (see Chapter 16). Special Agents also receive a minimum of 40 hours of in-service training annually, including courses in subjects such as evidence photography, archaeological crime scene processing, domestic terrorism, legal updates, judgment pistol shooting, firearms proficiency, defensive tactics, and investigative techniques.

Contact: Office of Law Enforcement, Bureau of Land Management, Department of the Interior; Washington, DC 20240. Phone: 202-208-3710. World Wide Web: http://www.blm.gov/.

SPECIAL AGENT (GS-1811)
NATIONAL PARK SERVICE
U.S. DEPARTMENT OF THE INTERIOR

Overview: National Park Service (NPS) Special Agents are responsible for the investigation of a wide range of criminal offenses and civil matters pertaining to NPS programs and operations. Investigations focus on incidents which occur on the grounds of national parks and monuments, scenic parkways, preserves, trails, campgrounds, battlefields, sea shores, lakeshores, recreational areas and historic sites which encompass the National Park System. Offenses investigated include violations of the Archaeological Resources Protection Act, Endangered Species Act, and Migratory Bird Treaty Act; NPS recreation and use violations; hazardous waste disposal and other environmental crimes; marijuana cultivation and other drug offenses; assault; rape; homicide; robbery; weapons offenses; larceny; vandalism; arson; and other property and personal crimes. NPS Special Agents also participate in local and regional drug task force operations, and conduct investigations jointly with other federal, state, and local law enforcement or regulatory agencies. NPS Special Agents are authorized to conduct surveillance and undercover operations, carry firearms, make arrests, execute search warrants and serve subpoenas. This position is covered under special retirement provisions for law enforcement officers and qualifies for 25 percent Law Enforcement Availability Pay. Similar NPS positions are staffed by personnel under the working title of "Criminal Investigator."

Qualifications: Applicants must be U.S. citizens, at least twenty-one years of age, and under the age of thirty-seven. (Candidates over age thirty-seven who have previous service creditable under special law enforcement retirement provisions may also be eligible.) Eyesight requirements include "sufficiently good vision in each eye, with or without correction." Corrected or uncorrected near vision must be sufficient to read printed material the size of typewritten characters. Hearing loss must not exceed 35 decibels at 1000, 2000, and 3000 Hz. Requirements for appointment to GS-5 level include completion of a four-year course of study leading to a bachelor's degree, OR three years general experience, one year of which was equivalent to GS-4; for GS-7, one full year of graduate education, or superior academic achievement during undergraduate studies, OR one year of specialized experience equivalent to GS-5; for GS-9, a master's degree or two years of graduate education, OR one year of specialized experience equivalent to GS-7; for GS-11, a Ph.D. or equivalent doctoral degree, or three years of graduate education, OR one year of specialized experience equivalent to GS-9; and for GS-12 and above, one year of specialized experience equivalent to the next lower grade level. In some cases, qualifying education may be substituted for experience, and vice versa. Tentative appointees must qualify for a security clearance, and pass a background investigation and drug screening test.

Training: NPS Special Agents attend the eight-week Criminal Investigator Training Program at the Federal Law Enforcement Training Center in Glynco, Georgia (see Chapter 16). In-service training may include courses which focus on environmental crimes, covert wildlife investigations, Archaeological Resources

Protection Act violations, drug trafficking, background investigations, interviewing techniques, criminal law, search and seizure, laws of arrest, firearms proficiency, arrest techniques, defensive tactics, and other subjects.

Contact: National Park Service, Department of the Interior, P.O. Box 37127; Washington, DC 20013. Phone: 202-208-6843. World Wide Web: http://www.nps.gov/.

SPECIAL AGENT (GS-1811)
OFFICE OF INSPECTOR GENERAL
U.S. DEPARTMENT OF THE INTERIOR

Overview: The Department of the Interior (DOI) manages the nation's public lands and minerals, national parks, national wildlife refuges, and western water resources, and upholds federal trust responsibilities to Indian tribes. Special Agents of the DOI Office of Inspector General (OIG) conduct complex and sensitive criminal, civil, and administrative investigations involving DOI programs and operations. Investigation focus on offenses committed by contractors, grantees, and DOI personnel, including crimes such as embezzlement, false claims, obtaining loans by fraudulent means, government credit card fraud, conspiracy to defraud the government, violations of the Migratory Bird Treaty Act and other environmental laws, and workers' compensation fraud. Special Agents are authorized to conduct surveillance and undercover operations, carry firearms, make arrests, execute search warrants and serve subpoenas. Investigations may be conducted jointly with agencies such as the FBI, Bureau of Land Management Law Enforcement Branch, U.S. Fish and Wildlife Service, Defense Criminal Investigative Service, Environmental Protection Agency OIG, and other federal, state, and local law enforcement and regulatory agencies. This position is covered under special retirement provisions for law enforcement officers and qualifies for 25 percent Law Enforcement Availability Pay.

Qualifications: Applicants must be U.S. citizens, at least twenty-one years of age, and under the age of thirty-seven. (Candidates over age thirty-seven who have previous service creditable under special law enforcement retirement provisions may also be eligible.) Eyesight requirements include "sufficiently good vision in each eye, with or without correction." Corrected or uncorrected near vision must be sufficient to read printed material the size of typewritten characters. Hearing loss must not exceed 35 decibels at 1000, 2000, and 3000 Hz. Requirements for appointment to GS-5 level include completion of a four-year course of study leading to a bachelor's degree, OR three years general experience, one year of which was equivalent to GS-4; for GS-7, one full year of graduate education, or superior academic achievement during undergraduate studies, OR one year of specialized experience equivalent to GS-5; for GS-9, a master's degree or two years of graduate education, OR one year of specialized experience equivalent to GS-7; for GS-11, a Ph.D. or equivalent doctoral degree, or three years of graduate education, OR one year of specialized experience equivalent to GS-9; and for GS-12 and above, one year of specialized experience equivalent to the next lower grade level. In some cases, qualifying education may be substituted for experience, and vice versa. Tentative appointees must qualify for a security clearance, and pass a drug screening test and medical exam.

Training: DOI-OIG Special Agents attend the eight-week Criminal Investigator Training Program at the Federal Law Enforcement Training Center in Glynco, Georgia (see Chapter 16). In-service training may include courses in DOI program investigations, surveillance and undercover operations, search and seizure, investigative techniques, conservation law, archaeological resources investigations, first aid and CPR, firearms proficiency, arrest techniques, and defensive tactics.

Contact: Office of Inspector General, Department of the Interior, 1849 C Street NW; Washington, DC 20240. Phone: 202-208-4356. World Wide Web: http://www.access.gpo.gov/doi/.

SPECIAL AGENT (GS-1812)
UNITED STATES FISH AND WILDLIFE SERVICE
U.S. DEPARTMENT OF THE INTERIOR

Overview: The U.S. Fish and Wildlife Service (FWS) is responsible for the conservation, protection, and enhancement of fish and wildlife and their habitat, including migratory birds, endangered species, certain marine mammals, and inland sport fisheries. FWS Special Agents investigate violations of federal fish and wildlife laws – such as those concerning the illegal taking, importing, and commercialization of wildlife – covered under the Endangered Species Act, Convention on International Trade in Endangered Species, Migratory Bird Treaty Act, Lacey Act, Marine Mammal Protection Act, Wild Bird Conservation Act, Eagle Protection Act, Airborne Hunting Act, and other laws. Violations are often clandestine in nature, committed by organized groups, and involve complex conspiracies. FWS Special Agents employ highly sophisticated investigation techniques, surveillance and undercover operations, and are authorized to carry firearms, make arrests, execute search warrants and serve subpoenas. Investigations may be conducted jointly with the National Marine Fisheries Service, Customs Service, FBI, USDA Animal and Plant Health Inspection Service, USDA Office of Inspector General, Food and Drug Administration, and other agencies. This position is covered under special retirement provisions for law enforcement officers and qualifies for 25 percent Law Enforcement Availability Pay.

Qualifications: Applicants must be U.S. citizens, at least twenty-one years of age, and under the age of thirty-seven. (Candidates over age thirty-seven who have previous service creditable under special law enforcement retirement provisions may also be eligible.) Eyesight requirements include distant vision of at least 20/200 (Snellen) in each eye without correction, and at least 20/20 in one eye and 20/30 in the other with correction. Near vision must be sufficient to read Jaeger Type 2 at 14 inches with correction. Normal depth perception and ability to distinguish shades of color are required. A history of Radial Keratotomy surgery is disqualifying. Hearing loss must not exceed 35 decibels at frequencies of 500, 1000, 2000 and 3000 Hz. Requirements for appointment to GS-5 level include completion of a four-year course of study leading to a bachelor's degree, OR three years general experience, one year of which was equivalent to GS-4; for GS-7, one full year of graduate education, or superior academic achievement during undergraduate studies, OR one year of specialized experience equivalent to GS-5; for GS-9, a master's degree or two years of graduate education, OR one year of specialized experience equivalent to GS-7; for GS-11, a Ph.D. or equivalent doctoral degree, or three years of graduate education, OR one year of specialized experience equivalent to GS-9; and for GS-12 and above, one year of specialized experience equivalent to the next lower grade level. In some cases, qualifying education may be substituted for experience, and vice versa. Tentative appointees must qualify for a security clearance, and pass a drug screening test and medical exam.

Training: FWS Special Agents attend the eight-week Criminal Investigator Training Program at the Federal Law Enforcement Training Center (FLETC) in Glynco, Georgia (see Chapter 16), followed by a ten-week FWS Special Agent Basic School which covers subjects such as treaties, law, FWS policies and regulations, wildlife identification, and law enforcement authority. In-service training may include courses concerning covert wildlife investigations, undercover operations, first aid and CPR, firearms proficiency, arrest techniques, and defensive tactics.

Contact: Division of Law Enforcement, U.S. Fish and Wildlife Service, P.O. Box 3247; Arlington, VA 22203. Phone: 703-358-1949. World Wide Web: http://www.fws.gov/~r9dle/div_le.html.

SPECIAL AGENT (GS-1811)
DRUG ENFORCEMENT ADMINISTRATION
U.S. DEPARTMENT OF JUSTICE

Overview: The Drug Enforcement Administration (DEA) is the lead federal agency responsible for enforcing the nation's narcotics and controlled substances laws and regulations. The DEA manages a national drug intelligence system in cooperation with federal, state, local, and foreign officials to collect, analyze, and disseminate strategic and operational drug intelligence information. DEA Special Agents enforce the Controlled Substances Act through complex investigations of individuals and organizations involved in the growing, manufacture or distribution of controlled substances. To accomplish its mission, DEA Special Agents are strategically placed along known routes of illicit drug trafficking, including 170 U.S. cities and 74 foreign posts of duty. Investigations frequently involve the pursuit of sophisticated organized criminal enterprises, surveillance and extensive undercover operations, and seizure of drug trafficking proceeds. Veteran DEA Special Agents may be assigned to posts overseas. DEA Special Agents often participate in task force and joint operations with agencies such as the IRS Criminal Investigation Division; Customs Service; Coast Guard; USDA Forest Service; USDA Office of Inspector General; Bureau of Alcohol, Tobacco and Firearms; HUD Office of Inspector General; Veterans Affairs Office of Inspector General, FBI; other federal, state, and local law enforcement agencies; and drug law enforcement counterparts in foreign countries. Special Agents are authorized to carry firearms, make arrests, execute search warrants and serve subpoenas. This position is covered under special retirement provisions for law enforcement officers and qualifies for 25 percent Law Enforcement Availability Pay. DEA Special Agents normally enter service at the GS-7 or GS-9 level, depending upon qualifications.

Qualifications: Applicants must be U.S. citizens, at least twenty-one and not more than thirty-six years of age at time of appointment; possess a bachelor's degree and at least three years of law enforcement experience, OR a bachelor's degree with a 2.95 GPA or better and at least three years of general experience; be in excellent physical condition; and have sharp hearing acuity. Eyesight requirements include uncorrected distant vision of at least 20/200 (Snellen), with correction to 20/20 in one eye and 20/40 in the other eye. A history of Radial Keratotomy surgery is disqualifying. Additional requirements include possession of a valid driver's license; willingness to accept assignments anywhere in the United States; and successful completion of the interview process, a polygraph examination, psychological suitability assessment, and background investigation. Those tentatively selected must qualify for a security clearance, and pass a personal interview, psychological evaluation, polygraph exam, Physical Task Test, drug screening test, and medical exam.

Training: Initial training for DEA Special Agents includes the sixteen-week DEA Basic Agent Training Program in Quantico, Virginia (see Chapter 16). In-service training may include courses in subjects such as search and seizure, operational and tactical procedures, clandestine laboratory operations, asset forfeiture, interviewing techniques, ethics and integrity, communication skills, legal issues and updates, first aid and CPR, firearms proficiency, arrest techniques, and defensive tactics.

Contact: Recruiting information can be obtained from any DEA Field Office, or by contacting Agent Recruiting, Drug Enforcement Administration; Washington, DC 20537. Phone: 202-307-1000 or 800-DEA-4288. World Wide Web: http://www.usdoj.gov/dea/.

SPECIAL AGENT (GS-1811)
FEDERAL BUREAU OF INVESTIGATION
U.S. DEPARTMENT OF JUSTICE

Overview: The Federal Bureau of Investigation (FBI) investigates violations of federal criminal law; protects the United States from foreign intelligence and terrorist activities; and provides leadership and law enforcement assistance to federal, state, local, and international agencies. As members of the principal investigative arm of the Justice Department, FBI Special Agents investigate more than 200 types of cases divided among seven programs, including Applicant Matters, Civil Rights, Counterterrorism, Financial Crime, Foreign Counterintelligence, Organized Crime and Drugs, and Violent Crime and Major Offenders. Within these program areas, FBI investigations focus on racketeering enterprises, domestic security, bank fraud and embezzlement, bank robbery, public corruption, fraud against the government, healthcare fraud, air piracy, interstate criminal activity, copyright matters, and other offenses. Investigations often involve undercover operations; physical and electronic surveillance; interaction with criminal informants; task force or joint operations with other federal, state, and local law enforcement and regulatory agencies; and cooperation with law enforcement counterparts in foreign countries. Operations are based in 56 field offices, 400 satellite offices known as Resident Agencies, 4 specialized field installations, and 23 foreign liaison posts known as Legal Attachés. FBI Special Agents are authorized to carry firearms, make arrests, execute search warrants and serve subpoenas. This position is covered under special retirement provisions for law enforcement officers and qualifies for 25 percent Law Enforcement Availability Pay. FBI Special Agents normally enter service at the GS-10 level.

Qualifications: Applicants must be U.S. citizens; at least twenty-three and not more than thirty-six years of age; and available for assignment anywhere within the FBI's jurisdiction. Eyesight requirements include uncorrected distant vision not worse than 20/200 (Snellen), with correction to 20/20 in one eye and 20/40 in the other eye. Standardized weight to height ratio and body fat requirements must also be met. All candidates must pass a color vision test, possess a driver's license, and hold a four-year degree from an accredited college or university. Candidates must qualify in at least one of four entry programs, including: *Law*, which requires possession of a JD degree from an accredited resident law school; *Accounting*, which requires a bachelor's degree in accounting or a related discipline; *Language*, which requires a bachelor's degree in any discipline and fluency in a foreign language for which the FBI has a current need; and *Diversified*, which requires a bachelor's degree in any discipline and three years full-time work experience, or an advanced degree and two years full-time work experience. Candidates must pass a battery of written tests (see Chapter 1), polygraph examination, drug screening test, medical examination, interview, and background investigation.

Training: FBI Special Agents attend a fifteen-week basic training program at the FBI Academy in Quantico, Virginia (see Chapter 16). FBI Special Agents also attend a wide variety of in-service seminars to enhance their knowledge, skills, and abilities throughout their careers.

Contact: Recruiting information can be obtained from any FBI Field Office, or by contacting the Federal Bureau of Investigation; Washington, DC 20535. Phone: 202-324-2727. World Wide Web: http://www.fbi.gov/.

SPECIAL AGENT (GS-1811)
OFFICE OF INSPECTOR GENERAL
U.S. DEPARTMENT OF JUSTICE

Overview: Special Agents of the U.S. Department of Justice (DOJ) Office of Inspector General (OIG) enforce criminal and civil laws, regulations, and ethical standards within the Department by investigating individuals and organizations who allegedly are involved in financial, contractual or criminal misconduct in DOJ programs and operations. Investigations may focus on offenses such as embezzlement, theft of government property, criminal wrongdoing by DOJ contractors and grantees, official misconduct by DOJ personnel, civil rights violations, workers' compensation fraud, misconduct by Assistant United States Attorneys, bribery of U.S. Immigration inspectors to facilitate drug smuggling, conspiracy to sell counterfeit immigration documents, physical and sexual abuse of prisoners, and other offenses. DOJ-OIG Special Agents are authorized to conduct surveillance and undercover operations, carry firearms, make arrests, execute search warrants and serve subpoenas; and are deputized as Special Deputy United States Marshals. Investigations may be conducted jointly with agencies such as the FBI, State Department, U.S. Postal Inspection Service, Immigration and Naturalization Service, and other federal, state, or local law enforcement agencies. This position is covered under special retirement provisions for law enforcement officers and qualifies for 25 percent Law Enforcement Availability Pay.

Qualifications: Applicants must be U.S. citizens, at least twenty-one years of age, and under the age of thirty-seven. (Candidates over age thirty-seven who have previous service creditable under special law enforcement retirement provisions may also be eligible.) Eyesight requirements include "sufficiently good vision in each eye, with or without correction." Corrected or uncorrected near vision must be sufficient to read printed material the size of typewritten characters. Hearing loss must not exceed 35 decibels at 1000, 2000, and 3000 Hz. Requirements for appointment to GS-5 level include completion of a four-year course of study leading to a bachelor's degree, OR three years general experience, one year of which was equivalent to GS-4; for GS-7, one full year of graduate education, or superior academic achievement during undergraduate studies, OR one year of specialized experience equivalent to GS-5; for GS-9, a master's degree or two years of graduate education, OR one year of specialized experience equivalent to GS-7; for GS-11, a Ph.D. or equivalent doctoral degree, or three years of graduate education, OR one year of specialized experience equivalent to GS-9; and for GS-12 and above, one year of specialized experience equivalent to the next lower grade level. In some cases, qualifying education may be substituted for experience, and vice versa. Tentative appointees must qualify for a top-secret security clearance, and pass a drug screening test and medical exam.

Training: DOJ-OIG Special Agents attend the eight-week Criminal Investigator Training Program at the Federal Law Enforcement Training Center in Glynco, Georgia (see Chapter 16). In-service training may include courses which focus on white-collar crime, financial investigations, personnel misconduct, computer hardware and software, investigative techniques, criminal and civil law, first aid and CPR, arrest techniques, defensive tactics, and firearms proficiency.

Contact: Office of Inspector General, Department of Justice, 10th Street and Constitution NW; Washington, DC 20530. Phone: 202-616-4500. World Wide Web: http://www.usdoj.gov/oig/.

SPECIAL AGENT (GS-1811)
UNITED STATES IMMIGRATION AND NATURALIZATION SERVICE
U.S. DEPARTMENT OF JUSTICE

Overview: The United States Immigration and Naturalization Service (INS) is responsible for enforcing laws regulating the admission of foreign-born persons to the United States, and for administering various immigration benefits, including the naturalization of resident aliens. INS Special Agents conduct a wide range of complex and sensitive investigations, such as those concerning multi-principal fraud, aliens involved in criminal activity, drug trafficking, and organized crime. Primary responsibilities include the enforcement of Immigration and Naturalization laws, investigation of alien smuggling operations, interviewing and interrogation of arrested alien smugglers and aliens, preparing sworn statements, intelligence gathering, and inspection of places of employment suspected of employing unauthorized alien workers. INS Special Agents are authorized to conduct surveillance and undercover operations, carry firearms, make arrests, execute search warrants and serve subpoenas. Investigations may be conducted jointly with agencies such as the Customs Service, FBI, State Department, DEA, U.S. Postal Inspection Service, USDA Office of Inspector General, and other federal, state, or local law enforcement agencies. This position is covered under special retirement provisions for law enforcement officers and qualifies for 25 percent Law Enforcement Availability Pay.

Qualifications: Applicants must be U.S. citizens, at least twenty-one years of age, and under the age of thirty-seven. (Candidates over age thirty-seven who have previous service creditable under special law enforcement retirement provisions may also be eligible.) Eyesight requirements include "sufficiently good vision in each eye, with or without correction." Corrected or uncorrected near vision must be sufficient to read printed material the size of typewritten characters. Hearing loss must not exceed 35 decibels at 1000, 2000, and 3000 Hz. Requirements for appointment to GS-5 level include completion of a four-year course of study leading to a bachelor's degree, OR three years general experience, one year of which was equivalent to GS-4; for GS-7, one full year of graduate education, or superior academic achievement during undergraduate studies, OR one year of specialized experience equivalent to GS-5; for GS-9, a master's degree or two years of graduate education, OR one year of specialized experience equivalent to GS-7; for GS-11, a Ph.D. or equivalent doctoral degree, or three years of graduate education, OR one year of specialized experience equivalent to GS-9; and for GS-12 and above, one year of specialized experience equivalent to the next lower grade level. In some cases, qualifying education may be substituted for experience, and vice versa. Tentative appointees must qualify for a security clearance, and pass a drug screening test and medical exam.

Training: INS Special Agents attend the fifteen-week Immigration Special Agent Training Course at the Federal Law Enforcement Training Center (FLETC) in Glynco, Georgia, which includes instruction in criminal and constitutional law, immigration and nationality law, search and seizure, laws of detention and arrest, admissions and confessions, laws of evidence, civil liability, investigative methods, interviewing and interrogation, evidence collection, interpersonal communications, firearms care and proficiency, driving, physical conditioning, and defensive tactics. This program is followed immediately by a five-week Spanish language course at FLETC. In-service training may include courses relating to legal updates, drug enforcement, first aid and CPR, firearms proficiency, arrest techniques, defensive tactics, and other subjects.

Contact: Immigration and Naturalization Service, Department of Justice, 425 I Street NW; Washington, DC 20536. Phone: 202-514-4316. World Wide Web: http://www.ins.usdoj.gov/.

SPECIAL AGENT (GS-1811)
OFFICE OF INSPECTOR GENERAL
U.S. DEPARTMENT OF LABOR

Overview: The U.S. Department of Labor (DOL) administers a variety of federal labor laws guaranteeing workers' rights to safe and healthful working conditions, a minimum hourly wage and overtime pay, freedom from employment discrimination, unemployment insurance, and workers' compensation. Special Agents of the DOL Office of Inspector General (OIG) conduct investigations to identify fraud and other forms of criminal or improper activity in DOL programs and operations. Investigations focus on wrongdoing in over 100 programs concerned with pension and welfare benefit plans, the unemployment insurance system, employment and training services, occupational safety and health, veterans employment and training services, mine safety, and provisions of the Federal Employees Compensation Act, Davis-Bacon Act, Black Lung Benefits Act, and other areas. Investigations often pertain to allegations of contract fraud, theft, bribery, kickbacks, false claims, healthcare provider fraud, and DOL employee integrity. The Labor Racketeering Section investigates organized crime activities, labor racketeering, extortion by labor union officials, and embezzlement from employee benefit plans. DOL-OIG Special Agents are authorized to conduct surveillance and undercover operations, carry firearms, make arrests, execute search warrants and serve subpoenas. Investigations may be conducted jointly with agencies such as the FBI, U.S. Postal Inspection Service, Housing and Urban Development OIG, and other federal, state, or local law enforcement and regulatory agencies. This position is covered under special retirement provisions for law enforcement officers and qualifies for 25 percent Law Enforcement Availability Pay.

Qualifications: Applicants must be U.S. citizens, at least twenty-one years of age, and under the age of thirty-seven. (Candidates over age thirty-seven who have previous service creditable under special law enforcement retirement provisions may also be eligible.) Eyesight requirements include "sufficiently good vision in each eye, with or without correction." Corrected or uncorrected near vision must be sufficient to read printed material the size of typewritten characters. Hearing loss must not exceed 35 decibels at 1000, 2000, and 3000 Hz. Requirements for appointment to GS-5 level include completion of a four-year course of study leading to a bachelor's degree, OR three years general experience, one year of which was equivalent to GS-4; for GS-7, one full year of graduate education, or superior academic achievement during undergraduate studies, OR one year of specialized experience equivalent to GS-5; for GS-9, a master's degree or two years of graduate education, OR one year of specialized experience equivalent to GS-7; for GS-11, a Ph.D. or equivalent doctoral degree, or three years of graduate education, OR one year of specialized experience equivalent to GS-9; and for GS-12 and above, one year of specialized experience equivalent to the next lower grade level. In some cases, qualifying education may be substituted for experience, and vice versa. Tentative appointees must qualify for a security clearance, and pass a drug screening test and medical exam.

Training: DOL-OIG Special Agents attend the eight-week Criminal Investigator Training Program at the Federal Law Enforcement Training Center in Glynco, Georgia (see Chapter 16). In-service training may include courses which focus on white-collar crime, labor laws, contract fraud, internal investigations, healthcare provider fraud, legal issues and updates, financial investigations, first aid and CPR, firearms proficiency, arrest techniques, and defensive tactics.

Contact: Office of Inspector General, Department of Labor, 200 Constitution Avenue NW; Washington, DC 20210. Phone: 202-219-5000. World Wide Web: http://www.usdoj.gov/oig/.

SPECIAL AGENT (GS-1811)
OFFICE OF INSPECTOR GENERAL
NATIONAL AERONAUTICS AND SPACE ADMINISTRATION

Overview: The National Aeronautics and Space Administration (NASA) develops, constructs, tests, and operates aeronautical and space vehicles, and conducts research relating to the exploration of space and flight within and outside the earth's atmosphere. Special Agents of the NASA Office of Inspector General (OIG) conduct complex investigations relating to NASA programs, operations, contractors, grantees, and employees. A significant amount of OIG activity is directed toward procurement irregularities and contract fraud. NASA-OIG investigations focus on offenses such as falsification of contractor's certified payrolls, fraudulent deviation from or failure to comply with NASA contract specifications, unlawful intrusion into NASA computer and electronic communication systems, embezzlement by NASA employees, conspiracy, theft, and mail fraud. Special Agents are authorized to conduct surveillance and undercover operations, carry firearms, make arrests, execute search warrants and serve subpoenas. Investigations may be conducted jointly with agencies such as the FBI, Defense Contract Audit Agency, U.S. Postal Inspection Service, Defense Criminal Investigative Service, Naval Criminal Investigative Service, Air Force OSI, Transportation Department OIG, Housing and Urban Development OIG, and other federal, state, or local law enforcement agencies. This position is covered under special retirement provisions for law enforcement officers and qualifies for 25 percent Law Enforcement Availability Pay.

Qualifications: Applicants must be U.S. citizens, at least twenty-one years of age, and under the age of thirty-seven. (Candidates over age thirty-seven who have previous service creditable under special law enforcement retirement provisions may also be eligible.) Eyesight requirements include "sufficiently good vision in each eye, with or without correction." Corrected or uncorrected near vision must be sufficient to read printed material the size of typewritten characters. Hearing loss must not exceed 35 decibels at 1000, 2000, and 3000 Hz. Requirements for appointment to GS-5 level include completion of a four-year course of study leading to a bachelor's degree, OR three years general experience, one year of which was equivalent to GS-4; for GS-7, one full year of graduate education, or superior academic achievement during undergraduate studies, OR one year of specialized experience equivalent to GS-5; for GS-9, a master's degree or two years of graduate education, OR one year of specialized experience equivalent to GS-7; for GS-11, a Ph.D. or equivalent doctoral degree, or three years of graduate education, OR one year of specialized experience equivalent to GS-9; and for GS-12 and above, one year of specialized experience equivalent to the next lower grade level. In some cases, qualifying education may be substituted for experience, and vice versa. Tentative appointees must qualify for a security clearance, and pass a drug screening test and medical exam.

Training: NASA-OIG Special Agents attend the eight-week Criminal Investigator Training Program at the Federal Law Enforcement Training Center in Glynco, Georgia (see Chapter 16). In-service training may include courses which focus on contract and procurement fraud, search and seizure in the workplace environment, handling and processing of seized computer evidence, export control laws and regulations, internal investigations, criminal and civil law, financial investigations, first aid and CPR, firearms proficiency, arrest techniques, and defensive tactics.

Contact: NASA Office of Inspector General, 300 E Street SW; Washington, DC 20546. Phone: 202-358-1000. World Wide Web: http://www.hq.nasa.gov/office/oig/hq/.

SPECIAL AGENT (GS-1811)
OFFICE OF INSPECTOR GENERAL
NATIONAL ARCHIVES AND RECORDS ADMINISTRATION

Overview: The National Archives and Records Administration (NARA) is responsible for managing federal government records, maintaining historically valuable documents, managing the Presidential Library System, and operating educational programs and exhibits for the benefit of the general public, researchers, scholars, educators and their students. NARA Office of Inspector General (OIG) Special Agents conduct investigations to identify fraud and other forms of criminal or improper activity in NARA programs and operations. Investigations often relate to contracts, contractors and their employees, and focus on offenses such as conspiracy, falsification of contractor's certified payrolls, and fraudulent deviation from or failure to comply with contract specifications. NARA-OIG Special Agents also investigate misconduct by Agency personnel, including offenses such as internal theft of historical documents or other government property, misuse of funds, or alteration of time and attendance records. Special Agents are authorized to conduct surveillance and undercover operations, carry firearms, make arrests, execute search warrants and serve subpoenas. Investigations may be conducted jointly with the FBI and other federal, state, or local law enforcement agencies. This position is covered under special retirement provisions for law enforcement officers and qualifies for 25 percent Law Enforcement Availability Pay.

Qualifications: Applicants must be U.S. citizens, at least twenty-one years of age, and under the age of thirty-seven. (Candidates over age thirty-seven who have previous service creditable under special law enforcement retirement provisions may also be eligible.) Eyesight requirements include "sufficiently good vision in each eye, with or without correction." Corrected or uncorrected near vision must be sufficient to read printed material the size of typewritten characters. Hearing loss must not exceed 35 decibels at 1000, 2000, and 3000 Hz. Requirements for appointment to GS-5 level include completion of a four-year course of study leading to a bachelor's degree, OR three years general experience, one year of which was equivalent to GS-4; for GS-7, one full year of graduate education, or superior academic achievement during undergraduate studies, OR one year of specialized experience equivalent to GS-5; for GS-9, a master's degree or two years of graduate education, OR one year of specialized experience equivalent to GS-7; for GS-11, a Ph.D. or equivalent doctoral degree, or three years of graduate education, OR one year of specialized experience equivalent to GS-9; and for GS-12 and above, one year of specialized experience equivalent to the next lower grade level. In some cases, qualifying education may be substituted for experience, and vice versa. Tentative appointees must qualify for a security clearance, and pass a drug screening test and medical exam.

Training: NARA-OIG Special Agents attend the eight-week Criminal Investigator Training Program at the Federal Law Enforcement Training Center in Glynco, Georgia (see Chapter 16). In-service training may include courses in contract and procurement fraud, internal investigations, criminal and civil law, financial investigations, computer hardware and software, arrest techniques, defensive tactics, and firearms proficiency.

Contact: Office of Inspector General, National Archives and Records Administration, 8601 Adelphi Road; College Park, MD 20740. Phone: 301-713-7300. World Wide Web: http://www.nara.gov/ig/.

SPECIAL AGENT
AMTRAK OFFICE OF INSPECTOR GENERAL
NATIONAL RAILROAD PASSENGER CORPORATION

Overview: The Investigations Division of the National Railroad Passenger Corporation (Amtrak) Office of Inspector General (OIG) is responsible for the detection and investigation of fraud, waste, and abuse concerning Amtrak programs and operations. Amtrak-OIG Special Agents conduct a wide range of criminal investigations pertaining to Corporation procurement activities and healthcare programs, including fraud committed by Amtrak contractors, vendors, and program participants. Offenses investigated include falsification of contractor's certified payrolls, fraudulent deviation from or failure to comply with contract specifications, product substitutions, inflated billings, kickbacks, false statements, and false claims. Special Agents also conduct employee integrity investigations involving allegations of serious misconduct by Amtrak personnel, including offenses such as embezzlement, conflict of interest, misuse of official position for personal gain, bribery, extortion, theft, acceptance of gratuities, and misuse of government property. Investigations may be conducted jointly with other federal, state and local law enforcement and regulatory agencies. Amtrak-OIG Special Agents are authorized to carry firearms, make arrests, execute search warrants and serve subpoenas. Salary for these personnel does not fall under the General Schedule pay system, although it is similar to GS-1811 Special Agent positions of other agencies.

Qualifications: Amtrak-OIG seeks candidates who have a high degree of integrity and responsibility, and with various professional and educational backgrounds depending upon the levels of positions being filled and the needs of the agency. Applicants must be U.S. citizens; pass a background investigation, drug screening test, and medical examination; and qualify for a security clearance.

Training: Amtrak-OIG Special Agents attend the eight-week Criminal Investigator Training Program at the Federal Law Enforcement Training Center (FLETC) in Glynco, Georgia (see Chapter 16). In-service training may include the two-week Criminal Investigations in an Automated Environment Training Program at

FLETC, and courses which focus on healthcare fraud, white-collar crime, financial investigations, contract and procurement fraud, criminal and civil law, personnel misconduct, interviewing techniques, firearms proficiency, arrest techniques, and defensive tactics, among others.

Contact: Office of Inspector General, Amtrak, 10 G Street NE; Washington, DC 20002. Phone: 202-906-3860. World Wide Web: http://www.amtrak.com/.

SPECIAL AGENT (GS-1811)
OFFICE OF INSPECTOR GENERAL
NATIONAL SCIENCE FOUNDATION

Overview: The National Science Foundation (NSF) is an independent agency created to increase the nation's base of scientific and engineering knowledge, research, and education programs to better prepare the nation for meeting the challenges of the future. Special Agents of the NSF Office of Inspector General (OIG) conduct investigations relating to NSF proposals, awards, programs, operations, grantees, and employees. Investigations often focus on violations of federal law committed by scientists, researchers and academic administrators, including offenses such as embezzlement or misuse of grant funds; obtaining Small Business Innovation Research grant funds as a result of duplicate proposals submitted to multiple agencies; bribery; improper and false claims; collusion; and conversion of government property. NSF-OIG Special Agents also conduct employee integrity investigations involving conflict of interest, unethical behavior, sexual harassment, abuses of authority, and mismanagement by NSF personnel. To accomplish its mission, NSF-OIG also employs scientists to respond to allegations, assist with investigations, and monitor administration of NSF programs. Investigations are routinely conducted with agencies such as the FBI, Defense Criminal Investigative Service, NASA-OIG, Energy Department OIG, Customs Service, Education Department OIG, Health and Human Services OIG, and other federal, state, and local law enforcement agencies. This position is covered under special retirement provisions for law enforcement officers and qualifies for 25 percent Law Enforcement Availability Pay.

Qualifications: Applicants must be U.S. citizens, at least twenty-one years of age, and under the age of thirty-seven. (Candidates over age thirty-seven who have previous service creditable under special law enforcement retirement provisions may also be eligible.) Eyesight requirements include "sufficiently good vision in each eye, with or without correction." Corrected or uncorrected near vision must be sufficient to read printed material the size of typewritten characters. Hearing loss must not exceed 35 decibels at 1000, 2000, and 3000 Hz. Requirements for appointment to GS-5 level include completion of a four-year course of study leading to a bachelor's degree, OR three years general experience, one year of which was equivalent to GS-4; for GS-7, one full year of graduate education, or superior academic achievement during undergraduate studies, OR one year of specialized experience equivalent to GS-5; for GS-9, a master's degree or two years of graduate education, OR one year of specialized experience equivalent to GS-7; for GS-11, a Ph.D. or equivalent doctoral degree, or three years of graduate education, OR one year of specialized experience equivalent to GS-9; and for GS-12 and above, one year of specialized experience equivalent to the next lower grade level. In some cases, qualifying education may be substituted for experience, and vice versa. Tentative appointees must pass a physical exam.

Training: NSF-OIG Special Agents attend the eight-week Criminal Investigator Training Program at the Federal Law Enforcement Training Center in Glynco, Georgia (see Chapter 16). In-service training may include courses concerned with NSF program fraud, money laundering, financial investigations, interviewing and interrogation, Affirmative Civil Enforcement, and employee integrity investigations.

Contact: Office of Inspector General, National Science Foundation, Room 1135; Arlington, VA 22230. Phone: 703-306-2100. World Wide Web: http://www.nsf.gov/. E-mail: info@nsf.gov.

SPECIAL AGENT (GS-1811)
OFFICE OF INSPECTOR GENERAL
U.S. OFFICE OF PERSONNEL MANAGEMENT

Overview: As the federal government's human resources agency, the U.S. Office of Personnel Management (OPM) is responsible for providing up-to-date employment information; for ensuring that the nation's civil service system remains free of political influence and that federal employees are selected and treated fairly and on the basis of merit; and for managing the federal retirement system and the Federal Employees Health Benefits (FEHB) Program. Special Agents of the OPM Office of Inspector General (OIG) investigate fraud, corruption, and other criminal or improper activities relating to the FEHB, Civil Service Retirement System, Federal Employees Retirement System, and other OPM programs and operations. The Agency is comprised of two branches, including the Health and Life Insurance Branch, and the Retirement and Special Investigations Branch. Investigations often pertain to the unlawful receipt of retirement benefits, such as those collected on behalf of deceased annuitants; inflated billings, waiver of copayments, and other fraudulent activities of FEHB healthcare providers, carriers, and subscribers; and schemes involving fraudulent prescription drug claims, disability insurance fraud, theft of government property, bribery, and kickbacks. OPM-OIG Special Agents are authorized to conduct surveillance and undercover operations, carry firearms, make arrests, execute search warrants and serve subpoenas. Investigations may be conducted jointly with agencies such as the FBI, Health and Human Services OIG, Veterans Affairs OIG, Pension Benefit Guaranty Corporation, and other law enforcement and regulatory agencies. This position is covered under special retirement provisions for law enforcement officers and qualifies for 25 percent Law Enforcement Availability Pay.

Qualifications: Applicants must be U.S. citizens, at least twenty-one years of age, and under the age of thirty-seven. (Candidates over age thirty-seven who have previous service creditable under special law enforcement retirement provisions may also be eligible.) Eyesight requirements include "sufficiently good vision in each eye, with or without correction." Corrected or uncorrected near vision must be sufficient to read printed material the size of typewritten characters. Hearing loss must not exceed 35 decibels at 1000, 2000, and 3000 Hz. Requirements for appointment to GS-5 level include completion of a four-year course of study leading to a bachelor's degree, OR three years general experience, one year of which was equivalent to GS-4; for GS-7, one full year of graduate education, or superior academic achievement during undergraduate studies, OR one year of specialized experience equivalent to GS-5; for GS-9, a master's degree or two years of graduate education, OR one year of specialized experience equivalent to GS-7; for GS-11, a Ph.D. or equivalent doctoral degree, or three years of graduate education, OR one year of specialized experience equivalent to GS-9; and for GS-12 and above, one year of specialized experience equivalent to the next lower grade level. In some cases, qualifying education may be substituted for experience, and vice versa. Tentative appointees must qualify for a security clearance, and pass a background investigation, personal interview, and physical exam.

Training: OPM-OIG Special Agents attend the eight-week Criminal Investigator Training Program at the Federal Law Enforcement Training Center in Glynco, Georgia (see Chapter 16). In-service training may focus on OPM programs, healthcare and disability insurance fraud, legal issues and updates, white-collar crime, arrest techniques, defensive tactics, and firearms proficiency.

Contact: Office of Inspector General, Office of Personnel Management, 1900 E Street NW, Room 6400; Washington, DC 20415. Phone: 202-606-1200. World Wide Web: http://www.opm.gov/.

SPECIAL AGENT
OFFICE OF INSPECTOR GENERAL
PEACE CORPS

Overview: The Peace Corps promotes world peace and friendship by providing qualified and trained volunteers to serve abroad in six program areas including education, agriculture, health, small business development, urban development, and the environment. Special Agents of the Peace Corps Office of Inspector

General (OIG) conduct criminal, civil, and administrative investigations concerning alleged or suspected violations of federal laws concerned with domestic and international Peace Corps programs and operations. Investigations focus upon offenses such as collusion, fraud, theft, forgery, acceptance of gratuities, credit card fraud, drug trafficking, and perjury. As personnel misconduct investigators, Peace Corps OIG Special Agents also perform criminal and non-criminal investigations of Corps employees, trainees and volunteers based in the United States and approximately ninety developing countries. The majority of investigations pertain to offenses committed overseas. As with other Peace Corps staff positions, OIG Special Agents are not permitted to serve a tour of duty exceeding five years. Salary for this position does not fall under the General Schedule pay system, although it is similar to GS-1811 Special Agent positions of other agencies. Peace Corps OIG Special Agents normally enter service at FP-5, which is similar to GS-9, and may advance to FP-3, which is similar to GS-13.

Qualifications: Applicants must be U.S. citizens, and must not have been employed in "certain intelligence-related activities." Eyesight and hearing requirements include "sufficiently good vision in each eye, with or without glasses, in order that they may perform duties satisfactorily"; and the ability to hear the conversational voice and whispered speech without the use of a hearing aid. Requirements include one year of specialized experience equivalent to the next lower grade level in the federal service related to the planning, organizing, and conducting of criminal, civil, or administrative investigations requiring the use of recognized investigative methods and techniques. In some cases, qualifying education may be substituted for experience.

Training: Peace Corps Special Agents attend the eight-week Criminal Investigator Training Program at the Federal Law Enforcement Training Center in Glynco, Georgia (see Chapter 16). In-service training may include courses which focus on Peace Corps programs, financial investigations, international issues, contract and procurement fraud, personnel investigations, criminal and civil law, and investigative techniques.

Contact: Peace Corps Office of Inspector General, 1990 K Street NW; Washington, DC 20526. Phone: 202-606-3950. World Wide Web: http://www.peacecorps.gov/.

SPECIAL AGENT (GS-1811)
OFFICE OF INSPECTOR GENERAL
PENSION BENEFIT GUARANTY CORPORATION

Overview: The Pension Benefit Guaranty Corporation (PBGC), a wholly owned government corporation, was established to encourage the growth of defined benefit plans, provide timely and uninterrupted payment of benefits, and maintain pension insurance premiums at the lowest level necessary to carry out the Corporation's obligations. The PBGC protects the retirement incomes of more than 40 million American workers in about 45,000 defined benefit pension plans. Special Agents of the PBGC Office of Inspector General (OIG) investigate violations of federal law relating to the Employee Retirement Income Security Act (ERISA); official misconduct by PBGC personnel; misuse of grant funds; or fraud committed by PBGC contractors, subcontractors, or vendors. ERISA investigations focus on fraud in pension insurance programs administered by PBGC, including the Single Employer Program and the Multiemployer Program. These investigations often involve allegations of fiduciary breaches, such as instances in which pension plan administrators unlawfully remove plan funds resulting in shortages, or pension plan participants who submit false information or commit other forms of fraud to unlawfully obtain retirement or disability benefits. Employee integrity investigations may focus on offenses such as bribery, conflict of interest, collusion, embezzlement, kickbacks, acceptance of gratuities, time and attendance fraud, and inflated claims for travel reimbursement. Investigations may be conducted jointly with the DEA, General Accounting Office, Federal Protective Service, Labor Department OIG, Office of Personnel Management, FBI, and other law enforcement and regulatory agencies. This position is covered under special retirement provisions for law enforcement officers.

Qualifications: Applicants must be U.S. citizens, at least twenty-one years of age, and under the age of thirty-seven. (Candidates over age thirty-seven who have previous service creditable under special law enforcement retirement provisions may also be eligible.) Eyesight requirements include "sufficiently good vision in each eye, with or without correction." Corrected or uncorrected near vision must be sufficient to read printed material the size of typewritten characters. Hearing loss must not exceed 35 decibels at 1000, 2000, and 3000 Hz. Requirements for appointment to GS-5 level include completion of a four-year course of study leading to a bachelor's degree, OR three years general experience, one year of which was equivalent to GS-4; for GS-7, one full year of graduate education, or superior academic achievement during undergraduate studies, OR one year of specialized experience equivalent to GS-5; for GS-9, a master's degree or two years of graduate education, OR one year of specialized experience equivalent to GS-7; for GS-11, a Ph.D. or equivalent doctoral degree, or three years of graduate education, OR one year of specialized experience equivalent to GS-9; and for GS-12 and above, one year of specialized experience equivalent to the next lower grade level. In some cases, qualifying education may be substituted for experience, and vice versa. Tentative appointees must qualify for a security clearance and pass a background investigation.

Training: PBGC-OIG Special Agents attend the eight-week Criminal Investigator Training Program at the Federal Law Enforcement Training Center in Glynco, Georgia (see Chapter 16). In-service training may include the three-week Inspector General Basic Training Program (see Chapter 16), and courses concerning ERISA provisions, white-collar fraud, interviewing techniques, criminal and civil law, computer hardware and software, and the investigation of fraud and personnel misconduct.

Contact: Pension Benefit Guaranty Corporation, 1200 K Street NW; Washington, DC 20005. Phone: 202-326-4000. World Wide Web: http://www.pbgc.gov/oig/.

SPECIAL AGENT
OFFICE OF INSPECTOR GENERAL
U.S. POSTAL SERVICE

Overview: Special Agents of the U.S. Postal Service (USPS) Office of Inspector General (OIG) conduct critical, multifaceted and sensitive criminal investigations pertaining to Postal operations and programs, with particular emphasis on white-collar and workers' compensation fraud involving Postal personnel. Primary responsibilities of USPS-OIG Special Agents include the investigation of internal financial fraud, such as cases which involve embezzlement, kickbacks, misappropriation of Postal funds, and bribery or attempted bribery of Postal personnel; conflict of interest offenses; fraudulent workers' compensation claims submitted by Postal personnel or healthcare providers; official misconduct by Postal executives; and various Service-wide criminal investigations. USPS-OIG Special Agents also investigate serious incidents and tort claims which could have significant liability implications on the Postal Service. Special Agents are authorized to conduct surveillance and undercover operations, carry firearms, make arrests, execute search warrants and serve subpoenas. Certain investigations may be conducted jointly with the U.S. Postal Inspection Service, as well as other federal, state, or local law enforcement agencies. This position is covered under special retirement provisions for law enforcement officers and qualifies for 25 percent Law Enforcement Availability Pay. Salary for this position does not fall under the General Schedule pay system, although it is similar to GS-1811 Special Agent positions of other agencies.

Qualifications: Applicants must be U.S. citizens, at least twenty-one years of age, and under the age of thirty-seven. (Candidates over age thirty-seven who have previous service creditable under special law enforcement retirement provisions may also be eligible.) General requirements include a bachelor's degree from an accredited college or university; good mental and physical condition, including weight proportionate to height; no criminal convictions; and ability to pass a physical examination and maintain physical condition as part of a wellness program. Eyesight requirements include "sufficiently good vision in each eye, with or without correction," and corrected or uncorrected near vision sufficient to read printed material the size of typewritten characters. Hearing loss must not exceed 35 decibels at 1000, 2000, and 3000 Hz. Although not required, desirable qualifications include prior graduation from the Criminal Investigator Training Program at the Federal Law Enforcement Training Center, or the U.S. Postal Inspection Service Academy, or an equivalent law enforcement training program; experience with white-collar crime investigations; unique or specialized knowledge of USPS operations; advanced academic degrees; or professional certifications by examination. Tentative appointees must pass a drug screening test and background investigation.

Training: USPS-OIG Special Agents attend the eight-week Criminal Investigator Training Program at the Federal Law Enforcement Training Center in Glynco, Georgia (see Chapter 16). In-service training may include courses in financial investigations, workers' compensation program fraud, personnel misconduct, internal fraud, investigative techniques, criminal and civil law, first aid and CPR, firearms proficiency, arrest techniques, and defensive tactics.

Contact: Office of Inspector General, U.S. Postal Service, 475 L'Enfant Plaza SW; Washington, DC 20260. Phone: 202-268-5623. World Wide Web: No Web site at this time.

SPECIAL AGENT (GS-1811)
OFFICE OF INSPECTOR GENERAL
RAILROAD RETIREMENT BOARD

Overview: The Railroad Retirement Board (RRB) administers comprehensive retirement-survivor and unemployment-sickness benefit programs for the nation's railroad workers and their families. Special Agents of the RRB Office of Inspector General (OIG) investigate a wide range of federal laws and irregularities pertaining to the administration of RRB programs, including provisions of the Railroad Retirement Act and Railroad Unemployment Insurance Act. Subjects of investigation include persons who fraudulently obtain or apply for disability, retirement, unemployment or health benefits. Investigations focus on offenses such as conspiracy, false statements, false claims, embezzlement, theft of government funds, and mail fraud. RRB-OIG Special Agents also conduct employee integrity investigations involving allegations of unethical behavior, conflict of interest, abuses of authority, and failure to report outside employment. Special Agents are authorized to conduct surveillance and undercover operations, carry firearms, make arrests, execute search warrants and serve subpoenas. Investigations may be conducted jointly with agencies such as the FBI, Health and Human Services OIG, U.S. Postal Inspection Service, Labor Department OIG, Social Security Administration OIG, and other federal, state, or local law enforcement and regulatory agencies. This position is covered under special retirement provisions for law enforcement officers and qualifies for 25 percent Law Enforcement Availability Pay.

Qualifications: Applicants must be U.S. citizens, at least twenty-one years of age, and under the age of thirty-seven. (Candidates over age thirty-seven who have previous service creditable under special law enforcement retirement provisions may also be eligible.) Eyesight requirements include "sufficiently good vision in each eye, with or without correction." Corrected or uncorrected near vision must be sufficient to read printed material the size of typewritten characters. Hearing loss must not exceed 35 decibels at 1000, 2000, and 3000 Hz. Requirements for appointment to GS-5 level include completion of a four-year course of study leading to a bachelor's degree, OR three years general experience, one year of which was equivalent to GS-4; for GS-7, one full year of graduate education, or superior academic achievement during undergraduate studies, OR one year of specialized experience equivalent to GS-5; for GS-9, a master's degree or two years of graduate education, OR one year of specialized experience equivalent to GS-7; for GS-11, a Ph.D. or equivalent doctoral degree, or three years of graduate education, OR one year of specialized experience equivalent to GS-9; and for GS-12 and above, one year of specialized experience equivalent to the next lower grade level. In some cases, qualifying education may be substituted for experience, and vice versa.

Training: RRB-OIG Special Agents attend the eight-week Criminal Investigator Training Program at the Federal Law Enforcement Training Center in Glynco, Georgia (see Chapter 16). In-service training may include courses which focus on fraudulent claims, technical investigative equipment, interviewing techniques, legal issues and updates, financial investigations, procurement fraud, internal investigations, arrest techniques, defensive tactics, firearms proficiency, and other topics.

Contact: Office of Inspector General, Railroad Retirement Board, 844 North Rush Street; Chicago, IL 60611. Phone: 312-751-4350. World Wide Web: http://www.rrb.gov/oiginves.html.

SPECIAL AGENT (GS-1811)
OFFICE OF INSPECTOR GENERAL
SMALL BUSINESS ADMINISTRATION

Overview: Small Business Administration (SBA) Office of Inspector General (OIG) Special Agents conduct investigations involving fraud and corruption pertaining to SBA programs and operations. Many of the subjects under investigation are applicants or participants in the SBA Loan Guarantee or Disaster Assistance Loan Programs who submit false tax returns or false information in order to obtain loans or benefits, use funds for purposes other than those for which loans were granted, or commit unlawful conversion of collateral pledged as security. Other investigations involve large contractors who misrepresent the size of their operations to qualify for small business loans. Investigations often focus on complex conspiracies, mail fraud, false statements and claims, and money laundering. Special Agents also conduct SBA employee integrity investigations which involve offenses such as bribery, conflict of interest, and abuses of authority. Special Agents are authorized to conduct surveillance and undercover operations, carry firearms, make arrests, execute search warrants and serve subpoenas. In addition to participating in federal task force operations, Special Agents conduct investigations with agencies such as the FBI; U.S. Postal Inspection Service; Health and Human Services OIG; Labor Department OIG; U.S. Secret Service; Bureau of Alcohol, Tobacco and Firearms; IRS Criminal Investigation Division; Air Force Office of Special Investigations; NASA-OIG, and other law enforcement agencies. This position is covered under special retirement provisions for law enforcement officers and qualifies for 25 percent Law Enforcement Availability Pay.

Qualifications: Applicants must be U.S. citizens, at least twenty-one years of age, and under the age of thirty-seven. (Candidates over age thirty-seven who have previous service creditable under special law enforcement retirement provisions may also be eligible.) Eyesight requirements include "sufficiently good vision in each eye, with or without correction." Corrected or uncorrected near vision must be sufficient to read printed material the size of typewritten characters. Hearing loss must not exceed 35 decibels at 1000, 2000, and 3000 Hz. Requirements for appointment to GS-5 level include completion of a four-year course of study leading to a bachelor's degree, OR three years general experience, one year of which was equivalent to GS-4; for GS-7, one full year of graduate education, or superior academic achievement during undergraduate studies, OR one year of specialized experience equivalent to GS-5; for GS-9, a master's degree or two years of graduate education, OR one year of specialized experience equivalent to GS-7; for GS-11, a Ph.D. or equivalent doctoral degree, or three years of graduate education, OR one year of specialized experience equivalent to GS-9; and for GS-12 and above, one year of specialized experience equivalent to the next lower grade level. In some cases, qualifying education may be substituted for experience, and vice versa. Tentative appointees must qualify for a security clearance, and pass a drug screening test and medical exam.

Training: SBA-OIG Special Agents attend the eight-week Criminal Investigator Training Program at the Federal Law Enforcement Training Center in Glynco, Georgia (see Chapter 16). In-service training may include courses in criminal and civil law, SBA loan programs, investigative techniques, financial investigations, personnel misconduct, first aid and CPR, firearms proficiency, arrest techniques, and non-lethal subject control techniques.

Contact: Personnel Specialist, Office of Inspector General, Small Business Administration, 409 Third Street SW; Washington, DC 20416. Phone: 202-205-6580. World Wide Web: http://www.sba.gov/ig/.

SPECIAL AGENT (GS-1811)
OFFICE OF INSPECTOR GENERAL
SMITHSONIAN INSTITUTION

Overview: In carrying out its mission to protect the integrity of the Smithsonian Institution (SI), Special Agents of the Office of Inspector General (OIG) investigate violations of federal laws and regulations, gross waste of funds, abuses of authority, and mismanagement concerning SI programs and operations. Investigations often pertain to theft of SI property or funds, fraud involving contracts and grants, false claims and statements, gratuities, bribery, kickbacks, misuse of funds, collusive bidding practices, destruction or removal of official records, and controlled substance use on SI property. SI-OIG Special Agents specialize in internal integrity investigations, including offenses relating to improprieties on the part of SI personnel in connection with SI programs; misuse of government vehicles or property; using public office for private gain; employment of relatives; sexual harassment or abuse; scientific misconduct; dealing in museum objects; procurement or contract irregularities; accepting bribes; conflict of interest; and abuses of authority. Special Agents are authorized to conduct surveillance and undercover operations, and serve subpoenas. Investigations may be conducted jointly with agencies such as the FBI, U.S. Fish and Wildlife Service, IRS Criminal Investigation Division, and other federal, state or local law enforcement agencies.

Qualifications: Eyesight requirements for SI-OIG Special Agents include "sufficiently good vision in each eye, with or without correction"; and corrected or uncorrected near vision sufficient to read printed material the size of typewritten characters. Hearing loss must not exceed 35 decibels at 1000, 2000, and 3000 Hz. Requirements for appointment to GS-5 level include completion of a four-year course of study leading to a bachelor's degree, OR three years general experience, one year of which was equivalent to GS-4; for GS-7, one full year of graduate education, or superior academic achievement during undergraduate studies, OR one year of specialized experience equivalent to GS-5; for GS-9, a master's degree or two years of graduate education, OR one year of specialized experience equivalent to GS-7; for GS-11, a Ph.D. or equivalent doctoral degree, or three years of graduate education, OR one year of specialized experience equivalent to GS-9; and for GS-12 and above, one year of specialized experience equivalent to the next lower grade level. In some cases, qualifying education may be substituted for experience, and vice versa. Tentative appointees must qualify for a security clearance, and pass a drug screening test and medical exam.

Training: Newly appointed SI-OIG Investigators attend the three-week Inspector General Basic Training Program at the Federal Law Enforcement Training Center in Glynco, Georgia (see Chapter 16). In-service training may include courses which focus on SI programs and operations, fraud involving SI contracts and grants, internal investigations, white-collar crime, financial investigations, legal issues and updates, investigative techniques, and other subjects.

Contact: Office of Inspector General, Smithsonian Institution, Suite 7600, 955 L'Enfant Plaza SW; Washington, DC 20560. Phone: 202-287-3326. World Wide Web: http://www.si.edu/newstart.htm.

SPECIAL AGENT (GS-1811)
OFFICE OF INSPECTOR GENERAL
SOCIAL SECURITY ADMINISTRATION

Overview: Special Agents of the Social Security Administration (SSA) Office of Inspector General (OIG) investigate criminal wrongdoing by Social Security applicants, beneficiaries, contractors, physicians, interpreters, representative payees, and SSA employees. Investigations pertain to offenses involving counterfeiting of Social Security cards; obtaining Social Security numbers based on false information; misusing Social Security numbers to obtain government benefits; using Social Security numbers for illegal work activity by non-citizens; theft and forgery of benefit checks; use of fraudulent medical records; feigning disabilities; and scams involving deceased payees. Offenses investigated include fraud, embezzlement, collusion, conflict of interest, gambling, sale or distribution of narcotics, and organized crime activities, among others. Employee integrity investigations may involve offenses relating to the fraudulent issuance or sale of Social Security cards; creation of fictitious identities; misappropriation of funds during collection and deposit of overpayments; and unauthorized access to confidential information. SSA-OIG Special Agents are authorized to conduct surveillance and undercover operations, carry firearms, make arrests, execute search warrants and serve subpoenas. Investigations may be conducted jointly with agencies such as the FBI, Health and Human Services OIG, Labor Department OIG, Railroad Retirement Board OIG, and other federal, state, or local law enforcement agencies. This position is covered under special retirement provisions for law enforcement officers and qualifies for 25 percent Law Enforcement Availability Pay.

Qualifications: Applicants must be U.S. citizens, at least twenty-one years of age, and under the age of thirty-seven. (Candidates over age thirty-seven who have previous service creditable under special law enforcement retirement provisions may also be eligible.) Eyesight requirements include "sufficiently good vision in each eye, with or without correction." Corrected or uncorrected near vision must be sufficient to read printed material the size of typewritten characters. Hearing loss must not exceed 35 decibels at 1000, 2000, and 3000 Hz. Requirements for appointment to GS-5 level include completion of a four-year course of study leading to a bachelor's degree, OR three years general experience, one year of which was equivalent to GS-4; for GS-7, one full year of graduate education, or superior academic achievement during undergraduate studies, OR one year of specialized experience equivalent to GS-5; for GS-9, a master's degree or two years of graduate education, OR one year of specialized experience equivalent to GS-7; for GS-11, a Ph.D. or equivalent doctoral degree, or three years of graduate education, OR one year of specialized experience equivalent to GS-9; and for GS-12 and above, one year of specialized experience equivalent to the next lower grade level. In some cases, qualifying education may be substituted for experience, and vice versa. Tentative appointees must qualify for a security clearance, and pass a background investigation, credit check, drug screening test, and physical exam.

Training: SSA-OIG Special Agents attend the eight-week Criminal Investigator Training Program at the Federal Law Enforcement Training Center in Glynco, Georgia (see Chapter 16). In-service training may include courses which focus on SSA program updates, healthcare fraud, criminal and civil law, white-collar crime, internal investigations, computer hardware and software, oleoresin capsicum spray, firearms proficiency, arrest techniques, and defensive tactics.

Contact: Office of Inspector General, Social Security Administration, 6401 Security Boulevard; Baltimore, MD 21235. Phone: 410-965-1234. World Wide Web: http://www.ssa.gov/oig/investns.htm

SPECIAL AGENT
BUREAU OF DIPLOMATIC SECURITY
U.S. DEPARTMENT OF STATE

Overview: Special Agents of the Bureau of Diplomatic Security (DS), U.S. Department of State, conduct criminal investigations related primarily to the enforcement of statutes protecting the integrity of U.S. passport and entry visa documents; perform background investigations of individuals seeking appointment or continued employment with the State Department; and provide protective services for the Secretary of State and selected foreign dignitaries during their visits to the United States. Passport and visa investigations are often related to international terrorism operations, fugitives, and drug trafficking enterprises operating in the United States and abroad. Counterterrorism and anti-crime investigations are often coordinated with the assistance of international law enforcement organizations, as well as agencies which participate in joint terrorism task forces in the United States. Following initial training, DS Special Agents serve in one of twenty-one field offices or Resident Agencies in the United States, and must be willing to accept assignments throughout the world. DS Special Agents are authorized to conduct surveillance and undercover operations, carry firearms, make arrests, execute search warrants and serve subpoenas. Investigations may be conducted jointly with agencies such as the FBI, Immigration and Naturalization Service, DEA, Customs Service, and other federal, state, or local law enforcement agencies. Salary for this position does not fall under the General Schedule pay system, although it is similar to GS-1811 Special Agent positions of other federal law enforcement agencies.

Qualifications: Applicants must be U.S. citizens, at least twenty-one years of age, and under the age of thirty-seven; possess a bachelor's degree from an accredited college or university; and have one year of specialized experience, or have completed one full year of graduate education. Foreign language ability is desirable. Applicants must submit a narrative autobiography which addresses their background, employment experience, personal interests, hobbies, and motivation for applying for a DS Special Agent position. The application process includes a writing exam which is evaluated for mastery of grammar, spelling, logic, organization, vocabulary and word selection. Applicants must also pass a medical exam, panel interview, and background investigation, and qualify for a top-secret security clearance.

Training: DS Special Agents complete a rigorous five-month training program. Initial training includes the eight-week Criminal Investigator Training Program at the Federal Law Enforcement Training Center in Glynco, Georgia (see Chapter 16). DS Special Agents then receive approximately three months of specialized training at various sites in the Washington, DC area, consisting of courses in passport and visa fraud, investigative techniques, personal security, firearms proficiency, emergency medical techniques, and driver training.

Contact: Bureau of Diplomatic Security, Department of State, P.O. Box 9317; Arlington, VA 22219. Phone: 202-663-0478. World Wide Web: http://www.heroes.net/.

SPECIAL AGENT (GS-1811)
OFFICE OF INSPECTOR GENERAL
U.S. DEPARTMENT OF STATE

Overview: Special Agents of the U.S. Department of State Office of Inspector General (OIG) conduct sensitive and complex criminal and general investigations concerning State Department programs, operations and personnel. Criminal investigations often focus on fraud or counterfeiting involving the use or issuance of U.S. passports and visas in the United States and abroad, and alien smuggling operations. Personnel integrity investigations pertain to State Department employees, including senior career and appointed government officials, as well as foreign citizens both here and abroad. These investigations encompass a range of allegations such as bribery, kickbacks, collusion, conflict of interest, embezzlement, and theft or conversion of government property. State Department OIG Special Agents are authorized to conduct surveillance and undercover operations, carry firearms, make arrests, execute search warrants and serve subpoenas. Investigations may be conducted jointly with agencies such as the FBI, Immigration and Naturalization Service, DEA, and other federal, state, or local law enforcement agencies, as well as those of foreign governments. This position is covered under special retirement provisions for law enforcement officers and qualifies for 25 percent Law Enforcement Availability Pay.

Qualifications: Applicants must be U.S. citizens, at least twenty-one years of age, and under the age of thirty-seven. (Candidates over age thirty-seven who have previous service creditable under special law enforcement retirement provisions may also be eligible.) Eyesight requirements include "sufficiently good vision in each eye, with or without correction." Corrected or uncorrected near vision must be sufficient to read printed material the size of typewritten characters. Hearing loss must not exceed 35 decibels at 1000, 2000, and 3000 Hz. Requirements for appointment to GS-5 level include completion of a four-year course of study leading to a bachelor's degree, OR three years general experience, one year of which was equivalent to GS-4; for GS-7, one full year of graduate education, or superior academic achievement during undergraduate studies, OR one year of specialized experience equivalent to GS-5; for GS-9, a master's degree or two years of graduate education, OR one year of specialized experience equivalent to GS-7; for GS-11, a Ph.D. or equivalent doctoral degree, or three years of graduate education, OR one year of specialized experience equivalent to GS-9; and for GS-12 and above, one year of specialized experience equivalent to the next lower grade level. In some cases, qualifying education may be substituted for experience, and vice versa. Tentative appointees must qualify for a top-secret security clearance, and pass a drug screening test and medical exam.

Training: State Department OIG Special Agents attend the eight-week Criminal Investigator Training Program at the Federal Law Enforcement Training Center in Glynco, Georgia (see Chapter 16). In-service training may include courses in financial fraud investigations, technical investigative equipment, computer software and databases, seizing computers, interviewing techniques, legal issues and updates, State Department program fraud, employee integrity investigations, first aid and CPR, firearms proficiency, arrest techniques, and defensive tactics.

Contact: Office of Inspector General, Department of State, 2201 C Street NW; Washington, DC 20520. Phone: 202-647-4000. World Wide Web: http://www.state.gov/. E-mail: oig.website@dos.us-state.gov.

SPECIAL AGENT
OFFICE OF INSPECTOR GENERAL
TENNESSEE VALLEY AUTHORITY

Overview: Special Agents of the Tennessee Valley Authority (TVA) Office of Inspector General (OIG) conduct criminal and administrative investigations pertaining to waste, fraud and abuse in the programs and operations of TVA, a wholly-owned government corporation which is the nation's largest single producer of electric power. Investigations focus on financial and internal matters relating to personnel misconduct, workers' compensation fraud, harassment and intimidation, contract fraud, environmental violations, nuclear issues, entitlement programs, and other offenses pertaining to TVA's servicing of large industries, federal installations, and 160 power distributors located in the Tennessee Valley region. Primary responsibilities include conducting interviews of complainants, witnesses, experts, and subjects of investigation; developing sources of information; obtaining and reviewing documentary and other evidence; coordinating investigative activities with United States Attorneys; and testifying before grand juries and in subsequent criminal proceedings. TVA-OIG Special Agents are authorized to conduct surveillance and undercover operations, and serve subpoenas. Salary for this position does not fall under the General Schedule pay system, although it is similar to GS-1811 Special Agent positions of other agencies.

Qualifications: Applicants must be U.S. citizens. Eyesight requirements include "sufficiently good vision in each eye, with or without correction." Corrected or uncorrected near vision must be sufficient to read printed material the size of typewritten characters. Hearing loss must not exceed 35 decibels at 1000, 2000, and 3000 Hz. Requirements for appointment to the Special Agent Trainee level include completion of a four-year course of study leading to a bachelor's degree, OR three years general investigative experience, one year of which was equivalent to the Special Agent Trainee level; a valid driver's license; and willingness to travel to different locations dependent upon needs of the Agency. Tentative appointees must qualify for a security clearance, and pass a drug screening test and physical exam.

Training: TVA-OIG Special Agents attend the eight-week Criminal Investigator Training Program at the Federal Law Enforcement Training Center in Glynco, Georgia (see Chapter 16). In-service training may include courses which focus on TVA operations, financial investigations, workers' compensation fraud, environmental offenses, white-collar crime, contract and procurement fraud, personnel misconduct, legal issues and updates, and investigative techniques.

Contact: Employee Service Center, Tennessee Valley Authority, 400 West Summit Hill Drive; Knoxville, TN 37902. Phone: 423-632-3222. World Wide Web: http://www.tva.gov. E-Mail: esc@tva.gov.

SPECIAL AGENT (GS-1811)
NATIONAL HIGHWAY TRAFFIC SAFETY ADMINISTRATION
U.S. DEPARTMENT OF TRANSPORTATION

Overview: In addition to carrying out programs relating to the safety of motor vehicles, drivers, occupants, and pedestrians, the National Highway Traffic Safety Administration (NHTSA) administers provisions of the Federal Odometer Law for the protection of purchasers of vehicles having altered odometers. Special Agents assigned to the NHTSA Odometer Fraud Staff are responsible for pursuing odometer fraud investigations and for the preparation of related criminal and civil cases. Investigations focus on the interstate movement of large numbers of vehicles and title documents through automobile dealerships and subsidiaries which engage in systematic and programmed odometer fraud. Responsibilities include examining the premises of businesses and persons suspected of fraud; interviewing and taking statements from victims and witnesses; seizing or impounding documents, equipment, and vehicles; participating in sting operations and large-scale task forces with other federal, state and local law enforcement and regulatory agencies; providing assistance to other law enforcement agencies when odometer fraud investigations develop evidence of violations of other criminal statutes; and testifying before grand juries and in criminal and civil trials. NHTSA Special Agents are authorized to conduct surveillance and undercover operations, carry firearms, make arrests, execute search warrants and serve subpoenas. This position is covered under special retirement provisions for law enforcement officers and qualifies for 25 percent Law Enforcement Availability Pay.

Qualifications: Applicants must be U.S. citizens, at least twenty-one years of age, and under the age of thirty-seven. (Candidates over age thirty-seven who have previous service creditable under special law enforcement retirement provisions may also be eligible.) Eyesight requirements include "sufficiently good vision in each eye, with or without correction." Corrected or uncorrected near vision must be sufficient to read printed material the size of typewritten characters. Hearing loss must not exceed 35 decibels at 1000, 2000, and 3000 Hz. NHTSA Special Agents are normally appointed at the GS-14 level, for which candidates must have one year of specialized experience equivalent to GS-13 in order to qualify. Tentative appointees must pass a drug screening test and medical exam, and qualify for a security clearance.

Training: NHTSA Special Agents attend a variety of training courses throughout their careers concerning motor vehicle titling, questioned documents, tracing funds through financial institutions, white-collar fraud, financial investigations, conspiracy, intelligence gathering, sources of information, investigative techniques, criminal and civil law, search and seizure, courtroom testimony, interviewing techniques, firearms proficiency, arrest techniques, defensive tactics, and other relevant subjects. NHTSA Special Agents may also attend courses presented at conferences sponsored by the National Odometer and Title Fraud Enforcement Agency.

Contact: Office of Human Resources, National Highway Traffic Safety Administration, Department of Transportation, 400 Seventh Street SW; Washington, DC 20590. Phone: 202-366-1784. World Wide Web: http://www.nhtsa.dot.gov/.

SPECIAL AGENT (GS-1811)
OFFICE OF INSPECTOR GENERAL
U.S. DEPARTMENT OF TRANSPORTATION

Overview: Special Agents of the Department of Transportation (DOT) Office of Inspector General (OIG) investigate allegations of fraud, waste, abuse and mismanagement in a broad range of DOT programs and operations. Investigations focus on Federal Aviation Administration contract and procurement functions, including contracts to build airport control towers, runways, terminals, and maintenance facilities, or fraud relating to the manufacturing and distribution of aircraft parts; the Federal Highway Administration, including highway and bridge construction, motor carrier safety programs, and transportation of hazardous materials; the Federal Railroad Administration, including Amtrak construction, procurement, and rail car safety programs; the Coast Guard, including construction and replacement of Coast Guard stations, aircraft hangars, and docking facilities; and operations of the Federal Transit Administration, National Highway Traffic Safety Administration, Maritime Administration, and other DOT components. Special Agents also conduct employee integrity investigations involving offenses such as bribery, conflict of interest, and abuses of authority. Special Agents conduct surveillance and undercover operations, and carry firearms, make arrests, execute search warrants and serve subpoenas. Investigations are conducted with agencies such as the FBI, U.S. Postal Inspection Service, EPA, Coast Guard Investigative Service, IRS Criminal Investigation Division, and Defense Criminal Investigative Service, among others. This position is covered under special retirement provisions for law enforcement officers and qualifies for 25 percent Law Enforcement Availability Pay.

Qualifications: Applicants must be U.S. citizens, at least twenty-one years of age, and under the age of thirty-seven. (Candidates over age thirty-seven who have previous service creditable under special law enforcement retirement provisions may also be eligible.) Eyesight requirements include "sufficiently good vision in each eye, with or without correction." Corrected or uncorrected near vision must be sufficient to read printed material the size of typewritten characters. Hearing loss must not exceed 35 decibels at 1000, 2000, and 3000 Hz. Requirements for appointment to GS-5 level include completion of a four-year course of study leading to a bachelor's degree, OR three years general experience, one year of which was equivalent to GS-4; for GS-7, one full year of graduate education, or superior academic achievement during undergraduate studies, OR one year of specialized experience equivalent to GS-5; for GS-9, a master's degree or two years of graduate education, OR one year of specialized experience equivalent to GS-7; for GS-11, a Ph.D. or equivalent doctoral degree, or three years of graduate education, OR one year of specialized experience equivalent to GS-9; and for GS-12 and above, one year of specialized experience equivalent to the next lower grade level. In some cases, qualifying education may be substituted for experience, and vice versa. Tentative appointees must qualify for a security clearance, and pass a drug screening test and medical exam.

Training: DOT-OIG Special Agents attend the eight-week Criminal Investigator Training Program at the Federal Law Enforcement Training Center in Glynco, Georgia (see Chapter 16). In-service training may include courses concerning DOT program investigations, hazardous materials, white-collar crime, contract and procurement fraud, internal investigations, legal issues and updates, arrest techniques, defensive tactics, and firearms proficiency.

Contact: Office of Inspector General, Department of Transportation, 400 Seventh Street SW; Washington, DC 20590. Phone: 202-366-2677. World Wide Web: http://www.dot.gov/oig/. E-mail: hrstaff@oig.dot.gov.

SPECIAL AGENT (GS-1811)
UNITED STATES COAST GUARD INVESTIGATIVE SERVICE
U.S. DEPARTMENT OF TRANSPORTATION

Overview: As members of the criminal investigation arm of the United States Coast Guard, civilian Special Agents of the Coast Guard Investigative Service (CGIS) conduct complex and sensitive criminal and personnel security investigations, counterintelligence operations, and provide personal protection to high-ranking Coast Guard officials. CGIS Special Agents are based in seven regional offices and twenty-three Resident Agencies throughout the continental United States. Investigations focus on the interdiction of drug trafficking activities, illegal immigrant smuggling operations, violent crimes, terrorism, piracy, marine environmental crimes, fishing violations, and the enforcement of other maritime criminal activity. CGIS Special Agents participate with the FBI, DEA, and other law enforcement agencies in the Organized Crime Drug Enforcement Task Force, and in personal protective operations with the Secret Service and State Department. Investigations may also be conducted with agencies such as the National Marine Fisheries Service, Transportation Department OIG, and other law enforcement and regulatory agencies. Special Agents are authorized to conduct surveillance and undercover operations, carry firearms, make arrests, execute search warrants and serve subpoenas. This position is covered under special retirement provisions for law enforcement officers and qualifies for 25 percent Law Enforcement Availability Pay. While the Coast Guard also maintains a staff of active duty military Special Agents, this is a civilian position and does not require active duty service.

Qualifications: Applicants must be U.S. citizens, at least twenty-one years of age, and under the age of thirty-seven. (Candidates over age thirty-seven who have previous service creditable under special law enforcement retirement provisions may also be eligible.) Eyesight requirements include "sufficiently good vision in each eye, with or without correction." Corrected or uncorrected near vision must be sufficient to read printed material the size of typewritten characters. Hearing loss must not exceed 35 decibels at 1000, 2000, and 3000 Hz. Requirements for appointment to GS-5 level include completion of a four-year course of study leading to a bachelor's degree, OR three years general experience, one year of which was equivalent to GS-4; for GS-7, one full year of graduate education, or superior academic achievement during undergraduate studies, OR one year of specialized experience equivalent to GS-5; for GS-9, a master's degree or two years of graduate education, OR one year of specialized experience equivalent to GS-7; for GS-11, a Ph.D. or equivalent doctoral degree, or three years of graduate education, OR one year of specialized experience equivalent to GS-9; and for GS-12 and above, one year of specialized experience equivalent to the next lower grade level. In some cases, qualifying education may be substituted for experience, and vice versa. Tentative appointees must qualify for a top-secret security clearance, and pass a drug screening test and medical exam.

Training: CGIS Special Agents attend the eight-week Criminal Investigator Training Program at the Federal Law Enforcement Training Center in Glynco, Georgia (see Chapter 16). In-service training may include courses which focus on drug trafficking, homicide, sexual assault, financial crimes, personal protective operations, driving techniques, counterterrorism, informant development, interviewing and interrogation, search and seizure, legal issues and updates, firearms proficiency, arrest techniques, defensive tactics, and other topics.

Contact: Coast Guard Investigative Service, Department of Transportation, 2100 Second Street SW; Washington, DC 20593. Phone: 202-267-2229. World Wide Web: http://www.dot.gov/dotinfo/uscg/.

SPECIAL AGENT (GS-1811)
BUREAU OF ALCOHOL, TOBACCO AND FIREARMS
U.S. DEPARTMENT OF THE TREASURY

Overview: Special Agents of the Bureau of Alcohol, Tobacco and Firearms (ATF) investigate violations of federal laws relating to explosives, arson, firearms, illicit distilled spirits and tobacco. ATF Special Agents give special emphasis to the enforcement of federal firearms laws to curb illegal trafficking and criminal use of firearms, as well as apprehension of armed narcotics traffickers and repeat offenders who possess firearms. Investigations often focus on violations of federal explosives laws and the Federal Alcohol Administration Act, bombings, arson-for-profit schemes affecting interstate commerce, ethnic street gangs, organized criminal enterprises, and interstate trafficking in contraband cigarettes. ATF Special Agents are authorized to conduct surveillance and undercover operations, carry firearms, make arrests, execute search warrants and serve subpoenas. Investigations may be conducted jointly with agencies such as the FBI, Marshals Service, DEA, Customs Service, IRS Criminal Investigation Division, USDA Office of Inspector General, HUD Office of Inspector General, and other federal, state, or local law enforcement and regulatory agencies. This position is covered under special retirement provisions for law enforcement officers and qualifies for 25 percent Law Enforcement Availability Pay.

Qualifications: Applicants must be U.S. citizens, at least twenty-one years of age, and under the age of thirty-seven. (Candidates over age thirty-seven who have previous service creditable under special law enforcement retirement provisions may also be eligible.) Eyesight requirements include uncorrected distant vision of at least 20/100 (Snellen) in each eye, correctable to 20/30 in one eye and 20/20 in the other; normal depth perception and peripheral vision; the ability to distinguish shades of color; and near vision sufficient to read Jaeger type 2 at 14 inches. Hearing loss must not exceed 30 decibels at 500, 1000, 2000 Hz. Ability to hear the whispered voice at fifteen feet without the use of a hearing aid is also required. Requirements for appointment to GS-5 level include completion of a four-year course of study leading to a bachelor's degree, OR three years general experience, one year of which was equivalent to GS-4; for GS-7, one full year of graduate education, or superior academic achievement during undergraduate studies, OR one year of specialized experience equivalent to GS-5; for GS-9, a master's degree or two years of graduate education, OR one year of specialized experience equivalent to GS-7; for GS-11, a Ph.D. or equivalent doctoral degree, or three years of graduate education, OR one year of specialized experience equivalent to GS-9; and for GS-12 and above, one year of specialized experience equivalent to the next lower grade level. In some cases, qualifying education may be substituted for experience, and vice versa. Tentative appointees must pass the Treasury Enforcement Agent Examination (see Chapter 1), a drug screening test, physical exam, and background investigation, and qualify for a top-secret security clearance.

Training: ATF Special Agents attend the eight-week Criminal Investigator Training Program at the Federal Law Enforcement Training Center in Glynco, Georgia (see Chapter 16), followed by an eight-week ATF New Agent Training course at FLETC which focuses on firearms laws, explosives, surveillance, undercover operations, technical investigative equipment, driving techniques, computers, report writing, defensive tactics, firearms proficiency, and other subjects pertaining to ATF enforcement operations. A variety of in-service courses are also attended.

Contact: Personnel Division; Bureau of Alcohol, Tobacco and Firearms; 650 Massachusetts Avenue NW, Room 4100; Washington, DC 20226. Phone: 202-927-8423. World Wide Web: http://www.atf.treas.gov/. E-mail: PersDiv@atfhq.atf.treas.gov.

SPECIAL AGENT (GS-1811)
INTERNAL REVENUE SERVICE
U.S. DEPARTMENT OF THE TREASURY

Overview: Special Agents of the IRS Criminal Investigation Division (IRS-CID) investigate violations of federal tax laws and related financial crimes. With expertise in following money trails to establish unreported income and the flow of assets, IRS-CID Special Agents investigate offenses such as money laundering, illegal political campaign contributions, bribery of public officials, illegal tax shelters, banking violations, savings and loan scandals, bankruptcy fraud, healthcare and insurance fraud, embezzlement, and telemarketing fraud. Investigations may focus on tax protesters, high-level drug trafficking enterprises, organized crime activities, and public corruption. IRS-CID Special Agents are an integral component of the nationwide Organized Crime Drug Enforcement Task Force, which targets drug kingpins and others involved in illegal narcotics-related activities. To combat international money laundering operations, IRS-CID Special Agents are located in Germany, Columbia, France, Mexico, and Canada. Special Agents are authorized to conduct surveillance and undercover operations, carry firearms, make arrests, execute search warrants and serve subpoenas. Investigations are conducted jointly with agencies such as the Secret Service; Customs Service; Bureau of Alcohol, Tobacco and Firearms; FBI; DEA; USDA Office of Inspector General; Transportation OIG; and the U.S. Postal Inspection Service. This position is covered under special retirement provisions for law enforcement officers and qualifies for 25 percent Law Enforcement Availability Pay.

Qualifications: Applicants must be U.S. citizens, at least twenty-one years of age, and under the age of thirty-seven. (Candidates over age thirty-seven who have previous service creditable under special law enforcement retirement provisions may be eligible). Eyesight requirements include uncorrected distant vision of at least 20/200 (Snellen) in each eye, correctable to 20/30 in one eye and 20/20 in the other; normal depth perception and peripheral vision; ability to distinguish shades of color; and near vision sufficient to read Jaeger type 2 at 14 inches. Hearing loss must not exceed 30 decibels at 500, 1000, 2000 Hz. Ability to hear the whispered voice at fifteen feet without the use of a hearing aid is also required. Basic requirements (qualifying for GS-5) include completion of a four-year course of study leading to a bachelor's degree, with at least 15 semester hours in accounting and 9 hours in related business subjects, OR three years of accounting or related business experience. Additional requirements for GS-7 include one year of graduate education in a closely related field, or superior academic achievement during undergraduate studies; for GS-9, a master's degree or two years of graduate education, OR one year of specialized experience equivalent to GS-7; for GS-11, a Ph.D. or equivalent doctoral degree, or three years of graduate education, OR one year of specialized experience equivalent to GS-9; and for GS-12 and above, one year of specialized experience equivalent to the next lower grade level. In some cases, education may be substituted for experience, and vice versa. Applicants must qualify for a security clearance and pass the TEA Examination (see Chapter 1), a drug screening test, and a medical exam.

Training: IRS-CID Special Agents attend the eight-week Criminal Investigator Training Program at the Federal Law Enforcement Training Center (FLETC) in Glynco, Georgia (see Chapter 16), followed by a twelve-week IRS course at FLETC which includes subjects such as tax law, financial fraud, money laundering, computer fraud, undercover operations, surveillance techniques, forensic sciences, and court procedures. A wide range of in-service courses are also attended.

Contact: IRS Criminal Investigation Division, 1111 Constitution Ave. NW; Washington, DC 20224. Phone: 202-622-5000. World Wide Web: http://www.treas.gov/irs/ci/.

SPECIAL AGENT (GS-1811)
OFFICE OF INSPECTOR GENERAL
U.S. DEPARTMENT OF THE TREASURY

Overview: Special Agents of the United States Department of the Treasury Office of Inspector General (OIG) conduct sensitive and complex criminal and administrative investigations concerning fraud, waste, and abuse in Treasury Department programs and operations. Investigations often involve contract and procurement fraud pertaining to Treasury Department vendors, contractors, and their employees, and include offenses such as theft, embezzlement, bribery, collusion, falsification of contractors' certified payrolls, and other crimes. Treasury OIG Special Agents are also responsible for the investigation of official misconduct by employees of Treasury Department offices and bureaus, which encompass a range of allegations such as bribery, embezzlement, theft of U.S. currency or postage stamps, accepting bribes and gratuities, and conflict of interest. Treasury OIG Special Agents are authorized to conduct surveillance and undercover operations, carry firearms, make arrests, execute search warrants and serve subpoenas. Many investigations are conducted jointly with various Treasury Department offices and bureaus, and other federal, state, or local law enforcement agencies. This position is covered under special retirement provisions for law enforcement officers and qualifies for 25 percent Law Enforcement Availability Pay.

Qualifications: Applicants must be U.S. citizens, at least twenty-one years of age, and under the age of thirty-seven. (Candidates over age thirty-seven who have previous service creditable under special law enforcement retirement provisions may also be eligible.) Eyesight requirements include "sufficiently good vision in each eye, with or without correction." Corrected or uncorrected near vision must be sufficient to read printed material the size of typewritten characters. Hearing loss must not exceed 35 decibels at 1000, 2000, and 3000 Hz. Requirements for appointment to GS-5 level include completion of a four-year course of study leading to a bachelor's degree, OR three years general experience, one year of which was equivalent to GS-4; for GS-7, one full year of graduate education, or superior academic achievement during undergraduate studies, OR one year of specialized experience equivalent to GS-5; for GS-9, a master's degree or two years of graduate education, OR one year of specialized experience equivalent to GS-7; for GS-11, a Ph.D. or equivalent doctoral degree, or three years of graduate education, OR one year of specialized experience equivalent to GS-9; and for GS-12 and above, one year of specialized experience equivalent to the next lower grade level. In some cases, qualifying education may be substituted for experience, and vice versa. Tentative appointees must qualify for a security clearance, and pass a background investigation, drug screening test and medical exam.

Training: Treasury OIG Special Agents attend the eight-week Criminal Investigator Training Program at the Federal Law Enforcement Training Center in Glynco, Georgia (see Chapter 16). In-service training may include courses in search and seizure, computer hardware and software, employee integrity investigations, criminal and civil law, financial investigations, program fraud investigations, investigations, arrest techniques, defensive tactics, and firearms proficiency.

Contact: Office of Inspector General, Department of the Treasury, 740 15th Street NW, Suite 510; Washington, DC 20220. Phone: 202-927-5230. World Wide Web: http://www.treas.gov/.

SPECIAL AGENT (GS-1811)
UNITED STATES CUSTOMS SERVICE
U.S. DEPARTMENT OF THE TREASURY

Overview: Investigations conducted by U.S. Customs Service (USCS) Special Agents focus primarily on the illegal shipment of arms and high technology to foreign entities, illicit transportation of currency in support of criminal enterprise, and schemes to defraud the government of revenue. In the interests of national security, USCS Special Agents investigate the illegal exporting of strategically sensitive technology to restricted nations, with particular emphasis on goods which may be utilized in the development of chemical, biological or nuclear weapons or related missile delivery systems. USCS Special Agents enforce laws related to child pornography, drug trafficking, money laundering, cargo theft, and schemes involving smuggled goods or contraband, and also assist the Secret Service with Presidential protection operations. Special Agents are authorized to conduct surveillance and undercover operations, carry firearms, make arrests, execute search warrants and serve subpoenas. Investigations may be conducted jointly with agencies such as the Immigration and Naturalization Service, Commerce Department Bureau of Export Administration, DEA, USDA Animal and Plant Health Inspection Service, USDA Office of Inspector General, IRS, Food and Drug Administration, U.S. Fish and Wildlife Service, FBI, and other agencies. This position is covered under special retirement provisions for law enforcement officers and qualifies for 25 percent Law Enforcement Availability Pay.

Qualifications: Applicants must be U.S. citizens, at least twenty-one years of age, and under the age of thirty-seven. (Candidates over age thirty-seven who have previous service creditable under special law enforcement retirement provisions may be eligible). Eyesight requirements include uncorrected distant vision of at least 20/200 (Snellen) in each eye, correctable to 20/30 in one eye and 20/20 in the other; normal depth perception and peripheral vision; the ability to distinguish shades of color; and near vision sufficient to read Jaeger type 2 at 14 inches. Hearing loss must not exceed 30 decibels at 500, 1000, 2000 Hz. Ability to hear the whispered voice at fifteen feet without the use of a hearing aid is also required. Requirements for appointment to GS-5 level include completion of a four-year course of study leading to a bachelor's degree, OR three years general experience, one year of which was equivalent to GS-4; for GS-7, one full year of graduate education, or superior academic achievement during undergraduate studies, OR one year of specialized experience equivalent to GS-5; for GS-9, a master's degree or two years of graduate education, OR one year of specialized experience equivalent to GS-7; for GS-11, a Ph.D. or equivalent doctoral degree, or three years of graduate education, OR one year of specialized experience equivalent to GS-9; and for GS-12 and above, one year of specialized experience equivalent to the next lower grade level. In some cases, qualifying education may be substituted for experience, and vice versa. Tentative appointees must qualify for a security clearance and pass the Treasury Enforcement Agent Examination (see Chapter 1), a drug screening test, and a medical exam.

Training: USCS Special Agents attend the eight-week Criminal Investigator Training Program at the Federal Law Enforcement Training Center in Glynco, Georgia (see Chapter 16), followed by an eight-week course presented by the Customs Service which focuses on search and seizure laws, Customs laws and regulations, arrest and search warrant execution, and search techniques. In-service training may include courses concerned with import and export violations, money laundering, financial investigations, asset forfeiture, firearms proficiency, and defensive tactics.

Contact: United States Customs Service, 1300 Pennsylvania Avenue NW; Washington, DC 20229. Phone: 202-927-1250. World Wide Web: http://www.customs.ustreas.gov/.

SPECIAL AGENT (GS-1811)
UNITED STATES SECRET SERVICE
U.S. DEPARTMENT OF THE TREASURY

Overview: U.S. Secret Service (USSS) Special Agents are charged with missions involving protection and investigation. Protection is provided for the President of the United States, Vice President, President-Elect and Vice President-Elect, and their immediate families; former Presidents and their spouses and minor children; visiting heads of foreign governments and their spouses traveling with them; other distinguished foreign visitors to the United States; official representatives of the United States performing special missions abroad; and major Presidential and Vice Presidential candidates and their spouses during an election year. Investigations focus on counterfeiting of U.S. currency, securities, and government identification documents; forgery of Social Security checks, savings bonds, USDA Food Stamps, and other government disbursements; fraud pertaining to credit cards, banks, electronic funds transfers, telecommunications, and telemarketing; money laundering; and computer crime. Special Agents are authorized to conduct surveillance and undercover operations, carry firearms, make arrests, execute search warrants and serve subpoenas. Investigations are conducted jointly with agencies such as the IRS Criminal Investigation Division, FBI, Customs Service, DEA, and USDA Office of Inspector General, among others. This position is covered under special retirement provisions for law enforcement officers and qualifies for 25 percent Law Enforcement Availability Pay.

Qualifications: Applicants must be U.S. citizens, at least twenty-one years of age, and under the age of thirty-seven. (Candidates over age thirty-seven who have previous service creditable under special law enforcement retirement provisions may also be eligible.) Eyesight requirements include uncorrected distant vision of at least 20/60 (Snellen) in each eye, correctable to 20/30 in one eye and 20/20 in the other; normal depth perception and peripheral vision; the ability to distinguish shades of color; and near vision sufficient to read Jaeger type 2 at 14 inches. Hearing loss must not exceed 30 decibels at 500, 1000, 2000 Hz. Requirements for appointment to GS-5 level include completion of a four-year course of study leading to a bachelor's degree, OR three years general experience, one year of which was equivalent to GS-4; for GS-7, one full year of graduate education, or superior academic achievement during undergraduate studies, OR one year of specialized experience equivalent to GS-5; for GS-9, a master's degree or two years of graduate education, OR one year of specialized experience equivalent to GS-7; for GS-11, a Ph.D. or equivalent doctoral degree, or three years of graduate education, OR one year of specialized experience equivalent to GS-9; and for GS-12 and above, one year of specialized experience equivalent to the next lower grade level. In some cases, qualifying education may be substituted for experience, and vice versa. Tentative appointees must qualify for a top-secret security clearance and pass the Treasury Enforcement Agent Examination (see Chapter 1), a background investigation, polygraph exam, drug screening test, and medical exam.

Training: USSS Special Agents attend the eight-week Criminal Investigator Training Program at the Federal Law Enforcement Training Center in Glynco, Georgia (see Chapter 16), followed by an eleven-week course which focuses on protection techniques; fraud involving credit cards, checks, and computers; and other subjects. In-service training consists of courses in defensive driving, criminal investigation, intelligence gathering, surveillance, undercover operations, computer crime, law, protective operations, interviewing techniques, firearms, and other topics.

Contact: U.S. Secret Service, 1800 G Street NW, Room 912; Washington, DC 20223. Phone: 202-435-5708 or 800-827-7783. World Wide Web: http://www.treas.gov/usss/.

SPECIAL AGENT (GS-1811)
OFFICE OF INSPECTOR GENERAL
U.S. DEPARTMENT OF VETERANS AFFAIRS

Overview: The U.S. Department of Veterans Affairs (VA) operates programs to benefit veterans and members of their families. Benefits include compensation payments for disabilities or death related to military service; pensions; education and rehabilitation; home loan guaranty; burial; and a medical care program incorporating nursing homes, clinics, and medical centers. Special Agents of the VA Office of Inspector General (OIG) conduct sensitive and complex criminal and general investigations to identify fraud and other forms of criminal or improper activity in VA programs and operations. Investigations focus on the VA Home Loan Guarantee Program, healthcare fraud, pension programs, payments for educational assistance, workers' compensation programs, fraudulent claims for disability benefits, scams involving deceased payees, fraudulent use of Social Security account numbers, bribery, kickbacks, theft of government equipment, product substitutions, embezzlement, antitrust violations, patient abuse, homicide, official misconduct by Department personnel, and other offenses. VA-OIG Special Agents are authorized to conduct surveillance and undercover operations, carry firearms, make arrests, execute search warrants and serve subpoenas. Investigations may be conducted jointly with agencies such as the Social Security Administration OIG, Secret Service, DEA, Army Criminal Investigation Command, FBI, and other federal, state, or local law enforcement agencies. This position is covered under special retirement provisions for law enforcement officers and qualifies for 25 percent Law Enforcement Availability Pay.

Qualifications: Applicants must be U.S. citizens, at least twenty-one years of age, and under the age of thirty-seven. (Candidates over age thirty-seven who have previous service creditable under special law enforcement retirement provisions may also be eligible.) Eyesight requirements include "sufficiently good vision in each eye, with or without correction." Corrected or uncorrected near vision must be sufficient to read printed material the size of typewritten characters. Hearing loss must not exceed 35 decibels at 1000, 2000, and 3000 Hz. Requirements for appointment to GS-5 level include completion of a four-year course of study leading to a bachelor's degree, OR three years general experience, one year of which was equivalent to GS-4; for GS-7, one full year of graduate education, or superior academic achievement during undergraduate studies, OR one year of specialized experience equivalent to GS-5; for GS-9, a master's degree or two years of graduate education, OR one year of specialized experience equivalent to GS-7; for GS-11, a Ph.D. or equivalent doctoral degree, or three years of graduate education, OR one year of specialized experience equivalent to GS-9; and for GS-12 and above, one year of specialized experience equivalent to the next lower grade level. In some cases, qualifying education may be substituted for experience, and vice versa. Tentative appointees must qualify for a security clearance, and pass a drug screening test and medical exam.

Training: VA-OIG Special Agents attend the eight-week Criminal Investigator Training Program at the Federal Law Enforcement Training Center in Glynco, Georgia (see Chapter 16). In-service training may include courses concerning VA program fraud investigations, workers' compensation fraud, investigative techniques, drug enforcement operations, legal issues and updates, white-collar crime, personnel misconduct investigations, firearms proficiency, arrest techniques, and defensive tactics.

Contact: Office of Inspector General, Department of Veterans Affairs, 810 Vermont Avenue NW; Washington, DC 20420. Phone: 202-273-4900. World Wide Web: http://www.va.gov/oig/.

SPECIAL AGENT PILOT (GS-1812)
UNITED STATES FISH AND WILDLIFE SERVICE
U.S. DEPARTMENT OF THE INTERIOR

Overview: Special Agent Pilots of the U.S. Fish and Wildlife Service (FWS) operate light aircraft in support of law enforcement and other FWS operations nationwide, including aerial surveillance to detect and enforce federal fish and wildlife law violations relating to the illegal taking, importing, and commercialization of wildlife. Aerial surveillance and other support functions may be carried out during the course of investigations which focus on clandestine operations, organized and sophisticated groups, and others involved in complex conspiracies. When not engaged in flight operations, FWS Special Agent Pilots conduct criminal investigations (see *FWS Special Agent*). Pilots are authorized to conduct surveillance and undercover operations, carry firearms, make arrests, execute search warrants and serve subpoenas. Joint operations are conducted with other federal, state, and local law enforcement and regulatory agencies. This position is covered under special retirement provisions for law enforcement officers and qualifies for 25 percent Law Enforcement Availability Pay.

Qualifications: Requirements include a current Federal Aviation Administration (FAA) Commercial Airman Certificate with ratings appropriate for the duties performed; an instrument rating; a minimum of 500 hours of flight time as pilot-in-command, and 25 hours of flight time as pilot-in-command at night; and an FAA Class II Medical Certificate. Applicants must be U.S. citizens, at least twenty-one years of age, and under the age of thirty-seven. (Candidates over age thirty-seven who have previous service creditable under special law enforcement retirement provisions may also be eligible.) Eyesight requirements include distant vision of at least 20/200 (Snellen) in each eye without correction, and at least 20/20 in one eye and 20/30 in the other with correction. Near vision must be sufficient to read Jaeger Type 2 at 14 inches with correction. Normal depth perception and ability to distinguish shades of color are required. A history of Radial Keratotomy surgery is disqualifying. Hearing loss must not exceed 35 decibels at frequencies of 500, 1000, 2000 and 3000 Hz. Requirements for appointment to GS-5 include completion of a four-year course of study leading to a bachelor's degree, OR three years general experience, one year of which was equivalent to GS-4; for GS-7, one full year of graduate education, or superior academic achievement during undergraduate studies, OR one year of specialized experience equivalent to GS-5; for GS-9, a master's degree or two years of graduate education, OR one year of specialized experience equivalent to GS-7; for GS-11, a Ph.D. or equivalent doctoral degree, or three years of graduate education, OR one year of specialized experience equivalent to GS-9; and for GS-12 and above, one year of specialized experience equivalent to the next lower grade level. Education may be substituted for experience, and vice versa. Tentative appointees must qualify for a security clearance, and pass a drug screening test and medical exam.

Training: FWS Special Agent Pilots attend the eight-week Criminal Investigator Training Program at the Federal Law Enforcement Training Center (FLETC) in Glynco, Georgia (see Chapter 16), followed by a ten-week course at FLETC which incorporates wildlife law enforcement, practical exercises, and other relevant

Chapter Seven

INTELLIGENCE SPECIALISTS

Three may keep a secret – if two of them are dead.
– BENJAMIN FRANKLIN

INTELLIGENCE SPECIALISTS IN FEDERAL LAW ENFORCEMENT play a vital role in the effort to protect our nation's citizens from foreign and domestic threats. These personnel are responsible for performing data collection, analysis, interpretation, and dissemination of information relating to criminal activity and other matters which directly or indirectly affect the national security. Depending upon the type of agency involved, the work of Intelligence Specialists revolves around intelligence pertaining to drug trafficking, terrorism, low-intensity conflict, alien smuggling, passport fraud, organized crime, money laundering, arson rings, cargo theft, espionage, and other offenses. Intelligence Specialists also determine the need for and write data collection manuals, process requests for intelligence information, determine the distribution of raw intelligence data and finished intelligence reports, and perform liaison functions within the intelligence community. While all intelligence organizations carry out similar processes, each agency is geared toward producing intelligence within its own sphere of operations.

Intelligence Specialists are required to have a basic knowledge and understanding of one or more of the natural or social sciences, engineering, military science, history, or political science. They must also have a fundamental knowledge of research techniques, the ability to express ideas orally and in writing, and a demonstrated potential for learning the methods and techniques characteristic of intelligence work.

Intelligence Specialists are classified in the GS-0132 series, and include official titles such as Intelligence Operations Specialist, Intelligence Research Analyst, and Intelligence Research Specialist. This chapter includes profiles of eleven careers which involve intelligence support activities for agencies including the Drug Enforcement Administration; Federal Bureau of Investigation; U.S. Immigration and Naturalization Service; U.S. Border Patrol; Naval Criminal Investigative Service; State Department Bureau of Intelligence and Research; State Department Office of Inspector General; U.S. Coast Guard; Bureau of Alcohol, Tobacco and Firearms; Financial Crimes Enforcement Network; and U.S. Customs Service.

INTELLIGENCE OPERATIONS SPECIALIST (GS-0132)
UNITED STATES IMMIGRATION AND NATURALIZATION SERVICE
U.S. DEPARTMENT OF JUSTICE

Overview: Intelligence Operations Specialists of the United States Immigration and Naturalization Service (INS), Department of Justice, are responsible for gathering and interpreting information relating to complex criminal organizations and illegal operations involving the smuggling of aliens, immigration fraud, and counterfeiting of immigration and other identity documents. The purpose of intelligence research projects is to detect trends, conduct analysis, and provide immediate response to field operations concerning illicit activities. Responsibilities of INS Intelligence Operations Specialists include the evaluation of raw intelligence data; performing file research in order to identify patterns, trends and associations; drawing logical conclusions based upon a wide range of incoming data; recognizing leads, detecting discrepancies, and identifying relevant evidence; operating computer systems and utilizing databases to facilitate the collection and development of information; and preparing written reports and oral presentations. Intelligence research results are utilized by INS Special Agents and Inspectors, Border Patrol Agents, and cooperating law enforcement agencies.

Qualifications: Applicants must be U.S. citizens. Requirements for appointment to GS-5 level include completion of a four-year course of study leading to a bachelor's degree, OR three years general experience, one year of which was equivalent to GS-4; for GS-7, one full year of graduate education, or superior academic achievement during undergraduate studies, OR one year of specialized experience equivalent to GS-5; for GS-9, a master's degree or two years of graduate education, OR one year of specialized experience equivalent to GS-7; for GS-11, a Ph.D. or equivalent doctoral degree, or three years of graduate education, OR one year of specialized experience equivalent to GS-9; and for GS-12, one year of specialized experience equivalent to GS-11. In some cases, qualifying education may be substituted for experience, and vice versa. Tentative appointees must pass a background investigation and drug screening test, and qualify for a top-secret security clearance.

Training: Initial training for INS Intelligence Operations Specialists includes either the two-week Criminal Intelligence Analysts Training Program at the Federal Law Enforcement Training Center in Glynco, Georgia (see Chapter 16); in-house training provided by INS staff; other courses pertaining to specific duties of the position; or a combination of these options. In-service training may include courses which focus on alien smuggling operations, counterfeiting and questioned documents, INS regulations, legal issues, and other subjects.

Contact: U.S. Immigration and Naturalization Service, Department of Justice, 425 I Street NW; Washington, DC 20536. Phone: 202-514-4316. World Wide Web: http://www.ins.usdoj.gov/.

INTELLIGENCE OPERATIONS SPECIALIST (GS-0132)
BUREAU OF INTELLIGENCE AND RESEARCH
U.S. DEPARTMENT OF STATE

Overview: The Bureau of Intelligence and Research is the focal point in the Department of State for coordination of sensitive civilian and military intelligence operations, analysis, and research for the Department and other federal agencies. Intelligence Operations Specialists of the Bureau serve as the contact for liaison on operational intelligence programs related to counterterrorism with the intelligence community, the National Security Council, and relevant State Department bureaus. Responsibilities include researching, analyzing, and evaluating intelligence reports; interpreting intelligence findings and making recommendations for actions to be taken; serving as a liaison representative with intelligence community organizations to ensure that State Department views on counterterrorism are well understood; drafting memoranda for Department principals attending National Security Council meetings on intelligence operational programs related to counterterrorism; and representing the Bureau at interagency meetings on operational counterterrorism practices. While a substantial effort is directed toward intelligence gathering, analysis, and dissemination for law enforcement purposes, intelligence operations involving national security matters are more prevalent.

Qualifications: Applicants must be U.S. citizens. Requirements for appointment to GS-5 level include completion of a four-year course of study leading to a bachelor's degree, OR three years general experience, one year of which was equivalent to GS-4; for GS-7, one full year of graduate education, or superior academic achievement during undergraduate studies, OR one year of specialized experience equivalent to GS-5; for GS-9, a master's degree or two years of graduate education, OR one year of specialized experience equivalent to GS-7; for GS-11, a Ph.D. or equivalent doctoral degree, or three years of graduate education, OR one year of specialized experience equivalent to GS-9; and for GS-12, one year of specialized experience equivalent to GS-11. In some cases, qualifying education may be substituted for experience, and vice versa. Tentative appointees must pass a background investigation and qualify for a security clearance.

Training: Intelligence Operations Specialists attend a one-week training program conducted by State Department staff which includes instruction in subjects such as crime reporting, drafting intelligence assessments, computer techniques, legal aspects of intelligence, sources of information, databases, information management, intelligence dissemination, and report writing. In-service training includes courses in foreign policy, advanced computer techniques, State Department regulations, and other subjects related to specific duties of the position.

Contact: PER/CSP/POD, P.O. Box 18657; Washington, DC 20036. Phone: 202-647-7284. World Wide Web: http://www.state.gov/www/careers/rfsspecds.html/.

INTELLIGENCE OPERATIONS SPECIALIST (GS-0132)
OFFICE OF INSPECTOR GENERAL
U.S. DEPARTMENT OF STATE

Overview: The Security and Intelligence Oversight division of the State Department Office of Inspector General (OIG) is responsible for evaluating the effectiveness of the intelligence oversight activities of the State Department and of mission chiefs worldwide, and for ensuring that intelligence operations and related activities are conducted in a manner consistent with law and executive directives. State Department OIG Intelligence Operations Specialists gather data and conduct interviews with Department, intelligence community, and other officials to develop working hypotheses and recommend issues to be examined during the course of intelligence inspections; plan and conduct intelligence oversight reviews; evaluate the ability of overseas posts to respond to threats from terrorism, organized crime, intelligence penetration, physical intrusion, and other criminal activity; determine whether adequate internal controls are in place to prevent or reduce the incidence of waste, fraud, and mismanagement; evaluate functional and individual performance in intelligence activities under review, highlighting potential problems and presenting viable solutions; draft detailed written reports; and meet with Department managers to present findings and resolve conflicts.

Qualifications: Applicants must be U.S. citizens. Requirements for appointment to GS-5 level include completion of a four-year course of study leading to a bachelor's degree, OR three years general experience, one year of which was equivalent to GS-4; for GS-7, one full year of graduate education, or superior academic achievement during undergraduate studies, OR one year of specialized experience equivalent to GS-5; for GS-9, a master's degree or two years of graduate education, OR one year of specialized experience equivalent to GS-7; for GS-11, a Ph.D. or equivalent doctoral degree, or three years of graduate education, OR one year of specialized experience equivalent to GS-9; and for GS-12, one year of specialized experience equivalent to GS-11. In some cases, qualifying education may be substituted for experience, and vice versa. Tentative appointees must pass a background investigation and qualify for a top-secret security clearance.

Training: State Department Intelligence Operations Specialists attend a variety of training courses throughout their careers involving Department operations and programs, intelligence gathering and dissemination, operations of federal intelligence organizations, memoranda of understanding, ambassador authority, and other subjects which focus on specific responsibilities of the position.

Contact: PER/CSP/POD, P.O. Box 18657; Washington, DC 20036. Phone: 202-647-7284. World Wide Web: http://www.state.gov/www/careers/rfsspecds.html/. E-mail: oig.website@dos.us-state.gov.

INTELLIGENCE RESEARCH ANALYST (GS-0132)
UNITED STATES COAST GUARD
U.S. DEPARTMENT OF TRANSPORTATION

Overview: As the primary maritime law enforcement agency in the United States, the U.S. Coast Guard (USCG) employs Intelligence Research Analysts to conduct extensive studies in support of a wide range of law enforcement and other USCG operations. Intelligence Research Analysts collect, analyze, and disseminate intelligence pertaining to individuals and organizations involved in drug trafficking activities, illegal immigrant smuggling operations, terrorism, piracy, marine environmental crimes, and other maritime criminal activity. Responsibilities also include production of all-source assessments on threats to USCG forces operating throughout the world, and representing the USCG in interagency operations with the national intelligence community on issues of terrorism, counterintelligence, crime, and low-intensity conflict. Intelligence is gathered from classified and unclassified library sources, documents, photographs, databases, and other sources. Research results are presented orally or in writing to senior USCG officers and civilian personnel, and to representatives of other organizations in high-level interagency meetings.

Qualifications: Applicants must be U.S. citizens. Requirements for appointment to GS-5 level include completion of a four-year course of study leading to a bachelor's degree, OR three years general experience, one year of which was equivalent to GS-4; for GS-7, one full year of graduate education, or superior academic achievement during undergraduate studies, OR one year of specialized experience equivalent to GS-5; for GS-9, a master's degree or two years of graduate education, OR one year of specialized experience equivalent to GS-7; for GS-11, a Ph.D. or equivalent doctoral degree, or three years of graduate education, OR one year of specialized experience equivalent to GS-9; and for GS-12, one year of specialized experience equivalent to GS-11. In some cases, qualifying education may be substituted for experience, and vice versa. Tentative appointees must pass a background investigation and qualify for a top-secret security clearance.

Training: Initial training for Intelligence Research Analysts includes a one-week course conducted by USCG staff in effective report writing and format. In-service training consists of courses pertaining to internal intelligence gathering and dissemination policies and procedures, intelligence information management, computer software and hardware systems, link analysis, event charting, and other subjects depending upon the needs of the Agency and individual personnel.

Contact: Civilian Personnel Management Division, U.S. Coast Guard, 2100 Second Street SW; Washington, DC 20593. Phone: 202-267-1890. World Wide Web: http:///www.dot.gov/dotinfo/uscg/.

INTELLIGENCE RESEARCH SPECIALIST (GS-0132)
DRUG ENFORCEMENT ADMINISTRATION
U.S. DEPARTMENT OF JUSTICE

Overview: In coordination with other federal, state, local, and foreign law enforcement organizations, Drug Enforcement Administration (DEA) Intelligence Research Specialists collect, analyze, and disseminate drug-related intelligence pertaining to individuals and organizations involved in the growing, manufacture, or distribution of controlled substances. Working closely with DEA Special Agents during the course of criminal investigations, DEA Intelligence Research Specialists gather and analyze information from a variety of sources including criminal investigations, seized documents, financial records, surveillance reports, cooperating sources, and court-ordered wiretaps. Complex research projects are managed in areas such as drug cultivation and production, methods of transportation, trafficking routes, major conspiracies, and the structure and analysis of trafficker organizations. Case development is enhanced through the use of sophisticated databases and unique methods of data manipulation. Research results are presented orally or in writing to case agents, supervisory personnel, U.S. Attorneys, grand juries and high-level decision-makers.

Qualifications: Applicants must be U.S. citizens. Requirements for appointment to GS-5 level include completion of a four-year course of study leading to a bachelor's degree, OR three years general experience, one year of which was equivalent to GS-4; for GS-7, one full year of graduate education, or superior academic

achievement during undergraduate studies, OR one year of specialized experience equivalent to GS-5; for GS-9, a master's degree or two years of graduate education, OR one year of specialized experience equivalent to GS-7; for GS-11, a Ph.D. or equivalent doctoral degree, or three years of graduate education, OR one year of specialized experience equivalent to GS-9; and for GS-12 or GS-13, one year of specialized experience equivalent to the next lower grade level. In some cases, qualifying education may be substituted for experience, and vice versa. Tentative appointees must qualify for a top-secret security clearance and pass a background investigation, drug screening test, writing evaluation and polygraph examination.

Training: Intelligence Research Specialists attend a seven-week formal training program at the DEA training center in Quantico, Virginia, which focuses on the mission and functions of the DEA, sources of information, legal aspects of intelligence, computer databases and software, information management, report writing, intelligence dissemination, and other aspects of drug trafficking intelligence operations. In-service training includes instruction in legal issues, operational and tactical procedures, personal integrity and responsibility, internal regulations, and other courses related to specific duties.

Contact: Direct inquiries to the DEA Field Office where employment is sought, or to the Drug Enforcement Administration; Washington, DC 20537. Phone: 202-307-1000 or 800-DEA-4288. World Wide Web: http://www.usdoj.gov/dea/.

INTELLIGENCE RESEARCH SPECIALIST (GS-0132)
FEDERAL BUREAU OF INVESTIGATION
U.S. DEPARTMENT OF JUSTICE

Overview: Intelligence Research Specialists of the Federal Bureau of Investigation (FBI) are responsible for the examination and interpretation of national security information in support of the criminal intelligence, foreign counterintelligence, counterterrorism, and organized crime missions of the FBI. Intelligence information is utilized for the preparation of strategic and operational analyses, espionage case studies, and threat assessments which are distributed within the FBI; to federal, state and local law enforcement agencies; and throughout the U.S. intelligence community. FBI Intelligence Research Specialists collect and analyze intelligence information from a wide range of sources such as criminal investigations, seized documents, financial records, surveillance reports, witness interviews, cooperating sources, and court-ordered wiretaps. Information is entered and processed through the use of sophisticated computer databases and various methods of data manipulation. Research results are presented orally or in writing to case agents, supervisory personnel, U.S. Attorneys, grand juries and high-level decision-makers.

Qualifications: Applicants must be U.S. citizens. Requirements for appointment to GS-5 level include completion of a four-year course of study leading to a bachelor's degree, OR three years general experience, one year of which was equivalent to GS-4; for GS-7, one full year of graduate education, or superior academic achievement during undergraduate studies, OR one year of specialized experience equivalent to GS-5; for GS-9, a master's degree or two years of graduate education, OR one year of specialized experience equivalent to GS-7; for GS-11, a Ph.D. or equivalent doctoral degree, or three years of graduate education, OR one year of specialized experience equivalent to GS-9; and for GS-12, one year of specialized experience equivalent to GS-11. In some cases, qualifying education may be substituted for experience, and vice versa. Tentative appointees must qualify for a top-secret security clearance, and pass a background investigation, drug screening test, and polygraph exam.

Training: Training for newly appointed FBI Intelligence Research Specialists includes courses, lectures and seminars pertaining to criminal intelligence, foreign counterintelligence, counterterrorism, legal issues, and analytical methodologies. In-service training includes conferences and courses which focus on subjects such as team building, polygraph examination, behavioral science matters, Arab/Israeli conflict, hostage rescue operations, communication skills, firearms and explosives, FBI laboratory operations, liaison with foreign law enforcement and government agencies, and the role of CIA analysts.

Contact: Recruiting information can be obtained from any FBI Field Office, or by contacting the Federal

Bureau of Investigation; Washington, DC 20535. Phone: 202-324-2727. World Wide Web: http://www.fbi.gov/.

INTELLIGENCE RESEARCH SPECIALIST (GS-0132)
UNITED STATES BORDER PATROL
IMMIGRATION AND NATURALIZATION SERVICE
U.S. DEPARTMENT OF JUSTICE

Overview: United States Border Patrol Intelligence Research Specialists are responsible for producing and analyzing immigration intelligence concerning threats to national security and Border Patrol personnel. Utilizing information from a wide variety of sources, Border Patrol Intelligence Research Specialists consolidate and evaluate incoming reports, intelligence data, and information involving Border Patrol operations; organize and summarize investigative material to identify needs, trends, patterns and profiles; ensure that necessary follow-up actions are initiated; establish working relationships with counterparts and colleagues throughout the intelligence community, exchange information, and provide free flow of intelligence on matters of mutual interest; and prepare finished studies of factual data as well as portions of or contributions to larger studies, statistical compilations, or intelligence techniques. Written reports and oral briefings are presented to the Chief Border Patrol Agent. Results are utilized by high-level Border Patrol staff to devise and implement appropriate responses to threats to national security and Border Patrol personnel.

Qualifications: Applicants must be U.S. citizens. Requirements for appointment to GS-5 level include completion of a four-year course of study leading to a bachelor's degree, OR three years general experience, one year of which was equivalent to GS-4; for GS-7, one full year of graduate education, or superior academic achievement during undergraduate studies, OR one year of specialized experience equivalent to GS-5; for GS-9, a master's degree or two years of graduate education, OR one year of specialized experience equivalent to GS-7; for GS-11, a Ph.D. or equivalent doctoral degree, or three years of graduate education, OR one year of specialized experience equivalent to GS-9; and for GS-12, one year of specialized experience equivalent to GS-11. In some cases, qualifying education may be substituted for experience, and vice versa. Tentative appointees must pass a background investigation and drug screening test, and qualify for a security clearance.

Training: Border Patrol Intelligence Research Specialists attend the two-week Criminal Intelligence Analysts Training Program at the Federal Law Enforcement Training Center in Glynco, Georgia (see Chapter 16). In-service training may include courses in legal issues, intelligence gathering, Border Patrol operations and regulations, and other subjects related to specific duties of the position.

Contact: United States Border Patrol, Immigration and Naturalization Service, 425 I Street NW; Washington, DC 20536. Phone: 202-616-1964. World Wide Web: http://www.ins.usdoj.gov/.

INTELLIGENCE RESEARCH SPECIALIST (GS-0132)
BUREAU OF ALCOHOL, TOBACCO AND FIREARMS
U.S. DEPARTMENT OF THE TREASURY

Overview: The Bureau of Alcohol, Tobacco and Firearms (ATF) employs Intelligence Research Specialists to conduct complex analytical studies in support of investigative operations and the national intelligence strategy of the Bureau. ATF Intelligence Research Specialists are responsible for collection, analysis, and evaluation of information relating to national and international organizations and individuals involved in the trafficking of firearms, explosives, and narcotics; arson rings; traditional and nontraditional organized crime enterprises; terrorist organizations; and others involved in complex criminal conspiracies. Utilizing information from a variety of sources, experienced ATF Intelligence Research Specialists are also responsible for the production of detailed strategic analyses which describe and predict violent criminal activity patterns. These studies typically include estimates of the scope of each type of criminal activity under various demographic, geopolitical and other scenarios, and assessments of their long-term impact on the ATF enforcement mission. Sophisticated computer systems and programs are utilized to facilitate the collection and development of information. Intelligence findings are communicated to law enforcement personnel, prosecuting attorneys, and grand juries in the form of written reports, charts, graphs, spreadsheets, and organized oral presentations.

Qualifications: Applicants must be U.S. citizens. Requirements for appointment to GS-5 level include completion of a four-year course of study leading to a bachelor's degree, OR three years general experience, one year of which was equivalent to GS-4; for GS-7, one full year of graduate education, or superior academic achievement during undergraduate studies, OR one year of specialized experience equivalent to GS-5; for GS-9, a master's degree or two years of graduate education, OR one year of specialized experience equivalent to GS-7; for GS-11, a Ph.D. or equivalent doctoral degree, or three years of graduate education, OR one year of specialized experience equivalent to GS-9; and for GS-12, one year of specialized experience equivalent to GS-11. In some cases, qualifying education may be substituted for experience, and vice versa. Tentative appointees must pass a background investigation and drug screening test, and qualify for a security clearance.

Training: ATF Intelligence Research Specialists attend the two-week Criminal Intelligence Analysts Training Program at the Federal Law Enforcement Training Center in Glynco, Georgia (see Chapter 16). In-service training includes various courses, conferences, and workshops pertaining to link analysis, analytical charting methods, concealed income analysis, case management, court testimony, pen register operations and analysis, firearms trafficking investigations, organized crime, legal issues and updates, and other subjects.

Contact: Personnel Division; Bureau of Alcohol, Tobacco and Firearms; 650 Massachusetts Avenue NW, Room 4100; Washington, DC 20226. Phone: 202-927-8423. World Wide Web: http://www.atf.treas.gov/. E-mail: persdiv@atfhq.atf.treas.gov.

INTELLIGENCE RESEARCH SPECIALIST (GS-0132)
FINANCIAL CRIMES ENFORCEMENT NETWORK
U.S. DEPARTMENT OF THE TREASURY

Overview: The Financial Crimes Enforcement Network (FinCEN) was created by the Treasury Department to provide a government-wide, multi-source intelligence and analytical network to support law enforcement and regulatory agencies in the detection, investigation, and prosecution of financial crimes, with particular emphasis on money laundering activities relating to drug trafficking operations. FinCEN Intelligence Research Specialists collect, analyze, and disseminate intelligence information gathered from a number of databases and other sources, such as the Treasury Department Financial Database, which includes reports filed under requirements of the Federal Bank Secrecy Act; databases administered by federal law enforcement and regulatory agencies; and commercial, publicly available databases containing business and marketing records, and demographic information. Intelligence information is disseminated to local and international law enforcement agencies to assist in building investigations, preparing prosecutions, and developing and implementing strategies to combat money laundering and other financial crimes. In addition to a permanent core of Intelligence Research Analysts, dozens of personnel are assigned to FinCEN on long-term details from various federal law enforcement and regulatory agencies.

Qualifications: Applicants must be U.S. citizens. Requirements for appointment to GS-5 level include completion of a four-year course of study leading to a bachelor's degree, OR three years general experience, one year of which was equivalent to GS-4; for GS-7, one full year of graduate education, or superior academic achievement during undergraduate studies, OR one year of specialized experience equivalent to GS-5; for GS-9, a master's degree or two years of graduate education, OR one year of specialized experience equivalent to GS-7; for GS-11, a Ph.D. or equivalent doctoral degree, or three years of graduate education, OR one year of specialized experience equivalent to GS-9; and for GS-12, one year of specialized experience equivalent to GS-11. In some cases, qualifying education may be substituted for experience, and vice versa. Tentative appointees must pass a background investigation and drug screening test, and qualify for a security clearance.

Training: FinCEN Intelligence Research Specialists attend the two-week Criminal Intelligence Analysts Training Program at the Federal Law Enforcement Training Center in Glynco, Georgia (see Chapter 16). In-service training may include courses in banking regulations, financial fraud, money laundering, legal issues, and other subjects related to specific duties of the position.

Contact: Financial Crimes Enforcement Network, Department of the Treasury, 2070 Chain Bridge Road; Vienna, VA 22182. Phone: 703-905-3848. World Wide Web: http://www.treas.gov/fincen/.

INTELLIGENCE RESEARCH SPECIALIST (GS-0132)
UNITED STATES CUSTOMS SERVICE
U.S. DEPARTMENT OF THE TREASURY

Overview: Intelligence Research Specialists of the U.S. Customs Service Office of Intelligence are responsible for the collection, analysis, and evaluation of information relating to the enforcement mission of the Customs Service. Utilizing information collected from Customs inspections, criminal investigations, and other sources, Customs Intelligence Research Specialists conduct extensive research operations pertaining to matters such as narcotics trafficking, terrorism, illegal shipment of arms and high technology to foreign entities, illicit transportation of currency in support of criminal enterprise, money laundering, counterfeit merchandise, import or export fraud, child pornography, smuggling of ozone-depleting substances and other prohibited goods, cargo theft, and other crimes. A variety of automated systems and databases are utilized to facilitate the collection and development of intelligence information. Research findings are communicated in the form of written reports, charts, graphs, spreadsheets, and organized oral presentations to Customs Service personnel, the United States Attorney's Office, grand juries, and other law enforcement agencies.

Qualifications: Applicants must be U.S. citizens. Requirements for appointment to GS-5 level include completion of a four-year course of study leading to a bachelor's degree, OR three years general experience, one year of which was equivalent to GS-4; for GS-7, one full year of graduate education, or superior academic achievement during undergraduate studies, OR one year of specialized experience equivalent to GS-5; for GS-9, a master's degree or two years of graduate education, OR one year of specialized experience equivalent to GS-7; for GS-11, a Ph.D. or equivalent doctoral degree, or three years of graduate education, OR one year of specialized experience equivalent to GS-9; and for GS-12, one year of specialized experience equivalent to GS-11. In some cases, qualifying education may be substituted for experience, and vice versa. Tentative appointees must pass a background investigation and drug screening test, and qualify for a security clearance.

Training: Customs Intelligence Research Specialists attend a five-week Customs Basic Intelligence School at the Federal Law Enforcement Training Center in Glynco, Georgia, which covers subjects such as Customs laws, legal aspects of intelligence operations, intelligence collection and cycles, link analysis and charting, event analysis, intelligence computer programs, crime scene investigation, interviewing and interrogation, oral briefing techniques, computer security, and terrorism. In-service training may include instruction concerning customs fraud, smuggling operations, legal issues and updates, advanced intelligence analysis, case methodologies, and other pertinent and timely subjects.

Contact: U.S. Customs Service, Department of the Treasury, 1300 Pennsylvania Avenue NW; Washington, DC 20229. Phone: 202-927-1250. World Wide Web: http://www.customs.ustreas.gov/.

INTELLIGENCE SPECIALIST (GS-0132)
NAVAL CRIMINAL INVESTIGATIVE SERVICE
U.S. DEPARTMENT OF DEFENSE

Overview: Intelligence Specialists of the Naval Criminal Investigative Service (NCIS) perform intelligence analysis and production tasks relative to criminal investigations, counterintelligence, and terrorism activities in support of Navy and Marine Corps operations worldwide. NCIS Intelligence Specialists develop, collate, and analyze data collected from criminal investigations and other sources; develop investigative targets; perform link analysis to determine relationships among information gathered by investigators; produce analytical reviews, flow charts, spreadsheets and time-lines of complex cases; operate automated databases; assist in prosecution of criminal cases; design preventive and proactive initiatives; monitor trends in criminal activity; participate in interagency conferences; maintain liaison with other agencies in the intelligence community to discuss mutual intelligence problems and operations; and review case files of counterintelligence investigations and operations to evaluate, extract, and disseminate information and provide analytical support. Research results are frequently provided to other federal, state, and local law enforcement agencies on a reciprocal basis. This is a civilian position and does not require active duty military service.

Qualifications: Applicants must be U.S. citizens. Requirements for appointment to GS-5 level include completion of a four-year course of study leading to a bachelor's degree, OR three years general experience, one year of which was equivalent to GS-4; for GS-7, one full year of graduate education, or superior academic achievement during undergraduate studies, OR one year of specialized experience equivalent to GS-5; for GS-9, a master's degree or two years of graduate education, OR one year of specialized experience equivalent to GS-7; for GS-11, a Ph.D. or equivalent doctoral degree, or three years of graduate education, OR one year of specialized experience equivalent to GS-9; and for GS-12, one year of specialized experience equivalent to GS-11. In some cases, qualifying education may be substituted for experience, and vice versa. Tentative appointees must pass a background investigation and drug screening test, and qualify for a top-secret security clearance. A polygraph exam may also be required.

Training: NCIS Intelligence Specialists complete approximately ten weeks of initial training which is conducted by the Defense Intelligence Agency in Washington, D.C. This training focuses on intelligence analysis fundamentals, tools and techniques utilized in data collection, terrorist threats and issues, counterterrorism analysis, civilian and military intelligence activities, functions and interdependent relationships among counterintelligence organizations, and other subjects. In-service training may include similar courses and updates, conferences, and symposia.

Contact: Naval Criminal Investigative Service, 716 East Sicard Street SE, Building 111, Washington Navy Yard; Washington, DC 20388. Phone: 202-433-9162. World Wide Web: http://www.ncis.navy.mil/.

Chapter Eight

UNIFORMED LAW ENFORCEMENT OFFICERS

Only in a police state is the job of a policeman easy.
– ORSON WELLES

UNIFORMED FEDERAL LAW ENFORCEMENT OFFICERS ENSURE compliance with and enforce laws, regulations, and agency rules while providing a visible deterrent to criminal activity on and around federal property. These officers are primarily responsible for preserving the peace and protecting civil rights; conducting patrols; preventing, detecting, and investigating crimes; arresting violators; assisting in the prosecution of criminals; and providing assistance to citizens in emergency situations. Many officers also perform tasks such as controlling traffic, investigating accidents, responding to crime scenes, engaging in search and rescue missions, screening visitors in federal buildings, monitoring electronic security devices that provide surveillance and alarm protection, working with juveniles, counseling persons in need of assistance, completing written reports, and managing activities related to wildlife and natural resources.

The work of uniformed officers is performed in a wide variety of settings which range from federally owned and leased office buildings to military installations, Indian reservations, hospitals, training academies, national parks and refuges, forests, public lands, international borders, campgrounds, recreational areas, historic residences and landmarks, train tracks and stations, roads and highways, power plants and hydroelectric dams, and printing facilities, among others. With very few exceptions, uniformed federal law enforcement officers are authorized to carry firearms and make arrests.

Thirty-four uniformed law enforcement officer careers are profiled in this chapter, including Border Patrol Agents, Canine Enforcement Officers, Capitol Police Officers, Customs Inspectors, Immigration Inspectors, Law Enforcement Officers, Law Enforcement Rangers, Mint Police Officers, Park Police Officers, Park Rangers, Police Officers, Postal Police Officers, Refuge Law Enforcement Officers, River Rangers, and Secret Service Uniformed Division Officers.

BORDER PATROL AGENT (GS-1896)
UNITED STATES BORDER PATROL
IMMIGRATION AND NATURALIZATION SERVICE
U.S. DEPARTMENT OF JUSTICE

Overview: The primary mission of the United States Border Patrol (USBP) is to detect and prevent the smuggling and unlawful entry of undocumented aliens into the United States, and to apprehend persons found in the United States in violation of immigration laws. As the mobile, uniformed enforcement arm of the Immigration and Naturalization Service, USBP Agents patrol 8,000 miles of international boundaries in vehicles, aircraft and boats, as well as on foot and horseback. In search of undocumented aliens, USBP Agents conduct surveillance, farm and ranch inspections, traffic observation, city patrols, respond to electronic sensor alarms, use infrared scopes and low-light camera systems at night, and follow tracks and other physical evidence. In an effort to intercept drug smugglers, USBP Agents carry out extensive drug interdiction efforts along the nation's land borders. Law enforcement efforts are often coordinated with other federal, state and local agencies. Initial tour-of-duty is normally along the U.S. border with Mexico. USBP Agents are authorized to conduct undercover operations, carry firearms and make arrests; are covered under special retirement provisions for law enforcement officers; and are eligible to receive Administratively Uncontrollable Overtime Pay.

Qualifications: Applicants must be U.S. citizens, at least twenty-one years of age, and under the age of thirty-seven. (Candidates over age thirty-seven who have previous service creditable under special law enforcement retirement provisions may also be eligible.) Eyesight requirements include uncorrected distant visual acuity of at least 20/70 (Snellen) in each eye, and at least 20/20 in both eyes with correction. Corrected or uncorrected near vision must be sufficient to read Jaeger Type 2 at 14 inches. Normal peripheral vision and ability to distinguish shades of color are required. A history of Orthokeratology or Radial Keratotomy surgery is disqualifying. Hearing loss must not exceed 30 decibels at 500, 1000, and 2000 Hz. Requirements for appointment to GS-5 level include a bachelor's degree, OR one year of general experience equivalent to GS-4; for GS-7, one full year of graduate education or superior academic achievement during undergraduate studies, OR one year of law enforcement-related experience equivalent to GS-5; and for GS-9, one year of law enforcement-related experience equivalent to GS-7. In some cases, qualifying education may be substituted for experience, and vice versa. Applicants must pass written examinations (see Chapter 1) and an oral interview, and tentative appointees must pass a drug screening test and medical exam.

Training: USBP Agents attend an eighteen-week Border Patrol Academy at the Federal Law Enforcement Training Center in Glynco, Georgia, which includes courses in immigration law, INS procedures, Spanish language, report writing, behavioral science, confrontation management, firearms, physical fitness, defensive tactics, driving, and other subjects. In-service training may include courses in Spanish language, criminal law, laws of arrest, search and seizure, patrol techniques, first aid, firearms proficiency, arrest techniques, and defensive tactics.

Contact: U.S. Border Patrol, Immigration and Naturalization Service, 425 I Street NW; Washington, DC 20536. Phone: 202-616-1964. World Wide Web: http://www.ins.usdoj.gov/.

CANINE ENFORCEMENT OFFICER (GS-1801)
UNITED STATES CUSTOMS SERVICE
U.S. DEPARTMENT OF THE TREASURY

Overview: Among the most unique operations of the United States Customs Service is the Canine Program Team, which consists of uniformed Canine Enforcement Officers (CEO) and narcotics or explosives detector dogs. Customs CEOs train and use detector dogs to enforce Customs laws and regulations at various air, sea and land border ports of entry throughout the United States. Canine Program Teams save countless staff-hours by efficiently detecting smuggled narcotics, weapons, explosives, merchandise, agricultural products and contraband in motor vehicles, mail, aircraft, unaccompanied baggage, and cargo ships. A Canine Enforcement

Team, composed of one dog and a CEO, is capable of checking hundreds of packages in thirty minutes. Duties may also include processing passengers at airports. CEOs are authorized to carry firearms and make arrests. Law enforcement efforts are often coordinated with Customs Inspectors and Special Agents, task force members, and other federal, state and local law enforcement agencies.

Qualifications: Applicants must be U.S. citizens. Eyesight requirements include distant visual acuity of at least 20/40 (Snellen) in one eye and 20/100 in the other eye, with or without correction; and the ability to distinguish shades of color. Near vision should test Jaeger 4 in both eyes, correction permitted. Hearing loss must not exceed 30 decibels at 500, 1000, and 2000 Hz. Applicants must be able to hear the spoken voice at 20 feet and the whispered voice at 15 feet in each ear without a hearing aid. Requirements for appointment to GS-5 level include a bachelor's degree, OR three years of general experience; and for GS-7, one full year of graduate education which included at least 15 semester hours of coursework in law enforcement or criminal justice, OR one year of specialized experience involving the training, handling, and employment of dogs in patrol duty or the detection of drugs or explosives, equivalent to GS-5. (Qualifying prior completion of canine patrol or sentry dog training may be substituted for law enforcement experience.) Customs Inspectors lacking dog handling experience may also qualify, subject to successful completion of the CEO basic training program. Tentative appointees must pass a drug screening test, physical exam, medical exam, and background investigation.

Training: Canine Enforcement Officers attend a fifteen-week Basic Narcotics Detection Course at the U.S. Customs Canine Enforcement Training Center in Front Royal, Virginia (see Chapter 16), which includes instruction in canine behavior and handling; detection of heroin, cocaine, marijuana, hashish, and methamphetamine; search techniques for vehicles, aircraft, freight, luggage, mail and other locations; Customs inspection and control procedures; passenger and cargo facilitation; Customs law; the Treasury Enforcement Communications System; firearms; and non-lethal defense techniques. In-service training may include courses and practical exercises similar to those of the Basic course, as well as other training needed to maintain or enhance canine enforcement skills.

Contact: U.S. Customs Service, Department of the Treasury, 1300 Pennsylvania Ave. NW; Washington, DC 20229. Phone: 202-927-1250. World Wide Web: http://www.customs.ustreas.gov/.

CAPITOL POLICE OFFICER
PATROL DIVISION
U.S. CAPITOL POLICE

Overview: Officers of the United States Capitol Police (USCP) are responsible for protecting life and property; preventing, detecting and investigating criminal acts; and enforcing traffic regulations within a 190-acre area which encompasses the United States Capitol Building, a large complex of congressional buildings, and a number of area parks and roadways. As the agency with the sole statutory responsibility for providing protective and law enforcement services for the U.S. Congress, USCP Officers monitor closed circuit television surveillance monitors, alarms, and intrusion detection devices; screen visitors and packages entering buildings; perform foot and vehicular patrols; respond to crimes in progress, disturbances, protests and demonstrations, bomb threats, and emergency situations; conduct traffic control and enforcement; assist the U.S. Secret Service with operations for the protection of the President, Vice President, immediate family members of the President and Vice President, and visiting dignitaries on Capitol grounds; and provide personal protection for members of Congress and their families in the Capitol complex and throughout the United States. In order to provide for the protection of national security information, the USCP conducts operations to ensure that Congress operates free from the threat of surreptitious and clandestine listening devices and monitoring systems. Special operations include assignments in the areas of Protective Services, Criminal or Special Investigations, Drug Enforcement, Containment and Emergency Response Team, Canine Patrol, Hazardous Devices and Electronic Countermeasures, and Mountain Bicycle Patrol. USCP Officers are authorized to carry firearms and make arrests. Salary for this position does not fall under the General Schedule pay system, although it is similar to GS-0083 Police Officer positions of other federal law enforcement agencies.

Qualifications: Applicants must be U.S. citizens; possess a high school diploma or GED certificate; and be at least twenty-one years of age and under the age of thirty-seven at the time of appointment. (The maximum entry age may be waived with prior qualifying federal law enforcement experience.) Uncorrected visual acuity must be no worse than 20/100 (Snellen), correctable to 20/20 in each eye. Weight must be proportionate to height. Applicants must pass a written exam, oral interview, polygraph exam, background investigation, physical exam, and psychological evaluation. The written exam assesses reading comprehension, arithmetic, writing, grammar, punctuation, and spelling skills.

Training: USCP Officers attend the nine-week Basic Police Training Program at the Federal Law Enforcement Training Center in Glynco, Georgia (see Chapter 16). Basic training is followed by a ten-week course at the Capitol Police Training Academy in Washington, D.C., which focuses on the District of Columbia Criminal Code and traffic laws. This course is followed by a ten-week field training program in which new Officers perform their duties accompanied by experienced Field Training Officers. In-service training may include courses in public relations, legal issues and updates, protective operations, firearms proficiency, first aid, physical fitness and defensive tactics, and other subjects.

Contact: Recruiting Section, United States Capitol Police, 119 D Street NE; Washington, DC 20510. Phone: 202-224-9819. World Wide Web: No Web site at this time.

CUSTOMS INSPECTOR (GS-1890)
UNITED STATES CUSTOMS SERVICE
U.S. DEPARTMENT OF THE TREASURY

Overview: United Sates Customs Inspectors are responsible for enforcement of the Tariff Act and other laws governing the importation or exportation of merchandise and other goods. Located at approximately 300 air, sea and land border ports of entry throughout the United States, Customs Inspectors conduct personal interviews and search persons, cargo, ships, aircraft, and motor vehicles entering or leaving the United States to ensure that all Customs requirements are met; seize narcotics, currency, equipment, vehicles, vessels, and contraband; and apprehend violators of applicable laws. To ensure compliance with tariff laws and to prevent smuggling, Inspectors clear individual baggage of international travelers and oversee the unloading of all types of commercial shipments. This places Inspectors in contact not only with travelers, but also with ship crew members, importers, and exporters. Responsibilities also include collection of duties, excise taxes, fees and penalties on imported goods and, at many ports of entry, inspection of persons arriving in the United States to ensure compliance with immigration laws. Customs Inspectors are authorized to carry firearms and make arrests. Operations may also be coordinated with Customs Special Agents and Canine Enforcement Officers, Immigration Inspectors and Special Agents, and other federal, state and local law enforcement officers.

Qualifications: Applicants must be U.S. citizens. Eyesight requirements include corrected or uncorrected distant vision of at least 20/40 (Snellen) in one eye and 20/100 in the other eye, as well as the ability to distinguish shades of color. Near vision should test Jaeger 4 in both eyes, correction permitted. Hearing loss must not exceed 30 decibels at 500, 1000, and 2000 Hz. Applicants must be able to hear the spoken voice at 20 feet and the whispered voice at 15 feet in each ear without a hearing aid. Requirements for appointment to GS-5 level include a bachelor's degree, OR three years of general experience, of which one year was equivalent to GS-4; for GS-7, one full year of graduate education or superior academic achievement during undergraduate studies, OR one year of specialized experience that entailed the performance of import/export or compliance/regulatory work which was equivalent to GS-5; and for GS-9, a master's degree or two years of graduate education, OR one year of specialized experience (as described above) which was equivalent to GS-7. Experience and education may be combined to meet minimum requirements. Tentative appointees must pass a drug screening test, physical exam, medical exam, personal interview, and background investigation.

Training: Customs Inspectors attend an eleven-week Customs Inspector Basic Training Program at the Federal Law Enforcement Training Center in Glynco, Georgia, which includes courses in Customs inspection, entry, and control procedures; passenger processing; Customs law; search and seizure; arrest authority and techniques; enforcement operations; the Treasury Enforcement Communications System; behavioral sciences;

bombs and explosives; detection of contraband, narcotics, and dangerous drugs; firearms; physical fitness; and non-lethal defense techniques. In-service training may include courses relating to border search techniques, inspection profiling, interviewing techniques, hazardous material cargo, blood-borne pathogens, law, and firearms.

Contact: United States Customs Service, 1300 Pennsylvania Ave. NW; Washington, DC 20229. Phone: 202-927-1250. World Wide Web: http://www.customs.ustreas.gov/.

IMMIGRATION INSPECTOR (GS-1816)
UNITED STATES IMMIGRATION AND NATURALIZATION SERVICE
U.S. DEPARTMENT OF JUSTICE

Overview: To ensure compliance with the Immigration and Nationality Act, United States Immigration and Naturalization Service (INS) Inspectors are responsible for the screening of all travelers arriving at ports of entry in the United States. The primary functions of Immigration Inspectors are to determine admissibility of persons seeking to enter the United States, and to detect the use of fraudulent citizenship or immigration documents. Inspections are performed at approximately 300 air, sea, and land border ports of entry in the United States, as well as pre-inspection locations outside the United States. Immigration Inspectors process between 330-500 million persons seeking entry to the U.S. each year. At many ports of entry, Immigration Inspectors also search persons, cargo, ships, aircraft, and motor vehicles entering the country to detect the presence of smuggled aliens and to ensure that Customs requirements are met; seize narcotics, currency, vehicles, vessels, equipment and contraband; and apprehend violators of applicable laws. Inspectors are authorized to carry firearms and make arrests. Operations may be coordinated with INS Special Agents, Border Patrol Agents, Customs Inspectors and Special Agents, and other federal, state and local law enforcement officers.

Qualifications: Applicants must be U.S. citizens. Requirements for appointment to GS-5 level include a bachelor's degree, OR three years general experience, one year of which was equivalent to GS-4; for GS-7, one full year of graduate education or superior academic achievement during undergraduate studies, OR one year of specialized experience equivalent to GS-5; for GS-9, a master's degree or two years of graduate education, OR one year of specialized experience equivalent to GS-7; and for GS-11, a Ph.D. or equivalent doctoral degree, or three years of graduate education, OR one year of specialized experience equivalent to GS-9. Experience and education may be combined to meet minimum requirements. Tentative appointees must pass a medical exam, drug screening test, background investigation, and qualify for a security clearance.

Training: Immigration Inspectors attend the thirteen-week Immigration Officer Basic Training Course at the Federal Law Enforcement Training Center (FLETC) in Glynco, Georgia (see Chapter 16), followed immediately by a five-week Spanish Language course at FLETC. Part-time/seasonal Inspectors attend a four-week basic course either at their duty-station or one of the INS training centers. In-service training may include instruction in subjects such as passport fraud and questioned documents, interviewing techniques, criminal law, laws of arrest, inspection procedures, first aid, firearms proficiency, and other subjects.

Contact: U.S. Immigration and Naturalization Service, Department of Justice, 425 I Street NW; Washington, DC 20536. Phone: 202-514-4316. World Wide Web: http://www.ins.usdoj.gov/.

LAW ENFORCEMENT OFFICER (GS-1802)
FOREST SERVICE
U.S. DEPARTMENT OF AGRICULTURE

Overview: Law Enforcement Officers of the USDA Forest Service conduct patrols to prevent, detect and enforce violations of federal laws and regulations concerning the protection and safe uses of National Forest System lands and resources. Forest Service Law Enforcement Officers have jurisdiction over 191 million acres of national forests, grasslands, and land utilization projects managed by the Forest Service in forty-four states, the Virgin Islands, and Puerto Rico. Primary responsibilities include general patrol; responding to motor vehicle accidents, plane crashes, and medical emergencies; engaging in search and rescue operations; and enforcing violations relating to natural resources laws, timber theft, arson, unauthorized mining claims, dumping of hazardous materials, marijuana cultivation, production of illegal drugs in clandestine laboratories, and provisions of the Archeological Resources Protection Act. Forest Service Law Enforcement Officers are authorized to carry firearms and make arrests. Operations may be coordinated with Forest Service Special Agents and other federal, state and local law enforcement agencies. This position is covered under special retirement provisions for law enforcement officers.

Qualifications: Applicants must be U.S. citizens; at least twenty-one years of age, and under the age of thirty-seven. (Candidates over age thirty-seven who have previous service creditable under special law enforcement retirement provisions may also be eligible.) Requirements for appointment to GS-5 include four years of education above high school, OR one year of specialized experience equivalent to at least GS-4; and for grades GS-6 through GS-11, one year of specialized experience equivalent to the next lower grade level. Applicants are rated on their experience, education, training, employment performance evaluations, and awards as they relate to the position. Experience and education may be combined to meet total experience requirements for positions at grade GS-5. Tentative appointees must pass a Physical Efficiency Battery (PEB), drug screening test, medical exam, and background investigation. The PEB consists of five physical fitness items performed during an evaluation session, and measures trunk flexibility (sit and reach test), body fat (skinfold technique), speed and agility (Illinois Agility Test), aerobic capacity (1.5 mile run), and upper body strength (bench press). A passing score of at least 70 percent must be attained in the PEB both prior to and during basic training.

Training: Forest Service Law Enforcement Officers attend the twelve-week Land Management Law Enforcement Training Program at the Federal Law Enforcement Training Center (FLETC) in Glynco, Georgia (see Chapter 16), followed by a two-week course at FLETC which covers various aspects of Forest Service law enforcement operations. In-service training may include courses concerned with officer survival, non-lethal control techniques, impact weapons, aerosol subject restraints, emergency vehicle operation, firearms proficiency, first aid, controlled substance investigations, criminal and civil law, photography, protection of archaeological resources, search and rescue management, and the Spanish language.

Contact: For further information, contact the regional or local Forest Service office where employment is sought, or: USDA Forest Service, P.O. Box 96090; Washington, DC 20090. Phone: 202-720-3760. World Wide Web: http://www.fs.fed.us. E-mail: mailroom/wo@fs.fed.us.

LAW ENFORCEMENT RANGER (GS-1801)
BUREAU OF LAND MANAGEMENT
U.S. DEPARTMENT OF THE INTERIOR

Overview: Law Enforcement Rangers of the Bureau of Land Management (BLM) enforce federal laws and regulations relating to public lands and resources managed by the Bureau. Law enforcement activities are conducted on 270 million acres of public lands and an additional 300 million acres where mineral rights are owned by the federal government. In carrying out the BLM Office of Law Enforcement mission, as well as objectives of the Federal Land Policy and Management Act of 1976, BLM Law Enforcement Rangers perform general patrol in marked vehicles or aircraft, or on foot, horseback, motorcycles, or all-terrain vehicles; respond to calls for service, accidents, and emergencies; engage in search and rescue operations; and enforce violations relating to natural resources offenses, trespassing, timber theft, arson, and crimes involving drug control laws as they relate to lands and resources managed by the Bureau. Field work is often performed over remote or rugged terrain; in conservation, wilderness, canyon, isolated and desert areas; on wild and scenic rivers; and at high altitudes where climatic conditions are variable and extreme. BLM Law Enforcement Rangers are authorized to carry firearms and make arrests. Operations may be coordinated with BLM Special Agents and other federal, state and local law enforcement agencies. This position is covered under special retirement provisions for law enforcement officers.

Qualifications: Applicants must be U.S. citizens; at least twenty-one years of age, and under the age of thirty-seven. (Candidates over age thirty-seven who have previous service creditable under special law enforcement retirement provisions may also be eligible.) Eyesight requirements include distant vision of at least 20/40 (Snellen) in one eye and 20/100 in the other eye, with or without correction; near vision sufficient to read printed material the size of typewritten characters, with or without correction; and the ability to distinguish shades of colors. Hearing loss must not exceed 30 decibels in either ear at 500, 1000, or 2000 Hz ranges. Requirements for appointment to GS-5 level include a bachelor's degree, OR three years general experience, one year of which was equivalent to GS-4; for GS-7, one full year of graduate education or superior academic achievement during undergraduate studies, OR one year of law enforcement-related experience equivalent to GS-5; for GS-9, a master's degree or two years of graduate education, OR one year of law enforcement-related experience equivalent to GS-7. In some cases, qualifying education may be substituted for experience, and vice versa. Tentative appointees must qualify for a top-secret security clearance, and pass a drug screening test and medical exam.

Training: BLM Law Enforcement Rangers attend the twelve-week Land Management Law Enforcement Training Program at the Federal Law Enforcement Training Center in Glynco, Georgia (see Chapter 16). Law Enforcement Rangers also receive at least forty hours of in-service training annually, including courses in subjects such as evidence photography, archaeological crime scene processing, domestic terrorism, legal updates, search and rescue techniques, judgment pistol shooting, firearms proficiency, defensive tactics, and the protection of natural resources.

Contact: Office of Law Enforcement, Bureau of Land Management, Department of the Interior; Washington, DC 20240. Phone: 202-208-3710. World Wide Web: http://www.blm.gov/.

MINT POLICE OFFICER
UNITED STATES MINT
U.S. DEPARTMENT OF THE TREASURY

Overview: The United States Mint (USM) produces and circulates coinage to allow the nation to conduct its trade and commerce. As the law enforcement and security force for USM operations, Mint Police Officers are responsible for the protection of USM assets, plant facilities, property, personnel, and visitors at facilities in Denver, Philadelphia, San Francisco, Fort Knox, and West Point. In carrying out the mission of the USM Police Division, Mint Police Officers perform static post, vehicular, and foot patrol duty; screen visitors entering USM facilities; observe closed-circuit surveillance monitors; maintain a control room post; respond to emergency situations, bomb threats, fires, crimes in progress, and calls for service; interview witnesses and suspects; prepare written reports; perform searches and seizures; escort visitors and contractors through restricted areas; and oversee the transfer of coinage to armored cars for shipment to Federal Reserve Banks. To protect the Mint from terrorism and other threats, Mint Police security reviews have been coordinated with the Secret Service, FBI, and Bureau of Alcohol, Tobacco and Firearms. Mint Police Officers are authorized to carry firearms and make arrests. Salary for this position does not fall under the General Schedule pay system, although it is similar to GS-0083 Police Officer positions of other federal law enforcement agencies.

Qualifications: Applicants must be U.S. citizens. Eyesight requirements include uncorrected distant vision of at least 20/70 (Snellen) in each eye, with correction to at least 20/20; corrected or uncorrected near vision sufficient to read Jaeger Type 2 at 14 inches; ability to distinguish basic colors; and normal depth perception. Hearing loss must not exceed 30 decibels in one ear at 500, 1000, or 2000 Hz. (Use of a hearing aid is permitted in the other ear.) Requirements for appointment to grade TR-6 include one year of specialized experience equivalent to TR-5, OR four years of undergraduate coursework leading to a bachelor's degree related to the duties of the position; and for grades TR-7 through TR-12, one year of specialized experience equivalent to the next lower grade level. Prior completion of a police academy training program may be substituted for three months of specialized experience or six months of general experience for appointment to grade TR-6. No substitution of education or training may be made for the required specialized experience for appointment to TR-7 and above. Tentative appointees must pass a drug screening test, medical exam, and background investigation. Selectees must qualify as a marksman with the 9mm semiautomatic handgun, 12-gauge shotgun, Uzi submachine gun, and non-lethal weapons.

Training: Mint Police Officers attend the nine-week Basic Police Training Program at the Federal Law Enforcement Training Center in Glynco, Georgia (see Chapter 16). In-service training may include courses in officer safety and survival, communications, interviewing, criminal law, laws of arrest and detention, terrorism, physical security, firearms proficiency, first aid, and defensive tactics. Weapons training includes instruction and qualification with pistols, shotguns, Uzi submachine guns, and non-lethal weapons.

Contact: United States Mint, Department of the Treasury, Judiciary Square Building, 633 Third Street NW; Washington, DC 20220. Phone: 202-874-9696. World Wide Web: http://www.treas.gov/mint/.

PARK POLICE OFFICER
UNITED STATES PARK POLICE
U.S. DEPARTMENT OF THE INTERIOR

Overview: As a law enforcement unit of the National Park Service, the United States Park Police (USPP) exercises jurisdiction over National Park Service areas and certain other federal and state lands. USPP Officers provide a wide range of uniformed patrol and law enforcement services in the vicinity of national parks, monuments, memorials, historic residences, highways and other federal property in Washington, D.C., and Maryland; within the Gateway National Recreation Area in New York City; and also on the grounds of the Golden Gate National Recreation Area in San Francisco. USPP Officers perform vehicular, horse-mounted and foot patrol duty; respond to emergencies and other calls for service; enforce traffic laws; investigate traffic accidents and crimes; perform crowd control at special events and large public gatherings; and frequently participate in protective operations for the President and Vice President of the United States and visiting dignitaries. Experienced USPP Officers may be assigned to the Special Forces Branch, which consists of a Special Weapons and Tactics (SWAT) team and motorcycle, aviation, and canine units; or the Criminal Investigations Branch, which comprises Sections including Major Crimes, Identification, Special Investigations, Narcotics and Vice, and Asset Forfeiture. USPP Officers are authorized to carry firearms and make arrests. Salary for this position does not fall under the General Schedule pay system, although it is similar to those of GS-0083 police officers of other federal agencies.

Qualifications: Applicants must be U.S. citizens; at least twenty-one years of age, and under the age of 35; and possess a high school diploma. Requirements also include two years of progressively responsible experience that has demonstrated the ability to learn and apply detailed and complex regulations and procedures, OR two years active duty military experience, OR two years of education above high school, OR a combination of acceptable experience and education of at least two years. Eyesight requirements include uncorrected distant vision of at least 20/100 (Snellen), and at least 20/20 with correction. Applicants must pass a written examination (see Chapter 1), oral interview, physical exam, medical exam, and drug screening test.

Training: Park Police Officers attend an eighteen-week USPP Basic Training Program at the Federal Law Enforcement Training Center (FLETC) in Glynco, Georgia, which is conducted by FLETC and USPP staff. This course includes instruction in subjects such as patrol procedures, crowd control, criminal law, report writing, hostage situations, communications, stress, narcotics, officer safety and survival, firearms, driver training, physical fitness, and defensive tactics. In-service training includes courses which cover automobile theft, domestic assault, police baton techniques, legal issues and updates, defensive tactics, CPR, firearms proficiency, and other subjects.

Contact: U.S. Park Police, National Park Service, 1100 Ohio Drive SW; Washington, DC 20240. Phone: 202-208-3710. World Wide Web: http://www.doi.gov/u.s.park.police/.

PARK RANGER (GS-0025)
NATIONAL PARK SERVICE
U.S. DEPARTMENT OF THE INTERIOR

Overview: National Park Service (NPS) Park Rangers are responsible for law enforcement and natural resources management duties at more than 300 locations that encompass the National Park System and other federally-managed sites. NPS Park Rangers are stationed at national parks and monuments, scenic parkways, preserves, trails, campgrounds, battlefields, sea shores, lakeshores, recreational areas, and historic sites nation-wide. Primary responsibilities include conducting patrols in vehicles or on foot, bicycles, or horseback; responding to traffic accidents, medical emergencies, and fires; performing traffic enforcement and control; investigating offenses such as larceny, assault, vandalism, trespassing, weapons offenses, and drug trafficking; responding to medical emergencies; and performing search and rescue operations and crowd control. Natural resource management responsibilities include the presentation of educational programs to park visitors concerning points of interest, historical and natural resources, and park activities; and tasks related to habitat and wildlife monitoring, rescue and rehabilitation. The mix of duties depends upon the size and particular needs of areas served. The NPS employs full-time, part-time and seasonal Rangers, including those with or without law enforcement authority. Full-time Rangers assigned to law enforcement details are authorized to carry firearms and make arrests, and are covered under special retirement provisions for law enforcement officers.

Qualifications: Applicants must be U.S. citizens, and at least twenty-one years of age. Appointees to permanent full-time positions assigned to law enforcement details must be under the age of thirty-seven. (Candidates over age thirty-seven who have previous service creditable under special law enforcement retirement provisions may also be eligible.) Requirements for appointment to GS-4 include six months of general experience and six months of specialized experience, OR two years of education above high school related to the occupation; for GS-5, four years of undergraduate coursework leading to a bachelor's degree, with twenty-four semester hours of coursework related to the occupation, OR one year of specialized experience equivalent to GS-4; for GS-7, one year of graduate education related to the occupation, OR superior academic achievement during undergraduate studies, OR one year of specialized experience equivalent to GS-5; for GS-9, two years of graduate education or a master's degree related to the occupation, OR one year of specialized experience equivalent to GS-7; for GS-11, three years of graduate education or a Ph.D. or equivalent doctoral degree related to the occupation, OR one year of specialized experience equivalent to GS-9; and for GS-12, one year of specialized experience equivalent to GS-11. In some cases, qualifying education may be substituted for experience, and vice versa. Tentative appointees must pass a drug screening test and background investigation.

Training: NPS Park Rangers attend the twelve-week Land Management Law Enforcement Training Program at the Federal Law Enforcement Training Center in Glynco, Georgia (see Chapter 16). Park Rangers also receive a minimum of forty hours of in-service training annually, including courses in subjects such as traffic accident investigation, criminal law, search and seizure, laws of arrest, patrol techniques, firearms proficiency, defensive tactics, and first aid.

Contact: National Park Service, Department of the Interior, P.O. Box 37127; Washington, DC 20013. Phone: 202-208-6843. World Wide Web: http://www.nps.gov/.

POLICE OFFICER
NATIONAL INSTITUTE OF STANDARDS AND TECHNOLOGY
U.S. DEPARTMENT OF COMMERCE

Overview: The National Institute of Standards and Technology (NIST) assists industry in developing technology to improve product quality, modernize manufacturing processes, ensure product reliability, and facilitate rapid commercialization of products based on new scientific discoveries. NIST Police Officers are responsible for the protection of NIST personnel, visitors, facilities, and property on campuses in Gaithersburg, Maryland, and Boulder, Colorado. Law enforcement and public welfare functions include general patrol; detection and investigation of federal and state crimes; traffic control and enforcement; parking control; responding to emergency situations, accidents, fires, and other incidents; accident investigation, and the apprehension of violators. Security duties include the prevention of theft, trespass violations, sabotage, espionage, fire, destruction of property, and accidents. NIST Police Officers are authorized to carry firearms and make arrests. Salary for this position does not fall under the General Schedule pay system, although it is similar to GS-0083 Police Officer positions of other federal law enforcement agencies.

Qualifications: Applicants must be U.S. citizens, have one year of specialized experience involving responsibility for protecting life and property, and have knowledge of criminal law and law enforcement operations. Experience must have been gained either through work with a public police force, as a military police officer, providing visitor protection and law enforcement in parks, as a criminal investigator, or in other work which provided the required knowledge or skills. Experience must have been equivalent to at least the GS-4 level in the federal service. Tentative appointees must qualify for a security clearance and pass a drug screening test, medical exam, and background investigation.

Training: NIST Police Officers attend the nine-week Basic Police Training Program at the Federal Law Enforcement Training Center in Glynco, Georgia (see Chapter 16). In-service training may include courses in security procedures, criminal law, laws of arrest, search and seizure, patrol techniques, traffic accident investigation, defensive tactics, firearms proficiency, and first aid.

Contact: Office of Human Resources Management, National Institute of Standards and Technology, Building 101, Room A123; Gaithersburg, MD 20899. Phone: 301-975-3058. World Wide Web: http://www.nist.gov/. E-mail: inquiries@nist.gov.

POLICE OFFICER (GS-0083)
UNITED STATES ARMY
U.S. DEPARTMENT OF DEFENSE

Overview: Civilian Police Officers of the U.S. Army perform a wide range of law enforcement and security functions at Army installations such as forts, posts, weapons testing facilities, and hospitals. Army Police Officers conduct vehicular and foot patrols; respond to crimes in progress, emergency situations, and accidents; disarm persons committing acts of violence; render first aid and CPR; intervene in domestic disputes and disturbances; detect and investigate federal and state crimes; conduct interviews and interrogations; apprehend violators; perform traffic control and enforcement; conduct traffic accident investigations; and perform physical security inspections and crime prevention tasks. Offenses investigated include assaults, larceny, malicious destruction of property, trespassing, weapons violations, armed robbery, homicide, drug trafficking, sabotage, espionage, and violations of the Uniform Code of Military Justice. Army Police officers are also responsible for controlling access to restricted areas containing highly sensitive or classified information, which if sabotaged or subjected to espionage could have an adverse impact on national security. The range of responsibilities varies depending upon the type of installation and needs of areas served. Army Police Officers are authorized to carry firearms and make arrests for federal and state offenses. While the Army maintains a corps of active duty military police officers, this position does not require active duty service.

Qualifications: Applicants must be U.S. citizens. Requirements for appointment to GS-4 include six months of general experience and six months of specialized experience, OR two years of education above high school with at least twelve semester hours of coursework related to law enforcement, criminal investigation or criminology; for GS-5, one year of specialized experience equivalent to GS-4, OR four years of undergraduate coursework leading to a bachelor's degree related to law enforcement, criminal investigation or criminology; and for GS-6 through GS-9, one year of specialized experience equivalent to the next lower grade level. Prior completion of a police academy training program may be substituted for three months of specialized experience or six months of general experience. No substitution of education or training may be made for the required specialized experience for appointment to GS-6 and above. Applicants must have "good near and distant vision," ability to distinguish basic colors, and ability to hear the conversational voice. Tentative appointees may be required to pass a drug screening test, medical exam, and background investigation.

Training: Depending primarily upon the threat level and nature of responsibilities at the assigned duty station, Army Police Officers attend either a state-certified police academy training program in the state where they will be employed; or the nine-week Basic Police Training Program at the Federal Law Enforcement Training Center in Glynco, Georgia (see Chapter 16); or an in-house training course conducted by Army or Defense Department staff. In-service training may include courses relating to search and seizure, traffic accident investigation, patrol techniques, legal updates, firearms proficiency, defensive tactics, first aid, and other subjects.

Contact: Apply directly to the Army installation where employment is sought, or contact Army Personnel and Employment Service, The Pentagon - Room 3D727; Washington, DC 20310. Phone: 703-695-3383. World Wide Web: http://www.army.mil/.

POLICE OFFICER (GS-0083)
DEFENSE LOGISTICS AGENCY
U.S. DEPARTMENT OF DEFENSE

Overview: The Defense Logistics Agency (DLA) provides supplies to all branches of the military and to a number of federal agencies, and supports their acquisition of weapons and other materiel. DLA Police Officers perform law enforcement and security functions nationwide at Agency installations, such as supply and distribution centers. Responsibilities include a wide range of tasks, such as vehicular and foot patrol; responding to incidents ranging from simple rule violations to felony offenses; taking charge of accident and crimes scenes; responding to calls for service, disturbances, emergency situations, and other incidents; traffic control and enforcement; traffic accident investigation; detection and preliminary investigation of federal and state crimes; and the apprehension of violators. DLA Police officers are also responsible for controlling access to restricted areas and crime prevention tasks. The mix of responsibilities depends upon the characteristics of the installation served. DLA Police Officers are authorized to carry firearms. This is a civilian position and does not require active duty military service.

Qualifications: Applicants must be U.S. citizens. Requirements for appointment to GS-4 include six months of general experience and six months of specialized experience, OR two years of education above high school with at least twelve semester hours of coursework related to law enforcement, criminal investigation or criminology; for GS-5, one year of specialized experience equivalent to GS-4, OR four years of undergraduate coursework leading to a bachelor's degree related to law enforcement, criminal investigation or criminology; and for GS-6 and above, one year of specialized experience equivalent to the next lower grade level. Prior completion of a police academy training program may be substituted for three months of specialized experience or six months of general experience. No substitution of education or training may be made for the required specialized experience for appointment to GS-6 and above. Applicants must have "good near and distant vision," ability to distinguish basic colors, and ability to hear the conversational voice. Tentative appointees may be required to pass a drug screening test, medical exam, and background investigation.

Training: Newly appointed DLA Police Officers attend either the nine-week Basic Police Training Program at the Federal Law Enforcement Training Center in Glynco, Georgia (see Chapter 16), or a state-certified police academy in the state where they will be employed. In-service training may include courses which focus on installation security procedures, driver training, traffic accident investigation, patrol techniques, vehicle stops, legal updates, firearms proficiency, defensive tactics, first aid, and other subjects.

Contact: Direct inquiries to the DLA installation where employment is sought, or contact Defense Logistics Agency, 8725 John J. Kingman Road, Suite 2533; Fort Belvoir, VA 22060. Phone: 703-767-7100. World Wide Web: http://www.dla.mil/.

POLICE OFFICER (GS-0083)
DEFENSE PROTECTIVE SERVICE
U.S. DEPARTMENT OF DEFENSE

Overview: Police Officers of the Defense Protective Service (DPS) perform a variety of law enforcement and security functions at Defense Department facilities in the National Capitol Region, such as the Pentagon, Hoffman Building, Army Materiel Command, and dozens of other buildings. DPS Police Officers perform vehicular and foot patrols; respond to calls for service, alarms and emergency situations; administer first aid and CPR; conduct bomb searches; regulate pedestrian and vehicular traffic, issue citations, and investigate traffic accidents; provide access control at sensitive locations to prevent unauthorized entry; interview complainants and interrogate suspects; prepare written incident and accident reports; and participate in building evacuation drills. Preliminary criminal investigations are also conducted by DPS Police Officers for offenses such as vandalism, armed robbery, assault, larceny, and weapons violations. DPS Police Officers are authorized to carry firearms and make arrests. This is a civilian position and does not require active duty military service.

Qualifications: Applicants must be U.S. citizens. Requirements for appointment to GS-4 include six months of general experience and six months of specialized experience, OR two years of education above high school with at least twelve semester hours of coursework related to the duties of the position; for GS-5, one year of specialized experience equivalent to GS-4, OR four years of undergraduate coursework leading to a bachelor's degree related to the duties of the position; and for GS-6 through GS-9, one year of specialized experience equivalent to the next lower grade level. Prior completion of a police academy training program may be substituted for three months of specialized experience or six months of general experience. No substitution of education or training may be made for the required specialized experience for appointment to GS-6 and above. Applicants must have "good near and distant vision," ability to distinguish basic colors, and ability to hear the conversational voice. Tentative appointees must pass a drug screening test, physical exam, and background investigation.

Training: DPS Police Officers attend the nine-week Basic Police Training Program at the Federal Law Enforcement Training Center in Glynco, Georgia (see Chapter 16). In-service training may include courses in subjects such as criminal law, laws of arrest, traffic accident investigation, firearms proficiency, defensive tactics, and first aid.

Contact: Human Resource Service Center, Department of Defense, 5001 Eisenhower Ave.; Alexandria, VA 22333. Phone: 703-614-4274. World Wide Web: No Web site at this time.

POLICE OFFICER (GS-0083)
UNITED STATES NAVAL ACADEMY
U.S. DEPARTMENT OF DEFENSE

Overview: United States Naval Academy (USNA) Police Officers are responsible for law enforcement and security functions on the grounds of the USNA in Annapolis, Maryland, a 338-acre campus located 33 miles east of Washington, D.C. USNA Police Officers perform vehicular and foot patrols; enforce federal, state and military criminal laws; respond to calls for service, alarms and emergency situations; administer first aid and CPR; take charge of crimes scenes; collect and preserve evidence; interview and take statements from victims, witnesses and suspects; enforce traffic laws and parking regulations; investigate traffic accidents; prepare written incident and accident reports; assist prosecutors with criminal actions; and testify in court proceedings. Incident response may require USNA Police officers to conduct preliminary criminal investigations concerning offenses such as larceny, assault, vandalism, weapons offenses, and trespass violations. USNA Police Officers are authorized to carry firearms and make arrests. This is a civilian position and does not require active duty military service.

Qualifications: Applicants must be U.S. citizens. Requirements for appointment to GS-4 include six months of general experience and six months of specialized experience, OR two years of education above high school with at least twelve semester hours of coursework related to the duties of the position; for GS-5, one year of specialized experience equivalent to GS-4, OR four years of undergraduate coursework leading to a bachelor's degree related to the duties of the position; and for GS-6 through GS-9, one year of specialized experience equivalent to the next lower grade level. Prior completion of a police academy training program may be substituted for three months of specialized experience or six months of general experience. No substitution of education or training may be made for the required specialized experience for appointment to GS-6 and above. Applicants must have "good near and distant vision," ability to distinguish basic colors, and ability to hear the conversational voice. Tentative appointees must pass a drug screening test, physical exam, and background investigation.

Training: Initial training for USNA Police Officers includes a two-week in-house training program which focuses on patrol procedures, motor vehicle stops, criminal law, juvenile law, laws of arrest, domestic violence, arrest and detention procedures, crowd control, bomb threats, traffic enforcement, traffic accident investigation, sex crimes, firearms, expandable batons, defensive tactics, and other subjects. USNA Police Officers may also attend the nine-week Basic Police Training Program at the Federal Law Enforcement Training Center in Glynco, Georgia (see Chapter 16). In-service training consists of at least forty hours of coursework annually, which includes subjects such as terrorism, use of force, report writing, hazardous materials, traffic radar, alcohol traffic enforcement, emergency vehicle operation, public relations, and legal updates.

Contact: Human Resources, U.S. Naval Academy, 181 Wainwright Road; Annapolis, MD 21402. Phone: 410-293-3822. World Wide Web: http://www.nadn.navy.mil/. E-mail: help@chinfo.navy.mil.

POLICE OFFICER (GS-0083)
UNITED STATES NAVY
U.S. DEPARTMENT OF DEFENSE

Overview: United States Navy (USN) Police Officers are responsible for law enforcement and security functions on the grounds of USN installations such as shipyards, air fields, supply centers, hospitals, and communication facilities. Navy Police Officers control the movement of persons and vehicles into and off of USN property and facilities; perform vehicular and foot patrols; respond to calls for service, alarms, and emergency situations; enforce federal, state and military criminal laws; perform undercover and surveillance operations; administer first aid and CPR; take charge of crime scenes and preserve evidence; interview victims, witnesses and suspects, and prepare written statements; enforce traffic laws and parking regulations; investigate traffic accidents; prepare written incident and accident reports; assist prosecutors with criminal actions; and testify in court proceedings. Navy Police Officers also respond to and conduct preliminary investigations of offenses such as theft, assault, armed robbery, sabotage, weapons offenses, and narcotics violations; and are authorized to carry firearms and make arrests. This is a civilian position and does not require active duty military service.

Qualifications: Applicants must be U.S. citizens. Requirements for appointment to GS-4 include six months of general experience and six months of specialized experience, OR two years of education above high school with at least twelve semester hours of coursework related to law enforcement, criminal investigation or criminology; for GS-5, one year of specialized experience equivalent to GS-4, OR four years of undergraduate coursework leading to a bachelor's degree related to law enforcement, criminal investigation or criminology; and for GS-6 through GS-9, one year of specialized experience equivalent to the next lower grade level. Prior completion of a police academy training program may be substituted for three months of specialized experience or six months of general experience. No substitution of education or training may be made for the required specialized experience for appointment to GS-6 and above. Applicants must have "good near and distant vision," ability to distinguish basic colors, and ability to hear the conversational voice. Tentative appointees must pass a drug screening test, physical exam, and background investigation.

Training: Initial training for Navy Police Officers includes either a state-certified police academy training program in the state where they will be employed; or the nine-week Basic Police Training Program at the Federal Law Enforcement Training Center in Glynco, Georgia (see Chapter 16); or an in-house police training course conducted by Navy staff. In-service training may include courses which focus on police science and technology, crime scene processing, criminal investigation, analysis of criminal behavior, tactical operations, police and community relations, criminal law, laws of arrest, search and seizure, traffic accident investigation, firearms proficiency, defensive tactics, first aid, and other subjects.

Contact: Direct inquiries to the Human Resources Office where employment is sought, or contact Office of Information, Department of the Navy; Washington, DC 20350. Phone: 703-697-7391. World Wide Web: http://www.navy.mil/. E-mail: help@chinfo.navy.mil.

POLICE OFFICER
METROPOLITAN POLICE DEPARTMENT
DISTRICT OF COLUMBIA

Overview: Police Officers of the District of Columbia Metropolitan Police Department (MPD) exercise jurisdiction over most areas within the District, with the exception of property under the control of federal entities which maintain their own police departments such as the Supreme Court, U.S. Capitol, Library of Congress, National Zoological Park, and Government Printing Office. While MPD Police Officers are not actually federal employees, they serve as the primary law enforcement agency within the District, which is a federal enclave, and operations are coordinated extensively with federal law enforcement agencies in the metropolitan D.C. area. MPD Police Officers perform all functions traditionally associated with urban police department operations, including vehicular and foot patrols; response to calls for service, crimes in progress and emergency situations; making arrests; traffic control and enforcement; community policing functions; crowd control at demonstrations and public events; VIP protection details; and crime prevention activities. Special assignments include bicycle patrol, motorcycle patrol, canine handler duties, harbor patrol, and assignment to the detective division. Salary for this position does not fall under the General Schedule pay system, although it is similar to GS-0083 Police Officer positions of federal law enforcement agencies.

Qualifications: Applicants must be U.S. citizens; at least twenty-one years of age at the time of appointment; and possess a high school diploma or GED certificate, or have had at least one year of experience as a sworn officer or member of a police department of a city with a population of 500,000 or more persons. Uncorrected visual acuity must be no worse than 20/60 (Snellen) in both eyes, correctable to 20/20. Successful applicants must pass a written exam, physical ability test, medical exam, drug screening test, psychological and psychiatric evaluation, polygraph test, and background investigation. Appointees must be willing to reside within a twenty-five mile radius of the U.S. Capitol.

Training: MPD Police Officers attend a twenty-four week Basic Police Officer Training Course at the MPD Academy, which includes courses in subjects such as criminal law, laws of arrest, search and seizure, traffic regulations, human relations, community policing, ethics, first aid, self defense, firearms proficiency, and emergency vehicle operation. In-service training may include courses in subjects such as criminal law, laws of arrest, traffic accident investigation, firearms proficiency, defensive tactics, and first aid.

Contact: Police Recruiting Unit, Metropolitan Police Department, 6 DC Village Lane SW, Building 1-A; Washington, DC 20032. Phone: 202-645-0445. World Wide Web: No Web site at this time.

POLICE OFFICER (GS-0083)
FEDERAL PROTECTIVE SERVICE
U.S. GENERAL SERVICES ADMINISTRATION

Overview: The Federal Protective Service (FPS) is the law enforcement and security arm of the Public Buildings Service, U.S. General Services Administration (GSA). The Public Buildings Service is responsible for the leasing and management of office space for most federal agencies in the United States, Puerto Rico, and the U.S. Virgin Islands. With responsibility for law enforcement and security operations on GSA-controlled property, FPS Police Officers patrol areas in and around federal facilities in cars, on motorcycles and bicycles, and on foot; monitor intrusion and fire alarm systems, x-ray equipment, metal detectors, and closed-circuit television systems; conduct traffic enforcement and control; respond to traffic accidents, calls for service, crimes in progress, emergency situations, protests, and demonstrations; administer first aid and CPR; conduct undercover and surveillance operations; secure crime scenes; collect and preserve evidence; interview victims and witnesses; interrogate suspects; and process prisoners. FPS Police Officers respond to criminal offenses such as trespassing, theft, robbery, burglary, arson, assault, rape, weapons offenses, vandalism, threats, gambling, drug activity, and homicide. The FPS Special Operations Response Team is trained to manage hostage situations, civil unrest, demonstrations, bomb threats, and counter-terrorism operations. Task force and other operations are conducted jointly with agencies such as the Drug Enforcement Administration, U.S.

Marshals Service, and other federal, state and local law enforcement agencies. FPS Police Officers are authorized to carry firearms and make arrests.

Qualifications: Applicants must be U.S. citizens. Requirements for appointment to GS-5 include one year of specialized experience equivalent to GS-4, OR four years of undergraduate coursework leading to a bachelor's degree related to law enforcement, criminal investigation or criminology; and for GS-6 through GS-9, one year of specialized experience equivalent to the next lower grade level. Prior completion of a police academy training program may be substituted for three months of specialized experience or six months of general experience. No substitution of education or training may be made for the required specialized experience for appointment to GS-6 and above. Applicants must have "good near and distant vision," ability to distinguish basic colors, and ability to hear the conversational voice. Tentative appointees must pass a drug screening test, physical exam, and background investigation.

Training: Newly appointed FPS Police Officers attend the nine-week Basic Police Training Program at the Federal Law Enforcement Training Center (FLETC) in Glynco, Georgia (see Chapter 16). In-service training may include the two-week Advanced Physical Security Training Program at FLETC, as well as courses pertaining to crime prevention, electronic security systems, oral briefing techniques, written communication skills, contract administration, security procedures and equipment, legal issues and updates, firearms proficiency, judgment pistol shooting, defensive tactics, and first aid.

Contact: Federal Protective Service, General Services Administration, 18th and F Streets NW; Washington, DC 20405. Phone: 202-501-0907. World Wide Web: http://www.gsa.gov/pbs/fps/fps.htm.

POLICE OFFICER
UNIFORMED POLICE BRANCH
U.S. GOVERNMENT PRINTING OFFICE

Overview: With operations centered around the largest general printing plant in the world, the U.S. Government Printing Office (GPO) produces and procures printed and electronic publications for Congress and the departments and establishments of the federal government. As the law enforcement branch of the GPO, uniformed Police Officers perform loss prevention functions and provide protection for GPO employees, visitors, buildings, and grounds. Responsibilities include vehicular and foot patrol; responding to intrusion, fire, and other emergency alarms; investigation of terrorist threats, disturbances, accidents, robberies, thefts, assaults, vandalism, and other crimes; coordination of bomb searches; standing guard at money handling facilities; protection of classified materials; rendering first aid and CPR; inspection of briefcases, packages and other containers brought into GPO by employees, visitors, and contractors to prevent the introduction of illegal materials; operation of x-ray and metal detection equipment used to screen incoming and outgoing personnel and property; and investigation of misconduct or violations of laws by GPO employees (not involving fraud, waste, abuse, or mismanagement). GPO Police Officers are authorized to carry firearms and make arrests. Salary for this position does not fall under the General Schedule pay system, although it is similar to GS-0083 Police Officer positions of other federal law enforcement agencies.

Qualifications: Applicants must be U.S. citizens. Requirements for appointment to grade PG-4 include six months of general experience and six months of specialized experience, OR two years of education above high school with at least twelve semester hours of coursework related to law enforcement, criminal investigation or criminology; and for PG-5, one year of specialized experience equivalent to PG-4 which has provided a broad knowledge of police operations, practices and techniques, OR four years of undergraduate coursework leading to a bachelor's degree. Specialized experience must have included making arrests, protecting life and property, maintaining law and order, preventing crime, and investigating accidents. Applicants are rated on the basis of their knowledge, skills, and abilities related to the position; as well as relevant experience, education, training, supervisory appraisal, and job-related awards. Tentative appointees must undergo a physical examination, and pass a background investigation.

Training: GPO Police Officers attend the nine-week Basic Police Training Program at the Federal Law

Enforcement Training Center in Glynco, Georgia (see Chapter 16), and may also attend various in-service training courses throughout their careers.

Contact: Employment Branch, Government Printing Office, 732 North Capitol Street NW; Washington, DC 20401. Phone: 202-512-1118. World Wide Web: http://www.gpo.gov/. E-mail: wwwadmin@www. access.gpo.gov.

POLICE OFFICER (GS-0083)
NATIONAL INSTITUTES OF HEALTH
U.S. DEPARTMENT OF HEALTH AND HUMAN SERVICES

Overview: The Police Branch of the National Institutes of Health (NIH) exercises law enforcement jurisdiction over the NIH campus in Bethesda, Maryland. The NIH enclave consists of 75 buildings on more than 300 acres, and includes a research hospital, outpatient clinic, pediatric treatment center, numerous research and education facilities, and the National Library of Medicine. Uniformed NIH Police Officers perform a wide range of law enforcement and security functions including patrol on foot, bicycles, or in marked and unmarked police cars; response to traffic accidents, calls for service, crimes in progress and emergency situations; coordinating special events and VIP security; traffic enforcement and control; rendering first aid and CPR; and providing police escorts. The Police Investigations Section is staffed by plainclothes detectives who process crime scenes and conduct criminal investigations, surveillance, interviews and interrogations. In addition, NIH Police Canine Teams assist with patrol functions and bomb detection operations. NIH Police Officers are authorized to carry firearms and make arrests.

Qualifications: Applicants must be U.S. citizens. Requirements for appointment to GS-5 include one year of specialized experience equivalent to GS-4, OR four years of undergraduate coursework leading to a bachelor's degree related to law enforcement, criminal investigation or criminology; and for GS-6 through GS-9, one year of specialized experience equivalent to the next lower grade level. Prior completion of a police academy training program may be substituted for three months of specialized experience or six months of general experience. No substitution of education or training may be made for the required specialized experience for appointment to GS-6 and above. Applicants must have "good near and distant vision," ability to distinguish basic colors, and ability to hear the conversational voice. Tentative appointees must pass a physical exam, credit check, and background investigation.

Training: NIH Police Officers attend the nine-week Basic Police Training Program at the Federal Law Enforcement Training Center in Glynco, Georgia (see Chapter 16). In-service training may include courses in traffic enforcement and accident investigation, VIP protection, criminal law, laws of arrest, search and seizure, firearms proficiency, defensive tactics, and first aid.

Contact: Human Resources Branch, National Institutes of Health, 31 Center Drive, Building 31; Bethesda, MD 20892. Phone: 301-496-5685. World Wide Web: http://www.nih.gov/od/ors/dps/police/.

POLICE OFFICER (GS-0083)
BUREAU OF INDIAN AFFAIRS
U.S. DEPARTMENT OF THE INTERIOR

Overview: Bureau of Indian Affairs (BIA) Police Officers are responsible for enforcement of federal, state, tribal and conservation laws on Indian lands, reservations, allotments, and communities throughout Indian country. BIA Police Officers perform vehicular and foot patrols in remote areas, at high altitudes, and over mountains and rugged terrain where climatic conditions are variable and extreme; respond to calls for service, disturbances, traffic accidents, fires, and emergency situations; operate traffic radar and perform traffic enforcement functions; conduct night surveillance using technical equipment in high-crime areas; coordinate traffic and crowd control activities at religious and ceremonial gatherings; and conduct preliminary investigations of offenses such as hunting and fishing violations, larceny, burglary, vandalism, assault, auto theft, child sexual abuse, murder, rape, robbery, liquor violations, and drug trafficking. BIA Police Officers are authorized to carry firearms and make arrests, and are covered under special retirement provisions for law enforcement officers. Indian lands which are served by tribes that maintain their own police departments are not patrolled by BIA Police Officers, although BIA Police assistance may be provided to tribal police agencies upon request.

Qualifications: Under the Indian Reorganization Act of 1934, qualified Indian applicants are given hiring preference for BIA positions, although applications from non-Indian candidates are encouraged. Applicants must be U.S. citizens; at least twenty-one years of age, and under the age of thirty-seven. (Candidates over age thirty-seven who have previous service creditable under special law enforcement retirement provisions may also be eligible.) Requirements for appointment to GS-5 include one year of specialized experience equivalent to GS-4, OR four years of undergraduate coursework leading to a bachelor's degree related to law enforcement, criminal investigation or criminology; and for GS-6 through GS-9, one year of specialized experience equivalent to the next lower grade level. Prior completion of a police academy training program may be substituted for three months of specialized experience or six months of general experience. No substitution of education or training may be made for the required specialized experience for appointment to GS-6 and above. Applicants must have "good near and distant vision," ability to distinguish basic colors, and ability to hear the conversational voice. Tentative appointees must pass a drug screening test, physical exam, and background investigation.

Training: BIA Police Officers attend the sixteen-week BIA Indian Police Academy at the Federal Law Enforcement Training Center in Artesia, New Mexico, which includes instruction in subjects such as Indian country law, conflict management, narcotics violations, officer safety and survival, criminalistics, search and seizure, collection and preservation of evidence, civil rights, detention and arrest, ethics, stress, firearms, defensive tactics, and driving. In-service training may include courses in crime scene investigation, domestic assault, traffic enforcement, accident investigation, police administration, criminal law, laws of arrest, firearms proficiency, defensive tactics, first aid, and other courses relating to law enforcement in the Indian community.

Contact: Direct inquiries to the personnel office where employment is sought, or contact BIA Office of Personnel, Department of the Interior, 1849 C Street NW; Washington, DC 20240. Phone: 202-208-3710. World Wide Web: http://www.doi.gov/bureau-indian-affairs.html.

POLICE OFFICER (GS-0083)
BUREAU OF RECLAMATION
U.S. DEPARTMENT OF THE INTERIOR

Overview: The mission of the Bureau of Reclamation (BR) is to manage, develop, and protect water and related resources in an environmentally and economically sound manner. BR Police Officers are responsible for law enforcement and security functions for the protection of BR facilities, employees, and visitors nationwide. With jurisdiction over water conveyances and distribution facilities, storage reservoirs, and hydroelectric power plants (including the Hoover Dam), BR Police Officers enforce federal and state laws; control access to restricted areas; perform vehicular and foot patrols; monitor alarm systems and intrusion control devices; respond to calls for service, alarms, disturbances, traffic accidents, fires, material spills, and emergency situations; operate fire apparatus; perform first aid and CPR; direct traffic and investigate motor vehicle accidents; secure crime scenes; preserve and collect evidence; conduct investigations, surveillance, interviews and interrogations; and exercise counterterrorism measures. BR Police Officers are authorized to carry firearms and make arrests.

Qualifications: Applicants must be U.S. citizens. Requirements for appointment to GS-4 include six months of general experience and six months of specialized experience, OR two years of education above high school with at least twelve semester hours of coursework related to law enforcement, criminal investigation or criminology; for GS-5, one year of specialized experience equivalent to GS-4, OR four years of undergraduate coursework leading to a bachelor's degree related to law enforcement, criminal investigation or criminology; and for GS-6 through GS-9, one year of specialized experience equivalent to the next lower grade level. Prior completion of a police academy training program may be substituted for three months of specialized experience or six months of general experience. No substitution of education or training may be made for the required specialized experience for appointment to GS-6 and above. Applicants must have "good near and distant vision," ability to distinguish basic colors, and ability to hear the conversational voice. Tentative appointees must pass a drug screening test, physical exam, physical fitness battery, psychological screening, and background investigation.

Training: BR Police Officers attend the twelve-week Land Management Law Enforcement Training Program at the Federal Law Enforcement Training Center in Glynco, Georgia (see Chapter 16). In-service training may include courses in traffic enforcement and accident investigation, search and seizure, criminal law, laws of arrest, firearms proficiency, defensive tactics, and first aid.

Contact: Personnel Office, Bureau of Reclamation Service Center, Building 67, Box 25007; Denver, CO 80225. Phone: 2303-236-3834. World Wide Web: http://www.usbr.gov/.

POLICE OFFICER (GS-0083)
FEDERAL BUREAU OF INVESTIGATION
U.S. DEPARTMENT OF JUSTICE

Overview: The Federal Bureau of Investigation (FBI) maintains a force of uniformed Police Officers whose primary mission is to maintain law and order, and to protect life, property, and the civil rights of FBI personnel and visitors at the FBI Headquarters building in Washington, D.C., as well as the FBI Training Academy on the grounds of the Marine Corps base in Quantico, Virginia. The secondary mission of FBI Police Officers is to protect government property and national security information from acts of sabotage, espionage, terrorism, trespass, theft, fire, and accidental or malicious damage or destruction. FBI Police Officers are assigned to fixed posts, roving patrols, and control desk duties on rotating shifts. Responsibilities also include responding to calls for service, crimes in progress, and emergency situations; identifying suspicious persons; administering first aid and CPR; securing crime scenes; collecting and preserving evidence; interviewing victims and witnesses; and processing prisoners. FBI Police Officers are authorized to carry firearms and make arrests.

Qualifications: Applicants must be U.S. citizens, a high school graduate, and at least twenty-one years of age. Requirements for appointment to GS-5 include four years of undergraduate coursework leading to a bachelor's degree related to law enforcement, criminal investigation or criminology, OR one year of specialized experience equivalent to GS-4; and for grades GS-6 through GS-9, one year of specialized experience equivalent to the next lower grade level. Prior completion of a police academy training program may be substituted for three months of specialized experience or six months of general experience. No substitution of education or training may be made for the required specialized experience for appointment to GS-6 and above. Applicants must have "good near and distant vision," ability to distinguish basic colors, and ability to hear the conversational voice. Tentative appointees must pass a polygraph exam, personal interview, drug screening test, physical exam, and background investigation.

Training: FBI Police Officers attend the nine-week Basic Police Training Program at the Federal Law Enforcement Training Center in Glynco, Georgia (see Chapter 16). In-service training includes firearms instruction and qualification, courses in defensive tactics and driving skills, and periodic legal training which is tailored to specific duties.

Contact: Federal Bureau of Investigation; Washington, DC 20535. Phone: 202-324-2727. World Wide Web: http://www.fbi.gov/.

POLICE OFFICER
LIBRARY OF CONGRESS POLICE
LIBRARY OF CONGRESS

Overview: The Library of Congress (LC) is the national library of the United States, offering diverse materials for research including the world's most extensive collections in many areas such as American history, music and law. LC Police Officers perform a variety of law enforcement and security functions within the buildings and grounds protected by the LC Police force. Responsibilities include protection of the lives, property and civil rights of LC staff and patrons; maintaining law and order; assisting in the protection of LC property and collections; conducting patrols to detect and report unlawful or unsafe actions and conditions; subduing unruly persons; rendering first aid and CPR in cases of accident or acute illness; participating in fire drills and inspections; and drafting official reports pertaining to accidents, incidents, conditions or unusual circumstances. LC Police Officers are authorized to carry firearms and make arrests. Salary for this position does not fall under the General Schedule pay system, although it is similar to GS-0083 Police Officer positions of other federal law enforcement agencies.

Qualifications: Applicants must be U.S. citizens and at least twenty-one years of age, and have a high school diploma or GED certificate. Requirements include at least eighteen months of full-time law enforcement or security experience. (Qualifying work experience includes service with a federal, state, or local police agency; private security organization; or service in the armed forces as a Military Police Officer.) One year of college or 720 classroom hours in criminal justice or law enforcement courses may be substituted for nine months of experience. Applicants must have "good near and distant vision," ability to distinguish basic colors, and ability to hear the conversational voice. Tentative appointees must pass a written examination, personal interview, medical exam, and background investigation.

Training: LC Police Officers attend the nine-week Basic Police Training Program at the Federal Law Enforcement Training Center in Glynco, Georgia (see Chapter 16). In-service training may include courses in criminal law, search and seizure, laws of arrest, interviewing techniques, firearms proficiency, defensive tactics, first aid, and other subjects.

Contact: Employment Office, Staffing and Recruitment Group, Library of Congress, 101 Independence Ave. SW; Washington, DC 20540. Phone: 202-707-2034. World Wide Web: http://www.lcweb.loc.gov/.

POLICE OFFICER
AMTRAK POLICE DEPARTMENT
NATIONAL RAILROAD PASSENGER CORPORATION

Overview: With police personnel assigned to 29 field locations in 16 states and the District of Columbia, the AMTRAK Police Department serves as the law enforcement and security arm of the federal government's National Railroad Passenger Corporation. AMTRAK Police Officers perform crime prevention functions and provide protection of passengers, property and personnel, while maintaining jurisdiction over more than 500 train stations in 45 states, and over a rail system of approximately 24,500 route miles. Primary responsibilities include performing foot, bicycle and vehicular patrols of train stations, railroad right of way and maintenance facilities to detect criminal activity, including vandalism to tracks, trains, signals, and other property; responding to incidents involving larceny, robbery, purse snatching, assault, weapons offenses, panhandling, drug trafficking, murder, arson, bomb threats, obstructions placed on tracks, and other crimes committed on trains, in train stations, or on AMTRAK property; riding trains; conducting surveillance; preserving the peace; performing preliminary criminal investigations; apprehending offenders; responding to emergency situations and accidents; and performing first aid and CPR. The Department also staffs a full-time Detective Division responsible for criminal investigations (see Chapter 6, *Detectives*), and both bicycle patrol and canine units. Many operations are conducted jointly with other federal, state, local, and transit law enforcement agencies. AMTRAK Police Officers are authorized to carry firearms and make arrests. Salary for this position does not fall under the General Schedule pay system, although it is similar to GS-0083 Police Officer positions of other federal law enforcement agencies.

Qualifications: Applicants must have U.S. citizenship or the right to work in the United States; be at least twenty-one years of age at the time of appointment; have a valid driver's license; and possess an associates degree or at least sixty semester credits from an accredited college or university. (A bachelor's degree is preferred.) No waiver will be granted for the substitution of previous work experience or training. Applicants must submit a resume and employment application form; and pass a written examination, personal interview, background investigation, psychological evaluation, medical examination, and drug screening test.

Training: Depending upon availability of training, newly appointed AMTRAK Police Officers attend either the nine-week Basic Police Training Program at the Federal Law Enforcement Training Center in Glynco, Georgia (see Chapter 16), or a state-certified police academy training program in the state where they will be employed. In-service training includes periodic courses in railroad operations and signal reading, drug interdiction, disaster response, crisis management, safety procedures, blood-borne pathogens, legal issues and updates, firearms proficiency, defensive tactics, arrest techniques, first aid, and other subjects.

Contact: Human Resources, AMTRAK Police Department, 30th Street Station, North Tower; Philadelphia, PA 19104. Phone: 215-349-1108. World Wide Web: http://www.amtrak.com/.

POLICE OFFICER (GS-0083)
NATIONAL ZOOLOGICAL PARK POLICE
SMITHSONIAN INSTITUTION

Overview: As one of the oldest branches of the Smithsonian Institution, the National Zoo encompasses 163 acres along Rock Creek in Northwest Washington, D.C., and contains more than 5,000 animals and nearly 500 species. Uniformed National Zoological Park Police (NZPP) Officers are responsible for a wide range of law enforcement and security functions on Zoo property, including vehicular and foot patrols; responding to calls for service, crimes in progress, and emergency situations; protecting animals and exhibits; maintaining order; inspection of Zoo rest rooms, locker rooms, buildings and other facilities; enforcement of Zoo rules; directing pedestrian and motor vehicle traffic; investigating traffic accidents; crowd control; administering first aid and CPR; locating lost children, missing persons and lost property; providing assistance to Zoo visitors; writing detailed incident and accident reports; and preparing criminal cases for prosecution. NZPP Officers are authorized to carry firearms and make arrests.

Qualifications: Applicants must be U.S. citizens. Requirements for appointment to GS-5 include one year of specialized experience equivalent to GS-4, OR four years of undergraduate coursework leading to a bachelor's degree related to law enforcement, criminal investigation or criminology; and for GS-6 through GS-9, one year of specialized experience equivalent to the next lower grade level. Prior completion of a police academy training program may be substituted for three months of specialized experience or six months of general experience. No substitution of education or training may be made for the required specialized experience for appointment to GS-6 and above. Applicants must have "good near and distant vision," ability to distinguish basic colors, and ability to hear the conversational voice. Tentative appointees may be required to pass a drug screening test, physical exam, and background investigation.

Training: NZPP Officers attend the nine-week Basic Police Training Program at the Federal Law Enforcement Training Center in Glynco, Georgia (see Chapter 16). In-service training may include courses in park policies, traffic accident investigation, criminal law, search and seizure, laws of arrest, firearms proficiency, defensive tactics, and first aid.

Contact: Office of Human Resources, National Zoological Park Police, 955 L'Enfant Plaza SW; Washington, DC 20560. Phone: 202-287-2499. World Wide Web: http://www.si.edu/natzoo/.

POLICE OFFICER
SUPREME COURT POLICE
SUPREME COURT OF THE UNITED STATES

Overview: Officers of the Supreme Court Police are responsible for the protection of personnel, visitors, and property at the Supreme Court of the United States in Washington, D.C. These Officers perform a variety of law enforcement and security functions, including foot and vehicular patrol of the Supreme Court Building, grounds, and adjacent streets; personal protection throughout the United States of the Chief Justice and Associate Justices of the Supreme Court, official Supreme Court guests, and officers or employees of the Supreme Court while engaged in their duties; building security and surveillance; courtroom security; responding to crimes in progress, disturbances, bomb threats, and emergency situations; policing protests and demonstrations on Supreme Court Building grounds; rendering first aid and CPR; and providing assistance to Supreme Court visitors. Supreme Court Police Officers are authorized to carry firearms and make arrests. Salary for this position does not fall under the General Schedule pay system, although it is similar to GS-0083 Police Officer positions of other federal agencies.

Qualifications: Applicants must be U.S. citizens; possess a high school diploma; and have a driver's license and an excellent driving record. Two years of college education and prior law enforcement or security experience is preferred. Applicants must be mature, reliable, and skilled in oral and written communications; have good interpersonal skills; and pass an oral interview, medical examination and background investigation.

Training: Supreme Court Police Officers attend the nine-week Basic Police Training Program at the Federal Law Enforcement Training Center in Glynco, Georgia (see Chapter 16). Basic training is followed by a six-month Orientation and Field Training Program at the Supreme Court which includes courses related to specific duties of the position, foot and vehicular patrol duty with an experienced Field Training Officer, and assignment to various posts of duty. In-service training may include courses in security procedures, personal protective operations, legal issues and updates, firearms proficiency, defensive tactics, and first aid.

Contact: Personnel Office, Supreme Court of the United States, 1 First Street NE; Washington, DC 20543. Phone: 202-479-3404. World Wide Web: No Web site at this time.

POLICE OFFICER
TVA POLICE
TENNESSEE VALLEY AUTHORITY

Overview: The Tennessee Valley Authority (TVA), a wholly-owned government corporation, is the nation's largest single producer of electric power, servicing large industries, federal installations, and 160 power distributors within an 80,000-square mile area in Tennessee, and parts of Mississippi, Alabama, Georgia, North Carolina, Virginia, and Kentucky. As fully-commissioned uniformed personnel, TVA Police Officers are responsible for maintaining order and the protection of TVA personnel, the public, and TVA property and facilities including three nuclear plants, 29 hydroelectric dams, 11 coal plants, 164 recreation facilities, 13 customer service centers, offices, and other facilities throughout the Tennessee Valley region. TVA Police Officers perform a wide range of law enforcement and security functions, including access control to prevent unauthorized entry to TVA property or restricted areas; conducting foot and vehicular patrols to prevent sabotage, theft of nuclear materials, civil disorders, vandalism, assaults, and other crimes; responding to crimes in progress, alarms, disturbances, bomb threats, accidents, and emergency situations; performing first aid and CPR; conducting traffic control and enforcement; and investigating crimes and accidents. TVA Police Officers are authorized to carry firearms and make arrests. Salary for this position does not fall under the General Schedule pay system, although it is similar to GS-0083 Police Officer positions of other federal law enforcement agencies.

Qualifications: Applicants must be U.S. citizens and at least twenty-one years of age; possess a high school diploma or GED; and have basic computer skills and at least one year of experience as a law enforcement officer or dispatcher. Eyesight and hearing requirements include the ability to see with sufficient clarity to monitor panels, light bars, screens, monitors, and other equipment and devices; and the ability to discriminate between differing sounds, such as various alarms and speech. Applicants must have knowledge of English grammar, spelling, and punctuation sufficient to accurately take notes and complete written reports; basic investigation techniques; and of law enforcement agencies and their operations. Applicants must pass a background investigation, psychological evaluation, medical exam, and drug and alcohol screening.

Training: TVA Police Officers attend the twelve-week Land Management Law Enforcement Training Program at the Federal Law Enforcement Training Center in Glynco, Georgia (see Chapter 16). In-service training may include courses in nuclear security, access control procedures, intrusion detection devices, traffic control and enforcement, accident investigation, legal issues and updates, interviewing techniques, firearms proficiency, first aid, and defensive tactics.

Contact: Employee Service Center, Tennessee Valley Authority, 400 West Summit Hill Drive; Knoxville, TN 37902. Phone: 423-632-3222. World Wide Web: http://www.tva.gov. E-Mail: esc@tva.gov.

POLICE OFFICER
BUREAU OF ENGRAVING AND PRINTING
U.S. DEPARTMENT OF THE TREASURY

Overview: The Bureau of Engraving and Printing (BEP) designs, prints, and finishes all of the nation's paper currency, as well as U.S. postage stamps, Treasury securities, naturalization certificates, Coast Guard water use licenses, Presidential appointment certificates, White House invitations, military identification cards, and other security documents. To protect these operations, BEP Police Officers are responsible for law enforcement and security functions at the headquarters facility in Washington, D.C., and a second currency manufacturing plant in Fort Worth, Texas. Responsibilities include the protection of Bureau assets, plant facilities, property, personnel, and visitors; maintaining order; static post and foot patrol duty; responding to crimes in progress and emergency situations; enforcement of federal laws, Treasury Department regulations, and Bureau security rules; writing detailed reports; screening visitors entering Bureau facilities; and monitoring alarm systems, intrusion control devices, and closed-circuit surveillance monitors. BEP Police Officers are authorized to carry firearms and make arrests. Appointment to Treasury grade TR-6 is equivalent to GS-5, and promotion to TR-7 is equivalent to GS-6.

Qualifications: Applicants must be U.S. citizens and at least twenty-one years of age. Requirements for appointment to Treasury grade TR-6 include one year of specialized experience equivalent to TR-5, OR four years of undergraduate coursework leading to a bachelor's degree related to law enforcement, criminal investigation or criminology; and to TR-7, one year of specialized experience equivalent to TR-6. Prior completion of a police academy training program may be substituted for three months of specialized experience or six months of general experience. Uncorrected visual acuity must be no worse than 20/60 (Snellen), correctable to 20/20 in both eyes. Applicants must be able to distinguish basic colors, and to hear the conversational voice. The application process also includes a written examination, drug screening test, medical exam, and background investigation. Appointees must meet firearms qualifications with handguns, shotguns, and submachine guns.

Training: BEP Police Officers attend the nine-week Basic Police Training Program at the Federal Law Enforcement Training Center in Glynco, Georgia (see Chapter 16). In-service training may include in-house instruction and other courses relating to BEP policies, physical security procedures, criminal law, laws of arrest, search and seizure, firearms proficiency, first aid, and defensive tactics.

Contact: Office of Human Resources, Bureau of Engraving and Printing, Department of the Treasury, 14th and C Streets SW; Washington, DC 20228. Phone: 202-874-3181. World Wide Web: http://www.treas.gov/bep/.

POLICE OFFICER (GS-0083)
OFFICE OF SECURITY AND LAW ENFORCEMENT
U.S. DEPARTMENT OF VETERANS AFFAIRS

Overview: The Department of Veterans Affairs (VA) operates hundreds of healthcare facilities in the United States, Puerto Rico, and the Philippines to benefit veterans and members of their families, including 173 medical centers, 39 domiciliaries, 376 outpatient clinics, 131 nursing home care units, and 205 Vietnam Veteran Outreach Centers. VA Police Officers are responsible for the physical protection of patients, visitors, and employees at VA facilities. Responsibilities include foot and vehicle patrols; enforcement of federal and state criminal laws and VA regulations; responding to calls for service, disturbances, assaults by patients and visitors, accidents, alarms, bomb threats, demonstrations, fires, crimes in progress, and emergency situations; making arrests; traffic and crowd control; accident investigation; performing first aid and CPR; writing detailed reports; conducting interviews and interrogations; collecting and preserving evidence; and the investigation of criminal incidents. The variety of responsibilities depends upon the size and particular needs of facilities served. Although VA Police Officers are authorized to carry chemical weapons and side-handle batons, authority to carry firearms varies from one VA facility to another.

Qualifications: Applicants must be U.S. citizens. Requirements for appointment to GS-4 include six months of general experience and six months of specialized experience, OR two years of education above high school related to the occupation; for GS-5, one year of specialized experience equivalent to GS-4, OR four years of undergraduate coursework leading to a bachelor's degree related to law enforcement, criminal investigation or criminology; and for GS-6 through GS-9, one year of specialized experience equivalent to the next lower grade level. Prior completion of a police academy training program may be substituted for three months of specialized experience or six months of general experience. No substitution of education or training may be made for the required specialized experience for appointment to GS-6 and above. Applicants must have "good near and distant vision," ability to distinguish basic colors, and ability to hear the conversational voice. Tentative appointees must pass a drug screening test, physical exam, psychological evaluation, and background investigation.

Training: VA Police Officers attend a four-week Basic Police Officer Training Course administered by the VA Office of Security and Law Enforcement, which includes instruction in subjects such as criminal law, laws of arrest, use of force encounters, human behavior, conflict resolution, and other topics pertaining to policing in a health care environment. Various in-service courses pertaining to law enforcement and security operations are also attended.

Contact: Inquiries should be directed to the facility where employment is sought, or to Office of Security and Law Enforcement, Department of Veterans Affairs, 810 Vermont Ave. NW; Washington, DC 20420. Phone: 202-287-2499. World Wide Web: http://www.va.gov/.

POSTAL POLICE OFFICER
UNITED STATES POSTAL INSPECTION SERVICE
U.S. POSTAL SERVICE

Overview: As the uniformed law enforcement branch of the Postal Inspection Service, Postal Police Officers perform a wide range of functions pertaining to the security of postal personnel, customers, buildings, vehicles, property, and mail; the enforcement of certain postal laws and regulations; while also providing a mobile response to emergency situations involving postal operations. Primary responsibilities include performing static post, vehicular and foot patrols on postal property; controlling access to postal facilities; exercising surveillance of persons in and around postal property to prevent assaults on postal employees and other crimes; preventing prohibited items from being brought onto postal premises and confiscating such items; monitoring electronic security devices that provide surveillance and alarm protection; responding to emergency situations and crimes in progress including accidents, injuries, illnesses, fires, disturbances, burglaries, robberies, bomb threats, and other circumstances threatening life or property; maintaining order to prevent assaults, injuries, and damage to property; collecting and preserving evidence; rendering first aid in emergency situations; ensuring the security of mail-handling areas; and escorting shipments of high-value mail while in transit between postal units and airports. Postal Police Officers are authorized to carry firearms and make arrests. Salary for this position is covered under the Postal Service pay scale, which is similar to GS-0083 Police Officers of federal law enforcement agencies.

Qualifications: Applicants must be U.S. citizens and at least twenty-one years of age. Eyesight requirements include uncorrected distant vision of at least 20/100 (Snellen) in each eye, correctable to 20/20 in one eye and 20/40 in the other, and good color perception. Incision Radial Keratotomy is a disqualifying condition. Applicants must be able to hear the conversational voice without the use of a hearing aid. Weight must be proportionate to height. A valid driver's license is required. Applicants must qualify for a security clearance and pass a written examination (see Chapter 1), drug screening test, personal interview, and background investigation.

Training: Postal Police Officers attend the nine-week Basic Police Training Program at the Federal Law Enforcement Training Center in Glynco, Georgia (see Chapter 16). In-service training may include courses pertaining to law enforcement and security operations, updates of criminal laws and Postal Service regulations, firearms proficiency, first aid, defensive tactics, and other courses related to specific responsibilities of the position.

Contact: U.S. Postal Inspection Service, 475 L'Enfant Plaza SW; Washington, DC 20260. Phone: 202-268-4267. World Wide Web: http://www.usps.gov/websites/depart/inspect/.

REFUGE LAW ENFORCEMENT OFFICER (GS-1802)
UNITED STATES FISH AND WILDLIFE SERVICE
U.S. DEPARTMENT OF THE INTERIOR

Overview: Uniformed Refuge Law Enforcement Officers of the United States Fish and Wildlife Service (FWS) are responsible for preventing and detecting violations of federal, state, and local fish and wildlife laws on more than 500 national wildlife refuges encompassing more than 30 million acres. FWS Refuge Officers respond to and investigate violations involving the illegal taking, importing, and commercialization of wildlife; poaching by individuals and local to interstate market hunting rings; illegal over-bagging of waterfowl; and other offenses. Responsibilities include patrolling refuge areas in vehicles and on foot; conducting surveillance; participating in raids; interviewing witnesses and interrogating suspects; documenting legal water uses; ensuring compliance with refuge water management plans; and monitoring upstream water use to protect refuge water rights from illegal diversions. Operations are often coordinated with FWS Special Agents and other federal, state, and local law enforcement agencies. Refuge Officers are authorized to carry firearms and make arrests.

Qualifications: Applicants must be U.S. citizens; and possess skill in documenting water use, operating gauging equipment, and applying water measurement techniques in order to identify illegal diversion. Requirements for appointment to GS-4 level include two years of education above high school, OR one year of general experience; for GS-5, four years of education above high school, OR one year of specialized experience equivalent to at least GS-4; and for grades GS-6 through GS-11, one year of specialized experience equivalent to the next lower grade level. Applicants are rated on their experience, education, training, employment performance evaluations, and awards as they relate to the position. Experience and education may be combined to meet total experience requirements for positions at grades GS-5 and below. Tentative appointees must pass a drug screening test, medical exam, and background investigation.

Training: Refuge Officers attend the twelve-week Land Management Law Enforcement Training Program at the Federal Law Enforcement Training Center in Glynco, Georgia (see Chapter 16). Officers then complete a two-week Refuge Officer Basic School at either FLETC or the FWS National Conservation Training Center in Shepherdstown, West Virginia, which covers topics such as law, treaties, waterfowl identification, tracking and sign recognition, Pressure Point Control Tactics, FWS policies, and enforcement problems unique to National Wildlife Refuges. In-service training may include courses in wildlife investigation, archaeological resources protection, marine law enforcement, Spanish language, legal issues and updates, firearms proficiency, first aid, and defensive tactics.

Contact: Division of Law Enforcement, U.S. Fish and Wildlife Service, P.O. Box 3247; Arlington, VA 22203. Phone: 703-358-1949. World Wide Web: http://www.fws.gov/~r9dle/div_le.html.

RIVER RANGER (GS-0025)
NATIONAL PARK SERVICE
U.S. DEPARTMENT OF THE INTERIOR

Overview: The primary responsibilities of National Park Service (NPS) River Rangers are to patrol water resources managed by the NPS, and enforce federal and state laws relating to the protection of natural and cultural resources. Uniformed NPS River Rangers conduct back-country patrols on Class II, III and IV white-water rivers, primarily in white-water rafts; perform search and rescue operations; provide emergency medical assistance to injured persons; participate in the river campground, back-country and boating permit programs; and maintain equipment utilized in law enforcement operations. When not engaged in river patrol functions, River Rangers may also conduct traditional vehicular and foot patrol duties; investigate and enforce laws such as larceny, assaults, vandalism, weapons offenses, and drug trafficking; present educational programs to park visitors concerning points of interest, historical and natural resources, and park activities; and perform a variety of tasks related to habitat and wildlife monitoring, rescue and rehabilitation. River Rangers are authorized to carry firearms and make arrests.

Qualifications: Applicants must be U.S. citizens, and at least twenty-one years of age. Requirements for appointment to GS-4 include six months of general experience and six months of specialized experience, OR two years of education above high school related to the occupation; for GS-5, four years of undergraduate coursework leading to a bachelor's degree, with twenty-four semester hours of coursework related to the occupation, OR one year of specialized experience equivalent to GS-4; for GS-7, one year of graduate education related to the occupation, OR superior academic achievement during undergraduate studies, OR one year of specialized experience equivalent to GS-5; for GS-9, two years of graduate education or a master's degree related to the occupation, OR one year of specialized experience equivalent to GS-7; for GS-11, three years of graduate education or a Ph.D. or equivalent doctoral degree related to the occupation, OR one year of specialized experience equivalent to GS-9; and for GS-12, one year of specialized experience equivalent to GS-11. In some cases, qualifying education may be substituted for experience, and vice versa. Tentative appointees must pass a drug screening test and background investigation.

Training: NPS River Rangers attend an orientation program which covers the mission, policies, procedures, and rules of the agency, followed by on-the-job training. River Rangers may also attend formal training courses located at Grand Canyon National Park or other NPS training centers, or at the Federal Law Enforcement Training Center in Glynco, Georgia.

Contact: National Park Service, Department of the Interior, P.O. Box 37127; Washington, DC 20013. Phone: 202-208-6843. World Wide Web: http://www.nps.gov/.

UNIFORMED DIVISION OFFICER
UNITED STATES SECRET SERVICE
U.S. DEPARTMENT OF THE TREASURY

Overview: Uniformed Division Officers of the United States Secret Service (USSS) are an integral component of USSS protective operations. Formerly known as the Executive Protective Service and the White House Police, Uniformed Division Officers are responsible for security at the White House Complex, the Vice President's residence, buildings in which Presidential offices are located, the U.S. Treasury Building and Annex, and foreign diplomatic missions and embassies located in the Washington, D.C. metropolitan area and throughout the United States. Uniformed Division Officers carry out their protective responsibilities through special support programs and a network of foot patrols, vehicular patrols and fixed posts, and are closely involved in almost every phase of the USSS protective mission. Officers screen visitors and operate magnetometers at the White House and at other sites to prevent persons from taking weapons into secure areas; monitor closed-circuit television surveillance monitors and intrusion detection devices; and utilize canine teams to respond to bomb threats, suspicious packages, and other situations where explosive detection is necessary. The Division also utilizes crime scene search technicians, and staffs an emergency response team and a countersniper unit. Officers are authorized to carry firearms and make arrests. Salary for this position does not fall under the General Schedule pay system, although it is similar to GS-0083 Police Officer positions of other federal law enforcement agencies.

Qualifications: Applicants must be U.S. citizens; at least twenty-one years of age and under the age of thirty-seven at the time of appointment; possess a high school diploma or GED certificate; and be in excellent health and physical condition. Weight must be proportionate to height. Uncorrected visual acuity must be no worse than 20/60 (Snellen), correctable to 20/20 in each eye. Law enforcement or military experience is beneficial but not required. Applicants must pass a written exam, oral interview, polygraph exam, background investigation, physical exam, and drug screening test, and qualify for a top-secret security clearance.

Training: Uniformed Division Officers attend the nine-week Basic Police Training Program at the Federal Law Enforcement Training Center in Glynco, Georgia (see Chapter 16), followed by ten weeks of specialized instruction at USSS training facilities in the Washington, D.C. area. Training for these Officers focuses on protective operations, physical security and law enforcement procedures, diplomatic immunity, international treaties and protocol, the District of Columbia Criminal Code, laws of arrest, search and seizure, psychology, police-community relations, firearms proficiency, first aid, physical fitness, defensive tactics, and other subjects. Classroom instruction is supplemented by on-the-job training and various advanced in-service training programs.

Contact: Uniformed Division, U.S. Secret Service, 1800 G Street NW; Washington, DC 20223. Phone: 202-435-5708 or 800-827-7783. World Wide Web: http://www.treas.gov/usss/.

Chapter Nine

LAW ENFORCEMENT
TECHNICIANS AND SPECIALISTS

Give us the tools, and we will finish the job.
– WINSTON CHURCHILL

THIS CHAPTER FOCUSES ON A WIDE VARIETY OF SPECIALIZED CAREERS which involve technical support for criminal investigation and law enforcement operations. Most of these positions are with the nation's largest law enforcement agencies, such as the U.S. Immigration and Naturalization Service; Federal Bureau of Investigation; U.S. Customs Service; U.S. Secret Service; Drug Enforcement Administration; U.S. Marshals Service; National Park Service; and Bureau of Alcohol, Tobacco and Firearms.

Law enforcement technicians and specialists provide skilled support in carrying out the missions of the agencies they serve. Depending on their particular expertise, these personnel perform tasks such as examining, preserving and identifying latent fingerprint evidence; conducting air patrol operations, search and rescue missions, and medical evacuations; combating the use of explosives by terrorists; examining handwriting and counterfeit documents; identifying and testing bombs, explosive devices, firearms, and ammunition; determining the cause and origin of explosions and fires; analyzing samples of blood, saliva, stains, gunshot residue, paint, fibers, controlled substances, and other evidence; taking surveillance photographs; and training law enforcement officers.

The career profiles included in this chapter cover a broad range of occupational classifications, including Airplane Pilot, Biologist/Forensic Examiner, Canine and Explosives Specialist, Chemist/Forensic Examiner, Customs Pilot, Document Analyst, Evidence and Seized Property Custodian, Explosives Enforcement Specialist, Fingerprint Specialist, Firearms Enforcement Technician, Forensic Chemist, Law Enforcement Training Instructor, Photographer, Seizure and Forfeiture Specialist, and Technical Enforcement Officer.

AIRPLANE PILOT (GS-2181)
NATIONAL PARK SERVICE
U.S. DEPARTMENT OF THE INTERIOR

Overview: National Park Service (NPS) Airplane Pilots are responsible for flight activities over the natural, historical, and recreational areas that encompass the National Park System. Flight assignments are carried out in support of law enforcement patrol operations, resource protection, wildfire detection, search and rescue operations, missions to transport personnel and supplies to remote districts, game census activities, mapping operations, and medical evacuations in areas under the jurisdiction of the Service. NPS Airplane Pilots operate aircraft equipped with floats, skis, or wheels; under hazardous conditions and over unfavorable mountainous terrain; through narrow or twisting canyons under challenging wind conditions; in extreme desert heat; and occasionally during unpredicted storms. In addition, air patrols, searches, and resource protection flights may be conducted at low altitudes (occasionally below 500 feet), and landings may be carried out in isolated areas on dirt roads that are considered marginal airstrips. Responsibilities of NPS Airplane Pilots also include maintaining airworthiness of aircraft, compliance with safety procedures and regulations, maintaining logs and flight reports, performing preflight and postflight checks, and assisting with aircraft maintenance.

Qualifications: Applicants must be U.S. citizens and possess a current Federal Aviation Administration (FAA) Commercial Pilot Certificate with ratings appropriate for the duties performed, an instrument rating, a current FAA Class I Medical Certificate, and must meet all Department of the Interior Office of Aircraft Services (OAS) requirements for pilots. Requirements for appointment to the GS-11 level and above include 1,500 hours of total flight time, including 1,200 hours as pilot-in-command; 75 hours of night flying experience, including at least 25 hours as pilot-in-command; 75 hours of actual or simulated instrument time, including at least 50 hours in actual flight; 100 hours as pilot-in-command during the previous twelve months; and 200 hours as pilot-in-command in low-level operations (within 500 feet of the surface of typical terrain), or ten hours of low-level flight instruction within the previous five years followed by a low-level flight check by an OAS pilot inspector. Applicants must submit a Form OAS-61, Record of Aeronautical Experience. A drug screening test is also required.

Training: NPS Airplane Pilots complete a wide range of training courses, seminars, and workshops throughout their careers. These programs cover subjects concerned with airplane and helicopter safety, aircraft capabilities and limitations, accident prevention, crash survival methods, water ditching, personal survival vests and flotation devices, emergency locator transmitters, hazardous materials, fuel handling procedures, sling load cargo transportation, departmental and agency aviation policies and procedures, and aviation resources. NPS Pilots are also required to complete a one-week refresher course every three years, which focuses on safety topics, policy information, aviation program updates, and other subjects.

Contact: National Park Service, Department of the Interior, P.O. Box 37127; Washington, DC 20013. Phone: 202-208-6843. World Wide Web: http://www.nps.gov/.

AIRPLANE PILOT (GS-2181)
UNITED STATES MARSHALS SERVICE
U.S. DEPARTMENT OF JUSTICE

Overview: United States Marshals Service (USMS) Airplane Pilots are responsible for flying aircraft in support of the USMS Justice Prisoner and Alien Transportation System (JPATS), one of the largest transporters of prisoners in the world. The JPATS handles hundreds of requests every day to move prisoners between judicial districts, correctional institutions and foreign countries. As the only government-operated, scheduled passenger airline in the United States, JPATS serves forty cities and moves prisoners more economically and with greater security than commercial airlines. In a cooperative effort between the USMS, Federal Bureau of Prisons (BOP) and the United States Immigration and Naturalization Service (INS), USMS Airplane Pilots transport prisoners for the USMS, BOP, INS, as well as the U.S. military and state and local governments, utilizing a fleet of turbine-powered, turboprop, and multi-engine fixed-wing aircraft. USMS Airplane Pilots are also responsible for supporting Special Operations Group missions; transporting cargoes of ammunition, pyrotechnics and chemical munitions; aircraft maintenance; writing reports; and performing other duties to accomplish the mission of the USMS Air Operations Branch. Aircraft are flown in and out of all types of airfields, over favorable and unfavorable terrain, and during day and nighttime hours.

Qualifications: Applicants must be U.S. citizens. Requirements for appointment to GS-11 level and above include possession of a current Federal Aviation Administration (FAA) Commercial Pilot Certificate with an airplane multi-engine land rating; at least one type of rating or equivalent military designation as pilot-in-command and/or second-in-command in fixed-wing turboprop jet aircraft with a gross takeoff weight of at least 50,000 pounds; at least 1,500 hours of total flight time, including 250 hours as pilot-in-command; at least 75 hours of night flying experience; at least 100 hours of flight time during the previous twelve months; and a current FAA Class I Medical Certificate. A background investigation and drug screening test is also required.

Training: Initial training for Airplane Pilots includes an orientation to USMS operations, and approximately three weeks of ground school simulation exercises in the types of aircraft to be operated. In-service training consists of annual ground school simulation refresher exercises, as well as courses which focus on subjects such as cockpit resources management, prisoner handling and transportation, safety and survival, firearms familiarization, and other topics.

Contact: Office of Human Resources, United States Marshals Service, 600 Army Navy Drive; Arlington, VA 22202. Phone: 202-307-9000. World Wide Web: http://www.usdoj.gov/marshals/.

BIOLOGIST/FORENSIC EXAMINER (GS-0401)
FEDERAL BUREAU OF INVESTIGATION
U.S. DEPARTMENT OF JUSTICE

Overview: Biologist/Forensic Examiners of the Federal Bureau of Investigation (FBI) plan, coordinate, direct, and perform a variety of examinations and comprehensive technical analyses in support of criminal investigations conducted by the FBI and other federal, state and local law enforcement agencies. Primary responsibilities include analyzing body fluids and body fluid stains recovered as evidence in violent crimes, which involves traditional serological techniques and biochemical analysis to identify and characterize blood, semen, saliva, and other body fluids; performing protein analyses or DNA analyses of samples; utilizing mitochondrial DNA analysis which is applied to evidence containing small or degraded quantities of DNA from hair, bones, teeth, and body fluids; comparing results of analyses to known samples obtained from crime victims or suspects; locating, identifying, reconstructing, and preserving pertinent items of evidence obtained at crime scenes for examination; conducting inventories of evidence; calibrating and operating analytical instruments to independently analyze and identify samples; preparing and presenting oral briefings and detailed written reports to case agents, supervisory personnel, U.S. Attorneys, and grand juries; and providing expert testimony in evidentiary hearings and criminal trials in support of their findings.

Qualifications: Applicants must be U.S. citizens. Basic eligibility requirements include a bachelor's degree in biochemistry, biological sciences, biotechnology or a related field with at least twenty-four semester hours in biochemistry or the biological sciences. Requirements for appointment to GS-7 include one full year of graduate education, or superior academic achievement during undergraduate studies, OR a bachelor's degree and one year of specialized experience; for GS-9, a master's degree or two years of graduate education, OR a bachelor's degree and one year of specialized experience equivalent to GS-7; for GS-11, a Ph.D. or equivalent doctoral degree, or three years of graduate education, OR a bachelor's degree and one year of specialized experience equivalent to GS-9; and for GS-12 or GS-13, a bachelor's degree or higher education and one year of specialized experience equivalent to the next lower grade level. Tentative appointees must pass a background investigation, drug screening test and polygraph exam, and qualify for a top-secret security clearance.

Training: Biologist/Forensic Examiners in the FBI Laboratory must successfully complete training necessary for certification as an FBI Forensic Examiner. These personnel attend a variety of professional seminars, workshops and courses throughout their careers which focus on laboratory techniques and procedures utilized in the examination and analysis of evidence. Training may be presented by FBI staff, colleges and universities, and other organizations.

Contact: Laboratory Division, Federal Bureau of Investigation, 935 Pennsylvania Ave. NW, Room 3437; Washington, DC 20535. Phone: 202-324-2727. World Wide Web: http://www.fbi.gov/.

CANINE AND EXPLOSIVES SPECIALIST
FEDERAL AVIATION ADMINISTRATION
U.S. DEPARTMENT OF TRANSPORTATION

Overview: Federal Aviation Administration (FAA) Canine and Explosives Specialists are responsible for implementing the FAA Canine Explosives Detection Team Program, which operates to combat the use of explosives by terrorists or others against civil aviation, whether as weapons in hijacking attempts or as bombs to destroy aircraft. Officially classified as Civil Aviation Security Specialists (with unique training and expertise), FAA Canine and Explosives Specialists are placed in strategic locations throughout the United States so that any aircraft receiving an in-flight threat could quickly be diverted to an airport which supports a Canine and Explosives Detection Team. The Program includes 130 teams, each consisting of one detector dog and one handler, based in 35 locations. Utilizing highly-trained detector dogs, FAA Canine and Explosives Specialists respond to bomb threats, reports of suspicious packages and containers, and intelligence information from a variety of sources. Inspections are performed in and around aircraft, vehicles, airport terminal and hangar facilities, cargo and cargo processing areas, and passenger luggage to detect bombs, explosives and incendiary devices. Detection Team members are evaluated and certified annually in areas of proficiency pertaining to the inspection of wide- and narrow-body aircraft, luggage, airport terminals, cargo, and vehicles. While salary does not fall under the General Schedule pay system, salaries for grades FG-5 through FG-13 are similar to those of GS-5 through GS-13 positions.

Qualifications: Applicants must be U.S. citizens. Requirements for appointment to FG-5 level include completion of a four-year course of study leading to a bachelor's degree, OR three years general experience, one year of which was equivalent to FG-4; for FG-7, completion of one full year of graduate education, or qualification under the Outstanding Scholar Program, OR one year of specialized experience equivalent to FG-5; for FG-9, a master's degree or two years of graduate education, OR one year of specialized experience equivalent to FG-7; for FG-11, a Ph.D. or equivalent doctoral degree, or three years of graduate education, OR one year of specialized experience equivalent to FG-9; and for FG-12 and FG-13, one year of specialized experience equivalent to the next lower grade level. In some cases, qualifying education may be substituted for experience, and vice versa. Tentative appointees must pass a background investigation and qualify for a security clearance.

Training: Initial training for Canine and Explosives Specialists includes a three-week Civil Aviation Security core course conducted at an FAA training facility in Oklahoma City, Oklahoma. This course focuses on FAA regulations and civil aviation laws, airport security, air carrier compliance with laws and regulations, security procedures, and other subjects relating to security in an aviation environment. In-service training is conducted primarily at the FAA training facility in Oklahoma City, or the Federal Law Enforcement Training Center in Glynco, Georgia, and may include courses pertaining to canine search techniques, identification of explosives, investigation of aviation offenses, security procedures and updates, criminal law, and other areas of specialization.

Contact: Office of Civil Aviation Security, Federal Aviation Administration, Department of Transportation, 800 Independence Ave. SW; Washington, DC 20591. Phone: 202-267-8007. World Wide Web: http://www.cas.faa.gov/.

CHEMIST/FORENSIC EXAMINER (GS-1320)
FEDERAL BUREAU OF INVESTIGATION
U.S. DEPARTMENT OF JUSTICE

Overview: Chemist/Forensic Examiners of the Federal Bureau of Investigation (FBI) are responsible for a wide range of forensic science activities in support of criminal investigations conducted by the FBI and other federal, state and local law enforcement agencies. These personnel investigate, analyze, and interpret the composition, molecular structure, and properties of substances, the transformations which they undergo, and the amounts of matter and energy included in these transformations. Primary responsibilities include conducting inventories and performing examinations and comprehensive technical analyses of evidence, such as biological tissues and fluids, pharmaceuticals, controlled substances, accelerants, explosives, explosive residues, stains, inks, bank security dyes, adhesives, paints, plastics, polymers, petroleum products, tapes, cosmetics, marking materials, and lubricants; locating, identifying, reconstructing, and preserving pertinent items of evidence obtained at crime scenes for examination; calibrating and operating analytical instruments to independently analyze and identify samples; preparing and presenting oral briefings and detailed written reports to case agents, supervisory personnel, United States Attorneys, and grand juries; and providing expert testimony in evidentiary hearings and criminal trials in support of their findings.

Qualifications: Applicants must be U.S. citizens. Basic eligibility requirements include a bachelor's degree in chemistry, toxicology, pharmacology, chemical engineering, physics, or an interdisciplinary degree in a related field with at least thirty semester hours in chemistry. Requirements for appointment to GS-7 include one full year of graduate education, or superior academic achievement during undergraduate studies, OR a bachelor's degree and one year of specialized experience; for GS-9, a master's degree or two years of graduate education, OR a bachelor's degree and one year of specialized experience equivalent to GS-7; for GS-11, a Ph.D. or equivalent doctoral degree, or three years of graduate education, OR a bachelor's degree and one year of specialized experience equivalent to GS-9; and for GS-12 or GS-13, a bachelor's degree or higher education and one year of specialized experience equivalent to the next lower grade level. Tentative appointees must pass a background investigation, drug screening test and polygraph exam, and qualify for a top-secret security clearance.

Training: Chemist/Forensic Examiners in the FBI Laboratory must successfully complete training necessary for certification as an FBI Forensic Examiner. These personnel attend a variety of professional seminars, workshops and courses throughout their careers which focus on laboratory techniques and procedures utilized in the examination and analysis of evidence. Training may be presented by FBI staff, colleges and universities, and other organizations.

Contact: Laboratory Division, Federal Bureau of Investigation, 935 Pennsylvania Ave. NW, Room 3437; Washington, DC 20535. Phone: 202-324-2727. World Wide Web: http://www.fbi.gov/.

CUSTOMS PILOT (GS-2181)
UNITED STATES CUSTOMS SERVICE
U.S. DEPARTMENT OF THE TREASURY

Overview: United States Customs Service (USCS) Pilots perform air surveillance and pursuit activities in support of USCS operations involving the interdiction of illegal drugs, contraband, and smuggled merchandise. Customs Pilots gather information regarding the smuggling of merchandise or contraband into or out of the United States; perform pre-flight aircraft and weather checks; fly high-performance single- and multi-engine planes or helicopters (depending upon the fleet to which they are assigned) during adverse weather conditions, over unfavorable terrain, at low altitudes and speeds, and during day and nighttime operations; maintain surveillance of aircraft, ground vehicles and vessels that are involved in smuggling activities; conduct interdictional surveillance and pursuit operations utilizing sophisticated sensor devices housed in aircraft to monitor the movement of persons, vehicles, and aircraft believed to be engaged in smuggling operations; pursue smugglers to remote landing spots over difficult terrain; support ground and sea components in order to intercept smuggling attempts; and prepare written reports of interdiction activities. Customs Pilots are authorized to carry firearms and make arrests, and to search violators of Customs and other federal laws. This position is covered under special retirement provisions for law enforcement officers and qualifies for 25 percent Law Enforcement Availability Pay.

Qualifications: Applicants must be U.S. citizens, at least twenty-one years of age, and under the age of thirty-seven. (Candidates over age thirty-seven who have previous service creditable under special law enforcement retirement provisions may also be eligible.) Requirements for appointment to GS-11 level and above include possession of a current Federal Aviation Administration (FAA) Commercial Pilot Certificate with an airplane single- and multi-engine land rating, an instrument rating, and/or instrument helicopter rating; at least 1,500 hours of total flight time, including 250 hours as pilot-in-command; at least 75 hours of night flying experience; 100 hours of flight time during the previous twelve months; 500 hours of multi-engine fixed-wing flight time; at least 75 hours of actual or simulated instrument time, including at least 10 hours in actual flight; and a current FAA Class I Medical Certificate. A background investigation and drug screening test are also required.

Training: Customs Pilots attend the eight-week Criminal Investigator Training Program at the Federal Law Enforcement Training Center in Glynco, Georgia (see Chapter 16). This program is followed by an additional eight-week course presented by Customs Service staff which focuses on search and seizure laws, Customs laws and regulations, arrest and search warrant execution, and search techniques. In-service training may include specialized courses in air operations and interdiction techniques, import and export violations, firearms proficiency, defensive tactics, and other subjects.

Contact: U.S. Customs Service, Department of the Treasury, 1300 Pennsylvania Avenue NW; Washington, DC 20229. Phone: 202-927-1250. World Wide Web: http://www.customs.ustreas.gov/.

DOCUMENT ANALYST (GS-1397)
FEDERAL BUREAU OF INVESTIGATION
U.S. DEPARTMENT OF JUSTICE

Overview: Federal Bureau of Investigation (FBI) Document Analysts plan, coordinate, direct, and conduct a variety of forensic science activities in support of criminal investigations for the FBI and other federal, state and local law enforcement agencies. Primary responsibilities include conducting inventories, examinations and comprehensive technical analyses of evidence such as handwriting, hand printing, typewriting, typewriter ribbons, printers, photocopiers, facsimiles, check writer impressions, dry seals, indented writing, watermarks, inks, erasures, paper products, altered or obliterated writing, burned or charred paper, and counterfeit documents; establishing authenticity, alteration, common authorship, characteristics, and other issues; performing document examinations using sequential morphological, chemical, microscopic, photographic, and computer imaging techniques in the examination of questioned and known documents; locating, identifying, reconstructing and preserving pertinent items of evidence obtained from crime scenes for examination; preparing and presenting oral briefings and detailed written reports to case agents, supervisory personnel, United States Attorneys, and grand juries; and providing expert testimony in evidentiary hearings and criminal trials in support of their findings.

Qualifications: Applicants must be U.S. citizens. Requirements for appointment to GS-7 include one full year of graduate education, or superior academic achievement during undergraduate studies, OR a bachelor's degree and one year of specialized experience; for GS-9, a master's degree or two years of graduate education, OR a bachelor's degree and one year of specialized experience equivalent to GS-7; for GS-11, a Ph.D. or equivalent doctoral degree, or three years of graduate education, OR a bachelor's degree and one year of specialized experience equivalent to GS-9, or certification by the American Board of Forensic Document Examiners; and for GS-12 or GS-13, a bachelor's degree, or higher education and one year of specialized experience equivalent to the next lower grade level. Tentative appointees must pass a background investigation, drug screening test and polygraph exam, and qualify for a top-secret security clearance.

Training: Training for FBI Document Analysts includes a variety of courses and professional seminars which are presented by FBI staff, academic institutions, ink and paper producers, and related professional organizations. Instruction focuses on ink and paper chemistry and dating procedures, various printing processes, laboratory techniques, and other aspects of forensic document examination. These personnel must successfully complete training necessary for certification as an FBI Forensic Examiner.

Contact: Laboratory Division, Federal Bureau of Investigation, 935 Pennsylvania Ave. NW, Room 3437; Washington, DC 20535. Phone: 202-324-2727. World Wide Web: http://www.fbi.gov/.

DOCUMENT ANALYST (GS-1397)
BUREAU OF ALCOHOL, TOBACCO AND FIREARMS
U.S. DEPARTMENT OF THE TREASURY

Overview: Document Analysts of the Bureau of Alcohol, Tobacco and Firearms (ATF) are responsible for conducting examinations of document evidence in support of enforcement operations of the Bureau. Primary responsibilities include conducting comparisons of questioned and known handwriting, hand printing, typewriting, photocopies and other documents to establish authenticity, alteration, or common authorship; performing document examinations using sequential morphological, chemical, microscopic, photographic, and computer imaging techniques in the examination of questioned and known documents; providing advice and assistance to United States Attorneys, state prosecuting attorneys, ATF Special Agents, and investigators from other federal, state and local law enforcement agencies on matters relating to forensic document examination; conducting research and development projects on the identification and analysis of document evidence leading to improved technology and methodology to solve evidence problems; preparing written reports of findings; furnishing depositions and affidavits; providing expert testimony in evidentiary hearings and criminal trials in support of their findings; assisting with the preparation of training materials; conducting training in effective procedures for the collection, preservation, labeling, packaging and submission of document evidence for laboratory examination; and representing ATF in national and local peer group professional organizations.

Qualifications: Applicants must be U.S. citizens. Requirements for appointment to GS-5 level include completion of a four-year course of study leading to a bachelor's degree, OR three years general experience, one year of which was equivalent to GS-4; for GS-7, one full year of graduate education, or superior academic achievement during undergraduate studies, OR one year of specialized experience equivalent to GS-5; for GS-9, a master's degree or two years of graduate education, OR one year of specialized experience equivalent to GS-7; for GS-11, a Ph.D. or equivalent doctoral degree, or three years of graduate education, OR one year of specialized experience equivalent to GS-9; and for GS-12 or GS-13, one year of specialized experience equivalent to the next lower grade level. Undergraduate or graduate education must have included major study in the areas of either physical or biological science, graphic arts, police science, criminology, or law. In some cases, qualifying education may be substituted for experience, and vice versa. A background investigation is required.

Training: Ongoing training for ATF Document Analysts includes a variety of courses, workshops, and seminars concerning questioned document examination, forensic handwriting analysis, physiology of handwriting, forensic science laboratory techniques, imaging methods, technical equipment, courtroom testimony, and other related subjects. Courses are offered by organizations such as the ATF National Academy, Federal Law Enforcement Training Center, colleges and universities, American Board of Forensic Document Examiners, and other professional forensic science organizations.

Contact: Personnel Division; Bureau of Alcohol, Tobacco and Firearms; 650 Massachusetts Avenue NW, Room 4100; Washington, DC 20226. Phone: 202-927-8423. World Wide Web: http://www.atf.treas.gov/. E-mail: PersDiv@atfhq.atf.treas.gov.

DOCUMENT ANALYST (GS-1397)
UNITED STATES SECRET SERVICE
U.S. DEPARTMENT OF THE TREASURY

Overview: Document Analysts in the Counterfeit Division of the United States Secret Service (USSS) analyze documents and paraphernalia associated with counterfeiting operations, and also provide other analytical services in support of USSS investigative and protective functions. Analyses often focuses on counterfeit currency, identification cards, credit cards, checks, bonds, and threatening correspondence directed toward persons protected by the USSS. Primary responsibilities include using magnifying devices, specialized lighting and energy sources, computers, energy dispersive x-ray, spectrum analyzers, and a wide range of techniques and procedures to examine, identify, and classify questioned and known documents; serving as an expert analyst during crime scene investigations; utilizing laboratory instruments applying the principles of organic and inorganic chemistry, ink and paper chemistry, physics, and related scientific and technical areas to identify, analyze and draw conclusions from examinations; participating in research to resolve difficult problems and issues from a variety of sources, and to analyze aspects of technological advances and their effect on USSS investigative and enforcement operations; coordinating activities and maintaining liaison with federal, state and local law enforcement agencies; preparing written reports of findings; testifying as an expert witness in federal and other criminal trials and hearings to present evidence pertaining to the analysis of document evidence; and maintaining the operation of forensic laboratories.

Qualifications: Applicants must be U.S. citizens. Requirements for appointment to GS-5 level include completion of a four-year course of study leading to a bachelor's degree, OR three years general experience, one year of which was equivalent to GS-4; for GS-7, one full year of graduate education, or superior academic achievement during undergraduate studies, OR one year of specialized experience equivalent to GS-5; for GS-9, a master's degree or two years of graduate education, OR one year of specialized experience equivalent to GS-7; for GS-11, a Ph.D. or equivalent doctoral degree, or three years of graduate education, OR one year of specialized experience equivalent to GS-9; and for GS-12 or GS-13, one year of specialized experience equivalent to the next lower grade level. Undergraduate or graduate education must have included major study in the areas of either physical or biological science, graphic arts, police science, criminology, or law. In some cases, qualifying education may be substituted for experience, and vice versa. Tentative appointees must pass a drug screening test and background investigation, and qualify for a top-secret security clearance.

Training: USSS Document Analysts attend in-house training and professional conferences and workshops throughout their careers which focus on subjects such as handwriting and hand printing comparison, identification of machined impressions, ink analysis, obliterated writings, currency production, counterfeiting techniques, and questioned document examination methods. Training is presented by USSS staff, paper and ink manufacturers, and organizations such as the U.S. Mint, Bureau of Engraving and Printing, American Numismatic Association, Institute of Paper Science and Technology, American Society of Questioned Document Examiners, International Association for Identification, and American Academy of Forensic Sciences.

Contact: Personnel Division, U.S. Secret Service, 1800 G Street NW, Room 912; Washington, DC 20223. Phone: 202-435-5708 or 800-827-7783. World Wide Web: http://www.treas.gov/usss/.

EVIDENCE AND SEIZED PROPERTY CUSTODIAN (GS-1802)
UNITED STATES FISH AND WILDLIFE SERVICE
U.S. DEPARTMENT OF THE INTERIOR

Overview: Evidence and Seized Property Custodians of the United States Fish and Wildlife Service (FWS) perform administrative functions concerning the seizure and maintenance of property and evidence in support of FWS law enforcement operations. Primary responsibilities include receiving evidence and seized property from FWS Special Agents and Wildlife Inspectors; making appropriate entries into manual logs and computer systems; maintaining records pertaining to evidence or property, such as evidence chain of custody receipts, property seizure notices, sales and donation records, and property or evidence destruction records; maintaining physical security of evidence storage facilities; coding and entering data in computer systems relating to forfeited or abandoned property, import and export declarations, and case reports; preparing and processing violation notices for federal court cases; working with appropriate authorities to carry out administrative property forfeiture proceedings, including the posting of forfeiture notices in newspapers; following through with disposal of forfeited or abandoned property; and maintaining related records and follow-up files.

Qualifications: Applicants must be U.S. citizens. Requirements for appointment to GS-4 level include two years of education above high school, OR one year of general experience; for GS-5, four years of education above high school, OR one year of specialized experience equivalent to at least GS-4; and for grades GS-6 and above, one year of specialized experience equivalent to the next lower grade level. Applicants are rated on their experience, education, training, employment performance evaluations and awards as they relate to the position. Qualifying experience and education may be combined to meet total experience requirements for positions at grades GS-5 and below.

Training: FWS Evidence and Seized Property Custodians complete ongoing on-the-job and in-house training on the subjects of evidence handling and tracking procedures, chain of custody requirements, computer system hardware and software, FWS policies and regulations, and other relevant topics.

Contact: Division of Law Enforcement, U.S. Fish and Wildlife Service, P.O. Box 3247; Arlington, VA 22203. Phone: 703-358-1949. World Wide Web: http://www.fws.gov/~r9dle/div_le.html.

EXPLOSIVES ENFORCEMENT SPECIALIST (GS-1801)
BUREAU OF ALCOHOL, TOBACCO AND FIREARMS
U.S. DEPARTMENT OF THE TREASURY

Overview: Explosives Enforcement Specialists of the Bureau of Alcohol, Tobacco and Firearms (ATF) provide direct technical support to ATF Special Agents and other law enforcement officers during the course of criminal investigations involving explosives and destructive incendiary devices. ATF Explosives Enforcement Specialists are responsible for providing on-site expertise to investigations concerning criminal and accidental explosions and arson; identifying bombs and other explosive devices; examining evidence; assembling, disassembling, and testing explosives and incendiary devices; using appropriate technical procedures and equipment to determine cause and origin of explosions or fires; writing reports and preparing documentation on the effects of bombs and destructive devices; making explosion and arson classifications for industry and other agencies; assisting in the preparation of court cases which involve arson and explosives incidents; and providing testimony in evidentiary hearings and criminal trials in support of findings and expert opinion.

Qualifications: Applicants must be U.S. citizens. Requirements for appointment to GS-5 level include completion of a four-year course of study leading to a bachelor's degree, OR three years general experience, one year of which was equivalent to GS-4; for GS-7, one full year of graduate education, or superior academic achievement during undergraduate studies, OR one year of specialized experience equivalent to GS-5; for GS-9, a master's degree or two years of graduate education, OR one year of specialized experience equivalent to GS-7; for GS-11, a Ph.D. or equivalent doctoral degree, or three years of graduate education, OR one year of specialized experience equivalent to GS-9; and for GS-12, one year of specialized experience equivalent to GS-11. In some cases, qualifying education may be substituted for experience, and vice versa. Tentative appointees must pass a background investigation and drug screening test, and qualify for a security clearance.

Training: ATF Explosives Enforcement Specialists attend courses throughout their careers which focus on subjects such as weapon familiarization and caches, pyrotechnics, arson and explosives investigation, search techniques, commercial and homemade explosives, radio-controlled explosive devices, car bombs, triggering devices, low-intensity conflict, booby traps, chemical and biological munitions, explosive ordnance disposal, evaluation and recovery of underwater explosives, photography, hazardous materials, terrorist attacks, hostage situations, and electronic devices. Training programs are conducted by ATF staff, the

Federal Law Enforcement Training Center, colleges and universities, and other recognized organizations and authorities.

Contact: Personnel Division; Bureau of Alcohol, Tobacco and Firearms; 650 Massachusetts Avenue NW, Room 4100; Washington, DC 20226. Phone: 202-927-8423. World Wide Web: http://www.atf.treas.gov/. E-mail: PersDiv@atfhq.atf.treas.gov.

FINGERPRINT EXAMINER (GS-0072)
FEDERAL BUREAU OF INVESTIGATION
U.S. DEPARTMENT OF JUSTICE

Overview: Fingerprint Examiners of the Federal Bureau of Investigation (FBI) are responsible for classifying, searching, verifying, and filing fingerprints and other vestigial prints for identification in support of criminal investigations for the FBI and other federal, state and local law enforcement agencies. Primary responsibilities include the examination of crime scene evidentiary materials by chemical or physical means, lasers, and alternative light sources for the detection and development of latent fingerprints, palm prints, footprints, and lip prints; developing, analyzing, preserving and identifying impressions of fingerprints and other body parts; and comparing latent prints with the known prints of suspects or victims. These personnel also assist in the identification of deceased victims of accidents or catastrophes involving United States citizens; prepare detailed reports of findings developed from examination and analysis of evidence; assist investigators and prosecuting attorneys with criminal case preparation; provide testimony in evidentiary hearings and criminal trials in support of findings and expert opinion; and maintain laboratory reports and records.

Qualifications: Applicants must be U.S. citizens. Requirements for appointment to the GS-7 level include one year of specialized experience equivalent to GS-5 that demonstrated the ability to classify inked fingerprints; for GS-9, one year of specialized experience equivalent to GS-7 that provided knowledge of the techniques for comparing and lifting latent fingerprints on evidentiary materials, in photographing latent and inked prints, and in making photographic enlargements for court demonstrations; for GS-11, one year of specialized experience equivalent to GS-9 performing difficult latent fingerprint examinations, preparing written laboratory reports based on examinations, and testifying as an expert witness in the area of latent fingerprint examinations; and for GS-12, one year of specialized experience equivalent to GS-11 analyzing complex fingerprint cases and imperfect or partial latent fingerprint impressions that contain only the minimum number of points necessary to make an identification, and conducting methods development projects to improve latent fingerprint examination capabilities. Tentative appointees must pass a physical examination, drug screening test and background investigation, and qualify for a security clearance.

Training: FBI Fingerprint Examiners attend an in-house training program which focuses on the examination and classification of fingerprints, identification procedures, and FBI policies and procedures relating to fingerprint classification. These personnel also complete a period of supervised work experience.

Contact: Laboratory Division, Federal Bureau of Investigation, 935 Pennsylvania Ave. NW, Room 3437; Washington, DC 20535. Phone: 202-324-2727. World Wide Web: http://www.fbi.gov/.

FINGERPRINT SPECIALIST (GS-0072)
NAVAL CRIMINAL INVESTIGATIVE SERVICE
U.S. DEPARTMENT OF DEFENSE

Overview: The Naval Criminal Investigative Service (NCIS) operates regional forensic laboratories and technical services offices in support of NCIS field operations, the United States Marine Corps, other Defense Department investigative organizations, and local law enforcement agencies in order to provide rapid and accurate forensic analysis of crime scene evidence. Primary responsibilities of NCIS Fingerprint Specialists include conducting visual, chemical, photographic and other scientific and instrumental examinations of physical evidence and developed latent impressions to form opinions regarding their identification; developing, analyzing, preserving and identifying impressions of fingerprints and other body parts; employing special microscopic and photographic processes for the examination of physical evidence; identifying glove impressions; performing digital image capture, image enhancement, and image retention of forensic evidence; preparing formal written reports on the results of examinations; assisting prosecuting attorneys with criminal case preparation; testifying in court; maintaining records; attending scientific conferences and symposia; and establishing and conducting formal training programs for criminal investigators. NCIS Fingerprint Specialists are stationed at NCIS Regional Forensic Laboratories in Norfolk, Virginia, and San Diego, California. This is a civilian position and does not require active duty military service.

Qualifications: Applicants must be U.S. citizens. Requirements for appointment to the GS-7 level include one year of specialized experience equivalent to GS-5 that demonstrated the ability to classify inked fingerprints; for GS-9, one year of specialized experience equivalent to GS-7 that provided knowledge of the techniques for comparing and lifting latent fingerprints on evidentiary materials, in photographing latent and inked prints, and in making photographic enlargements for court demonstrations; for GS-11, one year of specialized experience equivalent to GS-9 performing difficult latent fingerprint examinations, preparing written laboratory reports based on examinations, and testifying as an expert witness in the area of latent fingerprint examinations; for GS-12, one year of specialized experience equivalent to GS-11 analyzing complex fingerprint cases and imperfect or partial latent fingerprint impressions that contain only the minimum number of points necessary to make an identification, and conducting methods development projects to improve latent fingerprint examination capabilities; and for GS-13, one year of specialized experience equivalent to GS-12 working independently conducting visual, chemical, photographic, and other scientific and instrumental examinations of complex submissions of physical evidence and forming opinions regarding identification of latent prints or impressions. Tentative appointees must pass a drug screening test and background investigation, and qualify for a top-secret security clearance.

Training: Initial and in-service training for NCIS Fingerprint Specialists consists of a wide range of professional seminars, conferences, and symposia hosted by organizations such as the International Association for Identification and the American Academy of Forensic Sciences, among others.

Contact: Naval Criminal Investigative Service, 716 East Sicard Street SE, Building 111, Washington Navy Yard; Washington, DC 20388. Phone: 202-433-9162. World Wide Web: http://www.ncis.navy.mil/.

FINGERPRINT SPECIALIST (GS-0072)
BUREAU OF ALCOHOL, TOBACCO AND FIREARMS
U.S. DEPARTMENT OF THE TREASURY

Overview: Fingerprint Specialists of the Bureau of Alcohol, Tobacco and Firearms (ATF) Identification Section are responsible for the examination and identification of fingerprint evidence relating to complex, delicate, sensitive, and sensational criminal cases in support of the Bureau's enforcement of federal laws. Primary responsibilities of ATF Fingerprint Specialists include responding to major crime scenes to search for, collect, preserve, label and package evidence; performing latent fingerprint examination using visual, microscopic, photographic, computer image enhancement, complex sequential chemical and physical development techniques, and other scientific and instrumental examinations of latent impressions to form opinions regarding their identification; preparing reports of findings and expert opinions developed from examination and analyses of evidence; assisting prosecuting attorneys with criminal case preparation; providing testimony in evidentiary hearings and criminal trials in support of findings and expert opinion; and maintaining ATF forensic laboratory reports and records.

Qualifications: Applicants must be U.S. citizens. Requirements for appointment to the GS-7 level include one year of specialized experience equivalent to GS-5 that demonstrated the ability to classify inked fingerprints; for GS-9, one year of specialized experience equivalent to GS-7 that provided knowledge of the techniques for comparing and lifting latent fingerprints on evidentiary materials, in photographing latent and inked prints, and in making photographic enlargements for court demonstrations; for GS-11, one year of specialized experience equivalent to GS-9 performing difficult latent fingerprint examinations, preparing written laboratory reports based on examinations, and testifying as an expert witness in the area of latent fingerprint examinations; and for GS-12, one year of specialized experience equivalent to GS-11 analyzing complex fingerprint cases and imperfect or partial latent fingerprint impressions that contain only the minimum number of points necessary to make an identification, and conducting methods development projects to improve latent fingerprint examination capabilities. Tentative appointees must pass a physical examination, drug screening test and background investigation, and qualify for a security clearance.

Training: Training for ATF Fingerprint Specialists includes a wide range of basic and advanced courses, seminars, and workshops which focus on fingerprint classification, latent print comparison and identification, courtroom testimony, imaging methods, technical equipment, laboratory techniques, and other related subjects. Courses are offered by organizations such as the ATF National Academy, Federal Law Enforcement Training Center, FBI Academy, colleges and universities, International Association for Identification, and other professional forensic science organizations.

Contact: Personnel Division; Bureau of Alcohol, Tobacco and Firearms; 650 Massachusetts Avenue NW, Room 4100; Washington, DC 20226. Phone: 202-927-8423. World Wide Web: http://www.atf.treas.gov/. E-mail: PersDiv@atfhq.atf.treas.gov.

FINGERPRINT SPECIALIST (GS-0072)
UNITED STATES SECRET SERVICE
U.S. DEPARTMENT OF THE TREASURY

Overview: Fingerprint Specialists in the Forensic Sciences Division of the United States Secret Service (USSS) perform complex, delicate, and sensitive fingerprint identification assignments in support of USSS investigative and protective functions. Primary responsibilities include conducting complete examinations of a variety of surfaces to develop, examine, preserve and identify latent fingerprints; serving as a member of a response team dispatched to crime scenes; conducting visual, chemical, photographic and other scientific and instrumental examinations of latent impressions to form opinions regarding their identification; utilizing Automated Fingerprint Identification, Live Scan, and other state-of-the-art technology to develop, enhance and preserve latent fingerprints; preparing formal written reports on the results of examinations; conducting methods development projects to improve latent fingerprint examination capabilities; assisting prosecuting attorneys with criminal case preparation; testifying in court as an expert witness in the area of latent fingerprint examination; and maintaining laboratory reports and records.

Qualifications: Applicants must be U.S. citizens. Requirements for appointment to the GS-7 level include one year of specialized experience equivalent to GS-5 that demonstrated the ability to classify inked fingerprints; for GS-9, one year of specialized experience equivalent to GS-7 that provided knowledge of the techniques for comparing and lifting latent fingerprints on evidentiary materials, in photographing latent and inked prints, and in making photographic enlargements for court demonstrations; for GS-11, one year of specialized experience equivalent to GS-9 performing difficult latent fingerprint examinations, preparing written laboratory reports based on examinations, and testifying as an expert witness in the area of latent fingerprint examinations; and for GS-12, one year of specialized experience equivalent to GS-11 analyzing complex fingerprint cases and imperfect or partial latent fingerprint impressions that contain only the minimum number of points necessary to make an identification, and conducting methods development projects to improve latent fingerprint examination capabilities. Tentative appointees must pass a drug screening test and a background investigation, and qualify for a top-secret security clearance.

Training: USSS Fingerprint Specialists attend a variety of professional conferences and workshops throughout their careers which focus on new technology relating to the processing, examination, and comparison of fingerprints, palm prints, and footprints; fluorescent chemicals used with examination equipment and light sources; and updates of ongoing research concerning the examination of fingerprints and other evidence. Training is presented by groups such as the International Association for Identification, and other professional and scientific organizations.

Contact: Personnel Division, U.S. Secret Service, 1800 G Street NW, Room 912; Washington, DC 20223. Phone: 202-435-5708 or 800-827-7783. World Wide Web: http://www.treas.gov/usss/.

FIREARMS ENFORCEMENT TECHNICIAN (GS-0301)
BUREAU OF ALCOHOL, TOBACCO AND FIREARMS
U.S. DEPARTMENT OF THE TREASURY

Overview: Firearms Enforcement Technicians of the Bureau of Alcohol, Tobacco and Firearms (ATF) are responsible for the receipt, custody, and initial administrative processing of evidence in support of ATF criminal investigations. Primary responsibilities of ATF Firearms Enforcement Technicians include receiving personally delivered evidence and completing appropriate documentation; examining firearms to determine whether they are loaded; identifying various types of firearms and ammunition; recording evidence in master record books; assigning case numbers and preparing case jackets; maintaining the custody of evidence which is not in the possession of other Firearms Enforcement personnel; returning evidentiary materials upon completion of examinations; maintaining records of the disposition of processed materials; participating in coordination and administration of the Gun Control Act of 1968 by furnishing technical assistance to resolve unusual problems arising in the area of firearms enforcement; utilizing reference materials including military manuals, foreign publications and other firearms literature to assist in technical aspects of the position; and assisting with the maintenance of the ATF Firearms Reference Library.

Qualifications: Applicants must be U.S. citizens. Requirements for appointment to GS-5 level include completion of a four-year course of study leading to a bachelor's degree, OR three years general experience, one year of which was equivalent to GS-4; for GS-7, one full year of graduate education, or superior academic achievement during undergraduate studies, OR one year of specialized experience equivalent to GS-5; for GS-9, a master's degree or two years of graduate education, OR one year of specialized experience equivalent to GS-7; for GS-11, a Ph.D. or equivalent doctoral degree, or three years of graduate education, OR one year of specialized experience equivalent to GS-9; and for GS-12, one year of specialized experience equivalent to GS-11. In some cases, qualifying education may be substituted for experience, and vice versa. Tentative appointees must pass a drug screening test and background investigation, and qualify for a security clearance.

Training: ATF Firearms Enforcement Technicians attend a wide range of training programs throughout their careers, consisting primarily of in-house courses conducted by ATF staff, and advanced armorers schools presented by firearms manufacturers and other training organizations. Training often focuses on subjects such as firearms handling, examination, and identification; gunsmithing techniques; and mechanical aspects of firearms.

Contact: Personnel Division; Bureau of Alcohol, Tobacco and Firearms; 650 Massachusetts Avenue NW, Room 4100; Washington, DC 20226. Phone: 202-927-8423. World Wide Web: http://www.atf.treas.gov/. E-mail: PersDiv@atfhq.atf.treas.gov.

FORENSIC CHEMIST (GS-1320)
DRUG ENFORCEMENT ADMINISTRATION
U.S. DEPARTMENT OF JUSTICE

Overview: Drug Enforcement Administration (DEA) Forensic Chemists conduct complex analyses of samples to detect the presence of controlled substances in support of investigations concerning the illicit growing, manufacture or distribution of controlled substances. Primary responsibilities include conducting quantitative and qualitative analysis of samples; calibrating and operating analytical instruments to independently analyze and identify difficult, complex, new, unusual and unprecedented samples of controlled substances, adulterants and diluents; conducting research in the development of new methods of controlled substance analysis; developing intelligence data used to determine trends in international trafficking of illicit drugs; supporting DEA Special Agents, Task Force Officers and Diversion Investigators in criminal investigations; maintaining liaison with international, federal, state and local academic research organizations in order to exchange information; providing expert testimony in federal and state courts in criminal cases against sophisticated criminal organizations; and providing forensic support to the FBI, United States Customs Service, and other federal law enforcement agencies in drug investigations.

Qualifications: Applicants must be U.S. citizens. Requirements for appointment to GS-5 level include completion of a four-year course of study leading to a bachelor's degree, with a major in physical sciences, life sciences, or engineering that included thirty semester hours in chemistry, supplemented by coursework in mathematics and at least six semester hours of physics, OR a combination of education and experience, the coursework of which was equivalent to a major as indicated above; for GS-7, one full year of graduate education related to the position, or superior academic achievement during undergraduate studies, OR one year of specialized experience equivalent to GS-5; for GS-9, a master's degree or two years of graduate education related to the position, OR one year of specialized experience equivalent to GS-7; for GS-11, a Ph.D. or equivalent doctoral degree, or three years of graduate education related to the position, OR one year of specialized experience equivalent to GS-9; and for GS-12 or GS-13, one year of specialized experience equivalent to the next lower grade level. In some cases, qualifying education may be substituted for experience, and vice versa. Those tentatively selected must qualify for a security clearance, and pass a background investigation and drug screening test.

Training: Initial training for DEA Forensic Chemists consists of a six-month on-the-job orientation to laboratory procedures, evidence handling practices, chain of custody requirements, and various analytical techniques. This training is followed by a three-week DEA Forensic Chemist Basic School which focuses primarily on DEA policies, administrative paperwork, ethics, and laboratory procedures. In-service training includes in-house instruction relating to instrumental analysis, instrument maintenance and calibration, methods of analysis, and other subjects. These personnel also attend conferences, seminars and workshops presented by organizations such as the American Academy of Forensic Sciences.

Contact: Recruiting information can be obtained from any DEA Field Office, or by contacting Drug Enforcement Administration; Washington, DC 20537. Phone: 202-307-1000 or 800-DEA-4288. World Wide Web: http://www.usdoj.gov/dea/.

FORENSIC CHEMIST (GS-1320)
BUREAU OF ALCOHOL, TOBACCO AND FIREARMS
U.S. DEPARTMENT OF THE TREASURY

Overview: Forensic Chemists of the Bureau of Alcohol, Tobacco and Firearms (ATF) perform analyses of physical evidence or samples pertaining to criminal and regulatory enforcement cases using chemical, physical and instrumental techniques. Responsibilities include determining the chemical and physical properties of alcohol and tobacco products, firearms, explosives, fire debris and other substances; ascertaining the specific data to be obtained; identifying the approach, methods and procedures to be used; making adaptations and modifications of existing methods to satisfy unusual requirements and to solve specific problems; compiling accurate data and interpreting the results; preparing laboratory reports with conclusions supported by the analytical data; assisting prosecuting attorneys with criminal case preparation; and testifying in court as an expert witness. ATF Forensic Chemists assigned to the Explosives Section examine explosives, accelerants, gunshot residue, soil, hair, paint, fibers, glass, plastics and metals in connection with criminal cases to identify suspects and types of criminal offenses involved. Those assigned to the Alcohol and Tobacco Laboratory analyze alcoholic beverages, medicines, flavors, foods and products made with specially denatured alcohol to monitor industry practices and ensure compliance with applicable laws and regulations.

Qualifications: Applicants must be U.S. citizens. Requirements for appointment to GS-5 level include completion of a four-year course of study leading to a bachelor's degree, with a major in physical sciences, life sciences, or engineering that included thirty semester hours in chemistry, supplemented by coursework in mathematics and at least six semester hours of physics, OR a combination of education and experience, the coursework of which was equivalent to a major as indicated above; for GS-7, one full year of graduate education related to the position, or superior academic achievement during undergraduate studies, OR one year of specialized experience equivalent to GS-5; for GS-9, a master's degree or two years of graduate education related to the position, OR one year of specialized experience equivalent to GS-7; for GS-11, a Ph.D. or equivalent doctoral degree, or three years of graduate education related to the position, OR one year of specialized experience equivalent to GS-9; and for GS-12 or GS-13, one year of specialized experience equivalent to the next lower grade level. In some cases, qualifying education may be substituted for experience, and vice versa. Tentative appointees must pass a background investigation.

Training: ATF Forensic Chemists complete a variety of training courses throughout their careers which focus on pyrotechnics and explosives, investigative techniques, technical equipment and instrumentation, theoretical and analytical chemistry, forensic microscopy, gas chromatography, hazardous materials, fire debris, courtroom testimony, and other related subjects. These courses are presented by organizations such as the ATF National Academy, Federal Law Enforcement Training Center, EPA National Enforcement Training Institute, International Association of Bomb Technicians and Investigators, colleges and universities, and various manufacturers and vendors of technical equipment.

Contact: Personnel Division; Bureau of Alcohol, Tobacco and Firearms; 650 Massachusetts Avenue NW, Room 4100; Washington, DC 20226. Phone: 202-927-8423. World Wide Web: http://www.atf.treas.gov/. E-mail: PersDiv@atfhq.atf.treas.gov.

LAW ENFORCEMENT TRAINING INSTRUCTOR (GS-1712)
FEDERAL LAW ENFORCEMENT TRAINING CENTER
U.S. DEPARTMENT OF THE TREASURY

Overview: The Federal Law Enforcement Training Center (FLETC) employs a cadre of professional instructors who conduct training at the FLETC main campus in Glynco, Georgia, a satellite campus in Artesia, New Mexico, and a temporary facility in Charleston, South Carolina (see Chapter 16). FLETC Law Enforcement Training Instructors are responsible for conducting research and participating in analytical processes involved in the development and delivery of training programs; developing lesson plans, course materials and diverse instructional methods; conducting classroom and practical application sessions; and initiating training program content changes to achieve course objectives. Depending upon particular areas of expertise, FLETC Instructors are assigned to divisions including Behavioral Sciences; Driver and Marine; Enforcement Operations; Enforcement Techniques; Firearms; Legal; Physical Techniques; Program Support; Security Specialties; Training Operations; as well as the Financial Fraud Institute; FLETC Management Institute; and National Center for State, Local and International Law Enforcement Training.

Qualifications: Applicants must be U.S. citizens. Requirements for appointment to GS-7 level include one full year of graduate education, or superior academic achievement during undergraduate studies, OR one year of specialized experience equivalent to GS-5; for GS-9, a master's degree or two years of graduate education, OR one year of specialized experience equivalent to GS-7; for GS-11, a Ph.D. or equivalent doctoral degree, or three years of graduate education, OR one year of specialized experience equivalent to GS-9; and for GS-12 or GS-13, one year of specialized experience equivalent to the next lower grade level. Applicants must also have either five years experience in police or law enforcement work, or five years experience in teaching law enforcement training subjects, or an equivalent combination of police or law enforcement work and law enforcement training experience. In some cases, qualifying education may be substituted for experience, and vice versa. Tentative appointees must pass a background investigation and drug screening test.

Training: Newly appointed Instructors attend the two-week Basic Instructor Training Program at FLETC, which includes subjects such as adult learning, classroom management, instructional methodologies, effective listening, performance objectives, testing and evaluation, training aids, lesson plans, audio-visual equipment, and instructional systems design. In-service training may include courses or seminars in subjects such as research problem analysis, research methods, mentoring, and other training related to the Instructors' particular areas of expertise.

Contact: Personnel Division, Federal Law Enforcement Training Center, Department of the Treasury, Building 94; Glynco, GA 31524. Phone: 912-267-2287. World Wide Web: http://www.treas.gov/fletc/. E-mail: 102233.2271@compuserve.com.

PHOTOGRAPHER (GS-1060)
BUREAU OF ALCOHOL, TOBACCO AND FIREARMS
U.S. DEPARTMENT OF THE TREASURY

Overview: Bureau of Alcohol, Tobacco and Firearms (ATF) Photographers assigned to the Visual Information Branch, Office of Science and Information Technology, coordinate and provide a wide range of photographic services in support of ATF law enforcement and other Bureau activities. Primary responsibilities of ATF Photographers include developing technical specifications for the design and construction of new equipment to be utilized in forensic photography, such as equipment used in ATF criminal investigations to photograph evidence and crime scenes; operating a variety of standard and specialized cameras, complex photographic devices, and printing and processing equipment; developing and printing black-and-white and color prints, and 35mm slides; photographing crime scene evidence; and taking surveillance photographs utilizing an assortment of cameras and devices, special lenses and filters, pinhole cameras, and infrared equipment. Responsibilities also include photographing special events and awards ceremonies; taking training class photographs and official portraits; and photographing events or activities for public information and training purposes to be used in brochures, newsletters, multimedia presentations, training programs, and the ATF weapons catalog.

Qualifications: Applicants must be U.S. citizens. Requirements for appointment to GS-7 through GS-11 levels include one year of specialized experience equivalent to the next lower grade level. Specialized experience must have involved the operation of standard and specialized camera and film processing equipment related to the position. Applicants are rated on their experience, education, training, employment performance evaluations and awards as they relate to the position. Tentative appointees must pass a background investigation.

Training: ATF Photographers complete a wide range of training courses, seminars, and workshops throughout their careers. These programs cover camera systems and meters, special films, lenses, photographic equipment maintenance, flash photography, darkroom techniques, film processing, infrared photography, crime scene and arson photography, photographic surveillance equipment and techniques, night vision photography, and other topics. Training programs are conducted by ATF staff and organizations such as the Federal Law Enforcement Training Center, FBI, Evidence Photographers International Council, and various photographic equipment manufacturers.

Contact: Personnel Division; Bureau of Alcohol, Tobacco and Firearms; 650 Massachusetts Avenue NW, Room 4100; Washington, DC 20226. Phone: 202-927-8423. World Wide Web: http://www.atf.treas.gov/. E-mail: PersDiv@atfhq.atf.treas.gov.

SEIZURE AND FORFEITURE SPECIALIST (GS-0301)
UNITED STATES MARSHALS SERVICE
U.S. DEPARTMENT OF JUSTICE

Overview: Seizure and Forfeiture Specialists of the United States Marshals (USMS) provide technical support, information, and financial management services in the execution of the USMS National Asset Seizure and Forfeiture Program. Primary responsibilities include coordinating legal and administrative aspects of judicial and agency-initiated property seizures; attending pre-seizure meetings; receiving seizure and forfeiture-related writs, court orders and warrants, and reviewing them for accuracy; resolving various problems and discrepancies; receiving administrative documents from the Justice Department and other government agencies involved in the seizure and forfeiture process; maintaining an automated inventory and forfeiture case tracking system; compiling data for reports and records by extracting data from legal documents, seized property records, and automated systems; performing accounting functions concerning seized assets; reviewing invoices and receipts pertaining to seizure cases; monitoring reports on seized asset-related accounts; and providing direct support in procurement and property management efforts.

Qualifications: Applicants must be U.S. citizens. Requirements for appointment to GS-5 level include completion of a four-year course of study leading to a bachelor's degree, OR three years general experience, one year of which was equivalent to GS-4; for GS-7, one full year of graduate education, or superior academic achievement during undergraduate studies, OR one year of specialized experience equivalent to GS-5; for GS-9, a master's degree or two years of graduate education, OR one year of specialized experience equivalent to GS-7; for GS-11, a Ph.D. or equivalent doctoral degree, or three years of graduate education, OR one year of specialized experience equivalent to GS-9; and for GS-12, one year of specialized experience equivalent to GS-11. In some cases, qualifying education may be substituted for experience, and vice versa.

Training: Initial training for Seizure and Forfeiture Specialists consists of a one-week course presented by USMS staff which focuses on Agency policies, procedures, and rules; an overview of seizure and forfeiture processes; legal issues and statutes; procedures relating to the seizure of vehicles, boats, real estate, cash, and other assets; and property disposal methods. In-service training may include updates which focus on seizure and forfeiture program procedures; legal updates; computer hardware and software; problem solving; as well as courses pertaining to real estate sales and laws, including those offered by real estate brokers leading to licensure as a real estate agent.

Contact: Office of Human Resources, United States Marshals Service, 600 Army Navy Drive; Arlington, VA 22202. Phone: 202-307-9000. World Wide Web: http://www.usdoj.gov/marshals/.

Chapter Ten

GENERAL AND COMPLIANCE INVESTIGATORS

Injustice anywhere is a threat to justice everywhere.
– MARTIN LUTHER KING, JR.

CAREERS IN THE GENERAL AND COMPLIANCE INVESTIGATING SERIES involve inspectional, investigative, and advisory work to assure understanding of and compliance with federal laws, regulations, or other mandatory guidelines, and also to determine the character, practices, suitability, or qualifications of persons or organizations seeking, claiming, or receiving federal benefits, permits or employment. Investigative results are used to make or invoke administrative judgments, sanctions, or penalties. In some instances, general and compliance investigators work closely with criminal investigators and assist the United States Attorney's Office with criminal prosecution or civil action.

Responsibilities of general and compliance investigators vary widely, ranging from those who investigate compliance with labor laws, to others who investigate accidents involving aircraft, trains, marine vessels, and pipelines. Investigations also focus on federal food stamp and crop insurance programs, food safety, securities laws, pension and welfare plans, diversion of controlled substances, illegal immigrants, civil rights, consumer products, federal elections, environmental laws, payment of income taxes, corruption in labor unions, and provisions of other federal programs and operations.

These careers require a knowledge of investigative techniques; a knowledge of the laws, rules, regulations, and objectives of the employing agency; skill in interviewing, following leads, researching records, and preparing reports; and the ability to elicit information from persons in all walks of life. The work of general and compliance investigators often involves considerable field work and frequent travel.

Twenty-five careers which involve the investigation and enforcement of a wide variety of laws, program regulations, policies, and procedures are profiled in this chapter.

AIR SAFETY INVESTIGATOR (GS-1815)
FEDERAL AVIATION ADMINISTRATION
U.S. DEPARTMENT OF TRANSPORTATION

Overview: The Federal Aviation Administration (FAA) Office of Accident Investigation is the principal organization within the FAA with respect to aircraft accident investigation and all activities related to the National Transportation Safety Board. In addition to the investigation of aircraft accidents and incidents in the United States, FAA Air Safety Investigators perform investigations of aviation accidents worldwide involving aircraft of United States Registry; of aircraft which were either manufactured in the United States or built with U.S. components; and of aircraft which had U.S. citizens on board. FAA Air Safety Investigators serve in various areas of specialization which cover particular segments of aviation investigations. Depending upon their particular specialty, these personnel interview witnesses; examine aircraft wreckage, structures, power plants, navigational systems, components, equipment, and records; gather information pertaining to meteorology, air traffic control, air navigation, airport communications, air carrier operations, and pilot performance; monitor laboratory tests of failed or malfunctioning parts; conduct airworthiness studies; prepare detailed reports of the facts, conditions, and circumstances relating to each accident and a determination of the probable causes; provide testimony at public hearings; make recommendations to alleviate safety hazards and prevent similar accidents in the future; and perform other related functions. FAA Air Safety Investigators are eligible to receive Administratively Uncontrollable Overtime pay.

Qualifications: Requirements for appointment at the GS-9 level and above include a high school diploma or its equivalent; one year of specialized experience equivalent to the next lower grade level; a current first or second class medical certificate in accordance with FAA regulations; a valid driver's license; fluency in the English language; and no chemical dependencies or drug abuse that could interfere with job performance. Additional eligibility requirements depend upon areas of specialization, and include appropriate FAA pilot certificates and/or military ratings, and meeting specific flight hour requirements. Applicants for all grades and specializations must possess a Commercial Pilot Certificate with instrument rating, the appropriate military rating, or other certificate that meets or exceeds the requirements of the Commercial Pilot Certificate (such as an Airline Pilot Certificate). Candidates are required to appear for a personal interview and to show appropriate certificates and log books.

Training: Initial and in-service training for FAA Air Safety Investigators includes a variety of courses concerning accident investigation techniques and case studies, wreckage site evidence, technical investigative equipment, photography, fire investigations, aircraft design, metallurgy, forensic laboratory techniques, interviewing, investigator safety, new technology and equipment, helicopter investigations, and related subjects. Training is conducted primarily at the FAA Academy in Oklahoma City, Oklahoma.

Contact: Office of Accident Investigation, Federal Aviation Administration, 800 Independence Avenue SW, Room 838; Washington, DC 20591. Phone: 202-267-8190. World Wide Web: http://www.faa.gov/avr/aai/aaihome.htm.

AVIATION ACCIDENT INVESTIGATOR (GS-1801)
OFFICE OF AVIATION SAFETY
NATIONAL TRANSPORTATION SAFETY BOARD

Overview: The National Transportation Safety Board (NTSB) is an independent federal agency charged by Congress with investigating civil aviation accidents and significant accidents in other modes of transportation, and with issuing safety recommendations aimed at preventing future accidents. NTSB Aviation Accident Investigators are responsible for the investigation of aircraft accidents and incidents throughout the United States; of aviation accidents involving American aircraft operating anywhere in the world; and of accidents involving aircraft which were either manufactured in the United States or built with major components that were manufactured in the United States. Depending upon the nature of accidents, NTSB Aviation Accident Investigators examine aircraft wreckage, structures, systems, engines, and instruments; maintenance and flight records; pilot performance; evidence of fires and explosions; radar data; meteorology; flight data recorder information; air traffic control; witness accounts; and other evidence. Investigations sometimes involve work at unusual hours and for long periods of time in remote, rugged, and hostile settings. Investigations are often accomplished with the assistance of Federal Aviation Administration (FAA) Aviation Accident Investigators and specialists from regulatory agencies and other organizations outside of the NTSB who provide technical expertise. Investigative results are detailed in written reports which also serve as the basis for specific recommendations for corrective action.

Qualifications: Requirements for appointment at the GS-9 level and above include a high school diploma or its equivalent; one year of specialized experience equivalent to the next lower grade level; a current first or second class medical certificate in accordance with FAA regulations; a valid driver's license; fluency in the English language; and no chemical dependencies or drug abuse that could interfere with job performance. Additional eligibility requirements depend upon areas of specialization, and include appropriate FAA pilot certificates and/or military ratings, and meeting specific flight hour requirements. Applicants for all grades and specializations must possess a Commercial Pilot Certificate with instrument rating, the appropriate military rating, or other certificate that meets or exceeds the requirements of the Commercial Pilot Certificate (such as an Airline Pilot Certificate). Candidates are required to appear for a personal interview and to show appropriate certificates and log books.

Training: NTSB Aviation Accident Investigators receive ongoing training which focuses on aviation accident investigative techniques, NTSB operating rules and legal authority, air carrier operations, midair collisions and in-flight breakups, fracture recognition, turbine engines, propellers, forensic pathology and toxicology, interviewing techniques, air traffic control and radar, fire investigations, weather-related accidents, hazardous materials investigations, FAA accident support, accident report writing, safety recommendations, psychological stress management, and related subjects.

Contact: Office of Aviation Safety, National Transportation Safety Board, 490 L'Enfant Plaza SW; Washington, DC 20594. Phone: 202-314-6000. World Wide Web: http://www.ntsb.gov/.

CIVIL INVESTIGATOR (GS-1810)
NATIONAL ENFORCEMENT INVESTIGATIONS CENTER
OFFICE OF CRIMINAL ENFORCEMENT, FORENSICS AND TRAINING
U.S. ENVIRONMENTAL PROTECTION AGENCY

Overview: Under the Environmental Protection Agency's Office of Criminal Enforcement, Forensics and Training, Civil Investigators of the National Enforcement Investigations Center (NEIC) conduct investigations relating to violations of environmental laws such as the Clean Air Act, Clean Water Act, Resource Conservation and Recovery Act, Safe Drinking Water Act, Toxic Substances Control Act, and the National Emissions Standards for Hazardous Air Pollutants. In cooperation with multidisciplined teams of experts, NEIC Civil Investigators are responsible for developing evidence to substantiate violations; identifying, locating, and interviewing potential witnesses; identifying responsible parties and determining their ability to pay for environmental cleanup and proposed fines; developing links between various known and unknown corporate entities, such as parent corporations, subsidiaries, and successor companies, which help determine responsibility and liability for environmental violations; tracking unreported corporate or individual finances; preparing reports to support enforcement actions; and testifying in civil and criminal proceedings. Investigations are often conducted with the assistance of air, water and solid waste pollution control officials, and legal and technical representatives of other federal, state and local agencies.

Qualifications: Applicants must be U.S. citizens. Requirements for appointment to GS-5 level include completion of a four-year course of study leading to a bachelor's degree, OR three years general experience, one year of which was equivalent to GS-4; for GS-7, one full year of graduate education, or superior academic achievement during undergraduate studies, OR one year of specialized experience equivalent to GS-5; for GS-9, a master's degree or two years of graduate education, OR one year of specialized experience equivalent to GS-7; for GS-11, a Ph.D. or equivalent doctoral degree, or three years of graduate education, OR one year of specialized experience equivalent to GS-9; and for GS-12, one year of specialized experience equivalent to GS-11. In some cases, qualifying education may be substituted for experience, and vice versa.

Training: Initial and in-service training for NEIC Civil Investigators includes an orientation to the mission, policies, procedures and rules of the agency, and instruction concerning environmental laws and regulations, EPA agencies and enforcement operations, financial investigations, investigative techniques, and other courses conducted by EPA staff and outside organizations relating to the performance of EPA civil investigations.

Contact: National Enforcement Investigations Center, Office of Criminal Enforcement, U.S. Environmental Protection Agency, Building 53, Denver Federal Center; Denver, CO 80225. Phone: 303-236-5111. World Wide Web: http://es.epa.gov/oeca/oceft/neic/. E-mail: public-access@epamail.epa.gov.

COMPLIANCE INVESTIGATOR (GS-1801)
RISK MANAGEMENT AGENCY
U.S. DEPARTMENT OF AGRICULTURE

Overview: U.S. farmers have the option of purchasing federal crop insurance to protect against unexpected production losses from natural causes including drought, excessive moisture, hail, wind, flooding, hurricanes, tornadoes, and lightning. Compliance Investigators of the Department of Agriculture (USDA) Risk Management Agency (RMA) are responsible for the oversight of crop insurance program operations to ensure compliance of private insurance companies and farmers with laws and regulations related to the Crop Insurance Act of 1980. RMA Compliance Investigators perform on-site reviews of insurance company records and operations to ensure compliance with insurance agreements and related policies, procedures and guidelines; conduct farm inspections to ascertain crop production, losses, farming practices, and irregularities in claims for indemnity payments; inspect business records maintained by grain elevators, brokers and other entities to assess crop production and marketing levels; and writing investigative reports. Investigations may be conducted jointly with the USDA Office of Inspector General or other agencies.

Qualifications: Applicants must be U.S. citizens. Requirements for appointment to GS-5 level include completion of a four-year course of study leading to a bachelor's degree, OR three years general experience, one year of which was equivalent to GS-4; for GS-7, one full year of graduate education, or superior academic achievement during undergraduate studies, OR one year of specialized experience equivalent to GS-5; for GS-9, a master's degree or two years of graduate education, OR one year of specialized experience equivalent to GS-7; for GS-11, a Ph.D. or equivalent doctoral degree, or three years of graduate education, OR one year of specialized experience equivalent to GS-9; and for GS-12, one year of specialized experience equivalent to GS-11. In some cases, qualifying education may be substituted for experience, and vice versa.

Training: RMA Compliance Investigators attend the two-week Introduction to Criminal Investigations Training Program at the Federal Law Enforcement Training Center in Glynco, Georgia (see Chapter 16). In-service training may include specialized courses which focus on crop insurance program regulations, criminal and civil law, interviewing, investigative techniques, financial investigations, and other topics.

Contact: Risk Management Agency, Department of Agriculture, 1400 Independence Avenue SW; Washington, DC 20250. Phone: 202-720-2791. World Wide Web: http://www.act.fcic.usda.gov/.

COMPLIANCE OFFICER (GS-1801)
FOOD SAFETY AND INSPECTION SERVICE
U.S. DEPARTMENT OF AGRICULTURE

Overview: The Food Safety and Inspection Service (FSIS) of the Department of Agriculture is responsible for ensuring that the nation's commercial supply of meat, poultry, and egg products is safe, wholesome, and correctly labeled and packaged as required by the Federal Meat Inspection Act, the Poultry Products Inspection Act, and the Egg Products Inspection Act. FSIS Compliance Officers conduct random and planned compliance reviews and investigations relating to a multitude of commercial operations such as retail stores, restaurants, cold-storage warehouses, distributors, salvage operators, renderers, brokers, animal food manufacturers, and other handlers or processors of meat, poultry, and egg products. Reviews and

Investigations often support administrative actions, civil litigation, and referral for criminal prosecution pertaining to the sale of uninspected, adulterated, unwholesome, contaminated, misbranded or falsely labeled products; insanitary conditions in meat and poultry slaughter and processing facilities; and the slaughter, processing and sale of products from diseased or injured animals. FSIS Compliance Officers also promote and facilitate the efforts of the Compliance Division through contacts with government officials, private industry, and the general public. Investigations may be conducted jointly with the USDA Office of Inspector General or other agencies.

Qualifications: Applicants must be U.S. citizens. Requirements for appointment to GS-5 level include completion of a four-year course of study leading to a bachelor's degree, OR three years general experience, one year of which was equivalent to GS-4; for GS-7, one full year of graduate education, or superior academic achievement during undergraduate studies, OR one year of specialized experience equivalent to GS-5; for GS-9, a master's degree or two years of graduate education, OR one year of specialized experience equivalent to GS-7; for GS-11, a Ph.D. or equivalent doctoral degree, or three years of graduate education, OR one year of specialized experience equivalent to GS-9; and for GS-12, one year of specialized experience equivalent to GS-11. In some cases, qualifying education may be substituted for experience, and vice versa. Applicants must pass a background investigation and qualify for a security clearance.

Training: FSIS Compliance Officers attend a two-week basic training program conducted by FSIS staff which focuses on the Federal Meat Inspection Act, the Poultry Products Inspection Act, and the Egg Products Inspection Act; compliance review, inspection, and investigative techniques; FSIS personnel policies, procedures, and regulations; criminal, civil, and administrative actions; and cooperation with government and law enforcement agencies. In-service training may include updates of laws and regulations, and other subjects related to compliance reviews and investigative operations.

Contact: Personnel Division, Food Safety and Inspection Service, Department of Agriculture, Room 3133, South Building; Washington, DC 20250. Phone: 202-720-4827. World Wide Web: http://www.usda.gov/agency/fsis/.

DIVERSION INVESTIGATOR (GS-1801)
DRUG ENFORCEMENT ADMINISTRATION
U.S. DEPARTMENT OF JUSTICE

Overview: Diversion Investigators of the Drug Enforcement Administration (DEA) are charged with preventing and eliminating the diversion of and illicit trafficking in legitimate pharmaceutical drugs and chemicals throughout the United States. The duties of DEA Diversion Investigators encompass all front-line aspects of implementing DEA's responsibilities under both the Controlled Substances Act and the Chemical Diversion and Trafficking Act, and investigation of the diversion of controlled drugs and related substances from legitimate channels. The primary subjects of inspection or investigation are medical practitioners and their staff; pharmacies; and companies engaged in the manufacturing, distributing, importing or exporting of legitimately produced controlled substances and chemicals. Primary responsibilities include planning, organizing, and conducting investigations; examining books and records of registrants, such as physicians and pharmacists, to ascertain receipt and disposition of controlled drugs; evaluating security controls; conducting interviews; recognizing, collecting and preserving evidence; supporting DEA criminal investigative programs as intelligence is encountered related to diversion and excessive purchases of controlled drugs and diluents; and preparing detailed reports which support administrative, civil, and criminal proceedings.

Qualifications: Applicants must be U.S. citizens. Eyesight requirements include "sufficiently good vision in each eye, with or without correction." Corrected or uncorrected near vision must be sufficient to read printed material the size of typewritten characters. Hearing loss must not exceed 35 decibels at 1000, 2000, and 3000 Hz. Requirements for appointment to GS-5 level include completion of a four-year course of study leading to a bachelor's degree, OR three years general experience, one year of which was equivalent to GS-4; for GS-7, one full year of graduate education, or superior academic achievement during undergraduate studies, OR one year of specialized experience equivalent to GS-5; for GS-9, a master's degree or two years of graduate education, OR one year of specialized experience equivalent to GS-7; for GS-11, a Ph.D. or equivalent doctoral degree, or three years of graduate education, OR one year of specialized experience equivalent to GS-9; and for GS-12, one year of specialized experience equivalent to GS-11. In some cases, qualifying education may be substituted for experience, and vice versa. Tentative appointees must qualify for a security clearance, and pass a background investigation and drug screening test.

Training: DEA Diversion Investigators attend an eleven-week Diversion Investigator Training School at the DEA training facility in Quantico, Virginia, which includes instruction in controlled substances laws and regulations, pharmaceutical drug identification, drug manufacturing processes, auditing pharmacy records, drug diversion methods, interviewing methods, and investigative techniques. Periodic in-service training may focus on legal updates, interrogation methods, asset forfeiture, auditing and investigative techniques, and other specialized courses and updates as needed.

Contact: Recruiting information can be obtained from any DEA Field Office, or by contacting Drug Enforcement Administration; Washington, DC 20537. Phone: 202-307-1000 or 800-DEA-4288. World Wide Web: http://www.usdoj.gov/dea/.

FIELD INVESTIGATOR (GS-1801)
NATIONAL INDIAN GAMING COMMISSION
U.S. DEPARTMENT OF THE INTERIOR

Overview: The National Indian Gaming Commission (NIGC) is an independent agency within the Department of the Interior which is responsible for regulating and monitoring certain gaming activities conducted on Indian lands. The Commission was created by Congress to shield Indian gaming from organized crime and other corrupting influences, to ensure that Indian tribes are the primary beneficiaries of gaming operations, and to assure that gaming is conducted fairly and honestly. NIGC Field Investigators are responsible for monitoring the gaming activities of Indian tribes to ensure compliance with tribal, state, and federal gaming laws and regulations; conducting investigations of violations of the Indian Gaming Regulatory Act and the Commission's regulations; conducting background investigations of Indian gaming operation employees; preparing reports and testifying in administrative hearings and other proceedings; providing training and assistance to tribal agencies and gaming management contractors; maintaining liaison with tribal, local, state and federal law enforcement and regulatory agencies; and attending staff meetings to keep the Commission advised of developments in the Indian gaming industry.

Qualifications: Requirements for appointment to the GS-5 level include strong communication skills, both oral and written; and work experience with a tribal, local, state or federal law enforcement or regulatory agency with specific skills in gathering and analyzing information and conducting complex investigations. In addition, an undergraduate degree in criminal justice, public administration, business, or related field is preferred, as is knowledge or experience in some aspect of gaming operations.

Training: NIGC Field Investigators attend a wide range of training courses, seminars and conferences pertaining to Indian gaming laws and regulations, illegal gambling operations, gaming investigative techniques, regulatory authority, investigative jurisdiction, interviewing techniques, Indian cultural sensitivity, and other related subjects. Training is presented by NIGC staff, the FBI and other law enforcement agencies, companies which manufacture gaming equipment and devices, and other organizations.

Contact: Personnel Office, National Indian Gaming Commission, Department of the Interior, 1441 L Street NW, Suite 9100; Washington, DC 20005. Phone: 202-632-7003. World Wide Web: No Web site at this time.

FUTURES TRADING INVESTIGATOR (GS-1801)
DIVISION OF ENFORCEMENT
COMMODITY FUTURES TRADING COMMISSION

Overview: The Commodity Futures Trading Commission (CFTC) regulates trading on eleven U.S. futures exchanges which offer active futures and options contracts, as well as the activities of numerous commodity exchange members, public brokerage houses, futures industry sales personnel, commodity trading advisers, and commodity pool operators. The CFTC Division of Enforcement is the law enforcement arm of the Agency, with responsibility for the investigation and prosecution of violations of the Commodity Exchange Act and the Commission's regulations. Investigations focus on offenses such as price manipulations and illegal trade practices on contract markets regulated by the Commission; and fraud against customers involved in the trading of futures contracts, leverage contracts, and options. CFTC Investigators conduct interviews; serve subpoenas; review and analyze detailed financial, business, and accounting records obtained through subpoenas and inspections; draft memoranda and detailed investigative reports recommending legal actions; prepare charts, summaries and affidavits to be used in hearings and trials, and testify as to their content; provide technical assistance to CFTC attorneys in criminal prosecutions and administrative or civil enforcement actions; and work with other investigators, attorneys and auditors in task force operations. The Division is headquartered in Washington, DC, although CFTC investigators are also assigned to regional offices in New York, Chicago, and Los Angeles.

Qualifications: Applicants must be U.S. citizens. Requirements for appointment to GS-5 level include completion of a four-year course of study leading to a bachelor's degree, OR three years general experience, one year of which was equivalent to GS-4; for GS-7, one full year of graduate education, or superior academic achievement during undergraduate studies, OR one year of specialized experience equivalent to GS-5; for GS-9, a master's degree or two years of graduate education, OR one year of specialized experience equivalent to GS-7; for GS-11, a Ph.D. or equivalent doctoral degree, or three years of graduate education, OR one year of specialized experience equivalent to GS-9; and for GS-12 or GS-13, one year of specialized experience equivalent to the next lower grade level. In some cases, qualifying education may be substituted for experience, and vice versa.

Training: Initial training for CFTC Investigators includes an orientation program which covers the mission, policies, procedures and rules of the agency; evidence gathering techniques; as well as an introduction to the varieties of investigations encountered. In-service training includes courses or seminars pertaining to various aspects of futures and options trading, commodity exchanges, trading floor activities, interviewing and taking testimony from witnesses, organizing and presenting evidence for trial, fraud investigation, and investigative techniques.

Contact: Division of Enforcement, Commodity Futures Trading Commission, 1155 21st Street NW; Washington, DC 20581. Phone: 202-418-5320. World Wide Web: http://www.cftc.gov/enf/. E-mail: enforcement@cftc.gov.

IMMIGRATION AGENT (GS-1801)
UNITED STATES IMMIGRATION AND NATURALIZATION SERVICE
U.S. DEPARTMENT OF JUSTICE

Overview: Immigration Agents of the United States Immigration and Naturalization Service (INS) are responsible for a wide range of investigative, law enforcement, and administrative tasks pertaining to employer sanctions, criminal aliens and absconders, and other functions involving the enforcement of laws and regulations under the Immigration and Nationality Act. Primary responsibilities of Immigration Agents include the identification of violations relating to employer sanctions, aliens illegally employed in the United States, and criminal aliens; conducting investigations; locating and interviewing witnesses; locating, apprehending, and detaining absconders from deportation proceedings and aliens involved in criminal activity; preparing written reports; and assisting with deportation and other enforcement actions. Immigration Agents are authorized to conduct surveillance and undercover operations, carry firearms, and make arrests. Investigative and enforcement operations may be conducted jointly with Immigration Special Agents, various INS law enforcement personnel, and other federal, state, or local law enforcement agencies. This position is covered under special retirement provisions for law enforcement officers.

Qualifications: Applicants must be U.S. citizens. Requirements for appointment to GS-5 level include completion of a four-year course of study leading to a bachelor's degree, OR three years general experience, one year of which was equivalent to GS-4; for GS-7, one full year of graduate education, or superior academic achievement during undergraduate studies, OR one year of specialized experience equivalent to GS-5; for GS-9, a master's degree or two years of graduate education, OR one year of specialized experience equivalent to GS-7; and for GS-11, a Ph.D. or equivalent doctoral degree, or three years of graduate education, OR one year of specialized experience equivalent to GS-9. In some cases, qualifying education may be substituted for experience, and vice versa. Tentative appointees must pass a medical exam, drug screening test, background investigation, and qualify for a security clearance.

Training: Immigration Agents attend the thirteen-week Immigration Officer Basic Training Program at the Federal Law Enforcement Training Center (FLETC) in Glynco, Georgia (see Chapter 16), followed immediately by a five-week Spanish language course at FLETC. In-service training may include instruction concerning legal issues and updates, interviewing and investigative techniques, firearms proficiency, arrest techniques, defensive tactics, and other subjects.

Contact: U.S. Immigration and Naturalization Service, Department of Justice, 425 I Street NW; Washington, DC 20536. Phone: 202-514-4316. World Wide Web: http://www.ins.usdoj.gov/.

INVESTIGATOR (GS-1810)
ANIMAL AND PLANT HEALTH INSPECTION SERVICE
U.S. DEPARTMENT OF AGRICULTURE

Overview: The Animal and Plant Health Inspection Service (APHIS) of the Department of Agriculture (USDA) was established to conduct regulatory programs to protect and improve animal and plant health for the benefit of man and the environment. APHIS administers and enforces federal laws and regulations pertaining to animal and plant health and quarantine, humane treatment of animals, and the control and eradication of pests and diseases. Under the Investigative and Enforcement Services division of the Agency, APHIS Investigators conduct investigations of alleged violations of federal laws and regulations governing the interstate and international movement of plant materials and livestock; the welfare and treatment of animals; the manufacture and distribution of veterinary biological products; the transportation and interstate shipment of organisms; the standards established for accredited veterinarians working in federal or state cooperative programs; and standards for garbage and food that is fed to swine. Responsibilities also include meeting with individuals or groups representing industry, animal dealers and exhibitors, or other federal or state regulatory agencies and civic groups to explain federal programs and regulatory requirements; and training other APHIS employees in techniques for collecting evidence, conducting interviews, and enforcing APHIS regulations. Investigations may be conducted jointly with agencies such as the USDA Office of Inspector General, Customs Service, IRS Criminal Investigation Division, U.S. Fish and Wildlife Service, Food and Drug Administration, and other law enforcement or regulatory agencies.

Qualifications: Applicants must be U.S. citizens. Requirements for appointment to GS-5 level include completion of a four-year course of study leading to a bachelor's degree, OR three years general experience, one year of which was equivalent to GS-4; for GS-7, one full year of graduate education, or superior academic achievement during undergraduate studies, OR one year of specialized experience equivalent to GS-5; for GS-9, a master's degree or two years of graduate education, OR one year of specialized experience equivalent to GS-7; for GS-11, a Ph.D. or equivalent doctoral degree, or three years of graduate education, OR one year of specialized experience equivalent to GS-9; and for GS-12, one year of specialized experience equivalent to GS-11. In some cases, qualifying education may be substituted for experience, and vice versa.

Training: APHIS Investigators attend the two-week Introduction to Criminal Investigations Training Program at the Federal Law Enforcement Training Center in Glynco, Georgia (see Chapter 16), as well as an in-house orientation to the mission and rules of the Agency. In-service training may include specialized courses concerning APHIS program regulations and investigations, interviewing techniques, photography, white-collar crime, legal issues and updates, and various in-house training programs.

Contact: Investigative and Enforcement Services, APHIS, Department of Agriculture, 4700 River Road - Unit 85; Riverdale, MD 20737. Phone: 301-734-8684. World Wide Web: http://www.aphis.usda.gov/ies/.

INVESTIGATOR (GS-1810)
FOOD AND NUTRITION SERVICE
U.S. DEPARTMENT OF AGRICULTURE

Overview: The Food and Nutrition Service (FNS) administers the nutrition assistance programs of the Department of Agriculture (USDA). FNS Investigators plan and conduct investigations of retail firms that are authorized to participate in the USDA Food Stamp Program (FSP) and are suspected of unlawfully selling products or services for food stamps. Primary responsibilities include evaluating investigative alternatives and data to develop proper investigative strategies; examining records of program participation including food stamp redemption history, complaints, observed violations, and previous investigations to detect clues or links in evidence which are most likely to result in successful investigations; interacting with informants and law enforcement officers for undercover and investigative support; working in an undercover capacity and attempting to conduct violative food stamp transactions to obtain firsthand evidence; conducting interviews and preparing written investigative reports with the intent of justifying future criminal investigations by the USDA Office of Inspector General (OIG); and providing technical assistance to FNS Regional Offices, the USDA Office of General Counsel, and USDA-OIG relating to administrative hearings and judicial reviews. Senior Investigators also verify food stamp redemptions and subpoenaed sales records of firms with high redemptions; scrutinize firms that are authorized to participate in the FSP as retailers, but also conduct wholesale operations; and investigate authorized retailers that unlawfully acquire food stamps from firms not authorized to participate in the FSP. Investigations may be conducted jointly with the USDA-OIG or other agencies.

Qualifications: Applicants must be U.S. citizens. Requirements for appointment to GS-5 level include completion of a four-year course of study leading to a bachelor's degree, OR three years general experience, one year of which was equivalent to GS-4; for GS-7, one full year of graduate education, or superior academic achievement during undergraduate studies, OR one year of specialized experience equivalent to GS-5; for GS-9, a master's degree or two years of graduate education, OR one year of specialized experience equivalent to GS-7; for GS-11, a Ph.D. or equivalent doctoral degree, or three years of graduate education, OR one year of specialized experience equivalent to GS-9; and for GS-12, one year of specialized experience equivalent to GS-11. In some cases, qualifying education may be substituted for experience, and vice versa.

Training: FNS Investigators attend a two-week Introduction to Criminal Investigations Training Program at the Federal Law Enforcement Training Center in Glynco, Georgia (see Chapter 16). In-service training may include specialized courses concerning Food Stamp Program regulations and investigations, criminal and civil law, interviewing and investigative techniques, and other subjects.

Contact: Personnel Division, Food and Nutrition Service, Department of Agriculture, 3101 Park Center Drive, Room 620; Alexandria, VA 22302. Phone: 703-305-2276. World Wide Web: http://www.usda.gov/fcs/fcs.htm. E-mail: fcs-web@www.usda.gov.

INVESTIGATOR (GS-1810)
DEFENSE SECURITY SERVICE
U.S. DEPARTMENT OF DEFENSE

Overview: The Defense Security Service (DSS), formerly known as the Defense Investigative Service, provides security services to the Department of Defense (DoD) through the integration of personnel security, industrial security, information systems security and counterintelligence. DSS administers the National Industrial Security Program on behalf of the DoD and twenty-two other executive branch departments and agencies, and provides oversight to more than 11,000 cleared contractor facilities performing on classified contracts. DSS Investigators conduct security background investigations of civilian and military personnel being considered for assignments to positions requiring access to classified DoD information or highly sensitive DoD areas. Investigations focus on allegations of subversive affiliations, adverse suitability information, or any other situation that requires resolution to complete personnel security investigations. The majority of investigative activity consists of reviewing records and interviewing neighbors and employers of the subject of the investigation to verify education and employment; locating, analyzing and summarizing information; submitting factual data necessary to prove or disapprove a variety of developed allegations; completing and transmitting correspondence and written reports of investigative findings; and developing working relationships with individuals both within and outside of DSS.

Qualifications: Applicants must be U.S. citizens. Requirements for appointment to GS-5 level include completion of a four-year course of study leading to a bachelor's degree, OR three years general experience, one year of which was equivalent to GS-4; for GS-7, one full year of graduate education, or superior academic achievement during undergraduate studies, OR one year of specialized experience equivalent to GS-5; for GS-9, a master's degree or two years of graduate education, OR one year of specialized experience equivalent to GS-7; for GS-11, a Ph.D. or equivalent doctoral degree, or three years of graduate education, OR one year of specialized experience equivalent to GS-9; and for GS-12, one year of specialized experience equivalent to GS-11. In some cases, qualifying education may be substituted for experience, and vice versa. Tentative appointees must pass a drug screening test and background investigation, and qualify for a security clearance.

Training: Training for DSS Investigators consists of courses which focus on the elements of personnel security investigations; the *DSS Investigative Handbook* (Manual for Personnel Security Investigations); case management; record reviews; investigative leads; interviewing techniques; issue resolution; report writing; adjudicative procedures; polygraph examinations; DSS policies, procedures, regulations, and requirements; and other subjects. Instruction is presented through classroom lectures and practical exercises.

Contact: Defense Security Service, 1340 Braddock Place; Alexandria, VA 22314. Phone: 703-325-9471. World Wide Web: http://www.dss.mil.

INVESTIGATOR (GS-1810)
OFFICE FOR CIVIL RIGHTS
U.S. DEPARTMENT OF EDUCATION

Overview: The Department of Education (ED) Office for Civil Rights (OCR) is responsible for enforcing federal statutes that prohibit discrimination on the basis of race, color, national origin, gender, disability, or age in education programs and activities that receive federal financial assistance. Civil rights laws enforced by ED-OCR extend to all state education agencies, elementary and secondary school systems, colleges and universities, vocational schools, proprietary schools, state vocational rehabilitation agencies, libraries, and museums that receive Department funds. ED-OCR Investigators plan and conduct a range of investigative functions in support of civil rights compliance activities; identify allegations, issues, applicable theories of law, pertinent data, potential sources of evidence, investigative techniques to be employed, and the scope of cases under investigation; review records and data; interview witnesses; draft written reports of investigation; assist in complaint resolution through mediation to secure voluntary compliance with civil rights laws and ED regulations; and provide technical assistance, information and related services to education program recipients and other parties regarding their civil rights responsibilities and rights. Investigators are based in twelve ED-OCR offices located throughout the United States.

Qualifications: Applicants must be U.S. citizens. Requirements for appointment to GS-5 level include completion of a four-year course of study leading to a bachelor's degree, OR three years general experience, one year of which was equivalent to GS-4; for GS-7, one full year of graduate education, or superior academic achievement during undergraduate studies, OR one year of specialized experience equivalent to GS-5; for GS-9, a master's degree or two years of graduate education, OR one year of specialized experience equivalent to GS-7; for GS-11, a Ph.D. or equivalent doctoral degree, or three years of graduate education, OR one year of specialized experience equivalent to GS-9; and for GS-12, one year of specialized experience equivalent to GS-11. In some cases, qualifying education may be substituted for experience, and vice versa.

Training: Training for ED-OCR Investigators includes an orientation program which covers the mission, policies, procedures, and rules of the agency, followed by courses in report writing, interviewing techniques, and various investigative methods. On-the-job training and guidance is provided by senior EEO Specialists and staff attorneys on a variety of investigative functions and skills. In-service training may include courses in subjects such as EEO regulations, diversity, computer hardware and software, and computer Local Area Network (LAN) functions.

Contact: Office for Civil Rights, Department of Education, 330 C Street SW; Washington, DC 20202. Phone: 202-205-5413. World Wide Web: http://www.ed.gov/offices/OCR/. E-mail: ocr@ed.gov.

INVESTIGATOR (GS-1810)
OFFICE OF EMERGENCY AND REMEDIAL RESPONSE
U.S. ENVIRONMENTAL PROTECTION AGENCY

Overview: The Office of Emergency and Remedial Response (OERR) of the Environmental Protection Agency (EPA) manages the EPA Superfund Program, which was created by Congress to protect citizens from the dangers posed by abandoned or uncontrolled hazardous waste sites, and to develop long-term solutions for the nation's most serious hazardous waste problems. The EPA seeks to achieve prompt hazardous waste site cleanup and maximum liable party participation in performing and paying for cleanup. EPA-OERR Investigators plan and conduct investigations pertaining to Superfund sites in support of enforcement or civil actions under the Comprehensive Environmental Response, Compensation, and Liability Act of 1980. Primary responsibilities include assembling documentation necessary to support enforcement proceedings; conducting searches to identify liable parties that caused contamination; obtaining and analyzing financial records and information relating to liable parties to determine their financial status, viability, and ability to pay for cleanup; coordinating investigations and activities with other federal, state, or local agencies; preparing investigative reports; providing information to the EPA Criminal Investigation Division for criminal enforcement actions; testifying in enforcement actions and assisting the United States Attorney and EPA legal staff in preparation of cases for negotiations or litigation; and training state and local hazardous waste enforcement staff on interviewing and investigative techniques.

Qualifications: Requirements for appointment to GS-5 level include completion of a four-year course of study leading to a bachelor's degree, OR three years general experience, one year of which was equivalent to GS-4; for GS-7, one full year of graduate education, or superior academic achievement during undergraduate studies, OR one year of specialized experience equivalent to GS-5; for GS-9, a master's degree or two years of graduate education, OR one year of specialized experience equivalent to GS-7; for GS-11, a Ph.D. or equivalent doctoral degree, or three years of graduate education, OR one year of specialized experience equivalent to GS-9; and for GS-12 or GS-13, one year of specialized experience equivalent to the next lower grade level. In some cases, qualifying education may be substituted for experience, and vice versa. Tentative appointees must pass a medical examination.

Training: Initial training for EPA-OERR Investigators includes an orientation to the mission, policies, procedures, and rules of the agency, followed by instruction relating to EPA programs and operations, Superfund laws and regulations, and EPA enforcement actions. In-service training may include courses which focus on interviewing techniques, legal issues and updates, computer databases, financial investigations, money laundering, or other courses conducted by staff at the EPA, Federal Law Enforcement Training Center, or other organizations.

Contact: Office of Human Resources and Organizational Services, U.S. Environmental Protection Agency, 401 M Street SW; Washington, DC 20460. Phone: 202-260-4467. World Wide Web: http://www.epa.gov/superfund/oerr/oerrmain/. E-mail: public-access@epamail.epa.gov.

INVESTIGATOR (GS-1810)
OFFICE OF GENERAL COUNSEL
FEDERAL ELECTION COMMISSION

Overview: The Federal Election Commission (FEC) has exclusive jurisdiction in the administration and civil enforcement of laws regulating the acquisition and expenditure of campaign funds to ensure compliance by participants in the federal election campaign process. Investigators of the FEC Office of General Counsel (OGC) plan and conduct investigations concerning violations of the Federal Election Campaign Act (FECA) relating to public funding of presidential elections, public disclosure of the financial activities of political committees involved in federal elections, and limitations and prohibitions on contributions and expenditures made to influence federal elections. Primary responsibilities include reviewing complaints of FECA violations; locating records, individuals and entities; utilizing skip-tracing and other search strategies to obtain information, locate assets, and identify personal and business affiliations; interviewing witnesses and preparing affidavits; examining financial reports and documents; identifying money laundering activities; analyzing and summarizing results of investigations; preparing written investigative reports; conducting follow-up investigations to obtain supplemental evidence in cases being considered for litigation; assisting attorneys in settlement discussions in an attempt to obtain conciliation agreements that are mutually satisfactory and consistent with agency policy and authority; and participating in pretrial and trial proceedings.

Qualifications: Applicants must be U.S. citizens. Requirements for appointment to GS-5 level include completion of a four-year course of study leading to a bachelor's degree, OR three years general experience, one year of which was equivalent to GS-4; for GS-7, one full year of graduate education, or superior academic achievement during undergraduate studies, OR one year of specialized experience equivalent to GS-5; for GS-9, a master's degree or two years of graduate education, OR one year of specialized experience equivalent to GS-7; for GS-11, a Ph.D. or equivalent doctoral degree, or three years of graduate education, OR one year of specialized experience equivalent to GS-9; and for GS-12 or GS-13, one year of specialized experience equivalent to the next lower grade level. In some cases, qualifying education may be substituted for experience, and vice versa.

Training: The FEC-OGC actively recruits candidates to fill Investigator positions who are fully-trained and experienced in white-collar investigations. Initial and in-service training for FEC-OGC Investigators includes an orientation which covers the mission, policies, procedures and rules of the agency, and periodic instruction related to specific responsibilities of the position.

Contact: Personnel Division, Federal Election Commission, 999 E Street NW; Washington, DC 20463. Phone: 202-219-3690 or 800-424-9530. World Wide Web: http://www.fec.gov/.

INVESTIGATOR (GS-1810)
UNITED STATES ATTORNEY'S OFFICE
U.S. DEPARTMENT OF JUSTICE

Overview: The United States Attorneys serve as the nation's principal litigators under the direction of the Attorney General, with responsibility for conducting the prosecution of criminal cases brought by the federal government, the prosecution and defense of civil cases in which the United States is a party, and the collection of debts owed the federal government which are administratively uncollectible. Various United States

Attorney's Offices employ Investigators to perform investigative and support functions pertaining to Affirmative Civil Enforcement (ACE) litigation, healthcare fraud, and other matters. Investigations generally focus on fraud, waste, and abuse in government programs and operations, including Medicare and Medicaid fraud, defense and other procurement fraud, controlled substance violations, financial institution fraud, and other violations. Investigations tend to be highly complex and sensitive in nature, often relating to civil and criminal violations committed by prominent individuals and corporations. Primary responsibilities include determining applicable regulatory and statutory laws; conducting interviews of witnesses; planning and conducting surveillance of suspects; reviewing various business and financial records; devising methods for obtaining, preserving and presenting evidence; utilizing laboratories and other forensic services to identify handwriting, fingerprints, questioned documents and substances, sound and video recordings, and other evidence; coordinating investigative activities with federal, state and local agencies; and preparing interim and final reports on the progress of investigations.

Qualifications: Applicants must be U.S. citizens. Requirements for appointment to GS-9 level include a master's degree or two years of graduate education, OR one year of specialized experience equivalent to GS-7; for GS-11, a Ph.D. or equivalent doctoral degree, or three years of graduate education, OR one year of specialized experience equivalent to GS-9; and for GS-12 or GS-13, one year of specialized experience equivalent to the next lower grade level. In some cases, qualifying education may be substituted for experience, and vice versa. Tentative appointees must pass a background investigation and drug screening test.

Training: United States Attorney's Office Investigators attend periodic in-service training courses which are presented by Justice Department staff relating to Affirmative Civil Enforcement litigation, healthcare fraud issues, procurement and program fraud, coordinating civil and criminal intake proceedings, investigative resources, task force operations, and other topics.

Contact: Direct inquiries to the United States Attorney's Office where employment is sought, or to Executive Office for United States Attorneys, Department of Justice, 901 E Street NW, Suite 700; Washington, DC 20530. Phone: 202-307-1391. World Wide Web: http://www.usdoj.gov/usao/eousa/eousa.html.

INVESTIGATOR (GS-1810)
INVESTIGATIONS DIVISION
U.S. OFFICE OF SPECIAL COUNSEL

Overview: The United States Office of Special Counsel (OSC) is an independent federal investigative and prosecutorial agency whose enforcement authority includes the investigation of alleged prohibited personnel practices and Hatch Act violations in the federal government, as well as the litigation of cases arising out of investigations before the U.S. Merit Systems Protection Board. Investigations typically focus on personnel practices and other activities prohibited by civil service law, rule, or regulation, including provisions of the Civil Service Reform Act; violations of Hatch Act provisions relating to prohibited political activity by federal, state and local government employees; and certain cases involving the denial of federal employment or re-employment rights to veterans and military reservists seeking to return to the federal workplace following active duty with the armed services. Primary responsibilities of OSC Investigators include investigative planning and coordination with OSC attorneys; conducting interviews of witnesses and subjects of investigation; obtaining evidence by following up with pertinent leads; obtaining and reviewing documents and official records; and preparing comprehensive summaries, memoranda, and reports of investigation. OSC Investigators are based in the headquarters office in Washington, DC, as well as field offices located in Dallas and San Francisco.

Qualifications: Applicants must be U.S. citizens. Requirements for appointment to GS-9 level include a master's degree or two years of graduate education, OR one year of specialized experience equivalent to GS-7; for GS-11, a Ph.D. or equivalent doctoral degree, or three years of graduate education, OR one year of specialized experience equivalent to GS-9; and for GS-12 or GS-13, one year of specialized experience equivalent to the next lower grade level. In some cases, qualifying education may be substituted for experience, and vice versa.

Training: OSC Investigators receive on-the-job and periodic in-service training which focuses on personnel matters, agency adverse action procedures, personnel action requirements, position classifications, personnel investigations, interviewing techniques, and other relevant topics. Training is presented by OSC staff, the Federal Law Enforcement Training Center, and representatives of other government agencies.

Contact: Investigations Division, U.S. Office of Special Counsel, 1730 M Street NW; Washington, DC 20036. Phone: 202-653-7188 or 800-872-9855. World Wide Web: http://www.access.gpo.gov/osc/

LABOR INVESTIGATOR (GS-1801)
OFFICE OF LABOR-MANAGEMENT STANDARDS
EMPLOYMENT STANDARDS ADMINISTRATION
U.S. DEPARTMENT OF LABOR

Overview: The Office of Labor-Management Standards (OLMS) is responsible for administering and enforcing provisions of the Labor-Management Reporting and Disclosure Act of 1959 (LMRDA) to ensure basic standards of democracy and fiscal responsibility in labor organizations representing employees in private industry and the U.S. Postal Service. The Office also administers provisions of the Civil Service Reform Act of 1978 and the Foreign Service Act of 1980 concerned with standards of conduct for federal employee organizations. OLMS Labor Investigators conduct investigations and audits relating to improper or corrupt practices by labor unions and their officers and representatives, including violations of LMRDA provisions and related statutes. In order to protect and safeguard union funds and assets, criminal investigations often focus on allegations of embezzlement and other financial fraud by union officers or employees. Civil investigations include violations of the LMRDA which may have affected the outcome of labor union officer elections. Primary responsibilities of OLMS Labor Investigators include reviewing financial reports, union constitutions, and other documents; examining union operations and financial practices; meeting with union officials and their attorneys to observe and discuss union practices and techniques; negotiating for voluntary compliance with LMRDA provisions; supervising union elections; preparing investigative reports; referring investigative findings to the United States Attorney for possible criminal prosecution; and testifying as a witness before grand juries and in criminal and civil trials.

Qualifications: Requirements for appointment to GS-5 level include completion of a four-year course of study leading to a bachelor's degree, OR three years general experience, one year of which was equivalent to GS-4; for GS-7, one full year of graduate education, or superior academic achievement during undergraduate studies, OR one year of specialized experience equivalent to GS-5; for GS-9, a master's degree or two years of graduate education, OR one year of specialized experience equivalent to GS-7; for GS-11, a Ph.D. or equivalent doctoral degree, or three years of graduate education, OR one year of specialized experience equivalent to GS-9; and for GS-12, one year of specialized experience equivalent to GS-11. In some cases, qualifying education may be substituted for experience, and vice versa.

Training: Initial and in-service training for OLMS Labor Investigators includes an orientation to the mission, policies, procedures, and rules of the agency, as well as courses provided by Labor Department staff and outside organizations which focus on the investigation of union officer elections, white-collar fraud, embezzlement, financial disclosure reports, compliance auditing techniques, provisions of the LMRDA, financial investigations, legal issues and updates, interviewing techniques, report writing, and other subjects.

Contact: Office of Labor-Management Standards, Employment Standards Administration, Department of Labor, 200 Constitution Ave. NW; Washington, DC 20210. Phone: 202-219-7373. World Wide Web: http://www.dol.gov/dol/esa/.

MARINE ACCIDENT INVESTIGATOR (GS-1801)
OFFICE OF MARINE SAFETY
NATIONAL TRANSPORTATION SAFETY BOARD

Overview: Marine Accident Investigators of the National Transportation Safety Board (NTSB) are responsible for organizing, managing, and coordinating the investigation of major marine accidents, and also for developing and presenting reports with safety recommendations for adoption by the NTSB. Among accidents investigated are those involving the loss of six or more lives, the loss of vessels over 100 gross tons, or where damage exceeds $500,000; public and non-public vessel collisions with fatalities or at least $75,000 damage; small passenger vessels carrying more than six passengers; large passenger vessels, such as ocean cruise ships, excursion vessels, and ferries; tank ships and tank barges, commercial fishing vessels, oceangoing vessels, and inland tow vessels; and those involving serious hazardous material threats to life, property, or the environment. Results of investigations serve as the basis for specific recommendations for corrective action. NTSB Marine Accident Investigators examine safety issues relating to the adequacy of shipboard communications; design, installation, and testing of navigational and integrated bridge systems; bridge resource management; adequacy of emergency preparedness and evacuation plans; adequacy of fire prevention, detection, and control measures; boating safety standards; vessel towing procedures; port safety; human fatigue and performance; drug and alcohol use by marine personnel; and marine personnel training standards, among others. NTSB Marine Accident Investigators are required to remain on call and to respond to accident sites outside of normal work hours.

Qualifications: Applicants must be U.S. citizens. Requirements for appointment to GS-9 level include a master's degree or two years of graduate education, OR one year of specialized experience equivalent to GS-7; for GS-11, a Ph.D. or equivalent doctoral degree, or three years of graduate education, OR one year of specialized experience equivalent to GS-9; and for GS-12 and above, one year of specialized experience equivalent to the next lower grade level. Candidates must also possess knowledge and experience relating to areas such as marine engineering, steam or diesel propulsion plants, human performance, or other aspects of marine operations or accident investigation depending upon the nature of the position being filled. Tentative appointees must pass a personal interview, background investigation, and drug screening test.

Training: NTSB Marine Accident Investigators attend training programs throughout their careers which are offered by organizations such as the United Sates Coast Guard, Maritime Institute of Technology and Graduate Studies, United States Merchant Marine Academy, Transportation Safety Institute, RTM Simulation Training and Research Center, National Fire Academy, and the FBI. Training topics include marine accident investigation, accident photography, evidence preservation, arson investigation, interviewing techniques, tanker safety, bridge resource management, radar plotting, crude oil washing, public speaking, and many other subjects.

Contact: Office of Marine Safety, National Transportation Safety Board, 490 L'Enfant Plaza SW; Washington, DC 20594. Phone: 202-314-6000. World Wide Web: http://www.ntsb.gov/.

MARKET SURVEILLANCE SPECIALIST (GS-1801)
DIVISION OF ENFORCEMENT
U.S. SECURITIES AND EXCHANGE COMMISSION

Overview: The U.S. Securities and Exchange Commission (SEC) administers and enforces federal securities laws and SEC regulations to provide protection for investors and to ensure that securities markets are fair and honest. Market Surveillance Specialists of the SEC Division of Enforcement conduct investigations into possible violations of federal securities laws, and prosecute the Commission's civil suits in the federal courts as well as its administrative proceedings. Primary responsibilities include investigative planning and theory development; analyzing trading data, brokerage records and formal filings; selecting actively traded stocks to review for possible fraudulent or manipulative activity; reviewing exemptive applications, orders, and no-action requests; interviewing witnesses or interrogating suspects; taking testimony or obtaining written statements; preparing investigative reports, including detailed charts and schedules; making recommendations on further courses of actions to follow; and providing technical advice to staff on matters such as methods and practices involved in entering and executing orders for securities, the conduct of trading specialists and floor traders, activities of exchange members, and related technical and financial matters.

Qualifications: Applicants must be U.S. citizens. Requirements for appointment to GS-5 level include completion of a four-year course of study leading to a bachelor's degree, OR three years general experience, one year of which was equivalent to GS-4; for GS-7, one full year of graduate education, or superior academic achievement during undergraduate studies, OR one year of specialized experience equivalent to GS-5; for GS-9, a master's degree or two years of graduate education, OR one year of specialized experience equivalent to GS-7; for GS-11, a Ph.D. or equivalent doctoral degree, or three years of graduate education, OR one year of specialized experience equivalent to GS-9; and for GS-12 or GS-13, one year of specialized experience equivalent to the next lower grade level. In some cases, qualifying education may be substituted for experience, and vice versa.

Training: The SEC actively recruits candidates to fill Market Surveillance Specialist positions who are fully-trained and experienced in securities industry processes and functions. Initial training includes an in-house orientation which covers the mission, policies, procedures, and rules of the agency. Market Surveillance Specialists may also attend seminars which cover updates of federal securities laws and regulations, investigative techniques, or other subjects pertaining to specific responsibilities.

Contact: Office of Administrative and Personnel Management, U.S. Securities and Exchange Commission, 450 Fifth Street NW; Washington, DC 20549. Phone: 202-942-4500. World Wide Web: http://www.sec.gov/enforce.htm.

PENSION INVESTIGATOR (GS-1801)
PENSION AND WELFARE BENEFITS ADMINISTRATION
U.S. DEPARTMENT OF LABOR

Overview: As the national guardian of a vast private retirement and welfare benefit system, the Pension and Welfare Benefits Administration (PWBA) of the Department of Labor is charged with assuring responsible management of about 700,000 pension plans and six million health and welfare plans in the United States. PWBA Pension Investigators conduct civil and criminal investigations involving fiduciary breaches, benefits disputes, participants' rights, and reporting and disclosure provisions of Title I of the Employee Retirement Income Security Act of 1974 (ERISA). Primary responsibilities include identifying issues under investigation; case planning; examination of records involving financing and investment activities relating to employee benefits plans; locating pension and welfare plan participants and beneficiaries; conducting interviews; negotiating compliance with plan administrators, trustees, and attorneys; assembling and identifying exhibits for investigative reports, civil litigation, and criminal prosecutions; preparing investigative reports; making recommendations as to appropriate civil or criminal action; and conducting technical assistance sessions with plan administrators, employer and employee organizations, labor organizations, colleges and universities, and civic groups to promote understanding of ERISA.

Qualifications: Requirements for appointment to GS-5 level include completion of a four-year course of study leading to a bachelor's degree, OR three years general experience, one year of which was equivalent to GS-4; for GS-7, one full year of graduate education, or superior academic achievement during undergraduate studies, OR one year of specialized experience equivalent to GS-5; for GS-9, a master's degree or two years of graduate education, OR one year of specialized experience equivalent to GS-7; for GS-11, a Ph.D. or equivalent doctoral degree, or three years of graduate education, OR one year of specialized experience equivalent to GS-9; and for GS-12, one year of specialized experience equivalent to GS-11. In some cases, qualifying education may be substituted for experience, and vice versa.

Training: Initial training for Pension Investigators includes a three-week course presented by PWBA staff which focuses on ERISA provisions, Labor Department regulations, criminal laws concerning employee benefit plans, and investigative techniques. This training is followed by a two-week course pertaining to the operations of financial institutions; a two-week criminal enforcement course which covers criminal statutes and regulations concerning pension and health plans; and a two-week program which focuses on accounting methods. In-service training may include courses relating to investigations in an automated environment, forensic accounting, pension and welfare benefit program regulations, advanced interviewing techniques, white-collar crime, financial investigations, and other subjects.

Contact: Office of Human Resources, Pension and Welfare Benefits Administration, Department of Labor,

200 Constitution Ave. NW; Washington, DC 20210. Phone: 202-219-6471. World Wide Web: http://www.dol.gov/dol/pwba/.

PIPELINE ACCIDENT INVESTIGATOR (GS-1801)
OFFICE OF PIPELINE AND HAZARDOUS MATERIALS
NATIONAL TRANSPORTATION SAFETY BOARD

Overview: National Transportation Safety Board (NTSB) Pipeline Accident Investigators are responsible for a variety of tasks associated with the investigation of pipeline transportation accidents in the United States. Primary responsibilities include the investigation of accidents which involve the release of substances such as natural gas, propane, crude petroleum and petroleum products, or other highly volatile liquids; significant damage to the environment; fatalities or severe personal injuries; or extensive property damage. NTSB Pipeline Accident Investigators also conduct and review special pipeline transportation safety studies and investigations; evaluate pipeline transportation safety programs; exchange information with other organizations concerned with pipeline transportation safety; and report conclusions and findings in writing to the NTSB and other organizations. Results of investigations serve as the basis for specific recommendations for corrective action. Among the safety issues examined are the inspection and testing of pipelines; control of pipeline corrosion damage; vulnerability to premature failure of plastic piping used to transport natural gas; adequacy of federal and industry standards on pipeline design; damage to pipelines caused by excavation or construction activities; preparedness of pipeline operators to respond to threats to their pipelines and to minimize the potential for product releases; adequacy of gas company employee training programs; and safety performance of pipeline companies. Pipeline accident investigations sometimes involve work at unusual hours and for long periods of time in remote, rugged, and hostile settings. In addition, Investigators may be exposed to hazardous materials and bloodborne pathogens.

Qualifications: Applicants must be U.S. citizens. Requirements for appointment to GS-9 level include a master's degree or two years of graduate education, OR one year of specialized experience equivalent to GS-7; for GS-11, a Ph.D. or equivalent doctoral degree, or three years of graduate education, OR one year of specialized experience equivalent to GS-9; and for GS-12 and above, one year of specialized experience equivalent to the next lower grade level. Candidates must possess technical writing skills, as well as technical experience concerned with pipeline distribution, transmission, or liquid pipeline systems. Tentative appointees must pass a personal interview, background investigation, and drug screening test.

Training: Initial and in-service training for Pipeline Accident Investigators includes courses which focus on the inspection and safety evaluation of gas and liquid pipeline systems, risk assessment and management, odor and leak detection, gas pressure regulation, joining of pipeline materials, metallurgy and plastics, emergency response and preparedness, fault tree analysis, interviewing techniques, and other subjects. Training is presented by NTSB staff and organizations such as the Transportation Safety Institute, Federal Law Enforcement Training Center, as well as pipeline system operators, utility companies, and private consultants.

Contact: Office of Pipeline and Hazardous Materials, National Transportation Safety Board, 490 L'Enfant Plaza SW; Washington, DC 20594. Phone: 202-314-6000. World Wide Web: http://www.ntsb.gov/.

PRODUCT SAFETY INVESTIGATOR (GS-1801)
DIRECTORATE FOR FIELD OPERATIONS
U.S. CONSUMER PRODUCT SAFETY COMMISSION

Overview: The United States Consumer Product Safety Commission (CPSC) is an independent federal agency responsible for administering the Consumer Product Safety Act, Flammable Fabrics Act, Federal Hazardous Substances Act, Poison Prevention Packaging Act, and Refrigerator Safety Act to protect the public against unreasonable risks of injury from consumer products. In order to ascertain and ensure compliance with CPSC regulations, laws, and product standards, CPSC Investigators conduct inspections of manufacturers, distributors, wholesalers, and retailers who produce, assemble, distribute and sell consumer products.

Primary responsibilities include examining copies of consumer complaints; conducting site visits of production plants, company offices, distribution centers, and other facilities; examining production methods, product specifications, firm testing methods, quality control procedures, and product certification and labeling operations; inspecting plant assembly processes and records; field testing and evaluating products to determine compliance with applicable standards; identifying potential, substantial, and imminent product hazards; conducting interviews; obtaining affidavits and documents; preparing written reports reflecting significant observations and describing evidence collected; and advising business firms of their responsibilities under CPSC regulations and laws.

Qualifications: Requirements for appointment to GS-5 level include completion of a four-year course of study leading to a bachelor's degree, OR three years general experience, one year of which was equivalent to GS-4; for GS-7, one full year of graduate education, or superior academic achievement during undergraduate studies, OR one year of specialized experience equivalent to GS-5; for GS-9, a master's degree or two years of graduate education, OR one year of specialized experience equivalent to GS-7; for GS-11, a Ph.D. or equivalent doctoral degree, or three years of graduate education, OR one year of specialized experience equivalent to GS-9; and for GS-12, one year of specialized experience equivalent to GS-11. In some cases, qualifying education may be substituted for experience, and vice versa.

Training: CPSC Investigators attend a one-week New Investigator Training Course conducted by Commission staff, which includes instruction pertaining to CPSC operations; general investigative techniques; the inspection and investigation of manufacturers, distributors, wholesalers, and retailers; product quality control; collection of product samples and evidence; investigation of injuries and deaths; interviewing techniques; and CPSC laboratory operations. In-service training may include courses relating to matters such as infant suffocation; fire investigations; legal issues and updates; report writing; and computer hardware, software, and electronic mail.

Contact: Office of Human Resources Management, Consumer Product Safety Commission, 4330 East West Highway, Room 523; Bethesda, MD 20814. Phone: 301-504-0580. World Wide Web: http://www.cpsc.gov/.

RAILROAD ACCIDENT INVESTIGATOR (GS-2121)
OFFICE OF RAILROAD SAFETY
NATIONAL TRANSPORTATION SAFETY BOARD

Overview: Railroad Accident Investigators of the National Transportation Safety Board (NTSB) are responsible for the investigation of railroad accidents involving passenger, freight, rail transit, and commuter trains throughout the United States, and also for promoting railroad safety and eliminating safety hazards, improving investigative methods, and preventing railroad accidents. Primary responsibilities include examining train wreckage, track, and signals for evidence of structural failure or equipment malfunction; reconstructing components involved in accidents; conducting or observing equipment tests or crash simulations; examining train orders, operating rules, and other records that may provide information about causes of accidents; arranging for metallurgical or chemical analyses of wreckage; interviewing witnesses; applying knowledge of the interrelationships between railroad signals and train control, railroad track, locomotive power and equipment, railroad operating practices, and hazardous materials; and preparing written reports including findings as to the probable causes of accidents. Results of investigations also serve as the basis for specific recommendations for corrective action. Major safety issues examined by NTSB Railroad Accident Investigators include the adequacy of medical standards and examinations for locomotive engineers, railroad dispatching operations, train control systems, crashworthiness of locomotives and components, inspection and maintenance of equipment, and emergency response procedures, among others. Railroad accident investigations sometimes involve work at unusual hours and for long periods of time in remote, rugged, and hostile settings.

Qualifications: Requirements for appointment to the GS-9 level and above include at least one year of specialized experience which was equivalent to the next lower grade level. This experience must have demonstrated knowledge of the railroad industry, including economic and operating considerations and equipment; general safety and health principles and practices applicable to the industry; railroad accident investigation techniques; technical aspects concerned with railroad mechanical or operating systems; skill in written and oral communication, and the ability to write technical reports; and proficiency in the use of personal computers. Tentative appointees must pass a personal interview, background investigation, and drug screening test.

Training: Initial and in-service training for Railroad Accident Investigators includes a variety of courses which are presented by the NTSB and outside organizations such as railroad companies, locomotive manufacturers, and equipment suppliers. Training focuses on various accident reconstruction and investigative techniques, new technology, track structures and engineering, photography techniques, accident report writing, NTSB policies and procedures, and other subjects.

Contact: Office of Railroad Safety, National Transportation Safety Board, 490 L'Enfant Plaza SW; Washington, DC 20594. Phone: 202-314-6000. World Wide Web: http://www.ntsb.gov/.

REVENUE OFFICER (GS-1169)
INTERNAL REVENUE SERVICE
U.S. DEPARTMENT OF THE TREASURY

Overview: Revenue Officers of the Internal Revenue Service (IRS) are responsible for the collection of delinquent tax accounts and securing delinquent tax returns in order to protect the interests of the taxpaying public by obtaining maximum compliance with U.S. tax laws. Primary responsibilities include planning and conducting investigations and research; tracing the whereabouts of delinquent taxpayers; following leads and contacting third parties for information; interviewing taxpayers and witnesses; obtaining and analyzing financial statements and records; issuing summonses, liens, levies, seizures and referrals which legally require taxpayers to present various books and records; placing on public record evidence of tax liabilities; attaching bank accounts and payroll checks; seizing and selling private property; testifying in court; and helping taxpayers to understand their tax obligations. IRS Revenue Officers are assigned to field offices located in seven regions throughout the country. Much of their field work is conducted outside of office settings in meetings with taxpayers in varied environments.

Qualifications: Applicants must be U.S. citizens. Requirements for appointment to GS-5 level include completion of a four-year course of study leading to a bachelor's degree, OR three years general experience, one year of which was equivalent to GS-4; for GS-7, one full year of graduate education, or superior academic achievement during undergraduate studies, OR one year of specialized experience equivalent to GS-5; for GS-9, a master's degree or two years of graduate education, OR one year of specialized experience equivalent to GS-7; for GS-11, a Ph.D. or equivalent doctoral degree, or three years of graduate education, OR one year of specialized experience equivalent to GS-9; and for GS-12, one year of specialized experience equivalent to GS-11. In some cases, qualifying education may be substituted for experience, and vice versa. Tentative appointees must pass a tax audit and background investigation.

Training: Initial training for IRS Revenue Officers includes extensive classroom and on-the-job training in areas such as business law, tax law, financial statement analysis, investigative techniques, and collection enforcement procedures. During the on-the-job training phase, senior IRS Revenue Officers assist new Officers with the application of skills and techniques learned in the classroom with actual work assignments. Training is designed to prepare new Officers as rapidly as possible for independent performance and the responsibilities of the position. In-service training is also available to enhance advancement to higher-level positions.

Contact: Internal Revenue Service, Department of the Treasury, 1111 Constitution Ave. NW; Washington, DC 20224. Phone: 202-622-5000. World Wide Web: http://www.irs.treas.gov/.

Chapter Eleven

COMPLIANCE INSPECTORS AND SPECIALISTS

Adam was but human – this explains it all.
He did not want the apple for the apple's sake,
he wanted it only because it was forbidden.
– MARK TWAIN

CAREERS WHICH INVOLVE COMPLIANCE INSPECTION and examination are concerned with the enforcement of laws, regulations, and standards that are geared toward particular industries and organizations. These careers are highly specialized, and involve tasks such as preventing railroad accidents, obtaining compliance with wage and hour laws, inspecting underground and surface mining operations, detecting and controlling plant pests, inspecting establishments which produce alcohol and tobacco products, ensuring compliance with wildlife laws and treaties, determining tariff classifications and admissibility of merchandise, enforcing marine safety laws and regulations, and carrying out deportation proceedings.

The work of compliance inspectors and specialists requires a thorough knowledge of inspection and investigation techniques, and of the standards, laws, and regulations enforced; the ability to apply varied techniques to gain compliance, including investigation, negotiation, conciliation, education, persuasion, and litigation; and an understanding of business organization, recordkeeping systems, and practices related to the laws and regulations administered.

Careers which are profiled in this chapter are so diverse and specialized that six of the nine positions are classified in an exclusive occupational series, including GS-0249 Wage and Hour Compliance Specialists (Employment Standards Administration); GS-0436 Plant Protection and Quarantine Officers (Animal and Plant Health Inspection Service); GS-1822 Mine Safety and Health Inspectors (Mine Safety and Health Administration); GS-1854 ATF Inspectors (Bureau of Alcohol, Tobacco and Firearms); GS-1889 Customs Import Specialists (U.S. Customs Service); and GS-2121 Railroad Safety Inspectors (Federal Railroad Administration). Commercial Fishing Vessel Examiners, Deportation Officers, and Wildlife Inspectors are classified in the GS-1801 series.

ALCOHOL, TOBACCO AND FIREARMS INSPECTOR (GS-1854)
BUREAU OF ALCOHOL, TOBACCO AND FIREARMS
U.S. DEPARTMENT OF THE TREASURY

Overview: The Bureau of Alcohol, Tobacco and Firearms (ATF) employs ATF Inspectors to monitor and ensure consumer and industry compliance with laws and regulations relating to the production, processing, storage, distribution and tax system of distilled spirits, wine, beer, alcohol products, tobacco, firearms, and explosives in the United States. Primary responsibilities of ATF Inspectors include conducting inspections, examinations and investigations of breweries, wineries, distilled spirits plants, tobacco manufacturing facilities, and explosives plants; examining buildings, equipment, and finished products; taking inventory; analyzing records and reports, and evaluating reliability of recordkeeping systems; determining whether operations are in accordance with laws and regulations, whether tax liabilities have been correctly established and paid, and whether transactions requiring payment of excise taxes are reflected in tax returns; examining records of firearms and explosives transactions; determining whether beverage alcohol markets are free of illegal practices; conducting interviews of persons associated with industries regulated by the Bureau; and determining whether persons desiring to enter business in regulated industries meet established legal requirements for obtaining federal permits or licenses to conduct operations.

Qualifications: Applicants must be U.S. citizens. Requirements for appointment to GS-5 level include completion of a four-year course of study leading to a bachelor's degree, OR three years general experience, one year of which was equivalent to GS-4; for GS-7, one full year of graduate education, or superior academic achievement during undergraduate studies, OR one year of specialized experience equivalent to GS-5; for GS-9, a master's degree or two years of graduate education, OR one year of specialized experience equivalent to GS-7; for GS-11, a Ph.D. or equivalent doctoral degree, or three years of graduate education, OR one year of specialized experience equivalent to GS-9; and for GS-12, one year of specialized experience equivalent to GS-11. In some cases, qualifying education may be substituted for experience, and vice versa. Tentative appointees must pass a physical exam and background investigation.

Training: ATF Inspectors attend a five-week ATF Inspector Basic Training course at the Federal Law Enforcement Training Center in Glynco, Georgia, which includes instruction concerning firearms laws and regulations; firearms importing and exporting procedures; inspection of alcohol, tobacco and firearm plants and facilities; firearm tracing techniques; licensed firearms and explosives dealer operations; identification of firearms and explosives; industry tax stamps; ATF laboratory operations; and interviewing techniques. In-service training may include courses which focus on subjects such as firearms trafficking; alcohol, tobacco and firearm diversion; industry and legal updates; and explosive devices.

Contact: Personnel Division; Bureau of Alcohol, Tobacco and Firearms; 650 Massachusetts Avenue NW, Room 4100; Washington, DC 20226. Phone: 202-927-8423. World Wide Web: http://www.atf.treas.gov/. E-mail: PersDiv@atfhq.atf.treas.gov.

COMMERCIAL FISHING VESSEL EXAMINER (GS-1801)
UNITED STATES COAST GUARD
U.S. DEPARTMENT OF TRANSPORTATION

Overview: Commercial Fishing Vessel Examiners of the United States Coast Guard (USCG), Department of Transportation, are responsible for providing technical expertise, advanced training, and project leadership in the enforcement of marine safety, pollution prevention, and various vessel manning laws, regulations, treaties, and international conventions. Technical inspections of fishing vessels are performed in accordance with the Coast Guard commercial fishing vessel safety program. Primary responsibilities include determining that vessels have proper documentation and certification; examining vessel navigation, communication, alarm, lifesaving, pollution prevention systems, and machinery to ensure proper operation and compliance with standards and regulations; inspecting vessel hulls, internal structural members, fittings, tanks, holding areas, and structural fire protection systems to ensure that they are sound; conducting training for vessel owners and others to explain the intent and interpretation of regulations; drafting public affairs announcements; writing analytical reports; and working with commercial fishing industry personnel to ensure that vessels are operated safely, but without undue negative impact on the fishing community.

Qualifications: Applicants must be U.S. citizens. Requirements for appointment to GS-5 level include completion of a four-year course of study leading to a bachelor's degree, OR three years general experience, one year of which was equivalent to GS-4; for GS-7, one full year of graduate education, or superior academic achievement during undergraduate studies, OR one year of specialized experience equivalent to GS-5; for GS-9, a master's degree or two years of graduate education, OR one year of specialized experience equivalent to GS-7; for GS-11, a Ph.D. or equivalent doctoral degree, or three years of graduate education, OR one year of specialized experience equivalent to GS-9; and for GS-12, one year of specialized experience equivalent to GS-11. In some cases, qualifying education may be substituted for experience, and vice versa.

Training: Initial and in-service training for Coast Guard Commercial Fishing Vessel Examiners includes courses in subjects such as vessel stability, construction, and structural systems; maritime laws and regulations; safety equipment; visual distress signals; vessel firefighting and fuel systems; wooden boat inspections; Electronic Position Indicating Radio Beacons; vessel documentation and registration; enforcement operations; and other courses presented by USCG staff and other agencies or entities.

Contact: Civilian Personnel Management Division, U.S. Coast Guard, 2100 Second Street SW; Washington, DC 20593. Phone: 202-267-1890. World Wide Web: http://www.dot.gov/dotinfo/uscg/.

CUSTOMS IMPORT SPECIALIST (GS-1889)
UNITED STATES CUSTOMS SERVICE
U.S. DEPARTMENT OF THE TREASURY

Overview: Import Specialists of the United States Customs Service determine the admissibility, classification, appraisal value, and duty on the commercial importation of goods into the United States in accordance with tariff schedules and applicable laws. Primary responsibilities include reviewing entry documents submitted by importers or their representatives; examining samples of imported merchandise; determining the admissibility of merchandise and the accuracy of tariff classification and value declarations; interviewing importers and examining their business records; consulting with individuals who are knowledgeable about the physical characteristics or trade practices associated with particular varieties of imported merchandise and goods; examining and analyzing the results of Customs laboratory analyses; advising importers on probable (and in some cases binding) tariff classifications and rates of duty applicable to merchandise prior to its actual importation, and on the implications of various proposed changes in articles or business arrangements; and participating in operations with enforcement teams that investigate fraud, counterfeiting, and copyright violations.

Qualifications: Requirements for appointment to GS-5 level include completion of a four-year course of study leading to a bachelor's degree, OR three years general experience, one year of which was equivalent to GS-4; for GS-7, one full year of graduate education, or superior academic achievement during undergraduate studies, OR one year of specialized experience equivalent to GS-5; for GS-9, a master's degree or two years of graduate education, OR one year of specialized experience equivalent to GS-7; and for GS-11, a Ph.D. or equivalent doctoral degree, or three years of graduate education, OR one year of specialized experience equivalent to GS-9. In some cases, qualifying education may be substituted for experience, and vice versa. Tentative appointees must pass a drug screening test, physical exam, and background investigation.

Training: Customs Import Specialists attend a five-week Basic Import Specialist training program at the Federal Law Enforcement Training Center (FLETC) in Glynco, Georgia, which covers laws and regulations concerning the classification and appraisement of merchandise, customs duties, identification of merchandise country-of-origin, textile quota limitations, merchandise antidumping, entry documents, and other related subjects. In-service training includes a three-week course at FLETC which covers auditing and accounting techniques, examination of import entity books and records, money laundering, commercial fraud, interviewing techniques, and public speaking. Additional in-service courses are also provided which focus on specific responsibilities.

Contact: U.S. Customs Service, Department of the Treasury, 1300 Pennsylvania Ave. NW; Washington, DC 20229. Phone: 202-927-1250. World Wide Web: http://www.customs.ustreas.gov/.

DEPORTATION OFFICER (GS-1801)
UNITED STATES IMMIGRATION AND NATURALIZATION SERVICE
U.S. DEPARTMENT OF JUSTICE

Overview: During the course of the enforcement of federal laws which regulate immigration and nationality matters, the United States Immigration and Naturalization Service (INS) carries out the detention and deportation of certain criminal and non-criminal aliens. The mission of INS Deportation Officers is to provide for the control and removal of persons who have been ordered deported or otherwise required to depart from the United States. Deportation Officers must closely monitor deportation proceedings from initiation to conclusion; assist INS personnel and Assistant United States Attorneys with case processing; maintain close liaison with foreign consulates and embassies to facilitate the timely issuance of passports and travel documents required for deportation; investigate, locate and apprehend aliens who have absconded, and provide an armed escort where necessary; and respond to congressional inquiries. INS Deportation Officers are authorized to carry firearms. This position is covered under special retirement provisions for law enforcement officers.

Qualifications: Applicants must be U.S. citizens, at least twenty-one years of age, and under the age of thirty-seven. (Candidates over age thirty-seven who have previous service creditable under special law enforcement retirement provisions may also be eligible). Requirements for appointment to GS-5 level include completion of a four-year course of study leading to a bachelor's degree, OR three years general experience, one year of which was equivalent to GS-4; for GS-7, one full year of graduate-level education, OR superior academic achievement during undergraduate studies, OR one year of specialized experience equivalent to GS-5; for GS-9, a master's degree or two years of graduate-level education, OR one year of specialized experience equivalent to GS-7; for GS-11, a Ph.D. or equivalent doctoral degree, or three years graduate-level education, OR one year of specialized experience equivalent to GS-9; and for GS-12, one year of specialized experience equivalent to GS-11. In some cases, qualifying education may be substituted for experience, and vice versa. Tentative appointees must qualify for a security clearance, and pass a background investigation, drug screening test, and physical exam.

Training: INS Deportation Officers attend the thirteen-week Immigration Officer Basic Training Course at the Federal Law Enforcement Training Center (FLETC) in Glynco, Georgia (see Chapter 16), followed immediately by a five-week Spanish Language course at FLETC. In-service training may include specialized courses in deportation processing, laws of detention and arrest, immigration law, first aid, firearms proficiency, arrest techniques, and defensive tactics.

Contact: U.S. Immigration and Naturalization Service, Department of Justice, 425 I Street NW; Washington, DC 20536. Phone: 202-514-4316. World Wide Web: http://www.ins.usdoj.gov/.

MINE SAFETY AND HEALTH INSPECTOR (GS-1822)
MINE SAFETY AND HEALTH ADMINISTRATION
U.S. DEPARTMENT OF LABOR

Overview: The Mine Safety and Health Administration (MSHA) of the Labor Department administers provisions of the Federal Mine Safety and Health Act of 1977, and enforces compliance with mandatory safety and health standards as a means to eliminate fatal accidents; to reduce the frequency and severity of nonfatal accidents; to minimize health hazards; and to promote improved safety and health conditions in the Nation's mines regardless of size, number of employees, commodity mined, or method of extraction. Primary responsibilities of MSHA Inspectors include conducting safety and health inspections for metal and nonmetal mines, mills, and quarries; inspecting unknown mining operations or those that present unusual or unyielding safety or health problems; conducting investigations of mine accidents, disasters, and complaints of health and safety violations received from labor union officials, mine employees and the public; preparing reports of inspections and investigations including citations and orders; promoting safety by participating in safety meetings, providing instruction and demonstration in first aid and mine rescue, and conducting other training courses; and testifying at judicial hearings regarding notices of violations and orders of withdrawal.

Qualifications: Requirements for appointment to GS-5 level include completion of a four-year course of study above high school in any field, OR three years general experience related to mining operations, construction, excavation, electrical equipment or systems, heavy or engine-driven equipment, or heath and safety inspection or investigation in an industrial setting; for GS-7, one full year of graduate education in fields related to responsibilities of the position, OR one year of specialized experience equivalent to GS-5; for GS-9, two full years of graduate education or a master's degree in fields related to responsibilities of the position, OR one year of specialized experience equivalent to GS-7; and for GS-11 and GS-12, one year of specialized experience equivalent to the next lower grade level. Equivalent combinations of education and experience are qualifying for positions at grades GS-5 through GS-9. Uncorrected distant vision must be at least 20/50 (Snellen) in one eye and 20/70 in the other, correctable with eyeglasses (contact lenses are not acceptable) to at least 20/30 in one eye and 20/50 in the other. Near vision must be sufficient to read printed material the size of typewritten characters. Normal depth perception and field of vision are required, as is the ability to distinguish basic colors. Applicants, with or without the use of a hearing aid, must have no hearing loss in either ear of more than 40 decibels in the 500, 1000, or 2000 Hz ranges. Tentative appointees must pass a medical examination and drug screening test.

Training: MSHA Inspectors attend a twelve-week New Inspector Training program at the National Mine Health and Safety Academy in Beckley, West Virginia, which includes courses in law, investigations, courtroom procedures, safety and inspection procedures, accident prevention, industrial hygiene, mine emergency procedures, mining technology, underground ventilation, and other subjects. In-service training may include courses relating to subjects such as accident investigation, citations and orders, special investigations, mine hazards, and computers.

Contact: Mine Safety and Health Administration, Department of Labor, 4015 Wilson Blvd.; Arlington, VA 22203. Phone: 703-235-1452. World Wide Web: http://www.msha.gov/.

PLANT PROTECTION AND QUARANTINE OFFICER (GS-0436)
ANIMAL AND PLANT HEALTH INSPECTION SERVICE
U.S. DEPARTMENT OF AGRICULTURE

Overview: The Plant Protection and Quarantine (PPQ) division of the USDA Animal and Plant Health Inspection Service is responsible for programs pertaining to the control or eradication of plant pests and diseases in the United States. PPQ Officers enforce federal laws and regulations that prohibit or restrict the entry of foreign pests and plants, plant products, animal products and byproducts, soil, and other materials that may harbor crop-destroying pests or diseases. Inspections are performed at all major sea, air, border, and interior ports of entry in the United States, Puerto Rico, U.S. Virgin Islands, Bahamas, and Bermuda, as well as outlying ports and military installations. Responsibilities include the inspection of air freight, maritime cargo, overland freight, truck cargo, motor vehicles, and passengers and their baggage entering the United States; inspection and certification of domestic commodities for export; and regulation of the import and export of endangered plant species, and of genetically engineered organisms and products that present a plant pest risk. To increase efficiency, PPQ Officers utilize x-ray equipment and trained detector dogs at ports of entry and post offices for baggage and package inspections to detect fruits, vegetables, plants, soil, and meats that may carry pests and diseases.

Qualifications: Applicants must be U.S. citizens. Basic eligibility requirements for all levels include a bachelor's degree with a major in biology, agriculture, or a closely related field that included twenty semester hours of study in agronomy, cell biology, botany, entomology, forestry, horticulture, mycology, nematology, plant pathology, soil science, or related courses; OR a combination of education (as described above) and experience related to the position. Meeting basic eligibility requirements qualifies for appointment to GS-5. Additional requirements for appointment to GS-7 include one year of graduate-level education, OR superior academic achievement during undergraduate studies, OR one year of specialized experience equivalent to at least GS-5; for GS-9, a master's degree or two years of graduate-level education, OR one year of specialized experience equivalent to at least GS-7; and for GS-11, a Ph.D. or equivalent doctoral degree, or three years of graduate-level education, OR one year of specialized experience equivalent to at least GS-9. In some cases, qualifying education may be substituted for experience, and vice versa. Tentative appointees must also pass a background investigation and obtain a security clearance.

Training: Newly appointed Officers attend the PPQ New Officer Training Program, which consists of approximately nine weeks of technical instruction relating to specific duties of the position. Portions of this training program are conducted at the APHIS Professional Development Center in Frederick, Maryland, with the remainder being completed in the field. PPQ officers must also complete a prescribed training program and pass an examination to be certified as Regulatory Pest Control Applicators.

Contact: Inquiries should be directed to the facility where employment is sought, or to: Animal and Plant Health Inspection Service, Department of Agriculture; Washington, DC 20250. Phone: 202-720-2511. World Wide Web: http://www.aphis.usda.gov/ppq/.

RAILROAD SAFETY INSPECTOR (GS-2121)
FEDERAL RAILROAD ADMINISTRATION
U.S. DEPARTMENT OF TRANSPORTATION

Overview: The Federal Railroad Administration (FRA) is responsible for ensuring the safety of the nation's railroad system, which consists of more than 600 passenger, freight, and commuter railroads; 230,000 miles of railroad track; 89,000 track miles of signal and train control systems; 1.2 million freight cars; and 20,000 locomotives operating nationwide. FRA Railroad Safety Inspectors conduct inspections and accident investigations to ensure compliance with federal laws and railroad safety regulations. Inspection operations are divided into five areas of specialization including Track Inspection, Signals and Train Control, Motive Power and Equipment, Hazardous Materials, and Operating Practices. Responsibilities depend upon the area of specialization, although generally involve planning and conducting inspections of rail facilities, equipment, rolling stock, operations, and pertinent records; investigating complaints from railroad employees, legislative and governmental representatives, and the general public; conducting investigations of railroad collisions, derailments and other accidents resulting in serious injury or property damage; applying technical and regulatory standards, and knowledge of methods used in the installation, operation, maintenance and manufacturing of railroad equipment and systems; preparing investigative and accident reports; seeking correction of unsafe conditions; conducting safety meetings and training sessions relating to areas of specialization; and providing expert testimony during the course of civil litigation.

Qualifications: Requirements for appointment to GS-5 level include completion of a four-year course of study above high school leading to a bachelor's degree, with a major in engineering, electronics, physics, occupational or industrial safety, or other fields related to the position, OR three years general experience, one year of which was equivalent to at least GS-4, that provided knowledge of the construction, operation, overhaul, maintenance, repair, or installation of mechanical or electronic equipment used in an industrial setting; and the ability to read and understand written material, blueprints, specifications, or related technical material; for GS-7, one year of specialized experience equivalent to GS-5 that demonstrated knowledge of basic inspection techniques and safety practices related to the railroad industry; and for grades GS-9 through GS-12, one year of specialized experience equivalent to the next lower grade level that demonstrated knowledge of the railroad industry, including economic and operating considerations and equipment, general safety and health principles and practices applicable to the industry, and railroad accident investigation techniques. Tentative appointees must pass a background investigation and drug screening test.

Training: Initial training for FRA Railroad Safety Inspectors includes an orientation to the mission, policies, procedures, and rules of the agency. During the first two years of service, Inspectors also attend a variety of one- to two-week courses relating to each of the five areas of specialization, as well as courses concerning the inspection of bridges and steam engines, and railroad safety inspections and investigations. Additional in-service training courses presented by FRA staff and railroad industry firms are attended recurrently once specialization is achieved.

Contact: Federal Railroad Administration, Department of Transportation, 400 Seventh Street SW; Washington, DC 20590. Phone: 202-632-3124. World Wide Web: http://www.fra.dot.gov/.

WAGE AND HOUR COMPLIANCE SPECIALIST (GS-0249)
WAGE AND HOUR DIVISION
EMPLOYMENT STANDARDS ADMINISTRATION
U.S. DEPARTMENT OF LABOR

Overview: Wage and Hour Compliance Specialists of the Employment Standards Administration, Department of Labor, conduct investigations of commercial, industrial, agricultural, and other business enterprises and public institutions to monitor and ensure compliance with a variety of federal labor laws. Investigations are often conducted to substantiate violations pertaining to minimum or prevailing wage rates, overtime pay requirements, child labor restrictions, wage garnishments, domestic service in households, employment eligibility, migrant safety and health protection, certain forms of employment discrimination, and similar matters related to conditions of employment, wages, and hours worked. Primary responsibilities include conducting site visits of business establishments; interviewing employers or their representatives; observing work operations; reviewing business records; interviewing current or former employees to determine compliance with laws and regulations enforced and to substantiate violations; educating employers regarding requirements for compliance; and persuading employers to recognize violations and take appropriate corrective action for future compliance including payment of back wages or civil money penalties. Where voluntary compliance is not achieved, Wage and Hour Compliance Specialists recommend civil action to compel compliance, and in some cases work with attorneys to develop evidence and prosecute willful violators.

Qualifications: Requirements for appointment to GS-5 level include completion of a four-year course of study leading to a bachelor's degree, OR three years general experience, one year of which was equivalent to GS-4; for GS-7, one full year of graduate education, or superior academic achievement during undergraduate studies, OR one year of specialized experience equivalent to GS-5; for GS-9, a master's degree or two years of graduate education, OR one year of specialized experience equivalent to GS-7; for GS-11, a Ph.D. or equivalent doctoral degree, or three years of graduate education, OR one year of specialized experience equivalent to GS-9; and for GS-12, one year of specialized experience equivalent to GS-11. In some cases, qualifying education may be substituted for experience, and vice versa.

Training: Initial and in-service training for Wage and Hour Compliance Specialists includes courses conducted by Labor Department staff relating primarily to provisions of the Fair Labor Standards Act; Migrant and Seasonal Agricultural Worker Protection Act; Employee Polygraph Protection Act; Family and Medical Leave Act; Davis Bacon Act; Service Contract Act; wage garnishment provisions of the Consumer Credit Protection Act; and a number of employment standards and worker protections as provided in several immigration-related statutes.

Contact: Wage and Hour Division, Employment Standards Administration, 200 Constitution Ave. NW; Washington, DC 20210. Phone: 202-219-8305. World Wide Web: http://www.dol.gov/dol/esa/.

WILDLIFE INSPECTOR (GS-1801)
UNITED STATES FISH AND WILDLIFE SERVICE
U.S. DEPARTMENT OF THE INTERIOR

Overview: The United States Fish and Wildlife Service (FWS) maintains a force of uniformed Wildlife Inspectors to ensure that wildlife shipments entering or leaving the United States comply with federal wildlife trade laws and international treaties, and to intercept illegal shipments of federally protected wildlife. Stationed at ports of entry and other locations throughout the United States and its territories where wildlife import and export shipments occur, such as U.S. international airports and sea or land border points of entry, FWS

Wildlife Inspectors examine wild animals, packages, crates, or other containers that are either transported by air, sea, and land carriers, carried by individuals, or delivered through the mail. Primary responsibilities include examining documentation that accompanies shipments; physically inspecting the contents of shipments; seizing animals and wildlife products; participating in investigations; providing expertise to other agencies in wildlife law and species identification; testifying in court; and fulfilling administrative duties associated with the inspection and clearance of wildlife imports and exports. Inspections and investigations are often coordinated with FWS Special Agents, and investigative or compliance personnel of the U.S. Customs Service, USDA Animal and Plant Health Inspection Service, National Marine Fisheries Service, U.S. Immigration and Naturalization Service, and U.S. Coast Guard.

Qualifications: Applicants must be U.S. citizens. Requirements for appointment to GS-5 level include completion of a four-year course of study leading to a bachelor's degree, OR three years general experience, one year of which was equivalent to GS-4; for GS-7, one full year of graduate education, or superior academic achievement during undergraduate studies, OR one year of specialized experience equivalent to GS-5; for GS-9, a master's degree or two years of graduate education, OR one year of specialized experience equivalent to GS-7; for GS-11, a Ph.D. or equivalent doctoral degree, or three years of graduate education, OR one year of specialized experience equivalent to GS-9; and for GS-12, one year of specialized experience equivalent to GS-11. In some cases, qualifying education may be substituted for experience, and vice versa.

Training: Wildlife Inspectors attend a four-week Wildlife Inspector Basic Training Program at the Federal Law Enforcement Training Center in Glynco, Georgia. This course, which is conducted by FWS personnel, includes instruction pertaining to wildlife laws and treaties; FWS operational policies and port procedures; mammal, reptile, and amphibian identification; fish and wildlife handling and inspection techniques; identification of wildlife parts and manufactured wildlife products; and cooperative enforcement activities with the Customs Service, Department of Agriculture, and Canadian Wildlife Service. Annual in-service training include courses in problems and trends associated with the illegal importation of wildlife parts and products; legal updates and issues regarding the importation, exportation and inspection of fish and wildlife; officer safety techniques; and related subjects.

Contact: Division of Law Enforcement, U.S. Fish and Wildlife Service, P.O. Box 3247; Arlington, VA 22203. Phone: 703-358-1949. World Wide Web: http://www.fws.gov/~r9dle/div_le.html.

Chapter Twelve

SECURITY SPECIALISTS

When a man assumes a public trust,
he should consider himself as public property.
– THOMAS JEFFERSON

FEDERAL SECURITY SPECIALISTS PERFORM A VARIETY OF TASKS associated with the identification and protection of information, personnel, property, facilities, operations or material from unauthorized disclosure, misuse, theft, fraud, assault, vandalism, espionage, sabotage, or loss. The majority of security specialists are classified in the GS-0080 occupational series. Among the most common careers in this series are Physical Security Specialists and Personnel Security Specialists.

Physical Security Specialists design, install, operate and monitor devices and systems that are used to protect against fire, theft, vandalism, and illegal entry in order to safeguard personnel, property, and information. Physical Security Specialists are employed by agencies which include the U.S. Secret Service, U.S. Capitol Police, Agricultural Research Service, Federal Protective Service, and U.S. Marshals Service, among others.

Agencies such as the Bureau of Engraving and Printing, Drug Enforcement Administration, Comptroller of the Currency, and Federal Emergency Management Agency utilize Personnel Security Specialists to analyze and evaluate the character and background of employees, candidates for employment, and other persons having or proposed to be granted access to classified or other sensitive information, materials, or work sites.

Other security specialists are responsible for tasks related to the security of civil aviation operations, hospitals and research facilities, missile defense programs, nuclear facilities and materials, museums and galleries, banks, wharves and harbors, industrial operations, and other facilities and resources. Many security specialists review intelligence and counterintelligence reports, assess security vulnerabilities, design security systems based on their knowledge of the operating techniques of terrorist organizations, and train personnel in security requirements and procedures.

CIVIL AVIATION SECURITY SPECIALIST
FEDERAL AVIATION ADMINISTRATION
U.S. DEPARTMENT OF TRANSPORTATION

Overview: The civil aviation security program of the Federal Aviation Administration (FAA) exists to protect people, equipment, and cargo against criminal and terrorist attacks at airports or aboard aircraft nationwide and wherever U.S. air carriers operate throughout the world. The FAA Civil Aviation Security Division is responsible for enhancing explosives and weapons detection capabilities; increasing aircraft resilience to explosives; overseeing airport security systems; safeguarding air traffic control facilities; improving the performance of passenger screening personnel; and the continuous assessment of threats to domestic and international civil aviation. Civil Aviation Security Specialists coordinate and perform investigations, inspections, and advisory functions to assure compliance with federal regulations and FAA orders regarding all aspects of domestic and foreign air carrier and airport security, and corporate and general aviation security. Specialization may be achieved in areas such as airport security programs, canine and explosives detection, dangerous goods and cargo security, air carrier standard security programs, the Federal Air Marshal program, or other areas of expertise. Operations are coordinated with other FAA personnel; federal, state and local law enforcement officers; airport and airline officials; and various federal authorities. While salary does not fall under the General Schedule pay system, salaries for grades FG-5 through FG-13 are similar to those of GS-5 through GS-13 positions.

Qualifications: Applicants must be U.S. citizens. Requirements for appointment to FG-5 level include completion of a four-year course of study leading to a bachelor's degree, OR three years general experience, one year of which was equivalent to FG-4; for FG-7, completion of one full year of graduate education, or qualification under the Outstanding Scholar Program, OR one year of specialized experience equivalent to FG-5; for FG-9, a master's degree or two years of graduate education, OR one year of specialized experience equivalent to FG-7; for FG-11, a Ph.D. or equivalent doctoral degree, or three years of graduate education, OR one year of specialized experience equivalent to FG-9; and for FG-12 and FG-13, one year of specialized experience equivalent to the next lower grade level. In some cases, qualifying education may be substituted for experience, and vice versa. Tentative appointees must pass a background investigation and qualify for a security clearance.

Training: Initial training for Civil Aviation Security Specialists includes a three-week Civil Aviation Security core course conducted at the FAA Academy in Oklahoma City, Oklahoma. This course focuses on FAA regulations and civil aviation laws, airport security, air carrier compliance with laws and regulations, security procedures, and other subjects relating to security in an aviation environment. In-service training is conducted primarily at the FAA Academy or the Federal Law Enforcement Training Center, and may include courses pertaining to the investigation of aviation offenses, security procedures, legal updates, identification of explosives, and subjects relating to particular areas of specialization.

Contact: Office of Civil Aviation Security, Federal Aviation Administration, Department of Transportation, 800 Independence Ave. SW; Washington, DC 20591. Phone: 202-267-8007. World Wide Web: http://www.cas.faa.gov/.

CRIME PREVENTION SPECIALIST (GS-0301)
NATIONAL INSTITUTES OF HEALTH
U.S. DEPARTMENT OF HEALTH AND HUMAN SERVICES

Overview: The National Institutes of Health (NIH) Division of Public Safety is responsible for the administration and control of all physical security programs and the oversight of contract guard services on the NIH campus in Bethesda, Maryland. The NIH enclave consists of 75 buildings on more than 300 acres, and includes a research hospital, outpatient clinic, pediatric treatment center, numerous research and education facilities, and the National Library of Medicine. Operating within the Crime Prevention Branch of the Division of Public Safety, Crime Prevention Specialists conduct comprehensive physical security surveys of

NIH buildings and grounds to determine the effectiveness of security systems installed and ensure the protection of government equipment and experiments, NIH personnel, and visitors. Crime Prevention Specialists also develop close liaison with security professional groups and other government agencies; ensure that NIH is using the most advanced equipment in the field of physical security, especially electronic locking devices, closed-circuit television surveillance systems, and similar instrumentation and devices; and assist in reviewing construction plans for NIH facilities to ensure that adequate security measures are incorporated.

Qualifications: Requirements for appointment to GS-5 level include completion of a four-year course of study leading to a bachelor's degree, OR three years general experience, one year of which was equivalent to GS-4; for GS-7, one full year of graduate education, or superior academic achievement during undergraduate studies, OR one year of specialized experience equivalent to GS-5; for GS-9, a master's degree or two years of graduate education, OR one year of specialized experience equivalent to GS-7; for GS-11, a Ph.D. or equivalent doctoral degree, or three years of graduate education, OR one year of specialized experience equivalent to GS-9; and for GS-12, one year of specialized experience equivalent to GS-11. In some cases, qualifying education may be substituted for experience, and vice versa.

Training: Initial training for NIH Crime Prevention Specialists depends upon the experience and prior training of individual personnel, although it may include formal security or crime prevention training at the Federal Law Enforcement Training Center in Glynco, Georgia, or the National Crime Prevention Institute in Louisville, Kentucky. In-service training may include courses or seminars offered by the American Society for Industrial Security, colleges or universities, or private training organizations in subjects such as closed-circuit television systems, electronic and mechanical locking hardware, keying and access control systems, environmental security design, contract guard force management, or other subjects related to physical security and crime prevention.

Contact: Human Resources Branch, National Institutes of Health, 31 Center Drive, Building 31; Bethesda, MD 20892. Phone: 301-496-5685. World Wide Web: http://www.nih.gov/.

INDUSTRIAL SECURITY SPECIALIST (GS-0080)
BALLISTIC MISSILE DEFENSE ORGANIZATION
U.S. DEPARTMENT OF DEFENSE

Overview: The mission of the Ballistic Missile Defense Organization (BMDO) is to manage and direct the Defense Department's Ballistic Missile Defense acquisition programs, and to develop a national missile defense program for the United States. BMDO Industrial Security Specialists advise and assist in implementing the BMDO Foreign Disclosure Guidance. Responsibilities include oversight of the development, establishment, and management of the Joint National Test Facility (JNTF) Foreign Disclosure information program in support of BMDO and JNTF personnel, contacts, visitors, international conferences, multi-national war games, and assigned foreign exchange personnel; identifying potential information disclosure problems and developing approaches for problem avoidance; identifying and assisting investigative personnel in the event of unauthorized disclosure of data and items to foreign nationals; and planning and developing foreign disclosure processes, instructions and guidance relevant to national and agency principles, programs, policies, directives and regulations pertaining to national disclosure policy, foreign military sales, security assistance, technology transfer, and Export Control Act provisions. This is a civilian position and does not require active duty military service.

Qualifications: Applicants must be U.S. citizens. Requirements for appointment to GS-5 level include completion of a four-year course of study leading to a bachelor's degree, OR three years general experience, one year of which was equivalent to GS-4; for GS-7, one full year of graduate education, or superior academic achievement during undergraduate studies, OR one year of specialized experience equivalent to GS-5; for GS-9, a master's degree or two years of graduate education, OR one year of specialized experience equivalent to GS-7; for GS-11, a Ph.D. or equivalent doctoral degree, or three years of graduate education, OR one year of specialized experience equivalent to GS-9; and for GS-12, one year of specialized experience equivalent to

GS-11. In some cases, qualifying education may be substituted for experience, and vice versa. Tentative appointees must qualify for a security clearance, and pass a background investigation and drug screening test.

Training: Training for personnel in the Industrial Security Specialist occupational classification generally focuses on principles of personnel, physical and information security; security classifications and clearance levels; storage of classified or sensitive information; access controls; intrusion detection devices; espionage and sabotage; security plans and surveys; applicable laws and regulations; legal updates; report writing; and agency-specific issues and instructions. Training may be presented by agency or Defense Department staff; federal, state, or local law enforcement training programs or academies; colleges or universities; or other organizations.

Contact: Ballistic Missile Defense Organization, Department of Defense, The Pentagon; Washington, DC 20301. Phone: 703-697-4040. World Wide Web: http://www.acq.osd.mil/bmdo/bmdolink/html/. E-mail: external.affairs@bmdo.osd.mil.

INFORMATION SECURITY SPECIALIST (GS-0080)
DRUG ENFORCEMENT ADMINISTRATION
U.S. DEPARTMENT OF JUSTICE

Overview: Information Security Specialists assigned to the Drug Enforcement Administration (DEA) El Paso Intelligence Center (EPIC), located in El Paso, Texas, are responsible for the administration of the DEA Sensitive Compartmented Information (SCI) program. EPIC is a clearinghouse for tactical intelligence and the collection, analysis, and dissemination of information related to worldwide drug movement and alien smuggling. Primary responsibilities of DEA Information Security Specialists include ensuring that all SCI is properly accounted for, controlled, transmitted, packaged and safeguarded; maintaining all applicable SCI directives, regulations and manuals; enforcing and supporting related Executive Orders and Presidential Directives; directing SCI physical and technical security actions, procedures, and personnel access; serving as the point-of-contact for SCI material control and accountability; ensuring that SCI is disseminated only to authorized persons, and that material is destroyed in authorized destruction facilities; providing SCI support to appropriately cleared Defense Department contractors; conducting a continuing security education training program; and maintaining listings of available SCI electronic and hard-copy products and interfaces with other telecommunications centers.

Qualifications: Applicants must be U.S. citizens. Requirements for appointment to GS-5 level include completion of a four-year course of study leading to a bachelor's degree, OR three years general experience, one year of which was equivalent to GS-4; for GS-7, one full year of graduate education, or superior academic achievement during undergraduate studies, OR one year of specialized experience equivalent to GS-5; for GS-9, a master's degree or two years of graduate education, OR one year of specialized experience equivalent to GS-7; for GS-11, a Ph.D. or equivalent doctoral degree, or three years of graduate education, OR one year of specialized experience equivalent to GS-9; and for GS-12, one year of specialized experience equivalent to GS-11. In some cases, qualifying education may be substituted for experience, and vice versa. Tentative appointees must qualify for a security clearance, and pass a background investigation and drug screening test.

Training: Personnel in the Information Security Specialist occupational classification typically receive training relating to the collection, analysis, classification, dissemination and destruction of sensitive information and intelligence; access controls; report writing; technical security procedures; computer hardware systems and software programs; applicable laws and regulations; legal updates; agency policies and directives; and additional agency-specific issues and instructions. Training may consist of courses which are presented by agency staff; federal, state, or local law enforcement training programs or academies; colleges or universities; or other organizations.

Contact: Recruiting information can be obtained from any DEA Field Office, or by contacting Drug Enforcement Administration; Washington, DC 20537. Phone: 202-307-1000 or 800-DEA-4288. World Wide Web: http://www.usdoj.gov/dea/.

INFORMATION SECURITY SPECIALIST (GS-0080)
DIVISION OF FACILITIES AND SECURITY
U.S. NUCLEAR REGULATORY COMMISSION

Overview: The United States Nuclear Regulatory Commission (NRC) is an independent agency established by the United States Congress to ensure adequate protection of the public health and safety, the environment, and the common defense and security in the use of nuclear materials in the United States. Under the Division of Facilities and Security, the NRC Information Security Branch administers a number of programs pertaining to information and technical security, counterintelligence, communications, and foreign disclosure of information to protect classified and sensitive unclassified information and telecommunications. NRC Information Security Specialists serve as Special Security Officers with responsibility for transmitting and protecting intelligence information; recommending security measures and implementing policy for Sensitive Compartmented Information (SCI) and Special Access Program (SAP) information received and used within the NRC; disseminating SCI and SAP information to appropriate persons; maintaining all facilities which receive, process or store SCI and SAP information in the NRC in accordance with National directives and agency policy; preparing daily intelligence briefings for senior NRC officials, Commissioners and staff; and conducting liaison activities with various agencies and organizations in the intelligence community.

Qualifications: Applicants must be U.S. citizens. Requirements for appointment to GS-5 level include completion of a four-year course of study leading to a bachelor's degree, OR three years general experience, one year of which was equivalent to GS-4; for GS-7, one full year of graduate education, or superior academic achievement during undergraduate studies, OR one year of specialized experience equivalent to GS-5; for GS-9, a master's degree or two years of graduate education, OR one year of specialized experience equivalent to GS-7; for GS-11, a Ph.D. or equivalent doctoral degree, or three years of graduate education, OR one year of specialized experience equivalent to GS-9; and for GS-12, one year of specialized experience equivalent to GS-11. In some cases, qualifying education may be substituted for experience, and vice versa. Tentative appointees must qualify for a top-secret security clearance, and pass a background investigation and drug screening test.

Training: Personnel in the Information Security Specialist occupational classification typically receive training relating to the collection, analysis, classification, dissemination and destruction of sensitive information and intelligence; access controls; report writing; technical security procedures; computer hardware systems and software programs; applicable laws and regulations; legal updates; agency policies and directives; and additional agency-specific issues and instructions. Training may consist of courses which are presented by agency staff; federal, state, or local law enforcement training programs or academies; colleges or universities; or other organizations.

Contact: Office of Human Resources, U.S. Nuclear Regulatory Commission; Washington, DC 20555. Phone: 301-415-7000. World Wide Web: http://www.nrc.gov/.

MUSEUM SECURITY SPECIALIST (GS-1801)
OFFICE OF PROTECTION SERVICES
SMITHSONIAN INSTITUTION

Overview: Smithsonian Institution Museum Security Specialists are responsible for the security of the world's largest museum complex, including sixteen museums and galleries, and research facilities located in several states. Primary responsibilities include the investigation of criminal incidents involving theft of Smithsonian artifacts and property, vandalism, shoplifting violations that occur in museum shops, pickpocketing, purse snatching, sex offenses, assaults, homicides, armed robberies, narcotics crimes, and accidents where potential tort claims are likely. Investigations often require collection of evidence; interviews with victims, witnesses, and complainants; interrogation of suspects; preparation of detailed written reports; and testifying in court or at other hearings. Additional responsibilities include conducting surveillance and gathering intelligence concerning criminal activity and threats; advising museum managers on collections control and physical security matters; conducting security surveys and inspections; providing VIP protection; supervising the construction of alarm systems and control centers; and participating in the intrastate and interstate security escort of valuable artifacts in transit to or from Smithsonian facilities. Museum Security Specialists are authorized to carry firearms.

Qualifications: Applicants must be U.S. citizens. Requirements for appointment to GS-5 level include completion of a four-year course of study leading to a bachelor's degree, OR three years general experience, one year of which was equivalent to GS-4; for GS-7, one full year of graduate education, or superior academic achievement during undergraduate studies, OR one year of specialized experience equivalent to GS-5; for GS-9, a master's degree or two years of graduate education, OR one year of specialized experience equivalent to GS-7; for GS-11, a Ph.D. or equivalent doctoral degree, or three years of graduate education, OR one year of specialized experience equivalent to GS-9; and for GS-12, one year of specialized experience equivalent to GS-11. In some cases, qualifying education may be substituted for experience, and vice versa. Tentative appointees must pass a background investigation.

Training: Smithsonian Museum Security Specialists attend a wide range of introductory and in-service training courses and seminars, including a three-week museum security training program which focuses on the increasingly diverse set of security challenges within Smithsonian facilities. Museum Security Specialists are trained with the aid of Firearms Training Simulators (FATS), and receive instruction in control-room operations, human relations, confrontation management, security awareness, crime prevention, as well as other subjects relating to specific responsibilities of the position.

Contact: Office of Human Resources, Smithsonian Institution, 955 L'Enfant Plaza SW, Suite 2100; Washington, DC 20560. Phone: 202-287-3102. World Wide Web: http://www.si.edu/newstart.htm

PERSONNEL SECURITY SPECIALIST (GS-0080)
DEFENSE SECURITY SERVICE
U.S. DEPARTMENT OF DEFENSE

Overview: The Defense Security Service (DSS) is responsible for conducting highly complex and sensitive personnel security investigations of employees who require access to classified and sensitive Department of Defense (DoD) information or highly sensitive DoD areas. Subjects of investigations include military and civilian personnel of the DoD, Army, Navy, and Air Force, as well as employees of DoD contractors. DSS Personnel Security Specialists are responsible for a variety of tasks associated with DoD security clearance determinations, such as conducting in-depth reviews of investigative reports and related application documents for industrial security clearances; evaluating adverse information reports for DoD contractors and government agencies in accordance with the National Industrial Security Program (NISP) Operating Manual; reviewing security violations reported by DSS field offices and other Executive Department security offices; evaluating Personnel Security Questionnaires which indicate possible foreign representation on an individual; determining the degree and extent of investigative inquiry that is required in resolving allegations of adverse information; identifying and reviewing cases which contain major adverse information to determine whether a clearance suspension is warranted; and preparing written recommendations for security clearance suspension actions.

Qualifications: Applicants must be U.S. citizens. Requirements for appointment to GS-5 level include completion of a four-year course of study leading to a bachelor's degree, OR three years general experience, one year of which was equivalent to GS-4; for GS-7, one full year of graduate education, or superior academic achievement during undergraduate studies, OR one year of specialized experience equivalent to GS-5; for GS-9, a master's degree or two years of graduate education, OR one year of specialized experience equivalent to GS-7; for GS-11, a Ph.D. or equivalent doctoral degree, or three years of graduate education, OR one year of specialized experience equivalent to GS-9; and for GS-12, one year of specialized experience equivalent to GS-11. In some cases, qualifying education may be substituted for experience, and vice versa. Tentative appointees must qualify for a security clearance, and pass a background investigation and drug screening test.

Training: Training for DSS Personnel Security Specialists includes an overview of the National Industrial Security Program as implemented by the DoD; the NISP Operating Manual; the government acquisition cycle; communications security; international transfer of classified information; and personnel security clearances, facility clearances, and safeguarding of classified materials as they relate to the Government Contracting Activity and civilian contractors. Personnel Security Specialists may also attend related courses throughout their careers which provide additional information and updates.

Contact: Defense Security Service, 1340 Braddock Place; Alexandria, VA 22314. Phone: 703-325-9471. World Wide Web: http://www.dss.mil.

PERSONNEL SECURITY SPECIALIST (GS-0080)
SECURITY DIVISION
FEDERAL EMERGENCY MANAGEMENT AGENCY

Overview: The Federal Emergency Management Agency (FEMA) is responsible for emergency planning, preparedness, mitigation, response, and recovery relating to catastrophic disasters, and for programs providing recovery assistance and the protection of life and property. The mission of the Security Division is to protect FEMA personnel, facilities, and equipment to ensure a secure environment for the Agency and its emergency management partners. FEMA Personnel Security Specialists conduct investigations into the suitability, integrity and loyalty of FEMA employees, applicants for employment, contractors, and other designated personnel. Responsibilities include preparation, review, and evaluation of investigative reports to determine whether current or prospective employees meet security standards; processing requests concerning Special Access Program (SAP) and Sensitive Compartmented Information (SCI), including access to restricted data pertaining to North Atlantic Treaty Organization (NATO) and Department of Energy operations; processing clearance applications for national security and public trust positions; conducting pre-employment interviews, subject interviews, record checks, and other investigative functions; preparing recommendations for interim suspension of security clearances of cleared personnel on whom significant derogatory information becomes known; and conducting security briefings involving SAP information, foreign contacts, and counterintelligence. FEMA personnel are required to respond to emergencies on a twenty-four hour on-call basis.

Qualifications: Applicants must be U.S. citizens. Requirements for appointment to GS-5 level include completion of a four-year course of study leading to a bachelor's degree, OR three years general experience, one year of which was equivalent to GS-4; for GS-7, one full year of graduate education, or superior academic achievement during undergraduate studies, OR one year of specialized experience equivalent to GS-5; for GS-9, a master's degree or two years of graduate education, OR one year of specialized experience equivalent to GS-7; for GS-11, a Ph.D. or equivalent doctoral degree, or three years of graduate education, OR one year of specialized experience equivalent to GS-9; and for GS-12, one year of specialized experience equivalent to GS-11. In some cases, qualifying education may be substituted for experience, and vice versa. Tentative appointees must qualify for a security clearance, and pass a background investigation and drug screening test.

Training: Training for those in the Personnel Security Specialist occupational classification ordinarily consists of instruction which focuses on agency personnel standards, security clearance eligibility requirements, position sensitivity and security suitability determinations, adverse personnel action and derogatory information, interviewing techniques, report writing, applicable laws and regulations, legal updates, agency policies and procedures, and other agency-specific training. Personnel Security Specialists may attend courses which are presented by agency staff; federal, state, or local law enforcement training programs or academies; colleges or universities; or other organizations.

Contact: Federal Emergency Management Agency, 500 C Street SW; Washington, DC 20472. Phone: 202-646- 4600. World Wide Web: http://www.fema.gov/.

PERSONNEL SECURITY SPECIALIST (GS-0080)
DRUG ENFORCEMENT ADMINISTRATION
U.S. DEPARTMENT OF JUSTICE

Overview: Drug Enforcement Administration (DEA) Personnel Security Specialists conduct inquiries to determine whether DEA personnel or persons to be employed in sensitive positions meet security standards to the extent that their retention, hiring, or access to classified information is consistent with DEA integrity standards and national security. Primary responsibilities include reviewing and evaluating investigative reports and collateral information; conducting interviews of employees concerning minor derogatory allegations against them; determining the degree and extent of investigative inquiry that is required in resolving allegations of adverse information; examining relationship of facts to provisions of applicable laws and regulations, and their relevancy to the issues involved; developing detailed and objective summaries of the information considered; recommending approval or denial of clearances for access to classified information based on results of inquiries and knowledge of subversive activities and other factors pertinent to the administration of personnel security; and initiating necessary investigative action for updating or processing documentation for access clearances or re-certification through appropriate agencies.

Qualifications: Applicants must be U.S. citizens. Requirements for appointment to GS-5 level include completion of a four-year course of study leading to a bachelor's degree, OR three years general experience, one year of which was equivalent to GS-4; for GS-7, one full year of graduate education, or superior academic achievement during undergraduate studies, OR one year of specialized experience equivalent to GS-5; for GS-9, a master's degree or two years of graduate education, OR one year of specialized experience equivalent to GS-7; for GS-11, a Ph.D. or equivalent doctoral degree, or three years of graduate education, OR one year of specialized experience equivalent to GS-9; and for GS-12, one year of specialized experience equivalent to GS-11. In some cases, qualifying education may be substituted for experience, and vice versa. Tentative appointees must qualify for a security clearance, and pass a background investigation and drug screening test.

Training: Training for those in the Personnel Security Specialist occupational classification ordinarily consists of instruction which focuses on agency personnel standards, security clearance eligibility requirements, position sensitivity and security suitability determinations, adverse personnel action and derogatory information, interviewing techniques, report writing, applicable laws and regulations, legal updates, agency policies and procedures, and other agency-specific training. Personnel Security Specialists may attend courses which are presented by agency staff; federal, state, or local law enforcement training programs or academies; colleges or universities; or other organizations.

Contact: Recruiting information can be obtained from any DEA Field Office, or by contacting Drug Enforcement Administration; Washington, DC 20537. Phone: 202-307-1000 or 800-DEA-4288. World Wide Web: http://www.usdoj.gov/dea/.

PERSONNEL SECURITY SPECIALIST (GS-0080)
BUREAU OF ENGRAVING AND PRINTING
U.S. DEPARTMENT OF THE TREASURY

Overview: Personnel Security Specialists of the Bureau of Engraving and Printing (BEP) participate in a continuing program of personnel security controls, with responsibility for conducting comprehensive investigations concerned with the security suitability of individuals serving in sensitive positions or with access to classified information. Investigations focus on BEP job applicants, nongovernment personnel assigned at the BEP, and incumbents for promotion or retention in BEP positions. Primary responsibilities include collecting information from various sources, such as co-workers, neighbors, supervisors, and others to determine suitability for employment; analyzing results of investigative findings and making recommendations which may result in the granting of employment, denial or termination of employment, initiation of corrective measures, or criminal prosecution; conducting surveys and inspections of personnel security programs and systems, and preparing comprehensive reports of deficiencies and violations observed; making recommendations for corrective actions and for enhancing overall personal security controls; serving as a security liaison with representatives of other federal, municipal, and law enforcement agencies; and performing armed escort services. BEP Physical Security Specialists are authorized to carry firearms.

Qualifications: Applicants must be U.S. citizens. Requirements for appointment to GS-5 level include completion of a four-year course of study leading to a bachelor's degree, OR three years general experience, one year of which was equivalent to GS-4; for GS-7, one full year of graduate education, or superior academic

achievement during undergraduate studies, OR one year of specialized experience equivalent to GS-5; for GS-9, a master's degree or two years of graduate education, OR one year of specialized experience equivalent to GS-7; for GS-11, a Ph.D. or equivalent doctoral degree, or three years of graduate education, OR one year of specialized experience equivalent to GS-9; and for GS-12, one year of specialized experience equivalent to GS-11. In some cases, qualifying education may be substituted for experience, and vice versa. Tentative appointees must qualify for a security clearance, and pass a background investigation and drug screening test.

Training: BEP Personnel Security Specialists attend the eight-week Basic Criminal Investigator Training Program at the Federal Law Enforcement Training Center in Glynco, Georgia (see Chapter 16). In-service training may include specialized courses which focus on personnel investigations, security controls and systems, criminal and civil law updates, firearms proficiency, and other relevant topics.

Contact: Office of Human Resources, Bureau of Engraving and Printing, Department of the Treasury, 14th and C Streets SW; Washington, DC 20228. Phone: 202-874-3181. World Wide Web: http://www.bep.treas.gov/.

PERSONNEL SECURITY SPECIALIST (GS-0080)
COMPTROLLER OF THE CURRENCY
U.S. DEPARTMENT OF THE TREASURY

Overview: The Office of the Comptroller of the Currency (OCC) charters, regulates, and supervises national banks to ensure a safe, sound and competitive national banking system that supports the citizens, communities and economy of the United States. OCC Personnel Security Specialists are responsible for the implementation of policies and procedures for the OCC Personnel Security Program to ensure the continuous security evaluation of OCC personnel and contractors. Responsibilities include determining the suitability and security eligibility of individuals for entry and retention in sensitive and nonsensitive positions; conducting evaluations and recommending revisions to sensitivity level determinations for various positions; reviewing investigative reports and making recommendations whether to grant, deny, revoke, suspend or restrict security clearances; administering those portions of the federal government's National Industrial Security Program which relate directly to personnel security; coordinating with OCC contracting officers and representatives in the management of contracts requiring cleared personnel with access to classified information; and providing information and guidance on personnel security policies and procedures for adverse security determinations and related matters.

Qualifications: Applicants must be U.S. citizens. Requirements for appointment to GS-5 level include completion of a four-year course of study leading to a bachelor's degree, OR three years general experience, one year of which was equivalent to GS-4; for GS-7, one full year of graduate education, or superior academic achievement during undergraduate studies, OR one year of specialized experience equivalent to GS-5; for GS-9, a master's degree or two years of graduate education, OR one year of specialized experience equivalent to GS-7; for GS-11, a Ph.D. or equivalent doctoral degree, or three years of graduate education, OR one year of specialized experience equivalent to GS-9; and for GS-12, one year of specialized experience equivalent to GS-11. In some cases, qualifying education may be substituted for experience, and vice versa. Tentative appointees must pass a background investigation.

Training: Training for those in the Personnel Security Specialist occupational classification ordinarily consists of instruction which focuses on agency personnel standards, security clearance eligibility requirements, position sensitivity and security suitability determinations, adverse personnel action and derogatory information, interviewing techniques, report writing, applicable laws and regulations, legal updates, agency policies and procedures, and other agency-specific training. Personnel Security Specialists may attend courses which are presented by agency staff; federal, state, or local law enforcement training programs or academies; colleges or universities; or other organizations.

Contact: Comptroller of the Currency, Department of the Treasury, 250 E Street SW; Washington, DC 20219. Phone: 202-874-4700. World Wide Web: http://www.occ.treas.gov/.

PHYSICAL SECURITY SPECIALIST (GS-0080)
AGRICULTURAL RESEARCH SERVICE
U.S. DEPARTMENT OF AGRICULTURE

Overview: The Agricultural Research Service (ARS) of the Department of Agriculture (USDA) conducts research to develop new knowledge and technology needed to solve technical agricultural problems of broad scope and high national priority. Included among ARS research programs is support for the National Drug Control Strategy, for which it provides scientific expertise in the areas of illicit crop eradication and drug crop estimates. ARS Physical Security Specialists support the USDA Beltsville Agricultural Research Center (BARC), which includes more than 500 buildings located on 6,800 acres in Beltsville, Maryland. Responsibilities include conducting on-site surveys, analyses, and evaluation of the adequacy and performance of physical security structures and devices such as fences, barriers, lighting, intrusion detection systems, locks, and access controls; preparing written reports describing actions taken to correct security deficiencies; over-sight and coordination of contracts for the monitoring and maintenance of more than 70 intrusion alarm and access control systems and devices; reviewing access control data to determine whether systems are operating properly; assisting with the maintenance and repair of electronic security and access control systems; ensuring that security and access codes are issued to new employees, and that codes assigned to former employees are removed; and serving as liaison with other BARC organizations regarding physical security and fire alarm matters.

Qualifications: Applicants must be U.S. citizens. Requirements for appointment to GS-5 level include completion of a four-year course of study leading to a bachelor's degree, OR three years general experience, one year of which was equivalent to GS-4; for GS-7, one full year of graduate education, or superior academic achievement during undergraduate studies, OR one year of specialized experience equivalent to GS-5; for GS-9, a master's degree or two years of graduate education, OR one year of specialized experience equivalent to GS-7; for GS-11, a Ph.D. or equivalent doctoral degree, or three years of graduate education, OR one year of specialized experience equivalent to GS-9; and for GS-12, one year of specialized experience equivalent to GS-11. In some cases, qualifying education may be substituted for experience, and vice versa.

Training: Personnel in the Physical Security Specialist occupational classification normally receive training which covers agency policies and directives, intrusion detection systems and devices, security awareness, access control systems, physical security surveys, crime prevention, applicable laws and regulations, legal updates, investigative techniques, report writing, interviewing techniques, and agency-specific issues and instructions. Training may be presented by agency staff; federal, state, or local law enforcement training programs or academies; colleges or universities; or other organizations.

Contact: Human Resources Division, USDA Agricultural Research Service, 6305 Ivy Lane, Room 361; Greenbelt, MD 20770. Phone: 301-344-4638. World Wide Web: http://www.ars.usda.gov/.

PHYSICAL SECURITY SPECIALIST (GS-0080)
PHYSICAL SECURITY DIVISION
U.S. CAPITOL POLICE

Overview: United States Capitol Police (USCP) Physical Security Specialists are responsible for the design and installation of various electronic security systems utilized for the protection of the United States Capitol Building and a large complex of congressional buildings in the Washington, D.C. area. Primary responsibilities include designing, evaluating, installing and calibrating components and assemblies of electronic security systems, which includes testing and aligning digital circuits and replacing defective parts and devices; adapting security equipment to perform new or different functions; designing and assembling certain electronic equipment which is not available commercially; oversight of the installation of security equipment and systems by contractors; training USCP personnel in the operation of monitoring equipment and security devices; developing and designing engineering specifications for new electronic equipment and systems; assisting with the operation and maintenance of an electronics laboratory, including establishment of test procedures for bench operation and the inspection of equipment; and maintaining records of installations and related field tests.

Qualifications: Applicants must be U.S. citizens. Requirements for appointment to GS-5 level include completion of a four-year course of study leading to a bachelor's degree, OR three years general experience, one year of which was equivalent to GS-4; for GS-7, one full year of graduate education, or superior academic achievement during undergraduate studies, OR one year of specialized experience equivalent to GS-5; for GS-9, a master's degree or two years of graduate education, OR one year of specialized experience equivalent to GS-7; for GS-11, a Ph.D. or equivalent doctoral degree, or three years of graduate education, OR one year of specialized experience equivalent to GS-9; and for GS-12, one year of specialized experience equivalent to GS-11. In some cases, qualifying education may be substituted for experience, and vice versa. Tentative appointees must qualify for a top-secret security clearance and pass a background investigation.

Training: Personnel in the Physical Security Specialist occupational classification normally receive training which covers agency policies and directives, intrusion detection systems and devices, security awareness, access control systems, physical security surveys, crime prevention, applicable laws and regulations, legal updates, investigative techniques, report writing, interviewing techniques, and agency-specific issues and instructions. Training may be presented by agency staff; federal, state, or local law enforcement training programs or academies; colleges or universities; or other organizations.

Contact: Administrative Services Bureau, United States Capitol Police, 119 D Street NE; Washington, DC 20510. Phone: 202-225-7053. World Wide Web: No Web site at this time.

PHYSICAL SECURITY SPECIALIST (GS-0080)
FEDERAL PROTECTIVE SERVICE
U.S. GENERAL SERVICES ADMINISTRATION

Overview: The Federal Protective Service (FPS) is the law enforcement and security arm of the Public Buildings Service, a division of the U.S. General Services Administration (GSA). The Public Buildings Service is responsible for the leasing and management of office space for most federal agencies in the United States, Puerto Rico, and the U.S. Virgin Islands. FPS Physical Security Specialists determine security needs in GSA-operated buildings, including specific devices, systems, or services which would most effectively mitigate security risks to building tenants and visitors. Responsibilities include developing security plans, which include provisions for safes, alarms, locks, fences, intrusion detection and other devices; developing detailed reports on security surveys, crime assessments, agency consultations, crime awareness training, and security system design; recommending appropriate action where security requirements are not being observed; conducting training on office security, sexual assault, crime prevention, and Occupant Emergency Plans; conducting inspections to ensure proper fulfillment of security systems contracts; coordinating security, parking, traffic control, investigative and intelligence support functions with federal, state and local law enforcement agencies; and enforcing federal laws, building rules and regulations during emergencies and special investigative situations. FPS Physical Security Specialists are authorized to carry firearms.

Qualifications: Applicants must be U.S. citizens. Requirements for appointment to GS-5 level include completion of a four-year course of study leading to a bachelor's degree, OR three years general experience, one year of which was equivalent to GS-4; for GS-7, one full year of graduate education, or superior academic achievement during undergraduate studies, OR one year of specialized experience equivalent to GS-5; for GS-9, a master's degree or two years of graduate education, OR one year of specialized experience equivalent to GS-7; for GS-11, a Ph.D. or equivalent doctoral degree, or three years of graduate education, OR one year of specialized experience equivalent to GS-9; and for GS-12, one year of specialized experience equivalent to GS-11. In some cases, qualifying education may be substituted for experience, and vice versa.

Training: Personnel in the Physical Security Specialist occupational classification normally receive training which covers agency policies and directives, intrusion detection systems and devices, security awareness, access control systems, physical security surveys, crime prevention, applicable laws and regulations, legal updates, investigative techniques, report writing, interviewing techniques, and agency-specific issues and instructions. Training may be presented by agency staff; federal, state, or local law enforcement training programs or academies; colleges or universities; or other organizations.

Contact: Federal Protective Service, General Services Administration, 18th and F Streets NW; Washington, DC 20405. Phone: 202-501-0907. World Wide Web: http://www.gsa.gov/pbs/fps/fps.htm.

PHYSICAL SECURITY SPECIALIST (GS-0080)
UNITED STATES MARSHALS SERVICE
U.S. DEPARTMENT OF JUSTICE

Overview: Physical Security Specialists of the United States Marshals Service (USMS) are responsible for administration of security programs for the protection of federal court facilities and property, judges, United States Attorneys, law enforcement and court personnel, and court visitors. Responsibilities include conducting initial and continual on-site inspections of federal court buildings and grounds to determine security system requirements and assess the condition of existing devices and measures; evaluating, planning and creating specifications for security systems including intrusion detection devices, automated access control equipment, closed-circuit television monitoring devices, and duress systems; coordinating the installation, upgrading and maintenance of all interior and exterior physical security devices; using technical knowledge and skills to ensure that security devices operate properly and are resistant to false activations by man-made causes and naturally occurring phenomena; analyzing, testing and recommending experimental projects for security system modifications and enhancements; providing expertise in negotiating the technical aspects of physical security systems and equipment contracts; and performing technical evaluations of multi-phase contractor proposals and design plans.

Qualifications: Applicants must be U.S. citizens. Requirements for appointment to GS-5 level include completion of a four-year course of study leading to a bachelor's degree, OR three years general experience, one year of which was equivalent to GS-4; for GS-7, one full year of graduate education, or superior academic achievement during undergraduate studies, OR one year of specialized experience equivalent to GS-5; for GS-9, a master's degree or two years of graduate education, OR one year of specialized experience equivalent to GS-7; for GS-11, a Ph.D. or equivalent doctoral degree, or three years of graduate education, OR one year of specialized experience equivalent to GS-9; and for GS-12, one year of specialized experience equivalent to GS-11. In some cases, qualifying education may be substituted for experience, and vice versa.

Training: USMS Physical Security Specialists attend various courses, seminars, and workshops throughout their careers. Some of these training programs are presented by USMS staff, while others are offered by organizations such as the U.S. Army Corps of Engineers, Secret Service, or manufacturers of security systems and equipment.

Contact: Office of Human Resources, United States Marshals Service, 600 Army Navy Drive; Arlington, VA 22202. Phone: 202-307-9000. World Wide Web: http://www.usdoj.gov/marshals/.

PHYSICAL SECURITY SPECIALIST (GS-0080)
BUREAU OF ENGRAVING AND PRINTING
U.S. DEPARTMENT OF THE TREASURY

Overview: The Bureau of Engraving and Printing (BEP) designs, prints, and finishes all of the nation's paper currency, as well as U.S. postage stamps, Treasury securities, naturalization certificates, Coast Guard water use licenses, Presidential appointment certificates, White House invitations, military identification cards, and other security documents. Physical Security Specialists protect BEP operations through the development of security policy and the design, development, installation and evaluation of security systems and devices at the headquarters facility in Washington, D.C., a second currency manufacturing plant in Fort Worth, Texas, and at BEP contract sites. Responsibilities include planning and implementing protective methods and security procedures; operating state-of-the-art physical security equipment including closed-circuit television systems, intrusion detection devices, and related security systems; resolving complex security problems; analyzing security accountability discrepancies, security violations, and criminal activity; and assisting federal law enforcement agencies with investigative and other analytical activities involving the loss of accountability or theft of Bureau products. BEP Physical Security Specialists are authorized to carry firearms.

Qualifications: Applicants must be U.S. citizens. Requirements for appointment to GS-5 level include completion of a four-year course of study leading to a bachelor's degree, OR three years general experience, one year of which was equivalent to GS-4; for GS-7, one full year of graduate education, or superior academic achievement during undergraduate studies, OR one year of specialized experience equivalent to GS-5; for GS-9, a master's degree or two years of graduate education, OR one year of specialized experience equivalent to GS-7; for GS-11, a Ph.D. or equivalent doctoral degree, or three years of graduate education, OR one year of specialized experience equivalent to GS-9; and for GS-12, one year of specialized experience equivalent to GS-11. In some cases, qualifying education may be substituted for experience, and vice versa. Tentative appointees must qualify for a security clearance, and pass a background investigation and drug screening test.

Training: BEP Physical Security Specialists attend the eight-week Basic Criminal Investigator Training Program at the Federal Law Enforcement Training Center in Glynco, Georgia (see Chapter 16). In-service training may include specialized courses in security equipment and systems, investigative techniques, criminal and civil law, and firearms proficiency.

Contact: Office of Human Resources, Bureau of Engraving and Printing, Department of the Treasury, 14th and C Streets SW; Washington, DC 20228. Phone: 202-874-3181. World Wide Web: http://www.bep. treas.gov/.

PHYSICAL SECURITY SPECIALIST (GS-0080)
UNITED STATES SECRET SERVICE
U.S. DEPARTMENT OF THE TREASURY

Overview: In support of United States Secret Service (USSS) protective and investigative missions, USSS Physical Security Specialists provide technical expertise and hands-on support in the areas of physical security; technical surveillance; explosives countermeasures; fire safety; and chemical, biological and radiological (CBR) countermeasures. Responsibilities include conducting physical security surveys; installing and maintaining intrusion prevention and detection systems; conducting countermeasures in support of criminal investigations; installing and operating technical surveillance equipment; conducting fire safety surveys, evaluating fire protection systems, and implementing personnel evacuation plans; developing and implementing countermeasures to explosive and CBR threats against protected persons and facilities; testing, troubleshooting, and modifying electronic equipment; and analyzing technical problems and developing solutions pertaining to physical security equipment and systems. USSS Physical Security Specialists are assigned to the Washington, D.C. area, although may experience frequent travel and reassignment to USSS offices located throughout the United States or to foreign countries to perform liaison assignments. This position is covered under special retirement provisions for law enforcement officers.

Qualifications: Applicants must be U.S. citizens; at least twenty-one years of age, and under the age of thirty-seven. (Candidates over age thirty-seven who have previous service creditable under special law enforcement retirement provisions may also be eligible.) Requirements for appointment to GS-5 level include completion of a four-year course of study leading to a bachelor's degree, OR three years general experience, one year of which was equivalent to GS-4; for GS-7, one full year of graduate education, or superior academic achievement during undergraduate studies, OR one year of specialized experience equivalent to GS-5; for GS-9, a master's degree or two years of graduate education, OR one year of specialized experience equivalent to GS-7; for GS-11, a Ph.D. or equivalent doctoral degree, or three years of graduate education, OR one year of specialized experience equivalent to GS-9; and for GS-12, one year of specialized experience equivalent to GS-11. In some cases, qualifying education may be substituted for experience, and vice versa. Tentative appointees must qualify for a top-secret security clearance and pass a background investigation, polygraph exam, and drug screening test.

Training: Personnel in the Physical Security Specialist occupational classification normally receive training which covers agency policies and directives, intrusion detection systems and devices, security awareness, access control systems, physical security surveys, crime prevention, applicable laws and regulations, legal updates, investigative techniques, report writing, interviewing techniques, and agency-specific issues and instructions. Training may be presented by agency staff; federal, state, or local law enforcement training programs or academies; colleges or universities; or other organizations.

Contact: Personnel Division, U.S. Secret Service, 1800 G Street NW, Room 912; Washington, DC 20223. Phone: 202-435-5708 or 800-827-7783. World Wide Web: http://www.treas.gov/usss/.

PROTECTION OFFICER
FEDERAL RESERVE BANK
FEDERAL RESERVE BOARD

Overview: The Federal Reserve System serves as the nation's central bank, with responsibility for the execution of monetary policy, while also performing functions such as the transfer of funds, handling of government deposits and debt issues, supervising and regulating banks, and acting as a lender of last resort. Federal Reserve Bank (FRB) Protection Officers are responsible for the protection of FRB assets, property, employees, tenants, and visitors at facilities in Atlanta, Boston, Chicago, Cleveland, Dallas, Kansas City, Minneapolis, New York, Philadelphia, Richmond, San Francisco, and St. Louis, as well as branch banks located in twenty-five cities throughout the United States. Primary responsibilities include screening visitors and controlling access to the Bank and secure areas; inspecting briefcases, packages, and other containers brought into FRB facilities; conducting static post duty and foot patrols; maintaining a control room post; monitoring alarm systems, intrusion control devices, intercoms, and closed-circuit surveillance monitors; maintaining post logs; responding to intrusion and fire alarms, emergencies, disturbances, and other incidents; overseeing the transfer of assets to and from armored cars; participating in building evacuation drills; coordinating bomb searches; investigating thefts and other incidents; writing detailed reports; escorting personnel in possession of cash and securities to the post office and financial institutions; and administering CPR and first-aid. FRB Protection Officers are authorized to carry firearms. Salary for this position does not fall under the General Schedule pay system, although it is similar to those of police officers and security specialists of other federal agencies.

Qualifications: Requirements for appointment to FRB Protection Officer Trainee include possession of a high school diploma, OR experience in military or internal security, or other security-related field; good written and oral communication skills; and a stable employment history reflecting excellent performance and attendance. Tentative appointees must pass a background investigation.

Training: FRB Protection Officers attend approximately six weeks of initial training conducted by FRB staff pertaining to the mission, policies, procedures, and rules of the agency; Bank layout and design; security post and screening procedures; electronic security and surveillance systems; laws and regulations; firefighting equipment and procedures; conflict resolution; report writing; first-aid and CPR; firearms proficiency; use of force; and other matters related to the dynamics of particular facilities served. In-service training may include courses which focus on subjects such as information security; legal issues and updates; security equipment and procedures; tactical operations; response to bomb threats; bloodborne pathogens; CPR and first-aid techniques and equipment; and firearms proficiency.

Contact: Inquiries should be directed to the FRB personnel office where employment is sought, or to Division of Personnel, Board of Governors of the Federal Reserve System, Twentieth Street and Constitution Avenue NW; Washington, DC 20551. Phone: 202-452-3000. World Wide Web: http://www.bog.frb.fed.us/.

REGIONAL SECURITY OFFICER
BUREAU OF DIPLOMATIC SECURITY
U.S. DEPARTMENT OF STATE

Overview: Regional Security Officers of the Bureau of Diplomatic Security (DS) are responsible for the security of sensitive information, property, and foreign service personnel throughout the world. Operating from U.S. embassies and consulates, DS Regional Security Officers safeguard classified and sensitive information and materials in accordance with Presidential Directives or Executive Orders; implement security or safety-related aspects of new office building construction, counter-terrorist access controls, architectural security related design, or design of anti-intrusion devices; maintain an effective security program against terrorist, espionage, and criminal threats of U.S. interests, diplomatic installations, and personnel abroad; detect and investigate attempts by hostile intelligence to subvert U.S. personnel and interests overseas; conduct overseas investigations for the State Department and other federal agencies; and conduct security-related training for personnel of U.S. foreign affairs agencies and law enforcement officials of friendly foreign governments. DS Regional Security Officers are authorized to conduct surveillance and undercover operations, and carry firearms. Individual assignments often involve travel between Foreign Service posts in various countries. Salary for this position does not fall under the General Schedule pay system, although it is similar to GS-1811 Special Agent positions of other federal law enforcement agencies. Overseas salaries may be adjusted to include cost-of-living allowances, post differentials, danger pay, or other allowances specific to posts of assignment.

Qualifications: Applicants must be U.S. citizens; at least twenty-one years of age, and under the age of thirty-seven; possess a bachelor's degree from an accredited college or university; and have one year of specialized experience. (One full year of graduate education or a 3.0 grade point average during undergraduate studies may be substituted for one year of specialized experience.) Foreign language ability is desirable. Applicants must submit a narrative autobiography addressing their background, employment experience, personal interests, hobbies, and motivation for applying for a Regional Security Officer position. The application process also includes a writing exam, which is evaluated for mastery of grammar, spelling, logic, organization, vocabulary and word selection; a medical examination; a panel interview; and a background investigation. Tentative appointees must qualify for a security clearance.

Training: DS Regional Security Officers complete a rigorous five-month training program. Initial training includes the eight-week Basic Criminal Investigator Training Program at the Federal Law Enforcement Training Center in Glynco, Georgia (see Chapter 16). Officers then receive approximately three months of specialized training at various sites in the Washington, D.C. area, consisting of courses in passport and visa fraud, investigative techniques, personal security, firearms proficiency, emergency medical techniques, driver training, and other subjects.

Contact: Bureau of Diplomatic Security, Department of State, P.O. Box 9317; Arlington, VA 22219. Phone: 202-663-0478. World Wide Web: http://www.heroes.net/.

SECURITY SERVICES SPECIALIST (GS-0301)
UNITED STATES CUSTOMS SERVICE
U.S. DEPARTMENT OF THE TREASURY

Overview: The United States Customs Service (USCS) employs Security Services Specialists at USCS facilities, including Aviation Operations Centers, the Surveillance Support Center, and the National Aviation Center, to provide authoritative information and assistance to USCS management pertaining to physical, information, and operational security matters. USCS Security Services Specialists are responsible for a wide range of administrative duties concerning security logistics and property, aviation facility operations, communications security (COMSEC), physical security programs and systems, operations security, safeguarding of classified material, information security, and other security-related projects and programs. As COMSEC custodians, USCS Security Services Specialists are responsible for the management of COMSEC accounts, control of inventory, and the disposition of various materials. Responsibilities also include coordinating efforts with USCS Support Services Specialists and performing tasks concerning facilities management, logistics, and contracts management.

Qualifications: Applicants must be U.S. citizens. Requirements for appointment to GS-5 level include completion of a four-year course of study leading to a bachelor's degree, OR three years general experience, one year of which was equivalent to GS-4; for GS-7, one full year of graduate education, or superior academic achievement during undergraduate studies, OR one year of specialized experience equivalent to GS-5; for GS-9, a master's degree or two years of graduate education, OR one year of specialized experience equivalent to GS-7; for GS-11, a Ph.D. or equivalent doctoral degree, or three years of graduate education, OR one year of specialized experience equivalent to GS-9; and for GS-12, one year of specialized experience equivalent to GS-11. In some cases, qualifying education may be substituted for experience, and vice versa.

Training: Training for USCS Security Services Specialists consists of various courses relating to COMSEC, physical security, and other relevant topics. Many of these programs are presented at the Customs National Law Enforcement Communications Center in Orlando, Florida. Security Services Specialists may also attend seminars and workshops which are conducted by the Defense Department and other government agencies.

Contact: U.S. Customs Service, Department of the Treasury, 1300 Pennsylvania Avenue NW; Washington, DC 20229. Phone: 202-927-1250. World Wide Web: http://www.customs.ustreas.gov/.

SECURITY SPECIALIST (GS-0080)
UNITED STATES BUREAU OF THE CENSUS
U.S. DEPARTMENT OF COMMERCE

Overview: Security Specialists of the United States Bureau of the Census participate in the enhancement and administration of the Bureau's security program to ensure the protection and safeguarding of personnel, information and property. Responsibilities include the design, installation and maintenance of electronic security systems such as intrusion detection alarms, access control devices, and closed-circuit television equipment; monitoring security alarm systems and arranging for maintenance and adjustments of equipment; conducting site visits for the purpose of evaluating the performance of security systems; responding to emergencies and incidents such as assaults, robberies, and suspicious persons; conducting follow-up investigations involving crimes and various incidents; participating with the contract guard force, Federal Protective Service, United States Secret Service, FBI, and other law enforcement personnel during emergencies, civil disturbances, and bomb threat incidents; maintaining liaison with the Federal Protective Service with respect to building security, intelligence gathering, and terrorist threats; assisting in determining access requirements pertaining to national security information; reviewing security clearance determinations for Bureau employees and other persons with access to sensitive information, resources, material or works sites; and the implementation of the Bureau's security awareness program pertaining to the protection of property, restricted information, and national security material.

Qualifications: Applicants must be U.S. citizens. Requirements for appointment to GS-5 level include completion of a four-year course of study leading to a bachelor's degree, OR three years general experience, one year of which was equivalent to GS-4; for GS-7, one full year of graduate education, or superior academic achievement during undergraduate studies, OR one year of specialized experience equivalent to GS-5; for GS-9, a master's degree or two years of graduate education, OR one year of specialized experience equivalent to GS-7; for GS-11, a Ph.D. or equivalent doctoral degree, or three years of graduate education, OR one year of specialized experience equivalent to GS-9; and for GS-12, one year of specialized experience equivalent to GS-11. In some cases, qualifying education may be substituted for experience, and vice versa. Tentative appointees must qualify for a security clearance and pass a background investigation.

Training: Training for those in the Security Specialist occupational classification focuses on various aspects of personnel, physical and information security; security administration; access control systems; security awareness; security clearance and suitability determinations; computer hardware systems and software programs; applicable laws and regulations; legal updates; and other agency-specific training. Security Specialists may attend courses which are presented by agency staff; federal, state, or local law enforcement training programs or academies; colleges or universities; or other organizations.

Contact: Human Resources Division, Bureau of the Census, Department of Commerce; Washington, DC 20233. Phone: 301-457-1728. World Wide Web: http://www.census.gov/

SECURITY SPECIALIST (GS-0080)
OFFICE OF ADMINISTRATION
EXECUTIVE OFFICE OF THE PRESIDENT

Overview: The Office of Administration (OA) provides administrative support services to all units within the Executive Office of the President (EOP) including information, personnel, and financial management; data processing; library services; records maintenance; and general office operations such as mail, messenger, printing, procurement, and supply services. EOP Security Specialists perform a variety of administrative duties pertaining to personnel security and investigations in direct support of the OA Security Office. Responsibilities include maintaining an effective personnel security program primarily concerned with making suitability for employment determinations regarding employees and job applicants; conducting interviews and reviewing reports of investigations and other data to determine whether employees or job applicants meet national security standards; determining whether security clearances should be granted, suspended, revoked or denied; conducting security indoctrinations and debriefings for newly assigned and departing personnel; conducting monthly security briefings for all new employees in coordination with the United States Secret Service; performing tasks concerned with the physical protection of classified material to ensure that the material is not compromised or sabotaged; and implementing controls to ensure that only authorized personnel are granted access to sensitive information.

Qualifications: Applicants must be U.S. citizens. Requirements for appointment to GS-5 level include completion of a four-year course of study leading to a bachelor's degree, OR three years general experience, one year of which was equivalent to GS-4; for GS-7, one full year of graduate education, or superior academic achievement during undergraduate studies, OR one year of specialized experience equivalent to GS-5; for GS-9, a master's degree or two years of graduate education, OR one year of specialized experience equivalent to GS-7; for GS-11, a Ph.D. or equivalent doctoral degree, or three years of graduate education, OR one year of specialized experience equivalent to GS-9; and for GS-12, one year of specialized experience equivalent to GS-11. In some cases, qualifying education may be substituted for experience, and vice versa. Tentative appointees must qualify for a security clearance and pass a background investigation and drug screening test.

Training: Training for those in the Security Specialist occupational classification focuses on various aspects of personnel, physical and information security; security administration; access control systems; security awareness; security clearance and suitability determinations; computer hardware systems and software programs; applicable laws and regulations; legal updates; and other agency-specific training. Security Specialists may attend courses which are presented by agency staff; federal, state, or local law enforcement training programs or academies; colleges or universities; or other organizations.

Contact: Human Resources Management Division, Office of Administration, Executive Office of the President, 725 Seventeenth Street NW; Washington, DC 20503. Phone: 202-395-5892. World Wide Web: http://www.whitehouse.gov/WH/EOP/html/principals.html.

SECURITY SPECIALIST (GS-0080)
UNITED STATES GEOLOGICAL SURVEY
U.S. DEPARTMENT OF THE INTERIOR

Overview: The United States Geological Survey (USGS) is the nation's primary provider of earth and biological science information related to classification of public lands, topographic mapping, natural hazards, certain aspects of the environment, and mineral, energy, water and biological resources. USGS Security Specialists are responsible for planning, developing, and implementing programs pertaining to the protection of Sensitive

Compartmented Information (SCI) and related information storage and processing facilities. Responsibilities include coordination of SCI security operations; conducting periodic inspections of automated information systems security procedures to ensure that sensitive information, equipment and material are not compromised; inspection of security hardware and devices; investigation of security violations; monitoring operating procedures for inventory control accountability of classified information; managing the issuance, control and accountability of security badges, access key cards, locks, and keys; initiating, reviewing and analyzing security clearance documents to ensure that all required information is provided, and screening for any derogatory information and assessing impact of the information; identifying security training needs; and administering security briefings and education programs for USGS personnel, as well as other government agencies and contractors.

Qualifications: Applicants must be U.S. citizens. Requirements for appointment to GS-5 level include completion of a four-year course of study leading to a bachelor's degree, OR three years general experience, one year of which was equivalent to GS-4; for GS-7, one full year of graduate education, or superior academic achievement during undergraduate studies, OR one year of specialized experience equivalent to GS-5; for GS-9, a master's degree or two years of graduate education, OR one year of specialized experience equivalent to GS-7; for GS-11, a Ph.D. or equivalent doctoral degree, or three years of graduate education, OR one year of specialized experience equivalent to GS-9; and for GS-12, one year of specialized experience equivalent to GS-11. In some cases, qualifying education may be substituted for experience, and vice versa. Tentative appointees must qualify for a security clearance and pass a background investigation.

Training: Training for those in the Security Specialist occupational classification focuses on various aspects of personnel, physical and information security; security administration; access control systems; security awareness; security clearance and suitability determinations; computer hardware systems and software programs; applicable laws and regulations; legal updates; and other agency-specific training. Security Specialists may attend courses which are presented by agency staff; federal, state, or local law enforcement training programs or academies; colleges or universities; or other organizations.

Contact: U.S. Geological Survey, Department of the Interior, 12201 Sunrise Valley Drive; Reston, VA 20192. Phone: 703-648-6131. World Wide Web: http://www.usgs.gov/.

SECURITY SPECIALIST (GS-0080)
CRIMINAL DIVISION
U.S. DEPARTMENT OF JUSTICE

Overview: The Criminal Division of the Department of Justice employs Security Specialists to participate in the implementation of the Federal Witness Security Program, which is operated for the protection of government witnesses whose lives are in danger as a result of their testimony against organized crime figures, drug traffickers, terrorists and other major criminals. Responsibilities include preparing Program manuals and regulations; maintaining liaison and coordinating activities with the United States Attorney's Office, United States Marshals Service (USMS), Federal Bureau of Prisons, FBI, and other law enforcement agencies; arranging USMS interviews of prospective witnesses prepared for relocation to determine suitability for participation in the Program; making recommendations to approve or deny requests for Program participation; coordinating debriefing of witnesses after entry into the Program; inspecting special prison sites where prisoner-witnesses are housed; monitoring and coordinating investigations resulting from threats or attacks directed at relocated witnesses; establishing guidelines on travel by protected witnesses; resolving disputes among witnesses, prosecutors, and investigative agencies concerning job assistance, area of relocation, and termination of subsistence; conducting conferences and seminars for investigators and prosecutors to facilitate dissemination of Program information; and preparing responses to inquiries from the White House, Congress, media, and public.

Qualifications: Applicants must be U.S. citizens. Requirements for appointment to GS-5 level include completion of a four-year course of study leading to a bachelor's degree, OR three years general experience, one year of which was equivalent to GS-4; for GS-7, one full year of graduate education, or superior academic

achievement during undergraduate studies, OR one year of specialized experience equivalent to GS-5; for GS-9, a master's degree or two years of graduate education, OR one year of specialized experience equivalent to GS-7; for GS-11, a Ph.D. or equivalent doctoral degree, or three years of graduate education, OR one year of specialized experience equivalent to GS-9; and for GS-12, one year of specialized experience equivalent to GS-11. In some cases, qualifying education may be substituted for experience, and vice versa.

Training: Initial training for Security Specialists of the Criminal Division consists of an orientation to the mission, policies, procedures, and rules of the agency. In-service training may include courses such as report writing, computer security, information security, and other courses pertaining to specific responsibilities of the position. The majority of in-service training is provided by Justice Department staff, although some training is presented by outside organizations.

Contact: Criminal Division, Department of Justice, 1331 F Street NW, Suite 700; Washington, DC 20530. Phone: 202-514-2691. World Wide Web: http://www.usdoj.gov/criminal/criminal-home.html.

SECURITY SPECIALIST (GS-0080)
JUSTICE MANAGEMENT DIVISION
U.S. DEPARTMENT OF JUSTICE

Overview: Security Specialists serving in the Personnel Security Group of the Justice Management Division, United States Department of Justice (DOJ), conduct investigations into the suitability of DOJ employees and contractor personnel for employment, sensitive positions, or positions of trust. Primary responsibilities include conducting and directing investigations; assisting in the preparation of reviews and evaluations of investigative reports to determine whether current or prospective employees or contractors meet national security and employment suitability standards appropriate to the position sensitivity level; evaluating investigative reports to determine eligibility for granting access to national security information or sensitive compartmented information; responding to inquiries for verification of security clearances; maintaining computerized personal security records; assisting in the preparation of policies, orders, directives and manuals concerning personnel security and associated programs; reviewing component security program activities to determine the adequacy of compliance with the DOJ personnel security program; and generating reports and statistical information.

Qualifications: Applicants must be U.S. citizens. Requirements for appointment to GS-5 level include completion of a four-year course of study leading to a bachelor's degree, OR three years general experience, one year of which was equivalent to GS-4; for GS-7, one full year of graduate education, or superior academic achievement during undergraduate studies, OR one year of specialized experience equivalent to GS-5; for GS-9, a master's degree or two years of graduate education, OR one year of specialized experience equivalent to GS-7; for GS-11, a Ph.D. or equivalent doctoral degree, or three years of graduate education, OR one year of specialized experience equivalent to GS-9; and for GS-12, one year of specialized experience equivalent to GS-11. In some cases, qualifying education may be substituted for experience, and vice versa. Tentative appointees must pass a background investigation and drug screening test.

Training: Training for JMD Security Specialists consists of on-the-job and in-service instruction which includes an orientation to the mission, policies, procedures, and rules of the Agency; and seminars or courses relating to employee and contractor suitability determinations, adjudications guidelines and processes, alcohol and drug addition, indebtedness, derogatory information, and other topics.

Contact: Justice Management Division, Department of Justice, 1331 Pennsylvania Ave. NW, Suite 1175; Washington, DC 20530. Phone: 202-514-2000. World Wide Web: http://www.usdoj.gov/offices/jmd.html.

Chapter Thirteen

CORRECTIONAL OFFICERS AND SPECIALISTS

> If you want total security, go to prison.
> There you're fed, clothed, given medical care
> and so on. The only thing lacking is freedom.
> – DWIGHT D. EISENHOWER

THIS CHAPTER FEATURES TEN CAREERS ASSOCIATED WITH THE FEDERAL correctional system, including four positions with the Federal Bureau of Prisons. Careers that are profiled in this chapter include Clinical Psychologists, Correctional Officers, Correctional Program Specialists, Correctional Treatment Specialists, Detention Enforcement Officers, and Drug Treatment Specialists. Each plays a vital role in a coordinated effort to operate correctional facilities that are safe, humane and secure, and which provide work, counseling, and other opportunities to assist offenders in becoming law-abiding citizens.

Correctional Officers are stationed on the front lines of the correctional system by agencies such as the Federal Bureau of Prisons, Bureau of Indian Affairs, and National Park Service. These Officers are responsible for the confinement, supervision, safety, health, and protection of inmates, and for the overall operation of correctional facilities and programs. Detention Enforcement Officers of the U.S. Immigration and Naturalization Service and the U.S. Marshals Service are also responsible for correctional supervision of prisoners.

Clinical Psychologists, Correctional Treatment Specialists, and Drug Treatment Specialists assess, evaluate, and treat prisoners with a variety of problems and disorders through group and individual counseling, education, and other techniques. Correctional Program Specialists are employed by the Federal Bureau of Prisons and the Navy to develop, implement, and coordinate various programs relating to the treatment and rehabilitation of inmates.

Settings in which correctional officers and specialists perform their duties include federal correctional institutions, military and community-based facilities, camps, jails, medical facilities, and a national park. All institution-based correctional personnel are covered under special retirement provisions for law enforcement officers, and most are authorized to carry firearms and make arrests.

CLINICAL PSYCHOLOGIST (GS-0180)
FEDERAL BUREAU OF PRISONS
U.S. DEPARTMENT OF JUSTICE

Overview: The mission of the Federal Bureau of Prisons (BOP) is to protect society by confining offenders in prisons and community-based facilities that are safe, humane, and secure, and which provide work and other self-improvement opportunities to assist offenders in becoming law-abiding citizens. BOP Clinical Psychologists are responsible for the assessment, evaluation and treatment of prisoners with a variety of problems of personality, emotional adjustment, mental illness, or other disorders. Using professional knowledge of psychological principles, theories, methods, and techniques, BOP Clinical Psychologists administer and interpret psychological tests which are used for diagnosing mental and personality disorders; utilize data derived from these tests to determine physical and psychological diagnoses; assist in developing appropriate courses of treatment; develop and organize individual and group psychotherapy sessions and other rehabilitative programs; and prepare comprehensive written reports. BOP Clinical Psychologists are authorized to carry firearms and make arrests. This position is covered under special retirement provisions for law enforcement officers. Similar BOP positions are filled under the GS-0180 Counseling Psychologist series.

Qualifications: Applicants must be U.S. citizens, at least twenty-one years of age, and under the age of thirty-seven. (Candidates over age thirty-seven who have previous service creditable under special law enforcement retirement provisions may also be eligible. In special situations, a waiver may be granted up to age thirty-nine at locations where there is a shortage of applicants under thirty-seven.) Requirements for appointment to the GS-11 level include completion of all requirements for a Ph.D. or equivalent doctoral degree directly related to clinical psychology; and for GS-12 and GS-13, completion of all requirements for a Ph.D. or equivalent doctoral degree directly related to clinical psychology, and one year of specialized experience equivalent to the next lower grade level. Tentative appointees must qualify for a security clearance and pass a background investigation, personal interview, drug screening test and physical exam.

Training: Clinical Psychologists attend the three-week BOP Basic Training Program at the Federal Law Enforcement Training Center in Glynco, Georgia (see Chapter 16), followed by a two-week correctional institution familiarization course conducted by BOP staff. In-service training includes a minimum of forty hours of in-service courses annually, including subjects such as correctional supervision, therapeutic environments, group treatment processes, inmate suicide, legal issues and updates, inmate profiles, inmate and staff diversity, and interpersonal skills.

Contact: Federal Bureau of Prisons, Department of Justice, Suite 460, 320 First Street NW; Washington, DC 20534. Phone: 202-307-3198 or 800-347-7744. World Wide Web: http://www.bop.gov/.

CORRECTIONAL OFFICER (GS-0007)
BUREAU OF INDIAN AFFAIRS
U.S. DEPARTMENT OF THE INTERIOR

Overview: Bureau of Indian Affairs (BIA) Correctional Officers are responsible for the confinement, safety, health, and protection of criminal offenders in BIA custody, and for the overall operation of correctional facilities and programs. These personnel conduct preliminary interviews for physical and mental health classification assessments; conduct inmate supervision and counts; provide for facility safety and security, key control, inmate transportation, and perimeter security; perform inmate and cell searches; ensure compliance with correctional facility rules and regulations; coordinate and supervise services, activities, and programs relating to areas such as medical care, food service, laundry, counseling, recreation, library usage, counseling, religious services, and work programs; maintain fire safety; and prepare written reports. BIA Correctional Officers work closely with other criminal justice personnel, government and community officials, medical staff, and mental health professionals to ensure that inmate treatment plans are implemented according to correctional program standards and legal requirements. This position is covered under special retirement provisions for law enforcement officers.

Qualifications: Under the Indian Reorganization Act of 1934, qualified Indian applicants are given hiring preference for BIA positions, although applications from non-Indian candidates are encouraged. Applicants must be U.S. citizens, at least twenty-one years of age, and under the age of thirty-seven. (Candidates over age thirty-seven who have previous service creditable under special law enforcement retirement provisions may also be eligible.) Eyesight requirements include distant vision of at least 20/100 (Snellen) in each eye without correction, and at least 20/30 in each eye with correction. Normal hearing is required, including ability to hear the conversational voice and whispered speech without the use of a hearing aid. Requirements for appointment to GS-5 level include completion of a four-year course of study leading to a bachelor's degree, OR three years general experience, one year of which was equivalent to GS-4; for GS-6, one half year of graduate-level education with major study in criminal justice, social science, or other fields related to the position, OR one year of specialized experience equivalent to GS-5; for GS-7, one full year of graduate-level education (in the fields listed above), OR one year of specialized experience equivalent to GS-6; and for GS-8 and above, one year of specialized experience equivalent to the next lower grade level. In some cases, qualifying education may be substituted for experience, and vice versa. Tentative appointees must pass a drug screening test and background investigation.

Training: Initial training for BIA Correctional Officers includes a four-week Basic Detention Officer Training Program at Federal Law Enforcement Training Center in Artesia, New Mexico. Instruction includes topics such as cross-cultural awareness, Indian country jurisdiction, constitutional law, civil rights and liability, public law, crisis intervention, disturbance control, fingerprinting, alcohol and substance abuse, cell search, contraband control, suicide prevention, and physical conditioning. BIA Correctional Officers also attend a variety of in-service courses.

Contact: Direct inquiries to the personnel office where employment is sought or contact BIA Office of Personnel, Department of the Interior, 1849 C Street NW; Washington, DC 20240. Phone: 202-208-3710. World Wide Web: http://www.doi.gov/bureau-indian-affairs.html.

CORRECTIONAL OFFICER (GS-0007)
NATIONAL PARK SERVICE
U.S. DEPARTMENT OF THE INTERIOR

Overview: The National Park Service (NPS) employs Correctional Officers at Yosemite National Park to receive and process persons arrested on Park property, and to perform a variety of functions related to the detention, custody, security, counseling, and care and treatment of prisoners. Primary responsibilities include prisoner processing and fingerprinting; ensuring that security and custody procedures are followed relating to prisoner transportation, movement, detention, protection, and separation; informing prisoners of and ensuring compliance with NPS rules and regulations; performing regular shakedowns of cells; and serving as a court bailiff. As fully-commissioned law enforcement officers who are deputized as Special Deputy United States Marshals, NPS Correctional Officers occasionally participate in Park patrol and emergency operations, and are authorized to carry firearms and make arrests. Yosemite National Park is the only NPS location where Correctional Officers are employed. This position is covered under special retirement provisions for law enforcement officers.

Qualifications: Applicants must be U.S. citizens, at least twenty-one years of age, and under the age of thirty-seven. (Candidates over age thirty-seven who have previous service creditable under special law enforcement retirement provisions may also be eligible.) Eyesight requirements include distant vision of at least 20/100 (Snellen) in each eye without correction, and at least 20/30 in each eye with correction. Normal hearing is required, including ability to hear the conversational voice and whispered speech without the use of a hearing aid. Requirements for appointment to GS-5 level include completion of a four-year course of study leading to a bachelor's degree, OR three years general experience, one year of which was equivalent to GS-4; for GS-6, one-half year of graduate-level education with major study in criminal justice, social science, or other fields related to the position, OR one year of specialized experience equivalent to GS-5; for GS-7, one full year of graduate-level education (in the fields listed above), OR one year of specialized experience equivalent to GS-6; and for GS-8 and above, one year of specialized experience equivalent to the next lower grade level. In some cases, qualifying education may be substituted for experience, and vice versa. Tentative appointees must qualify for a security clearance and pass a personal interview, background investigation, drug screening test and physical exam.

Training: Those appointed to NPS Correctional Officer positions typically are fully-commissioned law enforcement officers who have already completed either state-certified police academy training or the twelve-week Land Management Law Enforcement Training Program at the Federal Law Enforcement Training Center in Glynco, Georgia. Officers also receive a minimum of forty hours of in-service training annually, including courses in subjects such as criminal law, laws of arrest, patrol techniques, firearms proficiency, defensive tactics, and first aid.

Contact: National Park Service, Department of the Interior, P.O. Box 37127; Washington, DC 20013. Phone: 202-208-6843. World Wide Web: http://www.nps.gov/.

CORRECTIONAL OFFICER (GS-0007)
FEDERAL BUREAU OF PRISONS
U.S. DEPARTMENT OF JUSTICE

Overview: Correctional Officers of the Federal Bureau of Prisons (BOP) perform a wide range of tasks concerning the custody, treatment, supervision, safety, and well-being of inmates in federal correctional institutions, camps, jails, and medical facilities. Primary responsibilities include guiding inmate conduct; monitoring activities such as exercise, dining, and showering; supervising work details; searching inmates and their living quarters for weapons, drugs, and contraband; inspecting locks, window bars, doors, and gates for signs of tampering; maintaining control room posts; monitoring closed-circuit television cameras and computerized tracking and detection systems; escorting inmates to and from visits with medical staff, other correctional personnel, and visitors; inspecting mail and visitors for prohibited items; carrying out plans for the treatment and modification of inmates' attitudes; instructing and counseling inmates on institutional and personal problems; and assisting with investigations involving crimes committed within correctional facilities. BOP Correctional Officers are authorized to carry firearms and make arrests. This position is covered under special retirement provisions for law enforcement officers.

Qualifications: Applicants must be U.S. citizens, at least twenty-one years of age, and under the age of thirty-seven. (Candidates over age thirty-seven who have previous service creditable under special law enforcement retirement provisions may also be eligible.) Eyesight requirements include distant vision of at least 20/100 (Snellen) in each eye without correction, and at least 20/30 in each eye with correction. Normal hearing is required, including ability to hear the conversational voice and whispered speech without the use of a hearing aid. Requirements for appointment to GS-5 level include completion of a four-year course of study leading to a bachelor's degree, OR three years general experience, one year of which was equivalent to GS-4; for GS-6, one-half year of graduate-level education with major study in criminal justice, social science, or other fields related to the position, OR one year of specialized experience equivalent to GS-5; for GS-7, one full year of graduate-level education (in the fields listed above), OR one year of specialized experience equivalent to GS-6; and for GS-8 and above, one year of specialized experience equivalent to the next lower grade level. In some cases, qualifying education may be substituted for experience, and vice versa. Tentative appointees must qualify for a security clearance and pass a personal interview, background investigation, drug screening test and physical exam.

Training: Correctional Officers attend the three-week BOP Basic Training Program at the Federal Law Enforcement Training Center in Glynco, Georgia (see Chapter 16), followed by a two-week correctional institution familiarization course conducted by BOP staff. In-service training includes a minimum of forty hours of in-service courses annually, including subjects such as correctional supervision, inmate suicide, hostage situations, interpersonal skills, use of force, legal issues and updates, inmate and staff diversity, and other topics related to specific duties.

Contact: Federal Bureau of Prisons, Department of Justice, Suite 460, 320 First Street NW; Washington, DC 20534. Phone: 202-307-3198 or 800-347-7744. World Wide Web: http://www.bop.gov/.

CORRECTIONAL PROGRAM SPECIALIST (GS-0006)
UNITED STATES NAVY
U.S. DEPARTMENT OF DEFENSE

Overview: United States Navy Correctional Program Specialists are responsible for developing, examining, and analyzing a wide range of programs concerning the treatment and rehabilitation of prisoners incarcerated in Navy correctional facilities. Responsibilities include developing programs and determining levels of staff expertise needed to meet program goals and prisoner needs; implementing, coordinating, and monitoring prisoner treatment efforts and initiating necessary changes; arranging for facilities, materials, instructors, and security; drafting policies concerning program procedures and operations; monitoring prisoners to determine their suitability for participation in programs and making recommendations for their release; participating as a member of various boards and panels to assess the effectiveness of program components and implementation strategies, and to assess prisoners' progress in rehabilitation; implementing corrections policies and regulations; and communicating with high-level Navy officials and others outside of the organization. Navy Correctional Program Specialists are covered under special retirement provisions for law enforcement officers. This is a civilian position and does not require active duty military service.

Qualifications: Applicants must be U.S. citizens. Requirements for appointment to GS-5 level include completion of a four-year course of study leading to a bachelor's degree, OR three years general experience, one year of which was equivalent to GS-4; for GS-7, one full year of graduate-level education, or superior academic achievement during undergraduate studies, OR one year of specialized experience equivalent to GS-5; for GS-9, a master's degree or two years of graduate-level education, OR one year of specialized experience equivalent to GS-7; for GS-11, a Ph.D. or equivalent doctoral degree, or three years graduate-level education, OR one year of specialized experience equivalent to GS-9; and for GS-12, one year of specialized experience equivalent to GS-11. In some cases, qualifying education may be substituted for experience, and vice versa. Tentative appointees must qualify for a security clearance and pass a background investigation, personal interview, drug screening test and physical exam.

Training: Initial training for Navy Correctional Program Specialists includes a 140-hour Correctional Specialist Course and a forty-hour preservice course. These in-house programs focus on naval policies and procedures, an overview of the correctional system, correctional issues, military law, civil liability, and other subjects. Additional training includes a four-week program which covers group and individual counseling methods, as well as various courses and workshops pertaining to correctional program development, interpersonal communication, interviewing techniques, hostage negotiation, self-defense, and other tasks. In-service training is presented by organizations such as the American Correctional Association, American Jail Association, and the FBI.

Contact: Direct inquiries to the Human Resources Office where employment is sought, or contact Office of Information, Department of the Navy; Washington, DC 20350. Phone: 703-697-7391. World Wide Web: http://www.navy.mil/. E-mail: help@chinfo.navy.mil.

CORRECTIONAL PROGRAM SPECIALIST (GS-0006)
FEDERAL BUREAU OF PRISONS
U.S. DEPARTMENT OF JUSTICE

Overview: While specific responsibilities vary widely among positions in this occupational series, Correctional Programs Specialists of the Federal Bureau of Prisons (BOP) are responsible for coordinating training programs that promote the health, spirituality, and well-being of prison inmates. Under the supervision of BOP Correctional Program Officers, Chief Psychologists, Chaplains, or Administrators, Correctional Program Specialists coordinate programs pertaining to recreation, religion, disease prevention, health education, physical fitness, rational thinking, criminal lifestyle confrontation, anger management, drug eradication, peer influences, ethics, relapse prevention, victim impact, and a variety of other subjects. Responsibilities include assisting with needs assessment and tasks analysis; developing program content; selecting and expelling inmates; scheduling; providing group counseling regarding BOP policies; preparing reports relevant to inmate histories and their progress in treatment; entering and retrieving data from computer systems; coordinating psychology services activities; purchasing equipment, materials and supplies; and other tasks relating to the overall operation of BOP programs. Correctional Program Specialists are authorized to carry firearms and make arrests. This position is covered under special retirement provisions for law enforcement officers.

Qualifications: Applicants must be U.S. citizens, at least twenty-one years of age, and under the age of thirty-seven. (Candidates over age thirty-seven who have previous service creditable under special law enforcement retirement provisions may also be eligible.) Requirements for appointment to GS-5 level include completion of a four-year course of study leading to a bachelor's degree, OR three years general experience, one year of which was equivalent to GS-4; for GS-7, one full year of graduate-level education, or superior academic achievement during undergraduate studies, OR one year of specialized experience equivalent to GS-5; for GS-9, a master's degree or two years of graduate-level education, OR one year of specialized experience equivalent to GS-7; for GS-11, a Ph.D. or equivalent doctoral degree, or three years graduate-level education, OR one year of specialized experience equivalent to GS-9; and for GS-12, one year of specialized experience equivalent to GS-11. In some cases, qualifying education may be substituted for experience, and vice versa. Tentative appointees must qualify for a security clearance and pass a background investigation, personal interview, drug screening test and physical exam.

Training: Correctional Program Specialists attend the three-week BOP Basic Training Program at the Federal Law Enforcement Training Center in Glynco, Georgia (see Chapter 16), followed by a two-week correctional institution familiarization course conducted by BOP staff. In-service training includes a minimum of forty hours of in-service courses annually, pertaining to subjects such as communicable diseases, drug and alcohol testing, correctional supervision, inmate suicide, interpersonal skills, interviewing techniques, legal issues and updates, inmate profiles, inmate and staff diversity, and other topics related to specific duties.

Contact: Federal Bureau of Prisons, Department of Justice, 320 First Street NW; Washington, DC 20534. Phone: 202-307-3198 or 800-347-7744. World Wide Web: http://www.bop.gov/.

CORRECTIONAL TREATMENT SPECIALIST (GS-0101)
UNITED STATES PAROLE COMMISSION
U.S. DEPARTMENT OF JUSTICE

Overview: The United States Parole Commission (USPC) is responsible for parole functions pertaining to eligible federal and District of Columbia (DC) prisoners and parolees. The USPC maintains the sole authority to grant, modify, or revoke parole; to conduct supervision of parolees and prisoners released upon the expiration of their sentences; and to determine supervisory conditions and terms. Serving in the capacity of Hearing Examiner, USPC Correctional Treatment Specialists conduct a wide range of parole hearings which involve eligible federal and DC prisoners, military prisoners confined in federal institutions, alleged parole or mandatory release violators, State Witness Protection cases, and Foreign Transfer Treaty cases. As a result of theses hearings, Correctional Treatment Specialists prepare case summaries and make recommendations for or against parole. In making its decisions, the USPC must take into account a number of factors, such as the need for just punishment, the offender's risk of recidivism, and the offender's conduct in the institution.

Qualifications: Applicants must be U.S. citizens, at least twenty-one years of age, and under the age of thirty-seven. (Candidates over age thirty-seven who have previous service creditable under special law enforcement retirement provisions may also be eligible.) Requirements for appointment to GS-5 level include a bachelor's degree that included at least twenty-four semester hours of coursework in the behavioral or social sciences, OR a combination of education and experience that included at least twenty-four semester hours of coursework in the behavioral or social sciences, and that provided the applicant with knowledge of one or more of the behavioral or social sciences equivalent to a bachelor's degree; for GS-7, one full year of graduate-level education, OR superior academic achievement during undergraduate studies, OR one year of specialized experience equivalent to GS-5; for GS-9, a master's degree or two years of graduate-level education, OR one year of specialized experience equivalent to GS-7; for GS-11, a Ph.D. or equivalent doctoral degree, or three years graduate-level education, OR one year of specialized experience equivalent to GS-9; and for GS-12, one year of specialized experience equivalent to GS-11. Graduate education must have been in corrections or a related field such as criminal justice, sociology, psychology, counseling, social work, or other coursework related to the position. In some cases, qualifying education may be substituted for experience, and vice versa. Tentative appointees must qualify for a security clearance and pass a background investigation, personal interview, drug screening test and physical exam.

Training: Newly appointed USPC Correctional Treatment Specialists are provided an orientation to the mission, policies, procedures, and rules of the agency, as well as an overview of the parole process, parole laws and regulations, professional contacts, and an introduction to Federal Bureau of Prisons and United States Probation operations. In-service training may include courses and criminal justice conferences pertaining to the parole process, legal issues and updates, parole case studies, and other pertinent matters relating to the position.

Contact: United States Parole Commission, Department of Justice, Suite 420, 5550 Friendship Boulevard; Chevy Chase, MD 20815. Phone: 301-492-5990. World Wide Web: http://www.usdoj.gov/uspc/.

DETENTION ENFORCEMENT OFFICER (GS-1802)
UNITED STATES IMMIGRATION AND NATURALIZATION SERVICE
U.S. DEPARTMENT OF JUSTICE

Overview: United States Immigration and Naturalization Service (INS) Detention Enforcement Officers are responsible for the receiving, processing, and security of undocumented and criminal aliens detained by the INS. The Detention and Deportation division of the INS operates nine facilities for the confinement of aliens awaiting proceedings to determine either their immigration status or whether they will be removed from the United States. Responsibilities of INS Detention Enforcement Officers include transporting detainees by car, van, plane, or bus to INS processing centers or correctional institutions; receiving prisoners and implementing processing procedures, including booking, issuing clothing and linen, assigning living quarters, and retrieving personal property; searching prisoners for concealed weapons, contraband, and other prohibited items; taking inventories of personal property; escorting detainees to places of employment, medical facilities, or consulates for interviews; delivering arrest warrants, bond letters, warrants of deportation, and orders to show cause; providing advice and information to detainees during their confinement; and accompanying detainees on flights out of the United States. INS Detention Enforcement Officers are authorized to carry firearms. This position is covered under special retirement provisions for law enforcement officers.

Qualifications: Applicants must be U.S. citizens, at least twenty-one years of age, and under the age of thirty-seven. (Candidates over age thirty-seven who have previous service creditable under special law enforcement retirement provisions may also be eligible.) Tentative appointees must qualify for a security clearance and pass a drug screening test, physical exam, and background investigation. Requirements for appointment to GS-5 level include four years of education above high school, OR one year of specialized experience equivalent to at least GS-4; and for grades GS-6 and above, one year of specialized experience equivalent to the next lower grade level. Applicants are rated on their experience, education, training, employment performance evaluations, and awards as they relate to the position. Experience and education may be combined to meet total experience requirements for positions at grade GS-5.

Training: INS Detention Enforcement Officers attend the eight-week Immigration Detention Enforcement Officer Basic Training Program at the Federal Law Enforcement Training Center in either Artesia, New Mexico or Glynco, Georgia. This course includes instruction pertaining to detention regulations and procedures, immigration status, transportation of prisoners, behavioral science, crowd control, constitutional law, civil rights, fingerprinting, driver training, firearms care and proficiency, and physical conditioning. In-service training may include specialized courses in subjects such as prisoner processing, laws of detention and arrest, immigration law, first aid, firearms proficiency, and defensive tactics.

Contact: Immigration and Naturalization Service, Department of Justice, 425 I Street NW; Washington, DC 20536. Phone: 202-514-4316. World Wide Web: http://www.ins.usdoj.gov/.

DETENTION ENFORCEMENT OFFICER (GS-1802)
UNITED STATES MARSHALS SERVICE
U.S. DEPARTMENT OF JUSTICE

Overview: The United States Marshals Service (USMS) houses approximately 20,000 prisoners each day in detention facilities throughout the United States, and completes more than 160,000 prisoner movements annually via coordinated air and ground systems. USMS Detention Enforcement Officers are responsible for the receiving, processing, detaining, tracking, and security of prisoners in USMS custody. Responsibilities include supervising prisoners; searching prisoners for concealed weapons, contraband, and other prohibited items; taking inventories of personal property; interviewing prisoners to obtain personal histories; entering personal data into automated database systems; taking photographs and fingerprints; operating busses or large passenger vans; transporting prisoners to and from federal or state detention facilities, cellblocks, and court-rooms; and maintaining courtroom discipline. USMS Detention Enforcement Officers are authorized to carry firearms. This position is covered under special retirement provisions for law enforcement officers.

Qualifications: Applicants must be U.S. citizens, at least twenty-one years of age, and under the age of thirty-seven. (Candidates over age thirty-seven who have previous service creditable under special law enforcement retirement provisions may also be eligible.) Requirements for appointment to GS-5 level include four years of education above high school, OR one year of specialized experience equivalent to at least GS-4; and for grades GS-6 and above, one year of specialized experience equivalent to the next lower grade level. Applicants are rated on their experience, education, training, employment performance evaluations, and awards as they relate to the position. Experience and education may be combined to meet total experience requirements for positions at grade GS-5. Tentative appointees must qualify for a security clearance and pass a drug screening test, medical exam, and background investigation.

Training: Training for USMS Detention Enforcement Officers includes an orientation to the mission, policies, procedures, and rules of the agency, followed by in-house instruction which focuses on prisoner processing, detention procedures, the USMS Prisoner Tracking System computer program, and other subjects. These personnel may receive periodic in-service training related to specific responsibilities of the position.

Contact: Human Resources, United States Marshals Service, 600 Army Navy Drive; Arlington, VA 22202. Phone: 202-307-9437. World Wide Web: http://www.usdoj.gov/marshals/.

DRUG TREATMENT SPECIALIST (GS-0101)
FEDERAL BUREAU OF PRISONS
U.S. DEPARTMENT OF JUSTICE

Overview: Drug Treatment Specialists of the Federal Bureau of Prisons (BOP) provide substance abuse counseling and education to inmates of BOP correctional institutions. Responsibilities include the development and evaluation of substance abuse programs; managing assigned caseloads of offenders who have histories of substance abuse; coordinating inmate training programs; developing social histories; identifying deficiencies and excesses in inmates' patterns of thought, feeling and behavior, and recommending or devising corrective measures; providing group and individual counseling; applying assessment and treatment techniques to help inmates overcome criminal lifestyle and drug abuse problems; evaluating the progress of program participants; planning aftercare programs; working with prisoners, their families, and interested persons in developing parole and release plans; completing progress reports and administrative paperwork; providing case reports to the U.S. Parole Commission; and interacting with U.S. Probation Officers and other agencies in developing and implementing release plans or programs. Drug Treatment Specialists are authorized to carry firearms and make arrests. This position is covered under special retirement provisions for law enforcement officers.

Qualifications: Applicants must be U.S. citizens, at least twenty-one years of age, and under the age of thirty-seven. (Candidates over age thirty-seven who have previous service creditable under special law enforcement retirement provisions may also be eligible.) Requirements for appointment to GS-5 level include a bachelor's degree that included at least twenty-four semester hours of coursework in the behavioral or social sciences, OR a combination of education and experience that included at least twenty-four semester hours of coursework in these subjects and that provided knowledge of one or more of the behavioral or social sciences equivalent to a bachelor's degree; for GS-7, one full year of graduate-level education, or superior academic achievement during undergraduate studies, OR one year of specialized experience equivalent to GS-5; for GS-9, a master's degree or two years of graduate-level education, OR one year of specialized experience equivalent to GS-7; for GS-11, a Ph.D. or equivalent doctoral degree, or three years graduate-level education, OR one year of specialized experience equivalent to GS-9; and for GS-12, one year of specialized experience equivalent to GS-11. Applicants must have completed three semester hours of undergraduate coursework or fifty hours of training in alcohol or drug abuse, or have six months of experience counseling drug or alcohol abusers. Tentative appointees must qualify for a security clearance and pass a background investigation, personal interview, drug screening test and physical exam.

Training: Drug Treatment Specialists attend the three-week BOP Basic Training Program at the Federal Law Enforcement Training Center in Glynco, Georgia (see Chapter 16), as well as a two-week correctional institution familiarization course conducted by BOP staff. This training is followed by a two-week Drug Abuse Treatment Specialist course which covers drug abuse program policies and procedures, group treatment processes, and other clinical issues. In-service training includes a minimum of forty hours of courses annually, pertaining to subjects such as cognitive skill building, creating therapeutic environments, group treatment processes, inmate suicide, interpersonal skills, inmate profiles, inmate and staff diversity, and other topics.

Contact: Federal Bureau of Prisons, Department of Justice, 320 First Street NW; Washington, DC 20534. Phone: 202-307-3198 or 800-347-7744. World Wide Web: http://www.bop.gov/.

Chapter Fourteen

PROBATION AND PRETRIAL SERVICES OFFICERS

There are a thousand hacking at the branches
of evil to one who is striking at the root.
– HENRY DAVID THOREAU

THIS CHAPTER PROVIDES PROFILES OF U.S. PRETRIAL Services Officers and U.S. Probation Officers of the Administrative Office of the United States Courts. These personnel are located within each of the ninety-four district courts in the fifty states, the District of Columbia, the Commonwealth of Puerto Rico, and the territories of Guam, the U.S. Virgin Islands, and the Northern Mariana Islands. All Officers are appointed by a specific district court, which is administered by a Chief Judge.

U.S. Pretrial Services Officers are responsible for investigating defendants who have been charged with federal criminal offenses, and for making recommendations on the amount of bail and the conditions to be met by defendants if released. Information may be gathered through interviews with defendants, arresting authorities, law enforcement automated criminal record systems, the United States Attorney's Office, and from family and community members. These Officers develop a supervision plan, evaluate information and arrive at an assessment of flight risk and danger to the community, supervise defendants released on bail to monitor compliance with the conditions of release, and maintain detailed records of case activity.

U.S. Probation Officers conduct investigations and prepare reports for the court with recommendations for sentencing of individuals convicted of federal offenses. The preparation of these reports requires interviewing offenders and their families; investigating the offense, prior record and financial status of the offender; and contacting law enforcement agencies, attorneys, crime victims, schools, churches, and civic organizations. U.S. Probation Officers also supervise and maintain contact with offenders; investigate employment, sources of income, lifestyle, and associates to assess risk and compliance; and refer offenders to outside agencies such as medical and drug treatment facilities, employment and training.

U.S. PRETRIAL SERVICES OFFICER
DIVISION OF PROBATION AND PRETRIAL SERVICES
ADMINISTRATIVE OFFICE OF THE U.S. COURTS

Overview: United States Pretrial Services Officers are responsible for gathering information and preparing reports for judges who must decide whether arrested persons should be released before trial in the federal court system; monitoring the conduct of those released pending trial; and assisting with pretrial diversion cases. Under the Division of Probation and Pretrial Services, U.S. Pretrial Services Officers conduct inquiries to assess the potential risk to the public posed by pretrial release of arrested persons. Inquiries typically examine defendants' character, family ties, mental condition, length of residence, and history of drug or alcohol abuse. U.S. Pretrial Services Officers also enforce court-imposed conditions of release, including drug testing and mental health treatment, curfew, home confinement with electronic monitoring, and restrictions on personal association, place of abode, and travel. Assistance is also provided in pretrial diversion cases, which involve court supervision agreements as an alternative to prosecution. As fully commissioned law enforcement personnel, U.S. Pretrial Services Officers are authorized to carry firearms, and are covered under special retirement provisions for law enforcement officers. Salary for this position does not fall under the General Schedule pay system. Starting salary at Court Personnel System grade CL-25 is similar to GS-7, and maximum salary for journeyman grade CL-28 is similar to GS-13.

Qualifications: Applicants must be U.S. citizens; at least twenty-one years of age, and under the age of thirty-seven. (Candidates over age thirty-seven who have previous service creditable under special law enforcement retirement provisions may also be eligible.) Requirements for appointment to grade CL-25 include a bachelor's degree from an accredited college or university in fields such as criminal justice, criminology, psychology, sociology, human relations, business, or public administration; and at least one year of specialized experience relating to probation, pretrial services, parole, corrections, criminal investigation, or work in substance abuse treatment. (Experience as a police patrol officer or security officer is not acceptable.) Qualifying specialized experience may be substituted by superior academic achievement during undergraduate studies, completion of a master's or juris doctorate degree, or one year of graduate education in a closely related field of study. Candidates must also be in good physical health, possess good writing and communication skills, and pass a background investigation.

Training: U.S. Pretrial Services Officers attend an orientation training program at their duty station, followed by an intensive six-day seminar at the Federal Judicial Center in Washington, D.C. These programs provide an overview of federal court operations, safety and security, sentencing guidelines, pre-sentence reports, Agency forms and standards, and terminology. In-service training may include courses relating to pretrial diversion programs, financial investigations, substance abuse, gangs in the penal system, ethnic sensitivity, report writing, law, court operations, computer automation, defensive tactics, firearms proficiency, and other subjects.

Contact: Inquiries should be directed to the office where employment is sought, or to Probation and Pretrial Services, Administrative Office of the U.S. Courts, One Columbus Circle NE; Washington, DC 20544. Phone: 202-273-1120. World Wide Web: http://www.uscourts.gov/.

U.S. PROBATION OFFICER
DIVISION OF PROBATION AND PRETRIAL SERVICES
ADMINISTRATIVE OFFICE OF THE U.S. COURTS

Overview: As fully commissioned law enforcement officers under the Division of Probation and Pretrial Services, United States Probation Officers are responsible for the investigation and supervision of criminal offenders on probation, parole, or supervised release in the federal court system. Primary responsibilities include the investigation of offenders' backgrounds; preparation of pre-sentence reports which include recommendations for sentencing; providing court testimony in support of investigative findings and the application of sentencing guidelines; and monitoring offenders under court supervision. To reduce risk to the community and maximize adherence to court-imposed conditions, U.S. Probation Officers investigate offenders' employment, sources of income, lifestyles, substance abuse, and associates. Their findings often result in referrals to outside agencies such as medical facilities, counseling and drug treatment programs, and employment and training sources. Investigations and supervision require frequent contact with the U.S. Parole Commission, Federal Bureau of Prisons, military authorities, and attorneys. U.S. Probation Officers are authorized to carry firearms, and are covered under special retirement provisions for law enforcement officers. Salary for this position does not fall under the General Schedule pay system. Starting salary at Court Personnel System grade CL-25 is similar to GS-7, and maximum salary for journeyman grade CL-28 is similar to GS-13.

Qualifications: Applicants must be U.S. citizens; at least twenty-one years of age, and under the age of thirty-seven. (Candidates over age thirty-seven who have previous service creditable under special law enforcement retirement provisions may also be eligible.) Requirements for appointment to grade CL-25 include a bachelor's degree from an accredited college or university in fields such as criminal justice, criminology, psychology, sociology, human relations, business, or public administration; and at least one year of specialized experience relating to probation, pretrial services, parole, corrections, criminal investigation, or work in substance abuse treatment. (Experience as a police patrol officer or security officer is not acceptable.) Qualifying specialized experience may be substituted by superior academic achievement during undergraduate studies, completion of a master's or juris doctorate degree, or one year of graduate education in a closely related field of study. Candidates must also be in good physical health, possess good writing and communication skills, and pass a background investigation.

Training: U.S. Probation Officers attend an orientation training program at their duty station, followed by an intensive six-day seminar at the Federal Judicial Center in Washington, D.C. Training subjects include an overview of federal court operations, safety and security, sentencing guidelines, pre-sentence reports, Agency forms and standards, and terminology. In-service training may include courses which focus on case management and investigation techniques, supervision of offenders, report writing, law, sentencing guidelines, court operations, computer automation, firearms proficiency, defensive tactics, and other subjects.

Contact: Inquiries should be directed to the office where employment is sought, or to Probation and Pretrial Services, Administrative Office of the U.S. Courts, One Columbus Circle NE; Washington, DC 20544. Phone: 202-273-1120. World Wide Web: http://www.uscourts.gov/.

Chapter Fifteen

COMMUNICATIONS TECHNICIANS AND DISPATCHERS

Never doubt that a small group of thoughtful,
committed citizens can change the world.
Indeed it's the only thing that ever has.
– MARGARET MEAD

COMMUNICATIONS TECHNICIANS AND DISPATCHERS ARE RESPONSIBLE for the operation and maintenance of radio telecommunication systems, telephones and telephone switching equipment, law enforcement computer database systems, and other electronic communication devices that are utilized in law enforcement, fire suppression, and other emergency response operations. Seventeen communications careers are profiled in this chapter.

Careers that involve the relay of radio communication traffic and critical data to law enforcement and other emergency personnel include Communications Equipment Operators, Emergency Communication Dispatchers, Emergency Vehicle Dispatchers, Law Enforcement Communications Assistants, Park Dispatchers, Public Safety Dispatchers, Radio Telecommunication Operators, and Telecommunications Equipment Operators. These personnel provide vital support to field operations of agencies such as the Drug Enforcement Administration, U.S. Army, U.S. Navy, National Park Service, U.S. Border Patrol, Bureau of Indian Affairs, and U.S. Marshals Service.

Electronics Technicians, Technical Enforcement Officers, and Telecommunications Specialists perform tasks which are related to the design, development, testing, installation, operation and maintenance of sophisticated electronic communication and surveillance equipment. These technicians perform analytical and technical tasks to ensure the efficient operation of multi-frequency mobile and base radio systems, repeaters, antennas, concealed miniature radio transmitters, electronic listening devices, video surveillance cameras, audio and video recording devices, and other technical investigative equipment. Agencies which employ these personnel include the Bureau of Alcohol, Tobacco and Firearms; USDA Forest Service; Federal Bureau of Prisons; Naval Criminal Investigative Service; Bureau of Land Management; U.S. Secret Service; Drug Enforcement Administration; and U.S. Customs Service, among others.

COMMUNICATIONS EQUIPMENT OPERATOR (GS-0392)
DRUG ENFORCEMENT ADMINISTRATION
U.S. DEPARTMENT OF JUSTICE

Overview: Drug Enforcement Administration (DEA) Communications Equipment Operators perform a wide range of communications functions in support of field operations and the administration of DEA programs. Responsibilities include the operation of UHF multi-frequency radio communication equipment; monitoring radios for DEA field traffic; responding to radio requests and researching information contained in automated law enforcement database systems relating to vehicle registrations, drivers license information, and criminal records; providing coordination and law enforcement data to DEA units and other agencies during land, sea and air pursuits, interceptions, and surveillance operations; patching city-to-city and car-to-base communications; dispatching emergency personnel; receiving, encoding, and transmitting messages on cryptographic equipment; maintaining logs of radio, telephone, or other communications; monitoring building security through closed-circuit television surveillance and audio systems; taking incoming telephone calls from the public; and responding to inquiries as appropriate.

Qualifications: Applicants must be U.S. citizens. Requirements for appointment to GS-4 level include two years of education above high school, OR one year of general experience; for GS-5, four years of education above high school, OR one year of specialized experience equivalent to at least GS-4; and for grades GS-6 and above, one year of specialized experience equivalent to the next lower grade level. Applicants are rated on their experience, education, training, employment performance evaluations, and awards as they relate to the position. Experience and education may be combined to meet total experience requirements for positions at grades GS-5 and below. Those tentatively selected must qualify for a security clearance and pass a background investigation and drug screening test.

Training: Personnel in the Communications Equipment Operator occupational classification typically receive on-the-job training and attend courses relating to automated law enforcement database systems, radio communication equipment, dispatching procedures, computer hardware and software, agency policies and directives, administrative paperwork, and agency-specific procedures. Training may be conducted by agency staff; federal, state, or local law enforcement training programs or academies; colleges or universities; or other organizations.

Contact: Direct inquiries to the DEA Field Office where employment is sought, or to Drug Enforcement Administration; Washington, DC 20537. Phone: 202-307-1000 or 800-DEA-4288. World Wide Web: http://www.usdoj.gov/dea/.

ELECTRONICS TECHNICIAN (GS-0856)
FOREST SERVICE
U.S. DEPARTMENT OF AGRICULTURE

Overview: Forest Service (FS) Electronics Technicians are responsible for the installation, testing, maintenance and repair of all fixed-station and mobile radio equipment utilized in FS law enforcement, fire suppression, emergency, and other communications. Responsibilities include performance of scheduled preventive maintenance checks, routine service work, and necessary technical corrections to ensure reliable technical and operational performance; making emergency and nonscheduled equipment repairs; operating and maintaining electronic testing equipment; maintaining a communications parts inventory; providing assistance with the implementation of FS communications plans; performing preinstallation technical inspection of new equipment to ensure compliance with FS specifications; assisting with the inspection of special use electronic sites and permits for compliance with regulations; training FS personnel in correct radio operating procedures, proper radio discipline, and minor servicing of equipment; and performing technical duties in establishing communications facilities for law enforcement, fire suppression, and other communications.

Qualifications: Applicants must be U.S. citizens. Requirements for appointment to GS-5 include completion of a four-year course of study leading to a bachelor's degree in electrical engineering, electronics engineering, or electronics technology; or three years of study in an accredited curriculum in electronics; or a four-year course of study leading to a bachelor's degree that included major study or at least twenty-four semester hours in any combination of courses in engineering, physical science, technology, or mathematics, of which at least twelve semester hours included electronics courses; OR one year of specialized experience equivalent to GS-4 as either an electronics technician, inspector or mechanic, or as a television or radio repair technician in a commercial shop. Requirements for GS-7 include one full year of graduate education directly related to the position, OR one year of specialized experience (as described above) equivalent to GS-5; for GS-9, two full years of graduate education directly related to the position, OR one year of specialized experience (as described above) equivalent to GS-7; and for GS-11, one year of specialized experience (as described above) equivalent to GS-9. In some cases, qualifying education may be substituted for experience, and vice versa. Those tentatively selected must pass a background investigation.

Training: Training for personnel in the Electronics Technician occupational classification normally covers a wide range of theories and techniques concerning the design, development, evaluation, testing, installation, use, and maintenance of electronic equipment utilized in law enforcement and public safety operations. Training may be presented by agency staff; federal, state, or local law enforcement training programs or academies; colleges or universities; or other organizations. The nature of training may depend upon the needs of individual personnel, agency requirements, and availability of courses.

Contact: For further information, contact the regional or local Forest Service office where employment is sought, or: USDA Forest Service, P.O. Box 96090; Washington, DC 20090. Phone: 202-720-3760. World Wide Web: http://www.fs.fed.us. E-mail: mailroom/wo@fs.fed.us.

ELECTRONICS TECHNICIAN (GS-0856)
BUREAU OF LAND MANAGEMENT
U.S. DEPARTMENT OF THE INTERIOR

Overview: Electronics Technicians of the Bureau of Land Management (BLM) are responsible for the maintenance and repair of all mobile and portable radio equipment utilized in law enforcement, fire suppression, emergency, and other communications. Responsibilities include maintenance of two-way radios, telephone systems and data communication equipment; setting up and testing of equipment; repair, modification and programming of mobile, base station, repeater and portable VHF, UHF, FM and AM radio systems; maintaining a variety of power sources used in remote locations, including AC power supplies and battery chargers, solar panel charge regulators, and rechargeable batteries; installing and removing mobile radios, cellular telephones, and associated antenna systems and accessories in vehicles; reviewing manufacturer's specifications and schematics to evaluate radio performance; performing initial acceptance checks on new radio equipment to ensure that equipment meets contracting specifications; maintaining records of repairs and inventory of equipment; providing radio training to BLM personnel; and assisting Telecommunications Specialists on various projects. Field work may be performed over remote or rugged terrain, in conservation or wilderness areas, and at high altitudes where climatic conditions are variable and extreme.

Qualifications: Applicants must be U.S. citizens. Requirements for appointment to GS-5 include completion of a four-year course of study leading to a bachelor's degree in electrical engineering, electronics engineering, or electronics technology; or three years of study in an accredited curriculum in electronics; or a four-year course of study leading to a bachelor's degree that included major study or at least twenty-four semester hours in any combination of courses in engineering, physical science, technology, or mathematics, of which at least twelve semester hours included electronics courses; OR one year of specialized experience equivalent to GS-4 as either an electronics technician, inspector or mechanic, or as a television or radio repair technician in a commercial shop. Requirements for GS-7 include one full year of graduate education directly related to the position, OR one year of specialized experience (as described above) equivalent to GS-5; for GS-9, two full years of graduate education directly related to the position, OR one year of specialized experience (as described above) equivalent to GS-7; and for GS-11, one year of specialized experience (as described above) equivalent to GS-9. In some cases, qualifying education may be substituted for experience, and vice versa. Those tentatively selected must pass a background investigation.

Training: Training for personnel in the Electronics Technician occupational classification normally covers a wide range of theories and techniques concerning the design, development, evaluation, testing, installation, use, and maintenance of electronic equipment utilized in law enforcement and public safety operations. Training may be presented by agency staff; federal, state, or local law enforcement training programs or academies; colleges or universities; or other organizations. The nature of training may depend upon the needs of individual personnel, agency requirements, and availability of courses.

Contact: Office of Law Enforcement, Bureau of Land Management, Department of the Interior; Washington, DC 20240. Phone: 202-208-3710. World Wide Web: http://www.blm.gov/.

ELECTRONICS TECHNICIAN (GS-0856)
FEDERAL BUREAU OF PRISONS
U.S. DEPARTMENT OF JUSTICE

Overview: The primary functions of Federal Bureau of Prisons (BOP) Electronics Technicians revolve around the installation, maintenance, and repair of communications and technical equipment to ensure the safety and well-being of inmates, visitors, and BOP personnel on the grounds of federal correctional institutions, penitentiaries, camps, jails and medical facilities. Primary responsibilities include planning, organizing, and executing projects for the installation, maintenance and repair of communications systems, security systems, and auxiliary equipment; troubleshooting, testing, installing, and repairing electronic and electro-mechanical equipment and systems; performing routine service work and necessary technical corrections to ensure reliable technical and operational performance; and interpreting and applying plans, specifications, blueprints and sketches for electronic projects. As fully commissioned federal officers, secondary responsibilities include maintaining security during emergency situations, staff shortages and training exercises. BOP Electronics Technicians are authorized to enforce criminal statutes and judicial sanctions, conduct investigations, carry firearms and make arrests. This position is covered under special retirement provisions for law enforcement officers.

Qualifications: Applicants must be U.S. citizens. Requirements for appointment to GS-5 include completion of a four-year course of study leading to a bachelor's degree in electrical engineering, electronics engineering, or electronics technology; or three years of study in an accredited curriculum in electronics; or a four-year course of study leading to a bachelor's degree that included major study or at least twenty-four semester hours in any combination of courses in engineering, physical science, technology, or mathematics, of which at least twelve semester hours included electronics courses; OR one year of specialized experience equivalent to GS-4 as either an electronics technician, inspector or mechanic, or as a television or radio repair technician in a commercial shop. Requirements for GS-7 include one full year of graduate education directly related to the position, OR one year of specialized experience (as described above) equivalent to GS-5; for GS-9, two full years of graduate education directly related to the position, OR one year of specialized experience (as described above) equivalent to GS-7; and for GS-11, one year of specialized experience (as described above) equivalent to GS-9. In some cases, qualifying education may be substituted for experience, and vice versa. Tentative appointees must qualify for a security clearance and pass a background investigation, personal interview, drug screening test and physical exam.

Training: BOP Electronics Technicians attend the three-week BOP Basic Training Program at the Federal Law Enforcement Training Center in Glynco, Georgia (see Chapter 16), as well as a two-week correctional institution familiarization course conducted by BOP staff. In-service training includes a minimum of forty hours of courses annually, pertaining to correctional issues and techniques, as well as training related to the installation, operation, maintenance, and repair of communications and technical equipment.

Contact: Federal Bureau of Prisons, Department of Justice, Suite 460, 320 First Street NW; Washington, DC 20534. Phone: 202-307-3198 or 800-347-7744. World Wide Web: http://www.bop.gov/.

ELECTRONICS TECHNICIAN (GS-0856)
BUREAU OF ALCOHOL, TOBACCO AND FIREARMS
U.S. DEPARTMENT OF THE TREASURY

Overview: Bureau of Alcohol, Tobacco and Firearms (ATF) Electronics Technicians provide support to ATF surveillance, undercover, and general field operations by ensuring that technical investigative equipment is maintained and utilized at optimum operational performance levels. Utilizing knowledge of the capabilities, limitations, operations, design characteristics, and functional use of a variety of technical investigative equipment and systems, ATF Electronics Technicians design, modify, repair, and test electronics systems and devices used in covert electronic surveillance applications. Responsibilities include ensuring that electronic audio and video surveillance devices and other technical investigative equipment functions properly and remains state-of-the-art; operating a wide range of electronics maintenance and repair equipment, as well as hand and power tools and machine shop equipment; providing operational and troubleshooting expertise to the ATF Criminal Enforcement Branch as well as field investigative personnel; preparing reports, technical documentation, and diagrams; and reviewing technical publications to stay abreast of electronic technological improvements.

Qualifications: Applicants must be U.S. citizens. Requirements for appointment to GS-5 include completion of a four-year course of study leading to a bachelor's degree in electrical engineering, electronics engineering, or electronics technology; or three years of study in an accredited curriculum in electronics; or a four-year course of study leading to a bachelor's degree that included major study or at least twenty-four semester hours in any combination of courses in engineering, physical science, technology, or mathematics, of which at least twelve semester hours included electronics courses; OR one year of specialized experience equivalent to GS-4 as either an electronics technician, inspector or mechanic, or as a television or radio repair technician in a commercial shop. Requirements for GS-7 include one full year of graduate education directly related to the position, OR one year of specialized experience (as described above) equivalent to GS-5; for GS-9, two full years of graduate education directly related to the position, OR one year of specialized experience (as described above) equivalent to GS-7; and for GS-11, one year of specialized experience (as described above) equivalent to GS-9. In some cases, qualifying education may be substituted for experience, and vice versa. Those tentatively selected must pass a background investigation.

Training: ATF Electronics Technicians attend training programs, seminars, and conferences throughout their careers which focus on the assembly, installation, disguising, application, and repair of technical investigative equipment. Training also includes instruction pertaining to the development and advancement of new technical surveillance techniques, electronic audio and video surveillance devices, and other technical investigative equipment. Training is conducted by the ATF Criminal Enforcement Branch in Washington, D.C.; various organizations which manufacture, sell, or service electronic surveillance devices; and other recognized authorities.

Contact: Personnel Division; Bureau of Alcohol, Tobacco and Firearms; 650 Massachusetts Avenue NW, Room 4100; Washington, DC 20226. Phone: 202-927-8423. World Wide Web: http://www.atf.treas.gov/. E-mail: persdiv@atfhq.atf.treas.gov.

EMERGENCY COMMUNICATION DISPATCHER (GS-0303)
UNITED STATES ARMY
U.S. DEPARTMENT OF DEFENSE

Overview: Emergency Communication Dispatchers of the United States Army are responsible for the control of all police, fire, and ambulance emergency response calls at Army installations. Primary responsibilities of these personnel include receiving emergency and non-emergency calls for service and determining their nature; dealing with members of the public requiring emergency services, including those who are in an agitated or excited state; dispatching, rendering assistance and guidance, and supplying critical information to police, fire, ambulance, and other emergency units; operating a variety of state-of-the-art radio transmitters and receivers, automated communication information and database systems, tape recorders, telephone systems, enhanced 911 emergency and non-emergency networks, commercial and Defense Department security alarm controls; preparing radio dispatch reports, police blotters, and other associated police and emergency response reports; filing documents and performing other administrative duties; and monitoring detention cell operations when cells are occupied by detained persons. This is a civilian position and does not require active duty military service.

Qualifications: Applicants must be U.S. citizens. Requirements for appointment to GS-4 include two years of education above high school, OR one year of general experience; for GS-5, four years of education above high school, OR one year of specialized experience equivalent to at least GS-4; and for GS-6 and above, one year of specialized experience equivalent to the next lower grade level. Applicants are rated on their experience, education, training, employment performance evaluations, and awards as they apply to the position. Education and experience may be combined to meet total experience requirements for positions at grades GS-5 and below. Tentative appointees must pass a background investigation, drug screening test, and medical exam; receive and maintain certification in first aid; and qualify for a security clearance.

Training: Personnel in the Emergency Communication Dispatcher occupational classification typically receive a combination of on-the-job training and classroom instruction which focuses on radio communication equipment, dispatching procedures, telephone techniques, pre-arrival instructions for providing CPR and other aid, automated law enforcement database systems, computer hardware and software, clerical tasks, and agency policies and procedures. Training may be presented by agency staff; federal, state, or local law enforcement training programs or academies; colleges or universities; or other organizations.

Contact: Apply directly to the Army installation where employment is sought, or contact Army Personnel and Employment Service, The Pentagon; Washington, DC 20310. Phone: 703-695-3383. World Wide Web: http://www.army.mil/.

EMERGENCY VEHICLE DISPATCHER (GS-2151)
UNITED STATES NAVAL ACADEMY
U.S. DEPARTMENT OF DEFENSE

Overview: United States Naval Academy (USNA) Emergency Vehicle Dispatchers are responsible for radio communication functions in support of law enforcement and security operations on the grounds of the USNA in Annapolis, Maryland, a 338-acre campus located 33 miles east of Washington, D.C. Primary responsibilities include receiving emergency and non-emergency telephone calls; monitoring radio transmissions of USNA police patrol units; receiving requests for police, fire and emergency medical services, and dispatching the appropriate response units; operating computer-aided multi-frequency radio communication equipment, radio control panels, portable radios, alert tone pagers, and base intercom systems; processing inquiries through the Criminal Justice Information System, which is an interagency computer network which includes the Maryland Interagency Law Enforcement System and the National Crime Information Center; monitoring computerized alarm systems that receive fire, burglary, bank and intruder alarms from more than 300 locations throughout the USNA complex; and maintaining communications with police and fire department officials on the scenes of accidents, medical emergencies, crimes, and other incidents. This is a civilian position and does not require active duty military service.

Qualifications: Applicants must be U.S. citizens. Requirements for appointment to GS-4 include two years of education above high school, OR one year of general experience; for GS-5, four years of education above high school, OR one year of specialized experience equivalent to at least GS-4; and for GS-6 and above, one year of specialized experience equivalent to the next lower grade level. Applicants are rated on their experience, education, training, employment performance evaluations, and awards as they apply to the position. Education and experience may be combined to meet total experience requirements for positions at grades GS-5 and below.

Training: Naval Academy Emergency Vehicle Dispatchers receive on-the-job training and attend courses relating to prioritization of calls for service, communication skills, crisis intervention, information gathering, suicide calls, liability and legal issues, dispatching procedures associated with crimes in progress, alarm panel operation, and automated law enforcement database systems. These personnel also receive training leading to Emergency Medical Dispatch (EMD) certification, which focuses on subjects such as listening skills, telephone techniques, pre-arrival instructions for CPR and other aid, child and elderly callers, disaster preparedness, pediatric considerations, and legal issues.

Contact: Office of Human Resources, U.S. Naval Academy, 181 Wainwright Road; Annapolis, MD 21402. Phone: 410-293-3822. World Wide Web: http://www.nadn.navy.mil/. E-mail: help@chinfo.navy.mil.

LAW ENFORCEMENT COMMUNICATIONS ASSISTANT (GS-1802)
UNITED STATES BORDER PATROL
IMMIGRATION AND NATURALIZATION SERVICE
U.S. DEPARTMENT OF JUSTICE

Overview: Law Enforcement Communications Assistants of the United States Border Patrol (USBP) perform a variety of crucial communications functions in support of USBP field operations to ensure the safety and well being of USBP Agents nationwide. Responsibilities include transmitting, receiving and relaying official messages via radio to operating units, sector patrol, aircraft, and section stations; coordinating and maintaining communications during emergency situations; receiving and relaying information pertaining to the location of illegal aliens; obtaining and processing information relating to driver's licenses, criminal records, vehicle registrations and immigration status from various automated law enforcement database systems, such as the National Crime Information Center, National Law Enforcement Telecommunications System, and Master Index Remote Access System; operating computer systems utilizing a complex myriad of codes and other access information to obtain information from automated databases; acting as Information Officer to the public, both telephonically and in personal contacts; relaying information by radio or telephone to other law enforcement agencies; and providing telephone coverage for anti-smuggling units.

Qualifications: Applicants must be U.S. citizens. Requirements for appointment to GS-4 level include two years of education above high school, OR one year of general experience; for GS-5, four years of education above high school, OR one year of specialized experience equivalent to at least GS-4; and for grades GS-6 through GS-11, one year of specialized experience equivalent to the next lower grade level. Applicants are rated on their experience, education, training, employment performance evaluations, and awards as they relate to the position. Experience and education may be combined to meet total experience requirements for positions at grades GS-5 and below. Those tentatively selected must pass a background investigation and drug screening test.

Training: Personnel in the Law Enforcement Communications Assistant occupational classification normally receive on-the-job training and attend courses pertaining to dispatching procedures, computer-aided radio communication equipment, telephone systems and procedures, automated law enforcement database systems, computer hardware and software, administrative records and reports, and agency policies and procedures. Training may be conducted by agency staff; federal, state, or local law enforcement training programs or academies; colleges or universities; or other organizations.

Contact: United States Border Patrol, Immigration and Naturalization Service, 425 I Street NW; Washington, DC 20536. Phone: 202-616-1964. World Wide Web: http://www.ins.usdoj.gov/.

PARK DISPATCHER (GS-2151)
NATIONAL PARK SERVICE
U.S. DEPARTMENT OF THE INTERIOR

Overview: National Park Service (NPS) Park Dispatchers are responsible for radio communication functions in support of law enforcement and security operations at locations managed by the NPS, such as national parks and monuments, trails, preserves, campgrounds, battlefields, sea shores, lakeshores, recreational areas, and historic sites. NPS Park Dispatchers serve as a point-of-contact between the public, the Communications Control

Center and operations personnel. Responsibilities include relaying information on multi-frequency park radio and multi-line telephone systems during routine and emergency situations; receiving reports and coordinating responses to law enforcement incidents, search and rescue operations, emergency medical situations, fires, air support operations, natural disasters, downed aircraft, and special events; analyzing situations and establishing priorities during concurrent incidents; coordinating operations with other law enforcement agencies, fire departments, and rescue organizations; operating complex law enforcement telecommunications computer systems tied in with the National Law Enforcement Telecommunications System, National Crime Information Center, and other law enforcement databases; monitoring fire alarm systems and intrusion detection devices; maintaining logs and confidential records pertaining to all law enforcement activities and communications transactions; and operating personal computers for word processing and data entry. Similar NPS positions are filled under series which include GS-0390 Communications Operator, GS-0390 Telecommunications Equipment Operator, GS-0392 Public Safety Communications Technician, or GS-0392 Telecommunications Technician.

Qualifications: Applicants must be U.S. citizens. Requirements for appointment to GS-4 include two years of education above high school, OR one year of general experience; for GS-5, four years of education above high school, OR one year of specialized experience equivalent to at least GS-4; and for GS-6 and above, one year of specialized experience equivalent to the next lower grade level. Applicants are rated on their experience, education, training, employment performance evaluations, and awards as they apply to the position. Education and experience may be combined to meet total experience requirements for positions at grades GS-5 and below. Tentative appointees must pass a background investigation.

Training: Personnel in the Park Dispatcher occupational classification ordinarily receive on-the-job training and attend courses relating to computer-aided radio communication equipment, dispatching procedures, automated law enforcement database systems, alarm panel controls, telephone systems and procedures, pre-arrival instructions for providing CPR and other aid, administrative records and reports, computer hardware and software, agency policies and directives, and other subjects. Training may be presented by agency staff; federal, state, or local law enforcement training programs or academies; colleges or universities; or other organizations.

Contact: Direct inquiries to the personnel office where employment is sought, or to National Park Service, Department of the Interior, P.O. Box 37127; Washington, DC 20013. Phone: 202-208-6843. World Wide Web: http://www.nps.gov/.

PUBLIC SAFETY DISPATCHER (GS-2151)
UNITED STATES NAVY
U.S. DEPARTMENT OF DEFENSE

Overview: United States Navy (USN) Public Safety Dispatchers are responsible for radio communication functions in support of law enforcement and security operations on the grounds of USN installations, such as shipyards, air fields, supply centers, hospitals, and communication facilities. Responsibilities include dispatching public safety personnel, vehicles, equipment, and supplies to routine and emergency situations via internal radio communication systems; performing data entry into computer-aided dispatch and local computer systems; retrieving information from automated law enforcement database systems; monitoring and operating emergency fire alarm and enhanced 911 telephone systems; summoning mutual aid from outside agencies to provide for support during major fires, multiple alarms, natural disasters, medical emergencies, and other incidents; maintaining records of dispatched units, personnel and equipment; preparing shift activity logs and related reports; monitoring closed-circuit television equipment and intrusion detection devices; and identifying equipment malfunctions and taking appropriate action to correct problems. Similar Navy positions are filled under the GS-0392 Police Dispatcher series. This is a civilian position and does not require active duty military service.

Qualifications: Applicants must be U.S. citizens. Requirements for appointment to GS-4 include two years of education above high school, OR one year of general experience; for GS-5, four years of education above high school, OR one year of specialized experience equivalent to at least GS-4; and for GS-6 and above, one year of specialized experience equivalent to the next lower grade level. Applicants are rated on their experience, education, training, employment performance evaluations, and awards as they apply to the position. Education and experience may be combined to meet total experience requirements for positions at grades GS-5 and below.

Training: Personnel in the Public Safety Dispatcher occupational classification ordinarily receive on-the-job training and attend courses relating to computer-aided radio communication equipment, dispatching procedures, pre-arrival instructions for providing CPR and other aid, automated law enforcement database systems, alarm panel controls, telephone systems and procedures, administrative records and reports, computer hardware and software, agency policies and directives, and other subjects. Training may be presented by agency staff; federal, state, or local law enforcement training programs or academies; colleges or universities; or other organizations.

Contact: Direct inquiries to the Human Resources Office where employment is sought, or contact Office of Information, Department of the Navy; Washington, DC 20350. Phone: 703-697-7391. World Wide Web: http://www.navy.mil/. E-mail: help@chinfo.navy.mil.

RADIO TELECOMMUNICATION OPERATOR (GS-0390)
BUREAU OF INDIAN AFFAIRS
U.S. DEPARTMENT OF THE INTERIOR

Overview: Bureau of Indian Affairs (BIA) Radio Telecommunication Operators perform a wide range of data processing and dispatching functions in support of BIA law enforcement operations on Indian lands, reservations, allotments, and communities throughout Indian country. Working under the direction of Supervisory BIA Police Officers, Radio Telecommunication Operators receive reports and dispatch appropriate police personnel to calls for service, crimes in progress, disturbances, traffic accidents, emergency medical situations, fires, search and rescue operations, special events, and other incidents; monitor police radio frequencies and respond to requests for telecommunication services; operate a variety of automated law enforcement database and communication systems, and relay results of inquiries to BIA police personnel in the field; receive telephone inquiries; communicate information to field units using police radio codes; and maintain confidential records, logs, and files pertaining to law enforcement activities, incoming and outgoing calls, and related communications. Similar BIA positions are filled under the GS-0390 Telecommunications Equipment Operator designation.

Qualifications: Under the Indian Reorganization Act of 1934, qualified Indian applicants are given hiring preference for BIA positions, although applications from non-Indian candidates are encouraged. Applicants must be U.S. citizens. Requirements for appointment to GS-4 include two years of education above high school, OR one year of general experience; for GS-5, four years of education above high school, OR one year of specialized experience equivalent to at least GS-4; and for GS-6 and above, one year of specialized experience equivalent to the next lower grade level. Applicants are rated on their experience, education, training, employment performance evaluations, and awards as they apply to the position. Education and experience may be combined to meet total experience requirements for positions at grades GS-5 and below. Tentative appointees must pass a background investigation.

Training: Personnel in the Radio Telecommunication Operator occupational classification typically receive a combination of on-the-job training and classroom instruction which covers message handling and dispatching procedures, pre-arrival instructions for providing CPR and other aid, radio communication equipment, automated law enforcement database systems, computer hardware and software, administrative tasks, and agency policies and procedures. Training may be presented by agency staff; federal, state, or local law enforcement training programs or academies; colleges or universities; or other organizations.

Contact: Direct inquiries to the personnel office where employment is sought, or contact: Office of

Personnel, Bureau of Indian Affairs, Department of the Interior, 1849 C Street NW; Washington, DC 20240. Phone: 202-208-3710. World Wide Web: http://www.doi.gov/bureau-indian-affairs.html.

TECHNICAL ENFORCEMENT OFFICER (GS-1801)
UNITED STATES CUSTOMS SERVICE
U.S. DEPARTMENT OF THE TREASURY

Overview: Technical Enforcement Officers of the U.S. Customs Service are responsible for the installation, operation, and maintenance of covert electronic and technical surveillance devices which are used to provide intelligence and evidence in ongoing criminal investigations. These personnel provide technical support to Customs Special Agents and other law enforcement officers in major operations which require the use of covert audio and video recording devices, cameras, electronic tracking devices, telephone surveillance equipment, transmitters and receivers, tactical radio communications systems, courtroom playback systems, and other related equipment. Primary responsibilities include attending briefings and assisting with the planning of enforcement operations; conducting site surveys to evaluate available applications; testing and evaluating electronic surveillance, tagging, and detecting equipment under laboratory and field conditions; installing, operating, adjusting, and repairing covert monitoring devices; operating special-purpose surveillance vehicles and electronic diagnostic equipment; resolving complex problems relating to electronic equipment; maintaining surveillance logs and inventories; and maintaining liaison with law enforcement personnel and agencies. Responsibilities may also include the surreptitious installation of electronic surveillance devices in the presence of targeted suspects while posing as a maintenance employee, radio technician, utility company employee, or other worker. Customs Technical Enforcement Officers qualify for Administratively Uncontrollable Overtime, and are authorized to carry firearms and make arrests.

Qualifications: Applicants must be U.S. citizens. Requirements for appointment to GS-5 level include completion of a four-year course of study leading to a bachelor's degree, OR three years general experience, one year of which was equivalent to GS-4; for GS-7, one full year of graduate education, or superior academic achievement during undergraduate studies, OR one year of specialized experience equivalent to GS-5; for GS-9, a master's degree or two years of graduate education, OR one year of specialized experience equivalent to GS-7; for GS-11, a Ph.D. or equivalent doctoral degree, or three years of graduate education, OR one year of specialized experience equivalent to GS-9; and for GS-12, one year of specialized experience equivalent to GS-11. In some cases, qualifying education may be substituted for experience, and vice versa. Tentative appointees must pass a background investigation and drug screening test, and qualify for a security clearance.

Training: Initial training includes the three-week Customs Basic Technical Enforcement Officer School at the Federal Law Enforcement Training Center in Glynco, Georgia. This course includes lecture, laboratory applications, and practical exercises which focus on electronic surveillance laws, search and seizure, audio recorders, surveillance receivers and transmitters, antennas, electronic tracking devices, video applications, covert installations, site planning, and troubleshooting. In-service training includes various courses pertaining to Customs laws, technical investigative equipment updates, database programs, firearms proficiency, use of force, and other subjects related to various aspects of technical investigative equipment.

Contact: United States Customs Service, 1300 Pennsylvania Avenue NW; Washington, DC 20229. Phone: 202-927-1250. World Wide Web: http://www.customs.ustreas.gov/.

TELECOMMUNICATIONS EQUIPMENT OPERATOR (GS-0390)
UNITED STATES MARSHALS SERVICE
U.S. DEPARTMENT OF JUSTICE

Overview: Telecommunications Equipment Operators of the United States Marshals Service (USMS) operate a variety of technical communications equipment and automated systems in support of USMS law enforcement and security operations nationwide. Responsibilities include the operation of telecommunication terminals linked to the National Crime Information Center (NCIC), the National Law Enforcement

Telecommunications System (NLETS), and the Justice Telecommunications System; entering data into Warrant Information Network databases and forwarding data to NCIC; receiving outstanding arrest warrant information, verifying that the data is in the proper format, and converting data into the proper format as needed; receiving fugitive apprehension information from other agencies; coordinating the arrest and detention of wanted persons via NLETS; processing teletype communications; handling telephone inquiries; monitoring closed-circuit television equipment and alarm systems to ensure building security; establishing and maintaining subject matter files; and receiving incoming messages and routing them to the proper addressee.

Qualifications: Applicants must be U.S. citizens. Requirements for appointment to GS-4 include two years of education above high school, OR one year of general experience; for GS-5, four years of education above high school, OR one year of specialized experience equivalent to at least GS-4; and for GS-6 and above, one year of specialized experience equivalent to the next lower grade level. Applicants are rated on their experience, education, training, employment performance evaluations, and awards as they apply to the position. Education and experience may be combined to meet total experience requirements for positions at grades GS-5 and below. Tentative appointees must qualify for a top-secret security clearance, and pass a background investigation and drug screening test.

Training: USMS Telecommunications Equipment Operators attend courses and receive continuous on-the-job training relating to the operation of various national and state law enforcement databases and telecommunications systems. This training is conducted by USMS staff and police agencies nationwide, and often leads to database operator certification by state police agencies. Additional training focuses on computer literacy and troubleshooting, word processing software, e-mail programs, telephone call handling procedures, and other relevant subjects.

Contact: Human Resources Division, United States Marshals Service, 600 Army Navy Drive; Arlington, VA 22202. Phone: 202-307-9437. World Wide Web: http://www.usdoj.gov/marshals/.

TELECOMMUNICATIONS SPECIALIST (GS-0391)
NAVAL CRIMINAL INVESTIGATIVE SERVICE
U.S. DEPARTMENT OF DEFENSE

Overview: Telecommunications Specialists of the Naval Criminal Investigative Service (NCIS) are responsible for the installation, maintenance, repair, and operation of communication equipment in support of NCIS criminal investigative, information security, law enforcement, physical and personnel security, and counterintelligence operations. Responsibilities include evaluation of radio frequency requirements; conducting site surveys, inspections, and special studies on radio frequency communication needs; testing and evaluating new equipment for the purpose of identifying required resources with which procurement decisions are made; recommending the implementation of projects designed to fulfill radio frequency mission requirements; maintaining close working relationships with Defense Department counterpart units; working with industry representatives to ensure that NCIS is kept abreast of advances in technology and plans which would impact or have applicability on the NCIS communication system; and conducting training to facilitate the successful use of radio communications equipment and systems to improve the investigative, counterintelligence, and security capabilities of NCIS personnel. This is a civilian position and does not require active duty military service.

Qualifications: Applicants must be U.S. citizens. Requirements for appointment to GS-5 level include completion of a four-year course of study leading to a bachelor's degree, OR three years general experience, one year of which was equivalent to GS-4; for GS-7, one full year of graduate education, or superior academic achievement during undergraduate studies, OR one year of specialized experience equivalent to GS-5; for GS-9, a master's degree or two years of graduate education, OR one year of specialized experience equivalent to GS-7; for GS-11, a Ph.D. or equivalent doctoral degree, or three years of graduate education, OR one year of specialized experience equivalent to GS-9; and for GS-12 or GS-13, one year of specialized experience equivalent to the next lower grade level. Undergraduate and graduate education must have included a major in electrical or electronic engineering, mathematics, physics, public utilities, statistics, computer science, telecommunications or information systems management, business administration, industrial management, or other fields related to the position. In some cases, qualifying education may be substituted for experience, and vice versa. Tentative appointees must qualify for a security clearance and pass a background investigation and drug screening test.

Training: NCIS Telecommunications Specialists receive ongoing classroom instruction and on-the-job training concerned with communication equipment and transmission media, and may also attend advanced courses and seminars, conferences, and symposia hosted by various professional organizations, colleges, and universities.

Contact: Naval Criminal Investigative Service, 716 East Sicard Street SE, Building 111, Washington Navy Yard; Washington, DC 20388. Phone: 202-433-9162. World Wide Web: http://www.ncis.navy.mil/.

TELECOMMUNICATIONS SPECIALIST (GS-0391)
DRUG ENFORCEMENT ADMINISTRATION
U.S. DEPARTMENT OF JUSTICE

Overview: Drug Enforcement Administration (DEA) Telecommunications Specialists originate and develop concepts, equipment and planning for the use of radio communications and technical investigative equipment and systems to improve the investigative capabilities and safety of DEA Special Agents. These personnel provide special technical expertise to the DEA and other domestic and foreign agencies in a coordinated effort to reduce the flow of illicit drugs into the United States. Responsibilities include participating in the planning of law enforcement operations; conducting site surveys to evaluate the possibility for communications and covert surveillance utilizing electronic devices; installing phone intercepts, video cameras, microphones, pen registers, microwave transmitters, transponders, and other communication and covert electronic devices; and coordinating the purchase, installation and repair of technical investigative equipment. In addition to operating in DEA field offices, Telecommunications Specialists are also assigned to the DEA El Paso Intelligence Center, which is a clearinghouse for tactical intelligence and the collection, analysis, and dissemination of information related to worldwide drug movement and alien smuggling.

Qualifications: Applicants must be U.S. citizens. Requirements for appointment to GS-5 level include completion of a four-year course of study leading to a bachelor's degree, OR three years general experience, one year of which was equivalent to GS-4; for GS-7, one full year of graduate education, or superior academic achievement during undergraduate studies, OR one year of specialized experience equivalent to GS-5; for GS-9, a master's degree or two years of graduate education, OR one year of specialized experience equivalent to GS-7; for GS-11, a Ph.D. or equivalent doctoral degree, or three years of graduate education, OR one year of specialized experience equivalent to GS-9; and for GS-12, one year of specialized experience equivalent to GS-11. Undergraduate or graduate education must have included a major in electrical or electronic engineering, mathematics, physics, public utilities, statistics, computer science, telecommunications or information systems management, business administration, industrial management, or other related fields. In some cases, qualifying education may be substituted for experience, and vice versa. Tentative appointees must qualify for a security clearance and pass a background investigation and drug screening test.

Training: Training for personnel in the Telecommunications Specialist occupational classification typically focuses on a broad range of technical and analytical functions pertaining to the planning, development, acquisition, testing, integration, installation, use, modification, and repair of telecommunications systems and technical investigative equipment utilized in law enforcement, investigative, and protective operations. Training may be presented by agency staff; federal, state, or local law enforcement training programs or academies; colleges or universities; or other organizations.

Contact: Direct inquiries to the DEA Field Office where employment is sought, or to Drug Enforcement Administration; Washington, DC 20537. Phone: 202-307-1000 or 800-DEA-4288. World Wide Web: http://www.usdoj.gov/dea/.

TELECOMMUNICATIONS SPECIALIST (GS-0391)
BUREAU OF ALCOHOL, TOBACCO AND FIREARMS
U.S. DEPARTMENT OF THE TREASURY

Overview: Telecommunications Specialists of the Bureau of Alcohol, Tobacco and Firearms (ATF) are divided among two areas of expertise, including both voice and radio communications systems. Voice Telecommunications Specialists are responsible for designing and maintaining systems that include telephones, switchboards, switching equipment, key systems, and data or radio interfaces. These personnel perform technical and analytical work to develop and enhance the Bureau's telecommunications equipment and services, which cover a broad range of state-of-the-art components. Radio Telecommunications Specialists plan and implement the application of radio communication systems and electronic surveillance equipment, including equipment installations in vehicles, aircraft and fixed station sites. Radio personnel are directly involved in field enforcement activities as they relate to the operation of multi-frequency mobile and base radio systems, repeaters, antennas, concealed miniature radio transmitters, electronic listening devices, video surveillance cameras, audio and video recording devices, and other technical investigative equipment. ATF Telecommunications Specialists explore emerging technologies; conduct site surveys to determine communications needs; coordinate the purchasing, testing, installation, operation, and maintenance of equipment; adapt advanced techniques and develop innovative procedures and equipment applications to meet unique needs which cannot be satisfied through conventional means; conduct training and orientation programs for user groups; and maintain liaison with communications equipment manufacturers, suppliers, and other experts in the field.

Qualifications: Applicants must be U.S. citizens. Requirements for appointment to GS-5 level include completion of a four-year course of study leading to a bachelor's degree, OR three years general experience, one year of which was equivalent to GS-4; for GS-7, one full year of graduate education, or superior academic achievement during undergraduate studies, OR one year of specialized experience equivalent to GS-5; for GS-9, a master's degree or two years of graduate education, OR one year of specialized experience equivalent to GS-7; for GS-11, a Ph.D. or equivalent doctoral degree, or three years of graduate education, OR one year of specialized experience equivalent to GS-9; and for GS-12 or GS-13, one year of specialized experience equivalent to the next lower grade level. Undergraduate and graduate education must have included a major in electrical or electronic engineering, mathematics, physics, public utilities, statistics, computer science, telecommunications or information systems management, business administration, industrial management, or other fields related to the position. In some cases, qualifying education may be substituted for experience, and vice versa. Tentative appointees must qualify for a security clearance and pass a background investigation.

Training: Training for ATF Telecommunications Specialists includes a wide range of courses which involve the design, installation, operation, maintenance, and repair of telephone and radio equipment and technical investigative devices. Many of these courses are conducted by technicians of telecommunications equipment manufacturers, or other recognized authorities.

Contact: Personnel Division; Bureau of Alcohol, Tobacco and Firearms; 650 Massachusetts Avenue NW, Room 4100; Washington, DC 20226. Phone: 202-927-8423. World Wide Web: http://www.atf.treas.gov/. E-mail: PersDiv@atfhq.atf.treas.gov.

TELECOMMUNICATIONS SPECIALIST (GS-0391)
UNITED STATES SECRET SERVICE
U.S. DEPARTMENT OF THE TREASURY

Overview: United States Secret Service (USSS) Telecommunications Specialists perform a range of functions associated with the planning, development, implementation and administration of all aspects of USSS radio, telephone, and other communications systems and facilities. Responsibilities include surveying, studying, and evaluating divisions, field offices, and resident agencies to determine radio communication requirements; locating contractors to perform the installation of antenna systems, electrical power, and related equipment;

installing, maintaining and repairing complex multi-frequency, multi-site radio communications systems; installing and maintaining integrated mobile radio systems consisting of voice privacy VHF and UHF mobile radios, cellular telephones, radio scanners, and warning lights; serving as a team leader or member on protective communications support missions throughout the United States or abroad; preparing written reports; and explaining system changes, proposals, and services provided for temporary communications. USSS Telecommunications Specialists are also involved in the planning, design, development, and implementation of a nationwide data telecommunications network which integrates highly sensitive and technical automated data processing functions, electronic mail, facsimile, and office automation functions.

Qualifications: Applicants must be U.S. citizens. Requirements for appointment to GS-5 level include completion of a four-year course of study leading to a bachelor's degree, OR three years general experience, one year of which was equivalent to GS-4; for GS-7, one full year of graduate education, or superior academic achievement during undergraduate studies, OR one year of specialized experience equivalent to GS-5; for GS-9, a master's degree or two years of graduate education, OR one year of specialized experience equivalent to GS-7; for GS-11, a Ph.D. or equivalent doctoral degree, or three years of graduate education, OR one year of specialized experience equivalent to GS-9; and for GS-12 or GS-13, one year of specialized experience equivalent to the next lower grade level. Undergraduate and graduate education must have included a major in electrical or electronic engineering, mathematics, physics, public utilities, statistics, computer science, telecommunications or information systems management, business administration, industrial management, or other fields related to the position. In some cases, qualifying education may be substituted for experience, and vice versa. Tentative appointees must qualify for a top-secret security clearance, and pass a background investigation and drug screening test.

Training: Training for personnel in the Telecommunications Specialist occupational classification typically focuses on a broad range of technical and analytical functions pertaining to the planning, development, acquisition, testing, integration, installation, use, modification, and repair of telecommunications systems and technical investigative equipment utilized in law enforcement, investigative, and protective operations. Training may be presented by agency staff; federal, state, or local law enforcement training programs or academies; colleges or universities; or other organizations.

Contact: United States Secret Service, 1800 G Street NW, Room 912; Washington, DC 20223. Phone: 202-435-5708 or 800-827-7783. World Wide Web: http://www.treas.gov/usss/.

Chapter Sixteen

FEDERAL TRAINING PROGRAMS AND FACILITIES

Education has for its object
the formation of character.
– HERBERT SPENCER

T RAINING THAT INTRODUCES THE MOST UP-TO-DATE INFORMATION and techniques is essential to prepare law enforcement officers for the demands of a complicated and ever-changing environment. To address these challenges, a number of prominent training facilities located throughout the United States offer innovative and specialized programs for the particular needs of federal law enforcement personnel.

The vast majority of federal criminal investigators and uniformed police officers complete introductory basic and in-service training at the Federal Law Enforcement Training Center (FLETC) in Glynco, Georgia. Many federal law enforcement technicians, specialists, inspectors, general and compliance investigators, and other support staff also complete courses at FLETC throughout their careers. In addition, most agencies take advantage of in-house courses as well as training programs offered by state and local police academies, colleges and universities, and privately-supported training organizations.

A few agencies operate independent academies primarily for the training of their own personnel, such as the Federal Bureau of Investigation (FBI), Drug Enforcement Administration (DEA), Postal Inspection Service, and Air Force Office of Special Investigations. In addition to conducting programs to meet their training requirements, these agencies also present specialized courses relating to their particular areas of expertise to personnel of other organizations.

FEDERAL LAW ENFORCEMENT TRAINING CENTER

The Federal Law Enforcement Training Center (FLETC) was established by the Treasury Department in 1970 as an interagency facility to serve the training needs of the federal law enforcement community. FLETC provides state-of-the-art instruction in a consolidated training environment to more than 70 participating federal agencies, and to other agencies on a space-available basis. The Center also presents more than 50 programs to state and local agencies, and provides training assistance to foreign governments. Nearly 300 unique training programs are conducted by a cadre of permanent staff instructors and experienced law enforcement personnel detailed to FLETC from participating agencies. More than 25,000 students are trained annually at FLETC facilities in Georgia, New Mexico, and South Carolina.

Training courses are divided among several instructional areas, including Behavioral Sciences, Driver and Marine, Enforcement Operations, Enforcement Specialties, Firearms, Legal Support, Physical Techniques, Program Support, Security Specialties, and Training Operations. Programs are also conducted at the FLETC Management Institute; Financial Fraud Institute; and National Center for State, Local and International Law

Enforcement Training. Instruction is presented primarily during daytime hours on weekdays, although some exercises are conducted during the evenings and on weekends. In many programs, professional role players are employed to provide a realistic atmosphere during practical exercises which focus on interviewing, arrest techniques, defensive tactics, undercover transactions, and other scenarios. Videotaped replays are also used to critique student performance.

While many participating agencies design and conduct training programs at the Center for their own employees to meet specific training requirements, the majority of FLETC courses are attended by a mix of personnel representing multiple agencies. This chapter provides an overview of mixed programs that are among the most widely attended by federal law enforcement officers, investigators, inspectors, technicians, and specialists. Although agency-specific in nature, the Federal Bureau of Prisons Basic Training Program is included as it is attended by employees of virtually every Bureau occupational category. Similarly, the Immigration Officer Basic Training Program is also profiled, as Officer Corps personnel in several Immigration and Naturalization Service careers attend this program.

Training Facilities

Glynco Main Campus

The main campus is located near Brunswick, Georgia, on the site of the former Glynco Naval Air Station, between Savanna and Jacksonville. Occupying more than 1,500 acres, it is the largest of the FLETC training centers, and the largest law enforcement training facility in the United States. Modern specialized facilities include classroom buildings, a computer laboratory, driver training ranges, marine facilities, computerized indoor and outdoor firearms ranges, automated judgment pistol shooting facilities, criminalistics teaching laboratories, raid houses, a physical techniques complex, a library, office and warehouse space, and various administrative and logistical support structures. Accommodations and amenities include dormitories and townhouses, a dining hall, recreation areas, a golf course, swimming pools, a post office, a convenience store, and laundry facilities. The Glynco campus has been operational since 1975, and provides the majority of FLETC programs.

Artesia Satellite Campus

The FLETC Artesia Center is located in southwestern New Mexico near Roswell. It offers similar facilities to those at Glynco, although on a much smaller scale, and is utilized primarily for meeting the basic training needs of the Bureau of Indian Affairs, Immigration and Naturalization Service (INS), United States Border Patrol, and the advanced training needs of agencies located principally in the western region of the United States. The Artesia campus has provided training since 1990, and has housing and associated support capacity for 320 students. Artesia Center facilities include firearms ranges, a physical techniques complex, driver training ranges, classroom facilities, office space, and a dining hall.

Charleston Temporary Campus

In response to the increasing size of the INS and Border Patrol, and the ensuing need to train thousands of new officers, a temporary FLETC satellite training center was established in Charleston, South Carolina, in 1996. This facility, on the grounds of the Charleston Naval Weapons Station, is utilized for the training of Immigration Officers and Border Patrol Agents, and is expected to remain operational as long as the build-up continues.

Criminal Investigator Training Program

The eight-week Criminal Investigator Training Program is designed to provide full-time Special Agents and other criminal investigators in the GS-1811 and GS-1812 series with an in-depth study of basic criminal investigative and law enforcement concepts and techniques. These personnel are provided the specific information and skills training necessary to equip them for investigative tasks, undercover and surveillance assignments, law enforcement techniques, and other functions performed by federal criminal investigators. This program is attended by personnel representing more than fifty federal agencies.

Primary subjects presented in this program include: Orientation to Federal Law Enforcement Agencies,

Criminal and Constitutional Law, Search and Seizure, Evidence, Detention and Arrest, Interviewing Techniques, Self-Incrimination, Surveillance, Informants, Sources of Information, Undercover Operations, High-Risk Vehicle Stops, Defensive Driving and Skid Control, Search Warrant Execution, Rapid Building Entry and Search Techniques, Crime Scene Investigation, Searching Computers, Non-Lethal Control Techniques, Fingerprinting, Photography, Drugs of Abuse, Questioned Documents, Organized Crime, Terrorism, Bombs and Explosives, Federal Firearms Violations, Firearms Safety, Marksmanship, Judgment Pistol Shooting, Reduced Light Shooting, Report Writing, Trial Preparation, Federal Court Procedures, Courtroom Testimony, Cultural Diversity, CPR, Physical Conditioning, and other topics.

Inspector General Basic Training Program

The Inspector General Basic Training Program is a three-week course that is designed to develop the specific skills identified as most critical by the Offices of the Inspectors General, with emphasis on the investigation of fraud, waste, and abuse in government programs. Developed by the FLETC Financial Fraud Institute in cooperation with the President's Council on Integrity and Efficiency, this course is frequently attended by Special Agents of the Offices of Inspectors General as a supplement to the eight-week Criminal Investigator Basic Training Program.

Instruction in this program includes practical exercises and classroom lectures in subjects such as: Federal Criminal Law, the Inspector General Act, Confidential Sources, the Whistleblower Act, Legal Issues in Obtaining Evidence, Investigative Case Planning, Personnel Misconduct Investigations, Technical Investigative Equipment, Electronic Sources of Information, Program and Entitlement Fraud, Contract Fraud, Link Analysis, Interviewing Techniques, Nonverbal Communication, Influence and Persuasion, Cognitive Interviewing, Kinesic Interviewing, Encountering Resistance in the Law Enforcement Interview, Legal Considerations of Interviews, Non-Lethal Control Techniques, Judgment Pistol Shooting, Tactical Speed Shooting, and Reduced Light Shooting.

Introduction to Criminal Investigations Training Program

The two-week Introduction to Criminal Investigations Training Program provides an overview of the procedures, techniques, legal concerns, and general problems associated with criminal investigations. This course is designed primarily for regulatory and compliance investigators, inspectors, paralegals, auditors, technical personnel, and others who conduct or participate in criminal investigations. Instruction consists of classroom lectures and practical exercises which examine the role of the criminal investigator, with particular emphasis on interviewing skills and legal requirements.

Courses presented in this program include: Introduction to Criminal Investigations, Orientation to Federal Law Enforcement Agencies, Federal Court Procedures, Criminal Law, Administrative Law, Civil Litigation, Privacy Act, Freedom of Information Act, Evidence, Search and Seizure, Civil Rights, Conspiracy, Assault, Bribery, Investigative Techniques, Surveillance, Informants, Sources of Information, Link Analysis, Investigative Computer Skills, Questioned Documents, Interviewing, Self-Incrimination, Entrapment, Report Writing, and Court Testimony.

Criminal Intelligence Analysts Training Program

Entry-level Criminal Intelligence Analysts and Specialists attend the two-week Criminal Intelligence Analyst Training Program to acquire and develop the basic skills and techniques required to perform analytical processes associated with intelligence research projects. Learning methodologies include demonstrations and lectures presented by FLETC instructors and guest speakers, and practical exercises designed to demonstrate the students' knowledge and understanding of the subject matter. Microcomputers also are used to demonstrate their importance as analytical tools.

Instruction in this program includes: Information Management, Intelligence Cycle and Process, Legal Aspects of Intelligence, Sources of Information, Databases, Collation and Evaluation of Information, Telephone Toll Analysis, Time Event Charting, Association Matrix, Financial Analysis, Report Writing, Courtroom Testimony, and Intelligence Dissemination.

Basic Police Training Program

The nine-week Basic Police Training Program provides a study of the basic law enforcement concepts and techniques that new federal police officers should understand and be able to perform in order to carry out their duties in a safe and effective manner. Instruction covers a wide range of topics relating to patrol techniques, vehicle operation, weapons proficiency, response to emergency situations, and the development of other skills required of uniformed law enforcement officers in a federal policing environment.

Participating agencies in the Basic Police Training Program include: AMTRAK Police, Bureau of Engraving and Printing, U.S. Capitol Police, Defense Protective Service, Government Printing Office, Federal Protective Service, Library of Congress, U.S. Mint, National Institutes of Health, National Institute of Standards and Technology, National Zoological Park Police, Postal Police, Secret Service Uniformed Division, Supreme Court Police, and others.

Federal Police Officers enrolled in this program receive instruction in areas such as: Police Authority, Patrol Procedures, Emergency Response Driving, High-Risk Vehicle Stops, Night Driving, Skid Control, Violent Groups, Crowd Control, Hostage Situations, Critical Incident Response, Radio Communications, Handling Abnormal Persons, Victimology, Criminal Law, Constitutional Law, Civil Rights, Search and Seizure, Detention and Arrest, Self-Incrimination, Crime Scene Preservation, Evidence, Interviewing Techniques, Description and Identification, Report Writing, Narcotics, Terrorism, Criminal Intelligence, Federal Firearms Violations, Court Testimony, VIP Protection, Physical Security Equipment, Fire Safety, Bombs and Explosives, Firearms Safety and Marksmanship, Weapons Detection, Non-Lethal Control Techniques, Impact Weapons Control, Physical Conditioning, First Aid and Trauma Management, CPR, and Orientation to Federal Law Enforcement Agencies.

Land Management Law Enforcement Training Program

Federal land management organizations whose officers perform law enforcement related duties in urban, rural or isolated areas attend the twelve-week Land Management Law Enforcement Training Program. This program is designed to meet the training needs of cultural and natural resource protectors engaged in professional law enforcement and visitor use management activities. Through classroom lectures, laboratory sessions, and practical exercises, students in this program learn and develop the particular skills required of officers responsible for protection in land management environments. Training is presented by FLETC staff as well as instructors detailed from the participating agencies, including the USDA Forest Service, Tennessee Valley Authority, National Park Service, U.S. Fish and Wildlife Service, National Marine Fisheries Service, and Bureau of Land Management.

Lectures, laboratory techniques, and practical exercises relate to subjects such as: Patrol Skills, Emergency Response and Pursuit Driving, High-Risk Vehicle Stops, Officer Safety and Survival, Non-Lethal Control Techniques, Automobile and Motorhome Search Tactics, Report Writing, Search Warrant Execution, Surveillance, Critical Incident Stress, Dangerous Motorcycle Gangs, Environmental and Animal Rights Extremist Groups, Threats Against Resource Management Agencies, Conflict Management, Interviewing Techniques, Criminal Law, Constitutional Law, Civil Rights, Archaeological Resources Crime, Search and Seizure, Evidence, Detention and Arrest, Fingerprinting, Self-Incrimination, Federal Court Procedures, Courtroom Testimony, Death Investigation, Narcotics, Marijuana Eradication, Booby Traps, Bombs and Explosives, Accident Investigation, Communications, Firearms Safety, Marksmanship, Judgment Pistol Shooting, Reduced Light Shooting, Ethics and Conduct, and Physical Conditioning.

Advanced Physical Security Training Program

The Advanced Physical Security Training Program is designed to provide full-time security specialists, law enforcement officers, and investigators an in-depth theoretical and practical knowledge of physical security systems and procedures. Training modules are presented systematically to form a common thread for conducting and developing security surveys. The final practical exercise includes student development of a security survey, a briefing on the results, and critique.

Subjects covered in this program include: Theory of Physical Security, Contingency Planning, Security

Design, Risk Assessment, Security Survey Process, Security Locks and Locking Devices, Access Control, Closed-Circuit Television Systems, Intrusion Detection Systems, Perimeter Security, Protective Lighting, Fire Safety, Bombs and Explosives, Weapons and Explosives Detection, Operations Security, Special Events Security, Domestic Terrorism, Security Legal Considerations, Security Information Resources, Guard Force Operations, and Violence in the Workplace.

Federal Bureau of Prisons Basic Training Program

Institution-based Bureau of Prisons (BOP) employees are required to complete the three-week BOP Basic Training Program, regardless of their duty position. The curriculum provides a common foundation of agency-specific training, and is taught by both FLETC and BOP staff. A wide range of methods are employed in the delivery of instruction, including group discussions, videotaped case studies, self studies, and practical exercises. In addition to academic subjects, students must actively participate and perform to standard levels in twenty hours of firearms training and sixteen hours of self-defense techniques.

Academic topics include: History and Organization of the BOP, Fundamentals of Correctional Law, Constitutional Law, Correctional Supervision, Inmate Discipline and Management, Sexuality in Prisons, Inmate Behavior and Diversity, Inmate Drug and Alcohol Abuse, Situation Assessment, Suicide Prevention, Hostage Situations, Use of Force, Interpersonal Communications, Interviewing Techniques, Problem Avoidance, Ethics, Managing Diversity, Stress Management, Computer Security, and other subjects.

Immigration Officer Basic Training Program

As members of the INS Officer Corps, newly appointed Immigration Inspectors, Deportation Officers, Immigration Agents, and Immigration Examiners attend the fourteen-week Immigration Officer Basic Training Program. The major components of this course consist of instruction pertaining to Immigration Law, Nationality Law, INS Operations, United States Customs Service Cross Training, and Spanish Language. Approximately 60 percent of the instruction is presented by INS staff members, such as courses in Spanish and Immigration Law, with the remaining 40 percent taught by FLETC staff instructors.

Primary subjects presented in this program include: History and Organization of the INS, Immigration and Nationality Law, Civil Liability, Inspection Techniques, Contraband Detection, Narcotics, Fraudulent Documents, Law Enforcement Authority, Interviewing and Interrogation, Self-Incrimination, Sworn Statements, Cross-cultural Communications, Spanish Language, Hostage Situations, Terrorism, Courtroom Testimony, Transportation of Prisoners, First Aid and CPR, Trauma Management, Firearms and Marksmanship, Emergency Vehicle Operation, Non-Lethal Control Techniques, Fingerprinting, and Stress Management.

Advanced Training Programs

In addition to basic training programs which make up the core of FLETC instruction, the Center also develops and offers advanced and specialized training in subjects that are common to two or more of its participating organizations. Examples include programs in Law Enforcement Photography, Marine Law Enforcement, Archeological Resources Protection, Wildfire Investigation, Criminal Investigations in an Automated Environment, Antiterrorism Management, and Physical Security Management. FLETC also conducts training for instructors of law enforcement agencies who teach subjects relating to Firearms, Emergency Response and Pursuit Driving, Physical Fitness, Non-Lethal Control Techniques, and Impact Weapons.

FLETC College Intern Program

The FLETC College Intern Program provides a unique opportunity for qualified students to gain firsthand experience while participating in the federal law enforcement training environment. Program participants devote approximately one-half of the internship participating in a variety of administrative assignments, while the other half consists of observation and participation in classroom and practical exercises in various training programs.

The Intern Program is offered four times annually at both the main campus in Glynco, Georgia, and the satellite facility in Artesia, New Mexico. Each session is ten weeks in length. Interns receive a daily allowance to help defray the cost of meals, incidental expenses, and travel costs, and are provided dormitory accommodations on site at no cost. In addition to Criminal Justice majors, Intern opportunities are available for majors in Adult Education, Business Administration, Communications, Computer Science, Journalism, Recreation, Graphic Design, Sports Medicine and other fields.

Assignments

Interns are assigned to a supervisor of either a FLETC division or a participating agency located on site. Assignments vary depending upon the needs of the Center and projects under way at the time, although they may involve tasks such as conducting research pertaining to law enforcement, corrections, or security issues to supplement classroom and practical training; creating computer databases and examining operational issues and trends; updating and revising lesson plans, handouts, and course materials; grading examinations; or assisting with other administrative assignments associated with various FLETC programs, operations, and participating agencies. Interns also observe a variety of classroom lectures and participate in virtually every aspect of practical training exercises, such as firearms qualification, search and arrest warrant execution, arrest techniques, undercover and surveillance operations, and physical techniques.

Qualifications

College seniors interested in applying must have completed 135 quarter hours or 90 semester hours of a baccalaureate program, and must be in the upper third of their class in academic standing. Students accepted or enrolled in a graduate program may also apply. The internship must be completed as part of the student's academic requirements and prior to graduation. Selection is highly competitive and is based upon grade point average (major and overall), leadership and community participation, work experience, professional experience related to the academic major, and their letter of interest together with their faculty member's letter of recommendation. Intern applicants must be citizens of the United States, and will be subjected to a background investigation prior to appointment.

Application Process

To apply, Intern applicants must: complete a Form OF-612 (Application for Federal Employment) or resume; complete an Intern Application and Interest Form; submit official college transcript(s); and have an appropriate college official complete an Intern Nomination form. Application packages are available from the FLETC Personnel Office. For further information, contact: Personnel Division, Building 94, Federal Law Enforcement Training Center; Glynco, Georgia 31524 (Telephone: 912-267-3500).

FBI ACADEMY

The FBI Academy is among the world's most respected law enforcement training centers. The FBI Training Division manages the Academy and trains FBI Special Agents and professional support staff, as well as local, state, federal, and international law enforcement personnel.

Training programs for FBI personnel include New Agent Training and a wide range of in-service and specialized courses for FBI Special Agents and support staff. Police training programs include the FBI National Academy, which is an eleven-week multidisciplinary program for seasoned law enforcement managers; the Executive Training program, which is attended by Chief Executive Officers of America's largest law enforcement organizations; and Operational Assistance, which trains law enforcement personnel how to respond in certain emergency situations. In addition to course offerings, FBI Academy faculty members conduct research and provide assistance to federal, state and local law enforcement agencies on many topics and investigative techniques.

Among the instructional components of the Training Division at the FBI Academy is the world renown FBI Behavioral Science Unit. Supervisory Special Agents and veteran police officers assigned to this Unit conduct specialized and applied training for the New Agent Training Program, the FBI National Academy, international police training programs, field police schools, FBI in-service courses, and other international courses and symposia. Instruction is presented on a variety of topics which focus on Applied Criminal Psychology,

Clinical Forensic Psychology, Community Policing and Problem-Solving Strategies, Crime Analysis, Death Investigation, Gangs and Gang Behavior, Interpersonal Violence, Law Enforcement Officers Killed and Assaulted in the Line of Duty, Research Methodology, Stress Management in Law Enforcement, and Violence in America.

Training Facilities

The FBI Academy is located on the United States Marine Corps Base at Quantico, Virginia. The facility is situated on 385 wooded acres of land providing the security, privacy, and safe environment necessary to carry out the diverse training and operational functions for which the FBI is responsible.

The main training complex has three dormitory buildings, classroom and audiovisual facilities, administrative offices, and a Forensic Science Research and Training Center, 1.1-mile pursuit and defensive driving track, dining hall, library, 1,000-seat auditorium, chapel, large gymnasium, outdoor track, and fully-equipped garage. Firearms training is conducted at indoor and outdoor firing ranges, four skeet ranges, and a 200-yard rifle range.

In addition to the main complex, a mock city known as "Hogan's Alley" is utilized for realistic practical training scenarios. The Hogan's Alley facility consists of facades replicating a typical small town, and is used primarily for FBI and DEA basic training to reinforce classroom instruction in a realistic environment. Hogan's Alley scenarios require students to apply principles learned in the academic, firearms, and physical training areas to successfully resolve the multidisciplinary practical exercises. Vehicles, radios, and other equipment are provided to scenario participants, and professional role players are utilized to confront the trainees with a variety of situations.

FBI New Agent Training Program

The New Agent Training Program provides sixteen weeks of intensive instruction for newly appointed FBI Special Agents. The program is designed to ensure that basic knowledge and skills are developed which will enable Agents to effectively discharge their complex responsibilities once they are assigned to investigative duties in one of the FBI's field offices. New Agent Training consists of instruction which is spread out over four major concentrations, including Academics, Firearms, Physical Training and Defensive Tactics, and Practical Exercises. A building-block approach is used to present course material. Students are expected to periodically demonstrate what they have learned in order to resolve multidisciplinary practical exercises which are staged at the Hogan's Alley facility.

The major components of the FBI New Agent Training Program include: Firearms, Practical Applications, Physical Training, Defensive Tactics, Law, Forensic Science, Interviewing Techniques, Informant Development, Communications, Tactical and Emergency Vehicle Operations, White-Collar Crime, Drug Investigations, Organized Crime, Behavioral Science, Computer Skills, Foreign Counterintelligence, Terrorism, Ethics, Equal Employment Opportunity, Cultural Diversity, and other academic and investigative subjects.

DEA TRAINING PROGRAM

The DEA has aggressively developed a comprehensive training program that reflects the diversity and sophistication of the Agency's complex mission. The goals and objectives of the DEA Office of Training are to support the Agency's federal drug law enforcement mission by developing and administering a comprehensive training program for all DEA employees, as well as for other drug law enforcement officials, including foreign drug control officers. Training for DEA personnel includes entry-level courses for newly appointed Special Agents, Diversion Investigators, Intelligence Research Specialists, and Chemists; instruction for supervisory and management personnel; ethics and integrity training; and various specialized and in-service courses.

The DEA also conducts a wide range of training programs for state and local law enforcement officers, including a two-week Basic Narcotics School that prepares newly assigned officers for the dynamics of drug investigations, as well as courses concerning clandestine laboratory investigations, cannabis eradication, drug trends, asset forfeiture, drug interdiction, and other subjects. In addition, the DEA's International Training

Section travels the world to provide drug law enforcement training to foreign police and drug enforcement counterparts.

Training Facilities

In 1985, the DEA moved its training programs from the Federal Law Enforcement Training Center in Glynco, Georgia, to the FBI Academy in Quantico, Virginia. With the expansion of the DEA in the 1990's, and in consideration of increasingly complex training requirements for DEA Special Agents and other law enforcement personnel conducting sophisticated drug investigations, the need for additional training space reached a critical level. In 1997, construction of the Justice Training Center was initiated on the grounds of the FBI Academy, for completion in early 1999. The new facility includes a dormitory, eight classrooms, a cafeteria, a warehouse, and office space for DEA Training staff.

DEA Basic Agent Training Program

To equip entry-level DEA Special Agents with the skills and abilities needed for the unique requirements of worldwide drug law enforcement, newly appointed Agents attend a sixteen-week training program which consists of academic, tactical, practical, firearms and legal instruction. This course covers all facets of drug law enforcement operations, from the hazards of undercover work, through the financial manipulations associated with money laundering, to the legal intricacies inherent in conspiracy law. Three major examinations are given, and an average score of 70 percent is required for graduation.

Throughout the program, training modules are delivered in a programmed sequence so that each practical exercise builds upon previous classroom instruction. For example, during approximately 80 hours of legal instruction, students are cross-examined by defense attorneys during a moot court scenario which simulates courtroom pressure. This exercise is videotaped and also includes a critique.

Instruction in the Basic Agent curriculum includes courses in: DEA Mission and History, Drug Identification, Law, Drug Smuggling, Analytical Investigations, Interviewing Techniques, Surveillance, Undercover Operations, Wiretaps, Raid Planning and Execution, Emergency Driving, Vehicle Stops, Arrest Techniques, Evidence Handling, Fingerprinting, Report Writing, Clandestine Laboratories, Drug Diversion, Money Laundering, Organized Crime, Crisis Management, Defensive Tactics, Firearms, First Aid and CPR, Photography, Ethics, Drug Demand Reduction, Courtroom Testimony, and other subjects.

U.S. POSTAL INSPECTOR TRAINING ACADEMY

As one of the nation's oldest and most prestigious federal law enforcement agencies, the U.S. Postal Inspection Service has a long and proud law enforcement tradition. Postal Inspectors are highly trained in an innovative atmosphere which targets multiple adult learning styles, extensive use of technology in the classroom, and a continuous thread of customer focus. The Postal Inspector Training Academy typically graduates between sixty and eighty Inspectors annually in classes of twenty students.

Training Facilities

The national academy for Postal Inspectors is located at the William F. Bolger Training Center in Potomac, Maryland, twelve miles northwest of Washington, D.C. This largely self-contained 525-bed complex is co-located with the Postal Service Leadership Center, and includes classrooms, a practical scenario building, an indoor firearms range, and exercise and dining facilities.

Postal Inspector Basic Training Program

In 1997, after providing basic training in a similar fashion to that of other federal law enforcement agencies for nearly thirty years, the Postal Inspection Service initiated an innovative fifteen-week course following the example of the Royal Canadian Mounted Police Training Academy. The new program mirrors Postal Inspection field operations by assigning trainees to teams, minimizing lecture in favor of group problem-solving techniques, and often giving more weight to students' creativity than their ability to memorize regulations.

Multiple adult learning styles and extensive use of technology are utilized throughout the program, with every team provided direct access to Postal databases and the Internet from their seats in the classroom. Instead of a series of lectures accompanied by blackboard illustrations, typical classroom sessions consist of teams engaged in brainstorming sessions and various exercises in search of solutions to problems posed in training modules. A continuous thread of customer focus is woven throughout the program that challenges students to view their efforts through the eyes of the community they serve. By better understanding the concepts and purposes behind each lesson, students are encouraged to develop approaches which result in solutions, not just apprehensions.

Training modules in this program focus on subjects such as: Ethics, Postal Inspection Operations, Intercultural Communications, Team Building, Customer Service, Problem Solving, Administrative Forms, Mail Processing and Delivery, the Criminal Justice System, Case Management, Electronic Surveillance, Informants, Undercover Operations, Controlled Substances, Interviewing and Interrogation, Statements and Affidavits, Report Writing, Financial Investigations, Internal Audits, Accounting, Search Warrants, Dynamic Building Entry, Laws of Arrest, Search and Seizure, Crime Scene Management and Processing, Evidence, Photography, Computer Searches, Crime Lab Operations, Legal Issues, Judicial Proceedings, Sentencing Guidelines, Fines and Forfeitures, Civil Fraud, Grand Jury Process, Pretrial Hearings, Computer Hardware and Software, International Security, Risk Assessment, Presentation Skills, Defensive Driving, Felony Vehicle Stops, Radio Communication, Firearms Proficiency, Defensive Tactics, Officer Survival, Physical Conditioning, First Aid and CPR, Bloodborne Pathogens, and Physical Conditioning.

U.S. AIR FORCE SPECIAL INVESTIGATIONS ACADEMY

The United States Air Force (USAF) Special Investigations Academy is an integral component of the Air Force Office of Special Investigations (AFOSI), the primary investigative agency for the Air Force. The Academy is staffed by a skilled team which is composed of veteran investigators, education specialists and administrators who have experience across the full AFOSI mission spectrum. Instruction is presented to AFOSI Special Agent candidates, criminal investigators from other federal law enforcement agencies, and law enforcement personnel from various foreign countries. In addition to conducting AFOSI Basic Training, Academy staff present advanced courses which focus on subjects such as Protective Service Operations, Fraud, Counterintelligence, Counterespionage, Technical Operations, Leadership, and Management. Academy instructors attend the widely acclaimed Academic Instructor School at Maxwell Air Force Base, Alabama, as well as other specialized programs.

Training Facilities

The USAF Special Investigations Academy is located at Andrews Air Force Base in Prince George's County, Maryland, approximately ten miles southeast of Washington, D.C. Training facilities include five classrooms, a computer lab, a library, an outdoor firearms range, automated judgment pistol shooting equipment, a gymnasium, a driver training range, dormitories, and a dining hall.

AFOSI Basic Special Investigators Course

Initial training for AFOSI Special Agents consists of an eleven-week Basic Special Investigators Course which is divided into four core areas, including Military Law, Collections, Investigations, and Operations. The AFOSI academy staff delivers most of the instruction, although outside experts also lecture on subjects relating to their particular areas of expertise. The student-instructor ratio is normally one instructor for six to eight students. Fifty percent of the instruction consists of intense classroom lectures, while the remaining portion involves detailed small-group instruction and practical exercises. Students are held to a tight schedule, and homework is extensive.

Topics of instruction in this program include: Prosecutive Jurisdiction, the Military Justice System, Military Rules of Evidence, Legal Rights of the Accused, Elements of Proof, Legal Defenses, Search and Seizure, Investigative Planning, Time Management, Sources of Information, Intelligence Oversight, Economic Crime Investigation, Collections Cycle, Procurement Process, Sexual Assault, Child Sexual Abuse,

Death Investigation, Environmental Crime Investigations, Narcotics, Undercover Operations, Interviewing and Interrogation, Witness Statements, Inspector General and Grand Jury Subpoenas, Crime Scene Processing, Digital Camera Systems, Forensic and Computer Evidence, Evidence Documentation, Reports of Investigation, Polygraph Support, Protective Service Operations, Defensive Tactics, Use of Force, Agent Survival, Judgment Pistol Shooting, Firearms Mechanical Drills and Live Fire, Chemical Weapons, Bloodborne Pathogens, Trial Coordination, Court Testimony, and other subjects that are designed to prepare AFOSI Special Agents for the challenges of investigative duty.

The Basic Special Investigators Course is capped with a three-day practical exercise which incorporates various types of cases, crime scene processing, protective service operations, and drug scenarios. This exercise culminates in a mock trial which provides experience in trial preparation and courtroom testimony.

SPECIALIZED TRAINING PROGRAMS AND FACILITIES

Canine Enforcement Training Center
U.S. Customs Service

Located on a 240-acre site in Front Royal, Virginia, the United States Customs Service's Canine Enforcement Training Center (CETC) provides training for all Customs Canine Enforcement Officer teams, and to other federal, state, local, and foreign law enforcement agencies on a space-available basis. The CETC maintains a staff which consists of instructors, animal caretakers, storage specialists, and administrative personnel. The Center's average canine population is between 100 and 150 dogs on a daily basis, with a yearly training output of 120 canine enforcement teams.

Programs offered by CETC staff include a twelve-week Basic Narcotic Detection Course (fifteen weeks for Customs officers); a ten-week Passenger Processing Course (thirteen weeks for Customs officers); an eight-week Technical Trainer Course for Canine Team Leaders; a ten-week Basic Currency Detection Course (for Customs officers only); a four-week Canine Narcotic Transition Course; a two-week Field Replacement Dog Course; a five-day Administration and Technical Application Course (for Customs supervisory personnel only); and a three-day Senior Management and Administration Course.

National Enforcement Training Institute
U.S. Environmental Protection Agency

Located within the Environmental Protection Agency's (EPA) Office of Enforcement and Compliance Assurance, the National Enforcement Training Institute (NETI) is responsible for training federal, state, local and tribal lawyers, inspectors, civil and criminal investigators, regulatory personnel, and technical experts in various aspects of environmental law enforcement. NETI provides training courses for enforcement personnel in a number of areas, such as case support, specific statute enforcement, compliance assurance, and environmental criminal enforcement. Besides providing training in EPA's Regional offices around the country and at other locations, NETI manages training sites in Washington, D.C.; Lakewood, Colorado; and at the Federal Law Enforcement Training Center in Glynco, Georgia.

NETI courses and workshops focus on environmental crimes and investigations; statutes and legal issues; solid and hazardous waste identification, inspection, enforcement and compliance; pollution prevention; enforcement and compliance relating to the Clean Air Act, Clean Water Act, Endangered Species Act, National Environmental Policy Act, Resource Conservation and Recovery Act, and National Historic Preservation Act; criminal intelligence analysis; wetlands and flood plains, and a broad range of other environmental issues.

Appendix 1

OCCUPATIONAL CLASSIFICATIONS FOR GENERAL SCHEDULE POSITIONS RELATED TO LAW ENFORCEMENT*

Miscellaneous Occupations
GS-0006   Correctional Administration
GS-0007   Correctional Officer
GS-0025   Park Ranger
GS-0072   Fingerprint Identification
GS-0080   Security Administration
GS-0083   Police Officer

Social Science, Psychology, And Welfare
GS-0101   Social Science
GS-0132   Intelligence
GS-0180   Psychology

Personnel Management and Industrial Relations
GS-0249   Wage & Hour Compliance

General Administration, Clerical, Office Services
GS-0301   Miscellaneous
GS-0303   Miscellaneous Clerk and Assistant
GS-0390   Communications Relay
GS-0391   Telecommunications
GS-0392   General Communications

Biological Sciences
GS-0401   General Biological Science
GS-0436   Plant Protection & Quarantine

Engineering and Architecture
GS-0856   Electronics Technician

Information and Arts
GS-1060   Photography

Business and Industry
GS-1169   Internal Revenue Officer

Physical Sciences
GS-1320   Chemistry
GS-1397   Document Analysis

Education
GS-1712   Training Instruction

Investigation Group
GS-1801   General Inspection, Investigation and Compliance
GS-1802   Compliance Inspection and Support
GS-1810   General Investigating
GS-1811   Criminal Investigating
GS-1812   Game Law Enforcement
GS-1815   Air Safety Investigating
GS-1816   Immigration Inspection
GS-1822   Mine Safety and Health
GS-1854   Alcohol, Tobacco and Firearms Inspection
GS-1889   Import Specialist
GS-1890   Customs Inspection
GS-1896   Border Patrol Agent

Transportation
GS-2121   Railroad Safety
GS-2151   Radio Dispatching
GS-2181   Aircraft Operation

*Includes all General Schedule occupational groups and series' of career profiles in this book.

Appendix 2

Vacancy Announcement

FEDERAL EMERGENCY MANAGEMENT AGENCY

Position Title:	CRIMINAL INVESTIGATOR	Announcement #:	MW-98-IG-192-SSM
Series/Grade:	GS-1811-9/11/12	Opening Date:	July 6, 1998
		Closing Date:	August 3, 1998

Organization:	Office of Inspector General	Duty Location:	Atlanta, Georgia
	Investigations Division	Number of Positions:	One

This is a Federal excepted service position. Appointments are term appointments, with full benefits, for up to four years with the possibility of a one-year extension.

AREA OF CONSIDERATION: All sources. Applications will be accepted from all qualified status and non-status candidates.

MAJOR DUTIES: Plans and conducts criminal investigations of persons suspected or convicted of offenses against the criminal laws of the United States. Incumbent assists in determining the depth of investigation and may request the use of engineers, auditors, and other personnel in the investigation. Prepares comprehensive and well-documented reports of investigative findings, and makes recommendations as to appropriate action. Responsible for assurance that each of his/her investigative files is maintained on a current basis. Personally maintains liaison with other law enforcement agencies at the local, state, and national levels for the purpose of obtaining their cooperation in furnishing information concerning illegal activities involving violations of criminal law related to FEMA personnel in the private sector which could assist in ferreting out violations. Serves as a team member engaged in investigations of interagency magnitude involving nationwide impact over designated geographical areas. Serves as a witness at civil hearings or criminal court trials and testifies before grand juries concerning evidence developed during criminal investigations.

QUALIFICATIONS REQUIRED: Applicants must meet the qualification requirements as contained in OPM's Qualifications Standards Operating Manual. The manual states that one year of specialized experience equivalent to the GS-7 is required for the GS-9 level or 2 full years or progressively higher level graduate education or Master's or equivalent grade degree; one year of specialized experience equivalent to the GS-9 is required for the GS-11 or 3 full years of progressively higher level graduate education or Ph.D. or equivalent doctoral degree; and, one year specialized experience equivalent to at least the next lower grade in the Federal service is required for the GS-12. Specialized experience is experience that equipped the applicant with the particular knowledge, skills and abilities to perform successfully the duties of the position, and that is typically in or related to the work of the position to be filled. To be creditable, specialized experience must have been equivalent to at least the next lower grade in the normal line of progression for the occupation in the organization. Education and experience may be combined as stated in the OPM Qualification Standards Operating Manual.

KNOWLEDGE, SKILLS, AND ABILITIES REQUIRED:

1. Knowledge of the principles and techniques of conducting investigations.

2. Ability to work independently for extended periods.

3. Ability to write concise and accurate reports.

4. Knowledge of U.S. Code Titles 18 and 31, rules of evidence, and administrative regulations.

SELECTIVE PLACEMENT FACTORS: In addition to the above requirements, applicants should have prior Federal investigative training and knowledge of the Federal Rules of Evidence. It is desirable that applicants have experience dealing with the U.S. Attorney's Office.

MAXIMUM ENTRY AGE: The date immediately proceeding an individual's 37th birthday is the maximum entry age for original appointment to a person in law enforcement as defined in Title 5 U.S.C. 8331(20) or in 5 U.S.C. 8401(17). Consideration will be restricted to candidates who have not yet reached age 37 at the time of referral for positions.

MEDICAL REQUIREMENTS: Successful completion of a medical examination within the last year is required prior to appointment. Re-certification of the physical is required on an annual basis. The history or presence of significant psychiatric disorder is disqualifying for law enforcement positions which entail the use of firearms. The duties of these positions require moderate to arduous physical exertion involving walking and standing, use of firearms, and exposure to inclement weather.

MOTOR VEHICLE OPERATIONS QUALIFICATIONS: Candidates must possess and maintain a valid automobile driver's license at the time of appointment, and qualify after appointment for authorization to operate motor vehicles in accordance with applicable OPM regulations and FEMA requirements.

HOW TO APPLY: Send applications to FEMA, Disaster Personnel Operations Division, P.O. Box 129; Berryville, VA 22611. Phone: 800-879-6076.

THIS IS A PUBLIC TRUST POSITION, WHICH REQUIRES A BACKGROUND INVESTIGATION PRIOR TO OR AFTER APPOINTMENT. SIGNIFICANT TRAVEL IS REQUIRED. THIS POSITION IS COVERED BY FEDERAL LAW ENFORCEMENT RETIREMENT PROVISIONS, 5 U.S.C. 8336(C), AND LAW ENFORCEMENT AVAILABILITY PAY.

For more information about the Federal Emergency Management Agency and other career opportunities we have to offer, please visit our web site at: www.fema.gov.

The Federal Government is an Equal Opportunity Employer

OPTIONAL APPLICATION FOR FEDERAL EMPLOYMENT - OF 612

You may apply for most jobs with a resume, this form, or other written format. If your resume or application does not provide all the information requested on this form and in the job vacancy announcement, you may lose consideration for a job.

1 Job title in announcement	2 Grade(s) applying for	3 Announcement number

4 Last name	First and middle names	5 Social Security Number

6 Mailing address		7 Phone numbers (include area code)
City	State	ZIP Code	Daytime ( )
		Evening ( )

WORK EXPERIENCE

8 Describe your paid and nonpaid work experience related to the job for which you are applying. Do **not** attach job descriptions.

1) Job title (if Federal, include series and grade)

From (MM/YY)	To (MM/YY)	Salary $	per	Hours per week

Employer's name and address	Supervisor's name and phone number
	( )

Describe your duties and accomplishments

2) Job title (if Federal, include series and grade)

From (MM/YY)	To (MM/YY)	Salary $	per	Hours per week

Employer's name and address	Supervisor's name and phone number
	( )

Describe your duties and accomplishments

50612-101   NSN 7540-01-351-9178   Optional Form 612 (September 1994)
U.S. Office of Personnel Management

9 May we contact your current supervisor?

YES [   ]   NO [   ] ▸ If we need to contact your current supervisor before making an offer, we will contact you first.

EDUCATION

10 Mark highest level completed. **Some HS** [   ]   **HS/GED** [   ]   **Associate** [   ]   **Bachelor** [   ]   **Master** [   ]   **Doctoral** [   ]

11 Last high school (HS) or GED school. Give the school's name, city, State, ZIP Code (if known), and year diploma or GED received.

12 Colleges and universities attended. Do **not** attach a copy of your transcript unless requested.

	Name	State	ZIP Code	Total Credits Earned Semester	Quarter	Major(s)	Degree (if any) - Year Received
1)	City						
2)							
3)							

OTHER QUALIFICATIONS

13 **Job-related** training courses (give title and year). **Job-related** skills (other languages, computer software/hardware, tools, machinery, typing speed, etc.). **Job-related** certificates and licenses (current only). **Job-related** honors, awards, and special accomplishments (publications, memberships in professional/honor societies, leadership activities, public speaking, and performance awards). Give dates, but do **not** send documents unless requested.

GENERAL

14 Are you a U.S. citizen?   YES [   ]   NO [   ] ▸ Give the country of your citizenship. ....

15 Do you claim veterans' preference? **NO** [   ]   **YES** [   ] ▸ Mark your claim of 5 or 10 points below.
   5 points [   ] ▸ Attach your DD 214 or other proof. **10 points** [   ] ▸ Attach an *Application for 10-Point Veterans' Preference* (SF 15) and proof required.

16 Were you ever a Federal civilian employee?

			Series	Grade	From (MM/YY)	To (MM/YY)

   NO [   ]   **YES** [   ] ▸ For highest civilian grade give:

17 Are you eligible for reinstatement based on career or career-conditional Federal status?

   NO [   ]   **YES** [   ] ▸ If requested, attach SF 50 proof.

APPLICANT CERTIFICATION

18 I **certify** that, to the best of my knowledge and belief, all of the information on and attached to this application is true, correct, complete and made in good faith. I **understand** that false or fraudulent information on or attached to this application may be grounds for not hiring me or for firing me after I begin work, and may be punishable by fine or imprisonment. I **understand** that any information I give may be investigated.

SIGNATURE   **DATE SIGNED**

Appendix 4

1998 GENERAL SCHEDULE ANNUAL SALARY RATES
(Including Locality Pay for "Rest of U.S." Geographic Areas)

	Step 1	Step 2	Step 3	Step 4	Step 5	Step 6	Step 7	Step 8	Step 9	Step 10
GS-1	$13,662	$14,118	$14,572	$15,024	$15,481	$15,748	$16,195	$16,647	$16,666	$17,093
GS-2	15,361	15,727	16,236	16,666	16,851	17,347	17,842	18,338	18,833	19,329
GS-3	16,761	17,319	17,878	18,437	18,996	19,554	20,113	20,672	21,231	21,789
GS-4	18,815	19,443	20,070	20,697	21,324	21,952	22,579	23,206	23,833	24,461
GS-5	21,051	21,753	22,456	23,158	23,860	24,562	25,264	25,966	26,668	27,370
GS-6	23,464	24,247	25,029	25,811	26,593	27,375	28,158	28,940	29,722	30,504
GS-7	26,075	26,943	27,812	28,681	29,549	30,418	31,287	32,155	33,024	33,893
GS-8	28,878	29,840	30,803	31,765	32,728	33,690	34,653	35,615	36,578	37,540
GS-9	31,897	32,961	34,024	35,088	36,152	37,215	38,279	39,343	40,406	41,470
GS-10	35,126	36,297	37,468	38,640	39,811	40,982	42,153	43,324	44,496	45,667
GS-11	38,593	39,879	41,165	42,452	43,738	45,024	46,310	47,596	48,882	50,168
GS-12	46,254	47,296	49,339	50,881	52,423	53,966	55,508	57,050	58,592	60,135
GS-13	55,004	56,837	58,670	60,504	62,337	64,170	66,003	67,837	69,670	71,503
GS-14	64,998	67,164	69,331	71,497	73,663	75,830	77,996	80,162	82,329	84,495
GS-15	76,456	79,005	81,554	84,103	86,652	89,201	91,750	94,299	96,848	99,397

1998 SALARY ADJUSTMENTS BY GEOGRAPHIC LOCALITY

In addition to the rates shown above, annual salary for employees in the following areas is increased by the Locality Pay percentages indicated:

Atlanta	6.18%	Huntsville	5.84%	Richmond	6.12%
Boston	8.61%	Indianapolis	5.63%	Sacramento	7.64%
Chicago	9.21%	Kansas City	6.06%	St. Louis	5.71%
Cincinnati	7.71%	Los Angeles	10.31%	San Diego	7.94%
Cleveland	6.35%	Miami	7.86%	San Francisco	12.06%
Columbus	6.90%	Milwaukee	6.19%	Seattle	7.34%
Dallas	6.90%	Minneapolis	7.32%	Washington, D.C.	7.27%
Dayton	6.19%	New York City	9.76%		
Denver	8.46%	Orlando	5.42%		
Detroit	9.36%	Philadelphia	7.67%		
Hartford	9.13%	Pittsburgh	6.21%		
Houston	11.96%	Portland	7.17%		

Appendix 5

1998 GENERAL SCHEDULE ANNUAL SALARY RATES
FOR LAW ENFORCEMENT OFFICERS
(Including Locality Pay for "Rest of U.S." Geographic Areas)

This Salary Schedule includes special pay enhancements for certain law enforcement officers at grades GS-3 through GS-10, which range from one to seven salary steps above General Schedule rates.

	Step 1	Step 2	Step 3	Step 4	Step 5	Step 6	Step 7	Step 8	Step 9	Step 10
GS-1	$13,662	$14,118	$14,572	$15,024	$15,481	$15,748	$16,195	$16,647	$16,666	$17,093
GS-2	15,361	15,727	16,236	16,666	16,851	17,347	17,842	18,338	18,833	19,329
GS-3	20,113	20,672	21,231	21,789	22,348	22,907	23,465	24,024	24,583	25,142
GS-4	22,579	23,206	23,833	24,461	25,088	25,715	26,342	26,970	27,597	28,224
GS-5	25,966	26,668	27,370	28,072	28,774	29,476	30,179	30,881	31,583	32,285
GS-6	27,375	28,158	28,940	29,722	30,504	31,287	32,069	32,851	33,633	34,415
GS-7	29,549	30,418	31,287	32,155	33,024	33,893	34,761	35,630	36,499	37,367
GS-8	30,803	31,765	32,728	33,690	34,653	35,615	36,578	37,540	38,503	39,465
GS-9	32,961	34,024	35,088	36,152	37,215	38,279	39,343	40,406	41,470	42,534
GS-10	36,297	37,468	38,640	39,811	40,982	42,153	43,324	44,496	45,667	46,838
GS-11	38,593	39,879	41,165	42,452	43,738	45,024	46,310	47,596	48,882	50,168
GS-12	46,254	47,296	49,339	50,881	52,423	53,966	55,508	57,050	58,592	60,135
GS-13	55,004	56,837	58,670	60,504	62,337	64,170	66,003	67,837	69,670	71,503
GS-14	64,998	67,164	69,331	71,497	73,663	75,830	77,996	80,162	82,329	84,495
GS-15	76,456	79,005	81,554	84,103	86,652	89,201	91,750	94,299	96,848	99,397

1998 SALARY ADJUSTMENTS BY GEOGRAPHIC LOCALITY

In addition to the rates shown above, employees in certain geographic areas receive Locality Payments. An itemized listing of Locality Pay percentages is shown in Appendix 4.

Appendix 6

1998 GENERAL SCHEDULE ANNUAL SALARY RATES FOR CRIMINAL INVESTIGATORS WHO RECEIVE LAW ENFORCEMENT AVAILABILITY PAY

(Including Locality Pay for "Rest of U.S." Geographic Areas)

This Salary Schedule applies only to personnel in the GS-1811 (Criminal Investigator / Special Agent) and GS-1812 (Game Law Enforcement) occupational series who receive Law Enforcement Availability Pay, a form of premium pay which amounts to 25 percent of base salary. The following Schedule includes base salary plus 25 percent Law Enforcement Availability Pay:

	Step 1	Step 2	Step 3	Step 4	Step 5	Step 6	Step 7	Step 8	Step 9	Step 10
GS-5	26,314	27,191	28,070	28,948	29,825	30,703	31,580	32,458	33,335	34,213
GS-7	32,594	33,679	34,765	35,851	36,936	38,023	39,109	40,194	41,280	42,366
GS-9	39,871	41,201	42,530	43,860	45,190	46,519	47,849	49,179	50,508	51,838
GS-11	48,241	49,849	51,456	53,065	54,673	56,280	57,888	59,495	61,103	62,710
GS-12	57,818	59,120	61,674	63,601	65,529	67,458	69,385	71,313	73,240	75,169
GS-13	68,755	71,046	73,338	75,630	77,921	80,213	82,504	84,796	87,088	89,379
GS-14	81,248	83,955	86,664	89,371	92,079	94,788	97,495	100,203	102,911	105,619
GS-15	95,570	98,756	101,943	105,129	108,315	111,501	114,688	117,874	121,060	124,246

1998 SALARY ADJUSTMENTS BY GEOGRAPHIC LOCALITY

In addition to the rates shown above, employees in certain geographic areas receive Locality Payments. An itemized listing of Locality Pay percentages is shown in Appendix 4.

Appendix 7

AGENCY CONTACT RECORD

Date of Contact _____

Name of Agency _____

Street Address _____

_____

City _____ State _____ Zip _____

Phone _____ Extension _____

Person Contacted _____ Title _____

Details: _____
_____
_____
_____
_____
_____
_____
_____
_____
_____
_____
_____
_____

Appendix 8

Targeted Action Verbs
For Federal Résumés And Application Forms

Law Enforcement Skills	Investigative Skills	Security Skills	Communication Security	Research Skills
arrested	analyzed	assisted	addressed	clarified
assisted	contacted	checked	advised	compiled
counseled	detected	controlled	arranged	computed
dispatched	determined	detected	authored	conducted
enforced	developed	discovered	coached	created
examined	discovered	eliminated	communicated	critiqued
fingerprinted	documented	enforced	coordinated	diagnosed
intervened	evaluated	ensured	corresponded	evaluated
interviewed	examined	escorted	counseled	examined
investigated	explored	evaluated	demonstrated	experimented
issued	identified	gathered	dispatched	explored
mediated	inspected	identified	displayed	identified
negotiated	interrogated	inspected	drafted	initiated
observed	interviewed	interviewed	edited	inspected
operated	investigated	investigated	educated	interpreted
patrolled	located	located	explained	logged
prepared	observed	notified	informed	measured
prosecuted	photographed	observed	instructed	observed
provided	pinpointed	operated	interviewed	organized
reported	proved	recognized	lectured	planned
resolved	reviewed	patrolled	mediated	recorded
responded	searched	prevented	motivated	researched
searched	seized	processed	negotiated	reviewed
seized	solved	protected	presented	solved
served	surveilled	recorded	published	sorted
settled	testified	reported	reported	studied
solved	traced	searched	resolved	summarized
testified	tracked	screened	trained	surveyed
transported	uncovered	secured	translated	tabulated
wrote	verified	solved	wrote	tested

TARGETED ACTION VERBS
FOR FEDERAL RÉSUMÉS AND APPLICATION FORMS

Clerical Skills	Technical Skills	Management Skills	Financial Skills	General Skills
accomplished	assembled	administered	allocated	accomplished
arranged	built	advised	analyzed	achieved
catalogued	calculated	analyzed	appraised	adapted
classified	calibrated	approved	audited	applied
collected	computed	assigned	balanced	arranged
compiled	constructed	authorized	budgeted	assembled
completed	designed	coordinated	calculated	assisted
composed	diagnosed	delegated	collected	attained
corresponded	engineered	developed	computed	coordinated
edited	experimented	directed	consolidated	created
filed	extracted	evaluated	decreased	demonstrated
generated	fabricated	improved	earned	developed
indexed	fixed	initiated	estimated	devised
labeled	formulated	managed	examined	established
logged	improved	mobilized	financed	expanded
monitored	installed	monitored	forecast	implemented
operated	invented	motivated	increased	improved
organized	modified	negotiated	marketed	increased
performed	operated	organized	monitored	initiated
persuaded	overhauled	projected	negotiated	maintained
planned	pinpointed	promoted	procured	organized
prepared	prepared	proposed	projected	participated
processed	programmed	recommended	purchased	performed
produced	remodeled	reviewed	reconciled	planned
recorded	repaired	revised	recorded	prepared
scheduled	restored	scheduled	saved	produced
sorted	revised	specified	solved	provided
systemized	tested	streamlined	sorted	reviewed
typed	treated	supervised	summarized	solved
updated	upgraded	trained	tabulated	utilized

INDEX

ABOUT THE AUTHOR

THOMAS ACKERMAN'S LAW ENFORCEMENT CAREER has covered a full spectrum of responsibilities while serving in the capacities of Federal Agent, Police Officer, Immigration Inspector, and Training Academy Instructor since 1980. His experience includes a variety of complex investigative and V.I.P. protection assignments, participation in multi-jurisdictional task force operations, undercover duties, uniformed patrol duty and community policing tasks, specialization in fatal motor vehicle accident investigation, and Emergency Medical Technician responsibilities. His first experience in law enforcement was an internship – like that of many college students aspiring to enter the field – which consisted of uniformed patrol duty with the Detroit Police Department in 1977. He's been hooked ever since, and presently serves as Special Agent with a federal agency in Michigan.

Thomas has spoken nationally and internationally at law enforcement training academies and criminal justice conferences on the subjects of law enforcement recruitment, selection, and training strategies, including the FBI National Academy, Swedish National Police College, American Society for Law Enforcement Trainers, Academy of Criminal Justice Sciences, and Midwestern Criminal Justice Association. He has lectured at the Federal Law Enforcement Training Center and many leading universities, participated in government-funded criminal justice research projects, and published articles in various law enforcement publications. He also serves as an instructor in the Police Reserve Officer Training Program at Schoolcraft College in Garden City, Michigan.

Thomas holds a bachelor's degree from the School of Political Science at Wayne State University, and a master's degree from the Michigan State University School of Criminal Justice. His master's thesis focused on the selection and training of police chiefs and patrol officer recruits of the Swedish National Police Force.

ORDER INFORMATION

Photocopy this page to order additional copies of this book.
All orders are shipped via 2-3 day Priority Mail.

Quantity	Title	Price Each	Total Price
	Guide to Careers in Federal Law Enforcement	$ 29.95	$
	Add 6% sales tax on books shipped to Michigan addresses		$
	Add $4.00 Shipping for each book		$
	Order Total		$

Customer Information:	Name
	Address
	City State Zip
	Phone: ( )

Mail this order form and a check or money order to:	Hamilton Burrows Press Suite 250 - A 2843 East Grand River Avenue East Lansing, MI 48823

Visit us on the World Wide Web!

http://www.federalcareers.com